Quest for Freedom

Quest for Freedom

THE TRANSFORMATION OF EASTERN EUROPE IN THE 1990S

by

Richard Krooth

and

Boris Vladimirovitz

McFarland & Company, Inc., Publishers
Jefferson, North Carolina, and London

"Boris Vladimirovitz" is the pseudonym of a
former member of the Supreme Soviet, USSR

British Library Cataloguing-in-Publication data are available

Library of Congress Cataloguing-in-Publication Data

Krooth, Richard.
    Quest for freedom : the transformation of Eastern Europe in the
1990s / by Richard Krooth and Boris Vladimirovitz.
        p.   cm.
    Includes bibliographical references and index.
    ISBN 0-89950-741-7 (lib. bdg. : 50# alk. paper) ∞
    1. Europe, Eastern—Politics and government—1989-   2. Former
Soviet republics—Politics and government.   3. Post-communism—
Europe, Eastern.   4. Post-communism—Former Soviet republics.
I. Vladimirovitz, Boris.   II. Title.
JN96.A2K76   1993
947'.0009'049—dc20   92-50425
                                                                    CIP

Manufactured in the United States of America

McFarland & Company, Inc., Publishers
  Box 611, Jefferson, North Carolina 28640

It is not only the will to be free
that delivers emancipation from the
imposition of others; but the need
to take charge of the material
conditions that chain populations
and nation states to the servitude
of their masters.

Contents

viii   Contents

Contents xiii

Acknowledgments

This study emerged from the authors' mutual concern with developments in the Soviet Union and Eastern Europe. After several years of cooperative work and discussions with others, we took the risk of presenting a working outline of the emerging contours of political economy in former Soviet Eurasia and Eastern and Western Europe.

We also attempted to frame the study with essential background materials that make the account both interesting and meaningful. Some parts of the study thus review historical information; others concentrate on momentary events that are linked to the past and a possible future that the authors conjecture by extrapolating from the known.

Like the subject matter itself, the facts presented, the method of presentation, and the conclusions projected will be controversial; and we thereby hope to contribute to the intense debate concerning the quest for freedom and development in the republics of the former Soviet Union and Europe, east and west.

Naturally a project such as this involves the cooperation, assistance, and expertise of many institutions, agencies, and people to bring it to a successful conclusion. So here we wish to recognize the help and contributions of others.

Information for the manuscript was gathered from queries, reports, and publications of many nations, institutions, groups, and individuals. The following is a brief list from the USSR, Eastern Europe, the United States, and Western Europe:

USSR: Institute of World Economy and International Relations; office of the Finance Minister of the Russian Federation; the Soviet Academy of National Economy; the Soviet Association of Joint Ventures; the Soviet Institute of International Economic and Political Studies; the offices of the mayors of Moscow and Leningrad; Institute of International Economic Studies under Director Oleg Bogomolov, 1989-91; COMECON Headquarters in Moscow; COMECON Conference, Moscow, 5 January 1991.

Assorted reports of the *New Times* (Moscow), 1989-91; *Interfax* (Moscow), November 1989 through January 1991; *Baltfax* (Vilnius, Riga), November 1989 through January 1991; Novotni Press Agency (Moscow);

Ogonyok (Moscow); *Komsomolskaya Pravda* (Moscow); *Pravda* (Moscow); Tass (Moscow); Boris Fedorov, 1989–90 Finance Minister, Russian Federation; then–Foreign Minister Eduard Shevardnadze and Soviet foreign policy negotiators; creators of the *Samizdat* culture; members of the Soviet opposition in various republics and in the Supreme Soviet.

Specific reports of President Mikhail Gorbachev, "Proposed Program," Supreme Soviet, 16 October 1990; C. P. Politburo, *Internal Memorandum*, November 1988; Yegor K. Ligachev, *Memorandum on Position of the Party, Politburo*, 6 February 1990; "C.I.A.–Soviet Economists Summary Report," Washington Economic Conference Proceedings, 23–27 April 1990; Bolis Kagarlitsky, Colloquium Series, 1990, Sociology Department, University of California, Berkeley, 22 March 1990.

Lithuania: *Izvestia* (Moscow), September–December 1989, January–April 1990; George Csicsery, "The Other War," *Express* (Berkeley, California), 8 February 1991; Pacific Film Archives, Clemov Soviet Collection (Berkeley, California: Pacific Film Archives, 1989–90); *Interfax* (Moscow), September–December 1989; *Baltfax* (Vilnius) January–April 1990.

Bulgaria: Office of the Deputy Prime Minister of Bulgaria; Bulgarian Public Prosecutor's Office; Bulgarian Socialist Party; Bulgarian Office of Foreign Economic Relations; Minister of Foreign Economic Relations; Richard W. Rahn, ed., *Action Plan for Bulgaria*, original draft edition, Washington, D.C.: United States Chamber of Commerce, September 1990; "Interview: Todor Zhivkov," *Trud* [Labor] (Sofia), 9 November 1990.

Germany: Commerzbank, A.G.; Deutsche Bank, A.G.; Deutsche Kreditbank; Dresdner Bank, A.G.; German Institute for the Economy of Berlin; Office of Prime Minister Modrow, former German Democratic Republic; Federal Republic of Germany, Bonn; from the USSR, Foreign Minister Shevardnadze, *Report* (Moscow: Politburo), 15 February 1990.

Hungary: Professor Ivan T. Berend, President of the Hungarian National Academy of Sciences; office of the Hungarian Privatization Minister; the Hungarian Economics Research Institute; Hungarian sociologist Andras Kovacs; Directorate, Central European Research Center; Hungarian Secretariat, Minister of Finance; and various other agencies of the Hungarian center-right government (Budapest) 1990–91.

Czechoslovakia: Czechoslovakian Finance Ministry; Economics Institute of the Czechoslovakian Academy of Sciences; Boriz Lazar, activist philosophy professor in the Public Against Violence in Slovakia.

Poland: Adam Michnik, Editor-in-Chief, *Gazeta Vyhoreza* (Warsaw); Adam Smith Institute (Warsaw); office of the Polish Prime Minister; Polish Finance Ministry; Polish Foreign Affairs Ministry; Polish Agricultural Ministry; *Solidarity Weekly* (Warsaw).

Rumania: National Salvation Front and Council of National Salvation Front; Radio Free Rumania (Bucharest); *Rumanian Mare* (Bucharest); Mihai Filmon, leader of the League of Rumanian Democracy (Harghita); Bishop Laszlo Tokes; office of the Minister for Economic

Orientation of Rumania; Slavomir Gvozdenovic, Editor of *Timisoara Literary Review*; National Prosecutor's Office; National Christian Peasant Party; National Defense Ministry; Interior Ministry; Timisoara's Committee for Social Democracy.

Yugoslavia: Office of the President and Vice President of Yugoslavia; Secretariat, Government Finance Ministry; Dragan Veselonov, President of the Serbian Peasants' Party; Central Intelligence Agency, *Yugoslavia: National Intelligence Estimate* (Washington, D.C.: C.I.A., November 1990); Roberto Boteri, Editor of *Slovenian Mladina*; Janos Vorzsak, 1990 Vice President of the Democratic Union of Hungarians in Rumania; Vuk Draskovic, Serbian Renewal Party; Professor Budomir Kosutic, Serbian Constitutional Committee.

United States and Western Europe: Reuters; UPI; *New York Times*; *Los Angeles Times*; *San Francisco Chronicle*; *Wall Street Journal*; *The Economist* (London); *The Sun* (London); *Financial Times* (London); the United States Institute of Peace (Washington, D.C.); National Geographic Society, Library and News Collection, Records Library, Translations Division, Pre-Press Division, and Maps and Reports (Washington, D.C.); Kennan Institute for Advanced Russian Studies, Woodrow Wilson International Center for Scholars; Soviet and East European Studies, Center for Strategic and International Studies; Brookings Institution (Washington, D.C.); Johns Hopkins University, Paul H. Nitze School of Advanced International Studies (Washington, D.C.); Heritage Foundation; Hoover Institute, Stanford University (Palo Alto, California); American University (Washington, D.C.).

Essential background information is listed in the bibliography, but several sources and recent studies provided useful reaffirmation of the materials presented: the 1990 World Economic Forum held in Davos, Switzerland; *Churchill–Eisenhower Correspondence, 1953–55*, edited by Peter G. Boylke; *The Long Pretense*, by Arnold Beichman; *Dangerous Capabilities: Paul Nitze and the Cold War*, by David Callahan.

Other opinions were gleaned from *Daedalus* ("To the Stalin Mausoleum," by pseudonymous "Z," who later surfaced as a Soviet expert at the University of California, Berkeley); Martin Malia, "The Soviet Union Has Ceased to Exist," *New York Times*, 31 August 1990; the weekly San Francisco Bay area KPFA radio program hosted by William M. Mandel, author and commentator on Soviet affairs; press statements of Jan Vanous, president of PlanEcon, Washington consultants; press statements of Harvard economist Jeffrey Sachs on the programs he helped design for Poland.

We would also like to thank those who contributed their expert knowledge in the period before this manuscript took formation. Notable here are Professors Richard Flacks and Richard Appelbaum, Sociology Department at the University of California, Santa Barbara; Professor Edgar W. Butler, Sociology Department at the University of California, Riverside; Dr. Hiroshi Fukurai, Board of Studies at the University of

California, Santa Cruz; Professor Paul Stevenson, Sociology Department at the University of Winnipeg; Professor William J. Chambliss, Sociology Department at George Washington University; University of Wisconsin history professors William Appelman Williams and Harvey Goldberg, both now deceased; Hans H. Gerth, who before his death was professor emeritus in the Sociology Department, University of Wisconsin.

Insightful comments, support, encouragement, and assistance were offered by Russian-speaking, contrarian Soviet historian Lester Radke; oral historian and professor Ann B. Krooth; and the following scholars and research associates in the Sociology Department at the University of California, Berkeley, during 1990–91: Professor Johannes Berger, University of Mannhein, West Germany; Associate Professor Penelope Canan, University of Denver; Emeritus Professor Charles Chakerian of Yale; Dr. Lixing Chen, working with the United Nations on urban studies in Yokohama, Japan; Dr. Mustafa Emirbayer, a Harvard Spencer Fellow; Professor Aryei Fishman, Bar-Ilan University, Israel; Professor Koichi Hasegawa, Tohoku University, Japan; Dr. Risto Heiskala, Academy of Finland; Dr. Andjelka Milic, University of Belgrad, Yugoslavia; Dr. Minoo Moallem, postdoctoral fellow of Montreal, Canada; Professor Shinsuke Ohtani, Matsuyama University, Japan; Dr. Michael Opielka, director of the West German Institute of Social Ecology, Hennef; Professor Kazuko Tanaka, Kokugakuin University, Tokyo; Professor Yasushi Yamamoto, University of Tokyo; and Elena Zdravomyslova, High Trade-Union School and the Leningrad branch of the Institute of Sociology, Academy of Science, USSR.

Funding for this study came in part from private sources and the Louis M. Rabinowitz Foundation, Inc.

Credits for technical help are due Wanda Clark, Marge Sauder, and other office staff in the Sociology Department, University of California, Riverside; and for facilitating University of California involvement with this study, Jean Margolis and the office staff in the Sociology Department, University of California, Berkeley.

Copyediting assistance and suggestions were provided by Karl Krooth, University of California, Santa Barbara and Berkeley, and McFarland & Company, Inc.

With the aid offered by these colleagues, critics, and friends, we have attempted to present the emerging patterns in the quest for freedom in the Soviet Union and Europe east and west. Needless to say, we alone are accountable for the contents, the facts presented, and the conclusions.

Richard Krooth
Boris Vladimirovitz

Introduction

For four and a half decades Communist theory calling for the withering of the state and democratic decentralization of economic and social power was never tried or implemented in the Soviet Union or Eastern Europe. Rather, regions or republics in each nation came under centrist controls emanating from the party-ruled urban domain, with political power carefully secured by buffer zones of communities isolated and kept apart.

Communist parties, with their centrist politburos and structured hierarchies, simply did not trust the masses they claimed supported the future promise of a Communist society. These parties had thus tenaciously refused to shift power to the lower reaches of the nation, and party-directed bureaucracies holding sinecures and vested interests would neither relinquish their advantages nor bring about reforms that might jeopardize their status or well-being. Democratic centralism, so-called, was thereby a powerful bureaucratic impediment to any democratic change.

Any basic reform would thus require a complete undoing of the structural relations of center and periphery, party and government, bureaucracy and people. But in the initial democratic "revolutions" of late 1989 to early 1991, such changes were only partly evident and not yet consummated in the Soviet Union or Eastern Europe, laying the frame for future turmoil, changes, and possibly new upheavals. After the first revolutions, then, others might follow.

The great transformation turned on the transition from bureaucratic centralism posturing as communism to commercial statism emphasizing the democratic forum as the medium of politics and market exchange as the scale of material values and the relations they embody.

The centrist state in soviet societies had vaunted an ideological egalitarianism that its own heavy-handed bureaucratic apparatus delayed, impeded, and prevented from being brought to fruition. And rather than offer the material and personal opportunities to fulfill human need, as Communist doctrine allowed, the Gosplan of bureaucratic centralism emphasized unrelenting work, production quotas regardless of output quality, and distribution for often unstated predefined purposes that

1

created sinecures for some, subsistence for the masses, and inequalities for all. The many levels of wages and salaries of work were to become the Gosplan filter for the various degrees of consumption that offered the better, the good, or the poorer life; and the state banks balanced the printing of the precise quantity of currency to regulate public access to amenities and to place the lion's share in the hands of the party, the apparat, and the military machine.

Despite Leninist thought on soviet democracy, this centrally determined distribution of material wealth could not be changed through the political venues of soviets and democratic forums. For state bureaucratic centralism and its Gosplan were under the control of the Communist party (CP) and its inner sanctum. Even the party that spoke of its own *internal* democratic centralism had long since eliminated the mechanisms for party democracy. The party Central Committee was the command station of the nation. And the only communism that remained was in the thoughts of the Communist beholder, for egalitarian relations were practically nowhere to be found.

As the facade of this hypocritical system was shattered in the desperate quest for freedom in Eastern Europe and the Soviet Union, the inheritors of bureaucratized governments affirmed the democratic forum as the medium of their political dialogue over programs for change. Yet they were slow to unhinge and destroy the old agencies of the state and to control the bureaucratic machinery of government. Even when various classes and parties coalesced as political factions appealing to voters to fill legislatures with those representing particular interests, the passage of laws was often contradictory, hybrid schemes that set the general frame for a commercial statism. For the new system of government guidance emphasized a financial, labor, production, and distribution mechanism that turned on market exchange, legislatively providing that privatized means of production would eventually be the focus of work, wages, and the means to buy the nation's output. And once set in motion, the new system assumed its own legislative elaboration of the parameters to be set for the output and dissemination of material values and the relations they embody.

True enough, the pace and patterns of this transition from bureaucratic centralism to commercial statism differed in the nations of Eastern Europe and the former Soviet Union. But the steps in each began to lead toward a similar end.

From 1985 to August 1991, the Gorbachev-led reforms in the Soviet Union were designed to maintain the CP and the Kremlin hierarchy above the local soviets and republics. So it was not really a revolution, only an upside-down exercise in talking about provincial helplessness at the hands of Moscow and creating an underground economy that jealous apparatchiks tried to control and then take advantage of.

The capstone of illusion was the Gorbachev advisors' "500 Day Plan" that implied that there might be a reversal of the structure of local-centrist political and production relations but actually concentrated on an alteration in the distribution system under central guidance creating a market. Even this might jeopardize sections of the party and apparat, though. So a compromise plan explicitly retained the Union structure while reallocating social output. Despite Supreme Soviet approval of this compromise as a "radical" step toward privatization of the means of production, it was framed as a *future* possibility, not a necessary part of a functioning market economy. And even with these limitations, the apparat, the Politburo, the KGB, and the army hierarchy blocked any forward movement toward implementation.

Crisis at the center leading to economic anarchy was the source of this exercise in false promises. Regional and local production in the late eighties and early nineties had been scaled back and withheld from the grasp of the Kremlin. Food and other goods were not available for sale or barter, the short supply coaxing prices to rise rapidly, and President Gorbachev to issue emergency *ukazy* to free up supplies of food and other goods, take up excess money (absorbing large-denominated ruble bills) momentarily to repress inflation, and pass austere measures to bottle up popular outrage and stifle protest.

This ill-formulated scheme further fragmented the economy. For the center could control neither the politics nor the output of republics or their ethnic communities. In the face of Kremlin rigidities, the seizure of local power in important life-support sectors was then extended, and a return to local autarchy bred the decentralization and minute cellularization of production and distribution as a portent of emancipation to come. It was as if the "500 Day Plan" had succeeded in spite of itself, for the sudden redistribution of incremental wealth led to the vertical disintegration of the hierarchical funneling of surplus from the republics and peripheries to the center.

The Baltics would soon be carrying on their own port trade with foreign countries; the Soviet Pacific republics would follow in step, as would the southern Ukraine, and the old prewar heartland, with its decaying systems of transport and supply, would be starved for goods and revenues. The Kremlin was being cut off from the life-giving surplus that supported the apparat, the army, the KGB, and the professional politicians who had shunned work for decades.

Yet the party did not fully comprehend the logic of popular belief: that party direction of the Kremlin had bred an oppressive system and social inequality.

Party promises for future change also depended on popular believability in the Communists' quest for material egalitarianism and individual social freedom. Few outside the Communist party believed the Communists sought these goals. And as the party rigidified, the illegitimacy of social relations defined by Soviet legal strictures was brought into focus. If the old codex of Soviet laws and procedures were not equitable, what assurances would there be that the Kremlin would pass new regulations that were just?

By early 1990, it was also obvious that the central Gosplan directing production and distribution had questionable viability. By guesswork in design and implementation, the party and Politburo had traditionally mobilized tiers of inflexible apparatchiks to extend control over the minutest detail in guiding rewards flowing to the center and limiting wage levels and production costs at local factories, mines, and farms. Surplus was appropriated for favored enterprises that produced arms, met military requirements, and supplied or otherwise propped up the apparat and party.

With the rumblings of discontent in the Soviet republics and Eastern Europe in 1989–90, however, ex post facto the party had second thoughts about the Soviet population continuing to accept the rigidities of apparat controls and funneling wealth.

Though the incentive system for work had nearly collapsed within the republics, the party seemed blind to its implications, continuing to "guide" unionwide economic affairs, overlaying its failing operations with mendacious statistics and designing makeshift pacification programs that had more or less worked poorly in the past. Wage levels were set at the apparat's discretion and after holding out against complaining workers to the point of conflict, could be raised to offset their escalating living costs. But the apparatchiks were also positioned to force up prices again, reducing living standards, the process repeating itself as need be to "protect" the Kremlin's revenues flows awarded its favorite charges.

Along the line, though, the party miscalculated the breadth of discontent, the depth of labor's production falls, and the extent of hoarding that blocked popular expectations for consumption. To bandage the wound draining the state sector of goods and revenues, the new "500 Day Plan" — minus its critical proposals for decentralized decision making — made Politburo sense.

There was never any government intention to bring the major means of land or factory production into the private sphere, but distribution was to be altered along the lines of a viable market that would free price levels, eliminate state subsidies, give labor the incentive to work harder to receive higher pay, offer profit rewards for those privatizing means of production, existence and commerce, and award added tax revenues to the government.

More pay for more work to cover higher prices to maintain living standards was the cheapest of Politburo alchemy. Yet its sorcery backfired as the underground economy took hold of "surplus" supplies of goods and sold them at hyperinflated prices, in turn redirecting funds away from the state sector. As government resources and services fell and budget deficits loomed, the Politburo met in conclave to design new methods to collect replacement revenues from the population at large, also exacerbating public dismay.

Thus was the central dictatorship stalled at dead center, unable to assuage popular disbelief in its rightful authority, to convince the many that its promises of future equality would be legally and equitably applied. Its legitimacy in question, it was hard pressed to control output, mobilize the nation's best work efforts, and centrally collect adequate revenues to support the apparat and the military—neither having ever acted or functioned like an impartial third force that would do no harm to the republics of workers. And the masses anticipated that the party and state apparat would operate immorally, illegally, and without compassion for their needs. Given such popular belief in their illegitimacy, the agents of the Kremlin could not promote a transition to a new ordering of economic and social life.

The Soviet "revolution" still in its infancy from 1985 to August 1991, the republics' legislatures set themselves against the center, local governments fought republic executive committees, and the people's deputies railed against Gorbachev's holding near-dictatorial presidential powers.

As the unresolved struggle pressed forward, local democratic organizations schooled by experience and determination rejected the nation's past authoritarian methods. Building upon the democratic forum, local elections also awarded popular controls in urban and rural domains. So any renewed attempts to restore the authoritarian regime would now have to face new democratic coalitions functioning at the locus of community life, and sending representatives to the Congress of People's Deputies and the Supreme Soviet.

The Kremlin might attempt to keep control over the republics by mobilizing Soviet "settler communities." But these bureaucratic "Bolsheviks" were now a hated lot, a new independent labor movement was in formation, and elections in the republics were displacing Communists who had exploited local populations. It had become increasingly difficult for the Kremlin to impose its unbending rule or martial law, thereby making a new form of confederation both essential and likely.

Regional failings also made a future cooperative federation possible. For minorities republics sought democracy for themselves, yet moved to nationalist and ethnic extremes by depriving others of their rights. Concentrating on their regional traditions, they emphasized their own needs and importance regardless of the needs of the nation they had come to reject, creating two paradigms of the future: nationalist, ethnic drives, as opposed to egalitarian civic commitments.

Other alternatives were still possible in the early 1990s. For previous alliances of neo–Stalinists and liberal Communists were coalescing against the democratic forces in ways that demanded a future moderate and conservative nationalist alliance favoring democracy, self-determination, and economic equity. These nationalists and the party Politburo controlling the army and KGB were together moving to appease the Russian Orthodox church and the patriots supporting the blood battle to maintain the territorial integrity of Mother Russia.

Though the Communist system had been in crisis for more than a decade and the old Leninist order began its collapse in 1989 under Gorbachev's reform communism, the party (CP), army generals, KGB, and bureaucratic oligarchies still could not bear real reform. And only when the population took to the streets and voted democracy was the old Communist order cornered. For *glasnost* was ultimately used to skate around CP power, the powerless consultive assemblies, and Communist dominance in the Supreme Soviet.

Yet there was no immediate destruction of communism to build a democratic forum or to elevate exchange relations as part of the global market. Modernization and an authoritarian commercial system under the guidance of the Bonapartist Gorbachev and a legitimist *nomenklatura* were able to assuage and appease gullible Western interests that promised aid and investments.

Gorbachev's Communist "junta" meanwhile refused to accommodate domestic needs. And the neo–Stalinists mobilized powerfully in late 1990 and early 1991. Their political alliance of apparat and army, the military involvement in politics, the maintenance of domestic order under KGB and Communist party direction — all these forces tightened the institutionalized control apparatus so that the mechanisms of repression were already in charge. Until Gorbachev opposed their plans, there was no need for a military takeover.

At this point, the civilian Congress of People's Deputies and committees of the Supreme Soviet had no influence on the CP–controlled military. The party and military may have lost prestige and budgetary resources in 1990–91 by comparison with the massive state support and resources equipping the army and KGB in the late 1920s; but the opposition controlled no army as such, had no nationwide political organization to act as a counterweight to the CP–army political structure, and under a declaration of martial law would appear to be relatively helpless.

President Gorbachev had blithely assumed that his radical thinking about national unity, new technology, work incentives, and markets would in itself promote change. He presumed that there was such an entity as the Soviet citizen who would rise above the citizen of the republics and ethnic communities. But Gorbachev lacked populist legitimacy and had no base to influence these republic and ethnic communities; his undemocratic ways looked to state authority using the institutional apparat, KGB, and army.

Only in the face of the failed August 1991 coup was the power balance changed as the army moved to back the Yeltsin-led democratic forces, pressuring the Communists to appease the republics demanding self-determination.

The progression transforming the old power equation began with the "500 Day Plan" that had provoked the party revolt restoring the status quo ante, ultimately leading to Gorbachev's new reforms, the failed putsch, the breakup of the Union, and the creation of a Commonwealth of Independent States. A variety of the "500 Day Plan" was then reinstated by Russia and the other independent republics, albeit with the equivocating backing of the multitude — opening new rounds of civil conflict sparked by economic breakdown and calmed by the massive infusion of Western aid and capital.

A new era thus opened amidst community and communal violence, strife between republics, their competitive military preparations, and weighty foreign influence. Still, looking ahead, future cooperation between the republics will undoubtedly be as essential as the accommodation of libertarian governments for public needs and economic modernization deploying old and new bureaucracies. And despite its experience and connections, the old centrist bureaucracy itself might require support from the very populace that before the 1991 coup saw the Kremlin as illegitimate.

Eastern Europe faced problems similar to and different from those besetting the former Soviet states.

Ethnic and social conflicts in Eastern Europe were partly based on the nineteenth-century inheritance of wartime antagonisms, peacetime partition of states and balkanized territories, unresolved economic deprivations and the failure of nation-states to consummate their industrial revolutions. After World War I, nearly fifty states and dozens of nationalities had been geographically fragmented and thrown into unresolvable irredentist conflicts. Again after World War II these diverse nations were repartitioned, then had to contend with Communist-installed governments pandering to both Moscow and nationalist sentiments, closing the way for the resolution of ethnic problems, needs, and demands. And the revolutions of 1989–91 once more freed nationalist nostalgia for insularity, division of nations by ethnic groupings, even hankerings for the old imperial status quo under the helotry of other states. Slovenia and Croatia thus declared their independence, suffered invasion and civil war, and looked to Western Europe as their proper home. Other Yugoslavian states followed suit, fearing Serbian domination yet battling against their minorities' quest for territory and rights. Slovaks also expressed their national consciousness and hope to become an independent state free of Czech controls. And East Germans were willing to live by West German law and order so long as economic equity was offered, their blind spot covering the rights of Poles and Czechs to secure borders and material equity.

At root, reforms in Eastern Europe were dependent on democratic institutions and Western capital, modern technology, and advanced production techniques.

The West might not be able to facilitate the balancing of vested interests and the building of party democracy and institutional legitimacy, but eventually it could provide access to the material means of production. Western conditions set for access to these means could also undermine the legitimacy of political institutions, however, for lenders and investors demanded that two of the essential conditions for production were the freeing of prices and regulation of wages. Though these promised to extend the capitalist ownership sector and expand market relations, they also reduced popular consumption and undercut popular support for the governments promoting reforms.

Private Western capital also hesitated to promote this transition to production unless state-funded international institutions took a lead role in stabilizing the unsteady economies of Eastern Europe. But even then, interest-drawing commercial debt to the West might not be adequately rescheduled, and direct foreign investments might not be committed if limitations were placed on the repatriation of profits.

That would leave Eastern Europe in the halfway house between state stimulation through closing inefficient factories, selling bankrupt enterprises and building human skills on one side and on the other soliciting debt relief, capital investments, and technical transfers from the West. But that would also ensure less than full-scale production, rising unemployment, and the questioning of governments taking too long to transact change. To appease popular needs, the state would again be forced to borrow great sums abroad to build infrastructure, and private capital still might hesitate, putting forth too few resources.

From 1990 to 1992, direct Western investments in Eastern Europe were evident. Billions of marks of long-term investments in the eastern wing of Germany were planned, as were proposals to stop eastern migration to the West by subsidizing both state-owned conglomerates and wage levels. In 1991–92, the German government also gave Russia $35 billion in aid, mostly to give Germany a free political rein by financing the withdrawal of Soviet troops from East Germany. And in the rest of Eastern Europe, where the Russians were withdrawing both their remaining troops and economic stake, domestic savings could not be mobilized without jeopardizing living standards and the political balance of power.

Thus were Western capital infusions critical.

The conditions set by Western capital also followed a tried formula that was at odds with promoting social welfare in borrowing nations. For the West assumed that economic transformation was the goal, neglecting the human, and thus political, context.

Stabilization was seen by Western sages as the first step, reducing excess demand for available goods through cutting both wages and employment, thereby reducing consumption and reaching an equilibrium where money spent on output made demand approximately equal to the value of commodities supplied to the market.

After stabilization, the next stage was to dismantle and convert the old economic and social structures. This was pursued with more initial vigor after the political revolutions in Eastern Europe than in Gorbachev's Soviet Union. For after scrapping the Soviet Shatalin Plan, there was no Kremlin mechanism to participate fully in foreign trade. Only following the coup of 1991, with the disintegration of the Leninist State, did Russia and the other newly independent republics rapidly pursue their global ties.

Both nationalist and republican Eastern European forces seeking self-determination and autarchy as a precondition to enter the global economy raised two alternatives: either the preservation of their territorial integrity, limiting their role in international commerce and borrowing, or decentralization and balkanization within republics, accompanying the extension of both trade and the division of labor between regions and with foreign states. In every nation, the policy of isolation was rejected and gave way to the real politik of becoming part of the global system.

Thus the third step in the calculations for Eastern European economic transformation was recovery based on the logic of Western advisors' five maxims:

1. In moving to a capitalist economy, owners must be legally secured in their ownership rights and seen by the population as legitimate.
2. In developing a capitalist base, both managerial talent and the concentration of ownership must be seen as essential.
3. In stimulating the deployment of capital, labor, and material, prices must be freed to rise in the domestic market.
4. In privatizing large-scale enterprises, upwardly adjusted prices are neccessary to signal the opportunity for profit maximization.
5. For understanding what price should be competitively paid for imports and competitively charged for commodity exports, the devaluation of domestic currency vis-à-vis more valuable hard foreign currencies is essential for the foreign trade sector to adjust to the structure of costs and prices in the world market.

Under the pressure of Western traders, lenders, and investors, would it become possible to move from centralized and bureaucratized state socialism to privatized ownership, the market economy, *and* democratic institutions promoting both commerce and social equity?

The answer depended on popular will and foresight as well as the extent to which each nation-state was able to mobilize the essential resources for a new commercial order without entrapment by domestic and foreign governments, lenders, investors, and traders.

The speed of commercial change was also critical in establishing statist legitimacy in the eyes of a long-deprived citizenry. For following Eastern Europe's unprecedented explosion of popular movements throwing out the old Communist parties, the popular quest for freedom had again come up against the remnants of the partly functioning bureaucratic center that impeded the move toward establishing viable market relations.

To outflank this army of apparatchiks, transitional organizations and institutions were essential. Previous legal structures had to be altered or destroyed and new ones built to secure the population, particularly those engaged in production, marketing, and politics.

The transition would also take time. Even for those new governments determined to destroy the previous forms of ownership and to replace production and distribution methods, their efforts would likely consume years, possibly decades. For indeed there was little capital and few market institutions left in Eastern Europe after forty-five years of bureaucratic socialism, requiring that the entire infrastructure for capital accumulation, production, and marketing be made anew. The Poles had joked in 1991 that the difference between an aquarium and fish soup was that you could turn an aquarium into soup but you could not reverse the process. Eastern Europe would have to design a new fish tank, fill it with fresh water, and generate or import aquatic life.

More deeply, though, the populations of Eastern Europe were only likely to go a short way toward change before hesitating, concerned over the fact that the new order and private market economy would bring inequality in remuneration and inequities in ownership rights and social benefits, that the new egalitarianism promised in political life would be based on vested interests and not extend to things economic. Toleration for inequality would not be simply a short-term state of mind; it would either shape and suffuse the future, or there would be no political party that could long pursue the transition to the market with its accompanying social inequalities.

Thus the newly elected governments could not long negotiate between those suffering downward mobility, those treading water, and those placing high economic hope in an uncertain future. Popular dismay rose as government plans for enforced economic decline raked the moment— eliminating subsidies, undermining the old fixed price structures, using inflation to cut living standards, lowering wages to cut production costs and thereby substitute local production for imports.

Poland had taken the lead in trying rapidly to guide the nation to market economy. To stop the gigantic drain of Poland's foreign exchange earned by exports, the Club of Paris, representing international lending agencies, cut Poland's indebtedness 50 percent, U.S. government loans were cut 70 percent, and Lech Walesa astutely solicited private foreign investments.

Poland's domestic measures were also monetary in nature, trying to eliminate 1,000 percent hyperinflation by balancing supply with money spent by consumers. Yet privatization of the means of production had barely begun, so there was no way that Polish-made goods could compete with imports on a price basis. The technologically backward "infant" industries of Poland still required protection to maintain output and employment — which was not part of the free-trade script foreign lenders or the Walesa government initially pursued. Only later did the Polish government realize it could either block foreign imports, stimulate domestic production, and create new jobs — or borrow conditional foreign funds, import cheaper goods undercutting Polish output and employment, and become an enemy of the very population it claimed to represent.

Transition after the forty-five year detour from the market system was meanwhile pursued differently by the nations of Eastern Europe.

Hungary made no attempt to return housing and the means of production to the original pre–World War II and pre–Communist-era owners, largely because the Communist regime had taken charge of big enterprises and given millions of people apartments or small means as owners, and to take them away would have created the base for a counterrevolution.

In contrast, the Czechoslovakian government planned to give production facilities back to the owners as of the 1938 pre–Nazi expropriations. And since the state owned these properties, the government expected little popular opposition.

Yet on one point all the new Eastern European governments moved in a common direction: to undermine the old Communist state with its social hierarchies. For the past was a grim reminder of the barriers to exercising one's skills, to economic rewards, to upward mobility and an avenue for a better life.

This past lack of opportunities hung heavy on present generations too. For societies that had had an aristocracy based on landholdings traditionally blocked peasant aspirations to own land and accumulate wealth. The gate into the middle class had also been closed as the middle strata was largely composed of foreign settlers and entrepreneurs, especially Eastern European Jews, who were neither socially accepted nor given full legal protection. Their practical annihilation during World War II became the foundation for the potential emergence of a new middle class that the Communists had made illegal but the new revolutions encouraged.

Thus Poland officially backed commercial dealings, blinking at the flourishing black market, a distinct break from the pre–World War II past when 10 percent of Poles had been landed nobility holding commerce and traders in check. And the portent of the future here and elsewhere was state support and subsidies for the emergent middle class of shopkeepers, small manufacturers, and traders.

Still, not so easily would the old centrist bureaucratic socialism pass into the night of memory. For the collapse of economic structures meant an immediate shortfall in both output and revenues to support state social services. And as these services collapsed, the new governments lacked the resources to build a social safety net. This meant that only debt relief, foreign borrowing, or the retooling of industry could salvage the industrial state, finance government benefits, and maintain social relations.

Yet for those nations seeking to put their economies on steady economic feet, domestic resources remained slim in the early 1990s. Privatization could be negotiated by the sale of bankrupt and other state-owned companies. But despite their low levels of capital accumulation, present book values, and sale prices, the population had little personal savings and could not buy back large enterprises. In Hungary alone, it would take one hundred years for the people to mobilize sufficient personal resources to purchase existing government-owned factories. Only small and medium-sized firms could set up operations, and foreign firms seeking joint ventures with Hungarian partners were sending Hungary capital and modern technology.

The government's future plan was to ensure that most means of production would be privately owned and that there would be little unemployment. And who would receive or buy the shares in Hungary and other Eastern European countries might be based in part on a planned "voucher system" with equal distribution of shares to the population. This would create a secondary market in shares with an eventual concentration of control or centralization of large-bloc interests. Hungary would sell shares directly to foreigners. Czechoslovakia initially wanted a strict domestic shares market, but concentration in trusts had already begun in early 1992, and likely foreigners would eventually ally with some domestic buyers.

Others sought a mixed economy—state-owned means of production that functioned within the market environment. Under such commercial statism, prices could be freed and imports allowed to compete with domestic goods, forcing out inefficient firms yet also creating unemployment and downward mobility for the working population.

Clearly, then, the paths to democracy and economic recovery differed among nation-states.

The linkage of political past and present meanwhile ran along a terrain that determined the economic transitions in store.

Center-right parties were largely installed after the first free elections in Eastern Europe. Social democratic parties were weak and weakening. Most workers' interests were not expressed in any political forum, opening the way for future labor parties to coalesce. Popular disaffection with Communists also promised to turn more attention to right-wing political parties. And unfilled economic and political needs set nationalist, anti-Gypsy, and anti-Semitic sentiments in motion.

These tendencies again played themselves out differently in each nation. In Hungary, a developed parliamentary system provided a democratic forum for the three leading and opposition parties (Christian Democrats, National Populists, and Liberal Democrats) to act together to deal with pressing matters, momentarily hiding their differences.

But the danger lay in possible economic failure during transition to the market. Would there be a return to the political frustrations of nineteenth-century capitalism with social conflicts and the polarization of wealth and poverty leading to a new authoritarianism with control over the working class while extracting surplus wealth?

In Poland, a faction of the leadership of Solidarity was willing to suspend democracy to introduce capitalism, which, they argued, would lead to future democracy. Even this would make success dependent on the massive infusion of Western capital and technology, they thought, and some would necessarily come as loans conditioned on government-imposed austerity, lowering living standards.

Yet egalitarian civil society in Eastern Europe remained dependent on prosperity and the population's welfare. Without Western aid and cooperation, economic uplift was hardly possible. And without prosperity and Western aid, civil relations might fall apart; national hatreds, anti–Semitism, and xenophobia might strengthen. And the decapitalized industries and still unfinished part of the European marketplace would possibly come under the control of returning right-wing autocratic parties, directing archaic, autarchic production through the immiserization of millions.

Richard Krooth
Boris Vladimirovitz

Part I:
The Historical Frame

Chapter 1
Tsar and Soviet

Back in the beginning of the century our major national intellect
S. Ye. Kryzhanovsky predicted: "The core Russia does not possess
a reserve of cultural and moral forces to assimilate all of the prov-
inces. This exhausts the Russian national nucleus."
But that was said in a rich, flourishing country, before millions
of people were killed, and not millions chosen at random, but the
selected ones, the elite. Today it sounds thousands of times more
convincing: we have no resources for the provinces, neither eco-
nomic nor spiritual. We have no resources for the Empire, and we
do not need them. Let them fall from our shoulders: It weakens
us, sucks all juices from us, speeds up our death....
The indubitable right of the republics I have cited for complete
separation must be declared formally and immediately. And if
any of them have doubts about seceding, with the same indubi-
table right we will have to declare our separation from them.
It has been in preparation for a long time. It is unavoidable. We
will have explosions here or there. Everyone can see we cannot live
together. And only by separating will we have a clear view of the
future.
—Aleksandr Solzhenitsyn, "How to Revitalize Russia"

How horrible, fantastic, incredible it is that we should be digging
trenches and trying on gas-masks here because of a quarrel in a far-
away country between people of whom we know nothing.
—British Prime Minister Neville Chamberlain,
on Hitler's Annexation of the Sudetenland, 1938

Though the tsars have long since been swept from the Russian landscape, the dilemma they faced remained in former Soviet society until the
attempted coup of 1991: too few state revenues and other resources to provide for a vast population and diverse ethnic regions; too many financial
and material drains to allow fulfillment of the nation's centralized plan for
unification, "Russification," and reorganization of its domain while positioning itself and pursuing its great power aspirations. These pressures led
to the disintegration of the Union in late 1991 and its replacement by a
Commonwealth of Independent Republics. And yet these republics were
in jeopardy of isolating themselves from what had once made them patch-
work parts of an interdependent whole.

17

Reflecting the great malaise that beset the Kremlin before the coup, its Eastern European emporium had collapsed, and it could no longer afford or support the aspirations of its populations for basic necessities, let alone consumer goods seen almost everywhere outside nations bred to the old Communist formulas. In its own republics and Eastern Europe, new conditions essential for independence and democracy had powerfully emerged, though those critical for survival were only barely discernible and volatility threatened future stability.

The West not only breathlessly hung in wait for the outcome of this historic interregnum, but it too had experienced a series of devastating crises—falling rates of profit, perennial negative cash flows, and an intense competitive spirit that threatened to lower domestic wages, burden its own populations with lower living standards, and foster the export of production operations, in part to overtake the East economically before it had put its own democracies in place.

In the future, the West might surmount its many crises, the republics of the former Soviet Union might raise their living standards, Eastern Europe might become economically viable, and all of Europe might become a common trade zone and investment sphere with critical needs in the East opening a transcontinental zone in which some enterprises would be successful at the expense of others. But the path will be costly for populations both east and west, with the largest beneficiaries likely to be great financial institutions and transnational corporations.

Here a brief review concentrates on the empires of the tsars and soviets and sets the frame for looking at the probable future transformation of Eurasia.

BREAKDOWN OF THE CENTRIST ECONOMY

The republics of the former Soviet Union today stand at the crossroads of internal and external change.

The breakdown of the Soviet centrist-directed economy has meant it could no longer afford to keep a standing army in the rest of Eastern Europe or deploy 25 to 40 percent of its population in military-related production. In Asia too, Soviet leader Gorbachev had promised unilateral withdrawal of 200,000 troops from the Far East. He had pulled Soviet forces out of Afghanistan and moved to reduce the Pacific fleet by a third and to withdraw all forces in Asia outside Soviet borders (including Vietnam's Cam Ranh Bay). He had advocated disengagement of forces along the Sino-Soviet border, established limited consular relations with Seoul to encourage North Korea to settle its differences with the South, encouraged Soviet-supplied Vietnamese troops to leave Cambodia, and resolved to remove 400 medium-range missiles from Soviet Asia.

Yet despite the lessening of these costly military burdens, for many reasons a new system of Soviet output and resource allocation had been difficult to put in place quickly. At the start of the nineties, Soviet bureaucracies remained the traditional "guardians" of the state, holding down production, distribution, and one in seven job positions in the nation. Under the central Gosplan, these bureaucracies were the instruments for interpreting, negotiating, and channeling central authority; allotting output quotas; enforcing a division of labor between the many republics; effectively segmenting the work force by mine, land, factory, transport, and other occupations, as well as by better-paid managers with advanced education, industrial workers with less, and migrants with practically none.

These apparatchiks guided the central plan, acting as the legal authorities demarcating lines that the population at large was to follow and not to cross. They granted franchises to uncompetitive monopolized industries, commanding an economy that produced too little food and too few goods for the nation's multitude possessed in 1990 of 165 billion rubles in so-called excess savings. Yet they hid their failings by enlarging the state supply of cash, which then fueled a crazed rush of consumers to buy everything for personal storage or barter, setting off rounds of hyperinflation. By such means, they were the real authors of what appeared to be "excess" demand by consumers queuing up with ration coupons for too few goods, resulting in the depreciation of the ruble; the extension of the black market into all spheres of production, finances, and trade; the effort of Communist party members to control warehouses and supplies for their comrades at the expense of all others; the breach of the government's own price ceilings; a continual decline in living standards; and a growing lack of popular support for the state Gosplan.

Under their bureaucratic tutelage, the consequences were obvious: the disintegration of the overall economy into autarchic entities; the balkanization of economic authority, with great urban centers like Moscow and Leningrad banning the sale of some foods and scarce consumer goods to anyone from outside the city limits; popular anger and discontent that promised to catapult the Gorbachev faction of the Communist party into a new commanding position not unlike that of the tsars of the past. There was a difference, though. For the old rulers affirmed central dictatorship over society at large, while the new ones sought to create the forms for a multiparty democracy and at the same time maintain central control over the reorganization of production, the division of labor, the distribution of output, and allocation for popular "welfare."

By state plan and ignorance, in 1988 the economy moved further out of sync. Gosplan apparatchiks ordered that enterprises link wages, bonuses, and benefits to prices to secure living standards. Prices were not frozen, however, so that enterprises controlling production and supplies in particular regions used their near-monopolistic powers not to enlarge production or improve quality but to invent "new" products, models, and brands not covered by the central plan, thus carrying higher price tags.

As too much money chased too few high-priced goods, as the marketplace was emptied of goods and people scrambled to hoard and raise hard currencies through the black market, the Gorbachev regime unsuccessfully attempted to impose an intermediate political solution to lower prices and enlarge output. Assuming the position of *prezident* with expanded powers to issue executive decrees and draft laws, he hoped to organize the ossified state and economy—by abolishing the bureaucratic ministries regulating individual enterprises; by denationalizing as much as three-quarters of state assets; by turning these firms into leased enterprises or joint-stock companies owned by the workers and managers, with enterprise stocks traded on a new stock market; by freezing wages; by freeing prices in an open market; by tightening money supply—and hopefully watching momentary demonetization, unemployment, and falling demand push down prices in the intermediate term.

THE CONSEQUENCES OF GLASNOST

The newly designed central plan was also an effort to maintain the integrity of the nation. The plan required the pacification of the nation's ethnic republics in the face of the exhaustion of Kremlin resources, the need to maintain the nation's internal structural apparatus, and the reduction of costs through closing down the Soviet foreign presence.

In fact, both ethnic groups and republics had acted against the central plan, redistributing labor and resources to benefit themselves. The disintegration of the Kremlin's authority was impending, for the opposition was questioning the purported "social contract" that had once regulated the ethnic republics by centrist propaganda and Communist party machinery. To maintain the status quo would now require central action, either by military force or economic blackmail. The Kremlin thus held out the bait of future "independent" republics in an egalitarian *federation* as the reason quick secession of the Baltic states and other republics should not go forward. But if the carrot was refused, the new rulers might also use the stick to keep the republics under their undiminished internal rule.

To hold the USSR together, in 1990 Gorbachev became the new *prezident*, chosen as an interim civic leader by an unrepresentative legislature. Rather than being above political biases, the new executive immediately cast a rigid shadow of the old Communist Politburo. And though he promised to cut the links with the Stalinists of the past, he was unable to open the gates for unfettered *glasnost* and *perestroika*. Rather, through his new position, the Communist party secularized its control, attempting to mobilize the forces for the old stability. And under his presidency, the nation began taking strategic steps to maintain the Soviet Union as a unitary whole rather than a disintegrating and disorganized body politic.

This secularization of party control was partly an act of democratization and partly one of centrally enforced order. Before 1985, Soviet rule had combined the functional positions of general secretary of the Communist party and the head of state, with any major disturbance in social order receiving immediate attention from this leader of the dictatorship. Thereafter, Gorbachev-guided *demokratia* had promised something different: that the centrist bureaucratic inheritance of Lenin and Stalin that finally produced the great Communist empire would be renounced; that there would be a severance of the functional positions of general secretary of the CP and the head of state; that a new set of maxims would regulate the nation's political center under dominating presidential powers.

Of course, there was little choice once *glasnost* drew out and highlighted many points of view for public debate. The Politburo quickly lost power to stop the questioning of the Soviet center or talk of secession of its republics. The KGB that had repressed national minorities since the days of Stalin could no longer use unbridled force to control Gorbachev-stimulated nationalist movements. And to go beyond the false promises of the past, the USSR sought to stop its international isolation by recognizing domestic and Eastern Europe's oppositional movements, also establishing new relations for the emigration of citizens and goods to and from other nations, creating the base for a scientific and cultural exchange with the West.

PERIPHERAL AND CENTRIFUGAL FORCES

The centrifugal pull of peripheral republics and Eastern Europe away from the Soviet center was meanwhile an effort to disperse and reorganize power. It challenged old myths of Soviet beneficence. It criticized the military, socioeconomic, and geopolitical Soviet dominance of the past.

The great lie of Soviet authority was now being scrutinized. Hypocrisy had bred a Communist doctrine sanctifying the myth of the people's approval of centralized power. The leading role of the Communist party and inviolability of political union had also been embodied in constitutional provisions that allegedly guaranteed the people autonomy and social freedom. But the Polish freedom movement led by Solidarity cut short the myth, to be followed by the cascading popular movements in the rest of Eastern Europe and the Soviet republics.

The illusion gone, its precepts were also battered as critical questions were raised about whose future democratic prerogatives would be enclosed in which social ordering of power. Which systems of moral order would prevail in the Soviet Union, its republics, and the various Eastern European nations? Would the Communist party gainsay an advantage over other parties in local constituencies simply by controlling the implementation of the central plan and running the local bureaucracies? In each nation or replublic led by a majority, would the rights and polity of minorities be secured? Would each seceding republic or nation that maintained its independence in the face of Kremlin threats be free to establish its own relations and foreign politics vis-à-vis other nations? Could each establishing its own economic autonomy be entitled to make trade or investment agreements with other republics or nations? Could republics seceding from the Soviet Union establish such outside ties even if it upset or disoriented the division of labor within the Soviet Union? And if the Soviet Union stood in the way of complete secession, how would economic and sociopolitical power be distributed?

Bypassing the Soviet party and bureaucracy was not only a question of the periphery and subjugated to assert their rights, though. There had to be methods to put the new beliefs in practice. *Glasnost* was soon to boil the fatuous lie out of the Soviet myth of a multicultural people's government. *Demokratia*, put in place by a parliament of people's deputies, finally revealed the dysfunctional role of the Communist party. Yet the party reasoned that *perestroika* could never be implemented if secession was actually allowed. So party hypocrisy reached full circle in appointing the new *prezident* to create an example of failure—to put a heavy price on Lithuanian secession: $33 billion in hard currencies; the loss of critical territory and a seaport; the end of subsidized, Soviet-delivered oil and raw materials; and a threatened embargo on Lithuanian imports of other republics' resources that the Kremlin also sold on world markets for hard currencies.

It was no idle threat, either, for 60 percent of Soviet hard currencies were earned from oil revenues, and these had fallen with the 1989–90 decline in Soviet production, a drop of 10 percent in world market prices, the slowdown of independence-minded refinery workers in Baku, and the need for more hard currencies to import grain due to the shortfall of Soviet crops under misguided central planners.

Under planned *perestroika*, moreover, new definitions of egalitarian production, fully requited trade, and democratic relationships between center and periphery were absent. By 1990, there was still no ideological framework to replace reliance on the generally defined concepts of Marxism-Leninism. Moscow simply sent tanks and imposed boycotts to try to quiet moves for independence and secession, each instance becoming a vignette of intimidation, not a rational plan for cooperation.

"Last night's session of Soviet tanks and military vehicles rumbling through the capital of Vilnius was unique," one episode was described by Lithuanian president Vytautas Landsbergis. "We felt we really were in an occupied country." If the Soviets had incited violence in Lithuania that night of March 23, he said, "it could explode all over the Soviet Union."

Perhaps this seemed an exaggeration. But the other Baltic republics did hold secessionist plans of their own; the Caucasus Mountain states of Georgia, Azerbaijan, and Armenia would not be far behind; and the Ukrainian nationalist alliance of the Rukh was calling for a fully independent state of 52 million people.

The Kremlin's undemocratic experiments with centralism simply did not square with grass-roots democracy and a widened forum of the peoples of the nation. The new *prezident* could not at once be the leader of the union, head of the Communist party, and the embodiment of the general interest of the country, its 15 republics, and some 50 distinct major and minor ethnic communities.

To accomplish this, there would have to be a uniform, equally applied federal rule of law that was neither imperial nor awarded favor to any republic over others, or rights to one ethnic group over others. Procedural justice would thus require both certain steps and certain outcomes, so that under a future legal system of equal-handed justice, no longer could there be a particular outcome for one region or people and a different outcome for others.

To diffuse separatist pressures, Gorbachev thus promised that one of his priorities would be to draft a new "union treaty," devolving real liberty to the republics in exchange for their voluntary agreement to cede powers like national defense to Moscow. The night of the party was over.

QUESTIONING THE LEGITIMACY OF THE UNION

Yet the day for restructuring the economy and the rights of ethnic Republics and minorities began painfully. After seventy-odd years of attempted central direction, it was hard to accept the new mood of promised flexibility and to grow into institutions still only hoped for or poorly formed. Increased autonomy for all republics was being enlarged by stripping the Communist party of one-party status, permitting other political parties, and experimenting with various forms of representative government. But Gorbachev's proposed treaty for a new union was too late to hold the Baltic republics' reclaiming the sovereignty they lost by forcible annexation in 1940. New force might hold them in check for a while. But then other republics might also attempt to secede, drawing away over one-third of the Union's population and over half its output.

The entire exercise in maintaining the Union turned on the question of legitimacy of the central government. There was still no explicit long-term plan for an unfettered, all–Union economy or market. Regional specialization had meant that nearly half of all trade and 70 to 80 percent of all commerce in agricultural output in the Soviet Union was interregional. But such trade also drained value from certain republics, made those in Central Asia poorer, and led to strong disbelief in the merits of central-government direction of the economy. The bitter experience of "reform" also taught the republics that the Kremlin could not maintain and support a uniform economic system and that it would not live up to its own laws offering cooperatives property rights, leases, or equitable taxation.

Yet the peripheral republics could not simply pull away without the Kremlin's imposition of painful sanctions. These republics might use the nationalities issue as the expressed motive for calls for secession or unhindered regional planning. But to stop regional economic disintegration, the initial steps would have to be more rigorous: to cut off central domination, to institute regional planning and control. These measures might be implemented through closing borders, regulating trade, establishing commercial relations with other nations, issuing currency exchangeable for currencies outside the Soviet Union, building up hard currency reserves, and importing capital equipment, raw materials, energy, and the like.

Such actions would involve a heavy loss of revenue and resources for the central government, the deficit-ridden Kremlin already experiencing a revenue fall of one-third in the eighties. Unable to support the periphery, Moscow had thus placed added tax and unequal exchange pressures upon the republics, ironically also fueling the popular wish to separate from the Union.

Since 1984, five years of such joust and parry had gone on while the old structures of power decayed and disintegrated of their own weight. The failings of the nation's economic frame had also accompanied rising popular disbelief in Kremlin authority and the party mandate. But new structures, different economic apparati, and codified ideological doctrines had not yet emerged to replace them.

Rather, the old party format for dealing with national groups and republics had exacerbated inequalities, taking revenues and goods from some to award them to others. Such centrist attempts to equalize education, welfare, and services between republics had been negotiated by a party bureaucracy that created a colonized periphery.

Not only had the central plan distorted the various republics' economic development; it had also created a division of labor that specialized production so that any fall in output, distribution, and revenue flows meant each had no alternative income sources. Republics that relied on extractive industries experienced perennial trade and revenue deficits. And as the crisis of tax collections by the center also spread, there were fewer financial benefits, goods, and services redirected to the peripheries, so that republics lacking energy and raw materials could not regulate their own scale and quality of production and distribution.

With the Kremlin no longer providing adequate services and fully covering deficits at the local level, popular anger and protest were followed by a scramble for security. In some places, local identification cards were issued to allow the holders to buy scarce resources. In other places, republic work cards were issued to authorize the provision of wage jobs only to republic citizens. And local protest under regional leadership also took the form of ethnic violence.

The future for the Kremlin was grim, for the central government and its voracious bureaucracy still required revenues and taxes from the constituent republics, without an equivalent return. Moscow might use the Gosplan to control regional banks, but Lithuania and other dissident states had plans to create their own banks and currencies. In Lithuania, Moscow could cut off subsidized oil and raw materials, forcing up Baltic prices and reducing the standards of living, but the Sajudis independence forces running the state were prepared to create their own industrial monopolies to make production efficient, contract with other nations for raw materials, sell their output abroad, and set both higher wages and higher prices to maintain living standards. In truth, 1990 independence in Lithuania was asserted without a detailed plan to control natural resources and land; mobilize sufficient finances by trade, foreign exchange, and taxation; and institute wage-price policies. And this led Lithuania to roll back its declaration of total independence for several months.

Still, Moscow was caught in a dilemma from which there was only one principled escape it initially refused to take: freeing the Baltic nations and other republics. The Kremlin was not losing its arrogance, only its ultimate central hold. For there were over 9 million square miles of Soviet land to direct, the largest mass on earth.

From the Urals to the Pacific, the Slavic landscape looked like the American West but was more than twice as large. The central Asian oasis, linking ancient civilization with a fluid commerce, was still a state-planned ecological calamity with one-crop cotton and produce economies, slave-like labor, shrinking seas, insufficient fresh-water supplies, and wind-borne pollutants spreading birth defects and disease. Near many of the nation's internal seas and great rivers, pesticides suffused the water table, children were poisoned, and mortality increased. By contrast, Soviet European republics were production centers powered by an industrial work force, importing food and raw materials but also spewing pollutants.

Nowhere were living conditions satisfactory: 50 to 80 percent of the population lived in shared housing in the various republics; Jews and Germans, Armenians and others, were migrating, seeking economic, social, and political security, and Byelorussia and other republics railed against centrist Russian control, some 90 percent of the Politburo positions still held by Russian Communists in early 1990.

The appointment of a constitutional *prezident* thus promised little immediate relief, only a return to the autocracy and "Great Russia" chauvinism of prerevolutionary tsarist rule, which had also embodied the impedimenta of inviolable law.

ORIGINS OF TSARIST AUTHORITY

Geography had placed emerging Russia between zones whose peoples held to different ethnic traditions and ways of survival. To bring them together under a single sovereign required a standing army, a growing bureaucracy, and an internal security apparatus using force in an attempt to hold together the ever-reappearing cleavage between peoples and territories within and outside the sovereign's boundaries. This was true both before and during tsarist rule and remains so even now. Looking to the past helps define the conundrums tsars, soviets, and commonwealth have had to face and attempt to resolve.

Russian leaders learned by experience that conquered territories had to be kept out of the grasp of competing empires and policed to stop domestic revolt. This was complicated by the periodic Russian quest for political dominance, military puissance, territorial expansion, and access to waterways, oceans, and overseas trade; by the search for know-how, technology, and labor-efficient production. Pursuing these Russian drives over the centuries inevitably violated the ill-defined boundaries of minority communities and nations, becoming the fount of repeated attempts of one people to free themselves from others on the Eurasian land mass.

The frame of this battle of might was the division of the Roman Empire into two wings. The wing east of the Valley of Drina, belonging to Constantinople, was predominantly Greek in language, rational in thought, and followed the Orthodox, or Right-Teaching, church. The Western wing, under Rome, used Latin script, was suffused by pride of power, and followed the Catholic, or Universal, church. As three ensuing centuries of tidal invasions by Hun, Goth, Avar, Bulgar, and Slav then swept southward with devastation over the Balkan peninsula, the only places of safety for the Greek Romans had been the walled towns like Constantinople and Salonika. Even here, ideological beliefs were in contest as the Eastern and Western churches competed for Slavic allegiance. Eastern emperor Michael sent Greek monks Cyril and Methodius to convert the Slavic immigrants to the Greek religion, ways, and newly invented Cyrillic alphabet to express the Slavic tongue. And the Curia sent its missionaries, using a slightly modified Latin alphabet to render the teachings of the Church of Rome.

A three-way challenge then emerged, pitting the Eastern and Western churches against Sultans and Tatars.

Over many centuries, Constantinople had ruled a territory composed predominantly of Slavs. But when the city fell before the armies of the Ottoman Sultans, they were powerfully opposed from the Russian East by a new *caesar*, or *tsar*, of the Slavic Orthodox Empire.

The heart of Russia had been ruled by the Tatars since the great Genghis Khan, its vast plains extending from the Central Asian steppes, plunging downward into river bottom lands. A nomadic ruler, Khan initiated two hundred years of Tatar wars, negotiating disputed territories, and these treaties usually favored the grand prince of Moscow, rewarding him, as the successor of Constantine's Byzantine troops in the East, in the rebellious crusade of the Orthodox faith against the pagan invaders.

The grand prince of Moscovy, Ivan the Terrible, thus came to wield Russian power. Turning the face of Russia eastward rather than west, Ivan established central Muscovy absolutism over the Russian Orthodox nation. "Russification" under the Orthodox church was thus set against the weakened imperial power of both the Roman church and the Muslim Ottoman Sultans.

Ivan made war on the Tatars and Lithuanians, and subjugated Novgorod and other independent principalities as their "sovereign," a distinct break from the past tradition of conqueror as "lord" entitled only to feudal booty. Yet Ivan also reduced the principalities of his own brothers and other appanage princes to feudal status owing service to him as their lord.

Hereditary privileges of the executive council of Boyars (*boyarskaya duma*) to participate in governing the nation nonetheless shackled the grand prince in making imperial appointments and moderating serfdom. So though Ivan promulgated the first Muscovite code of law (*sudebnik*) in 1497 defining the peasants' freedom to move, in fact 95 percent of the population was locked into the rural domain, could not exercise the toiler's right (*trudovoe pravo*) to title while working the land, and could not move until fully paying debts and rising taxes for Ivan's territorial adventures. Ivan thereby definitively supported serfdom and placed empire on Russia's horizon.

Russia rested for an intervening generation until the next great tsar, Ivan IV, actualized its heartland as a nation and emporium, strengthening serfdom while reducing the boyars and nobility to his villains (*kholopy*) and making them completely subject to his authority. Crowned tsar pursuing these aims, Ivan quickly became known for his cruelty as *Grozny*— the one to dread and inspire awe. And though Grozny's brutal ways were confessed as sins in Red Square on February 27, 1549, proclaiming a new era of Christian love and justice, the underlying significance was justification of his central control through the first assembly of the land (*zemsky sobor*) representing all classes except the peasants, to propose major reforms that did little more than ratify the autocrat's policies.

Draining the peasants of taxes, imposing obligatory military service, and effectively allowing the landlords to shift new imposts upon serfs frozen by law to the soil, *Grozny* initiated expansionist schemes demanding the backing of Russia's diverse multitude. With conquests in Kazan crushing the Muslims, Ivan planted the cross in Asia. Through victories in Astrakhan, he extended Moscovy rule over the whole of the Volga basin and the vast expanse beyond the Urals. His imperial quest still unsatiated, Ivan sought access to the Baltic, Western technology for arms production, and the science of waging war.

Nor was Russian opposition tolerated in this drive, Grozny extracting the domestic component of loyal servitude. He punished supposed traitors and seized the boyar estates, making them service tenures. And his terrorist rule was enforced by establishing an independent civil and military domain (*oprichnina*) within the tsardom.

Yet his ancient lineage was not to survive. For he chose as tsaritsa Anastasia, of Prussian ancestry, the fount of Russia's Romanov dynasty. And in a maddened rage, he accidentally killed his son, destroying the last link with Russia's ancient house of original Danish and Swedish invaders, the Burik, leaving the Romanov dynasty to rule its future.

RUSSIA BUILDS AN EMPIRE

The Russian Empire was growing, the early conquests in Kazan in 1552 followed by later forays into the Volga and China, the Ukraine, Baltic, north Caucases, Kazakstan, and the Crimea—bringing new lands and resistance.

For the next great tsar, Peter the Great (1672–1725), founder of modern Russia, transformed the nation into a great European power, looking Westward, rather than only to the East. Peter perceived as an outrage that a Moslem sultan court (*Ottoman Porte*) should control the Christian capital of the world, viewing Russia as defender of the Orthodox faith that should rule in the holy city of Constantine. Russia, he reasoned, would thereby also control the trade of the eastern Mediterranean, unlocking the gates of her vast southern granary and controlling the land route to the ancient seat of Babylon. For such goals, the tsar began to reach south, east, and southeast for access to Baltic warm-water harbors for trade.

Seeking sea power to supplant the great caravan trade of his Oriental dominions, Peter deployed Dutch mathematics, methods of shipbuilding, and military science; English sailing techniques; a naval fleet armed and equipped to defeat the Turkish court; an educated boyar elite studied in Western navigation; an army developed to Western standards; a force of foreign officers, seamen, engineers, and craftsmen in the tsar's service; and naval finances drawn from the landowners and a tax on the tobacco trade.

To enforce Russian unity in preparation for war, Peter destroyed his domestic opposition of terrorist secret police (*Streltsy*), built up his troops, and constructed St. Petersburg as a new fortress and port at the estuary of the Neva River (at the eastern end of the Gulf of Finland). This infrastructure in place, Peter then militarily defeated Sweden and linked Russia to Baltic commerce, forever changing the balance of power in Europe and eliciting a Western European defense against the feared Russian navy, armed puissance, and Baltic trade.

For Peter's measures, the Russian population was westernized, regimented, harnessed, sometimes rewarded, yet heavily burdened. A head tax was placed on the peasantry; domestic industries, both light and heavy, recruited a skilled work force and replaced items previously imported; and foreign exports were enlarged. For more effective central control, Peter decentralized government administration into eight provinces, with a central command post of a senate of nine tsar favorites overseen by an inspector-general and then a procurator-general responsible to Peter alone. Nine collegiate boards then replaced the single minister to run the empire's foreign, judicial, economic, military, industrial, and commercial affairs.

Government ranks were now based on ability and service, awarding titles and rights that the old system granted by birth. Education obliged the nobles' sons to attend professional academies and their daughters to be socially emancipated. The means of acquiring Western knowledge was also eased through the introduction of the civil Russian alphabet, Arabic numerals, and printed literature; civil institutions, hospitals, hospices for young and old; town planning and the creation of the Holy Governing Synod in place of the controlling patriarch to cleanse church abuses and serve the people.

These centrist-directed initiatives composed the domestic changes that backed Peter's exploration of the Pacific coast, annexation of the Kanchatka peninsula and Kurile Islands, and search for the link of Asia and America through the Bering strait.

THE EMPIRE THAT HOBBLED A NATION

Peter's successors, less determined to continue his policies, nonetheless conquered the Black Sea coast from Turkey, Finland from Sweden, and the largest share of a divided Poland. They kept Russia as a Western power, deploying German officials and experts, adopting French manners and customs, divisively separating themselves from the millions of toiling peasants and serfs largely unaffected by all the reforms of Peter and his progeny. Russia thereby bred two nations within its boundaries — a Europeanized aristocracy and an illiterate, impoverished peasantry. Yet this division could not last. Revolution was destined to destroy all existing Russian institutions save those rooted in community and ethnic traditions. It was this last force that would lead to the ultimate division and balkanization of the Soviet system.

The reasons for Russian expansion were many. The Baltics were seen as sixteenth- and seventeenth-century trade and shipping centers. The middle Volga and Ukraine were conquered for strategic positioning. Violent conquest of the Ukraine from Poland after 1709 was also a religious contest. But there was no policy to assimilate non–Russian people, and Ukrainian culture was allowed to flourish. As well, immigration of Russians was strictly limited to prevent "Russification." The Russian Orthodox church certainly encouraged conversions, but by and large it served Russians only on the periphery. Thus the expanding Russian empire had a dual character: sufficient coercion to penetrate and take charge of those conquered, but cooperation with obedient local elites that allowed retention of indigenous institutions, systems of legitimation, and culture.

Penetration through merchant activities, intermarriage, and bribes was sometimes crowned by conquest (as happened in Kazan). But keeping the colonized compliant required an administration that allowed loyal local authorities, such as the Siberian Hans, to use their own legal institutions and tax systems. Using this dual mandate, the Foreign Office in Moscow established treaty relations as if the conquered retained an aspect of sovereignty. Yet the underlying logic was to prevent provincial uprisings by ensuring there would be no new tax imposts and no debt-slavery of non–Russians, sometimes also ensuring the cooperation of local elites through the intermarrying of boyars as during the reigns of Ivan III and Ivan IV.

This policy resisting "Russification" changed at the end of the 18th century. Peter III's ascension in 1761 was followed the next year by his libertarian *ukazy* that emancipated the gentry from state military service, promoting their secular pursuit of education and culture. Yet Peter flew in the face of public sentiments, demanding Germany pay in land for Russia's recent military victories. Even among those favored, opposition to Peter's measures was strong, and government troops and priests, scheming to murder him, successfully aligned with his estranged wife, Catherine. Once she was proclaimed "autocrat," her reputation as libertarian spread but did not last. Catherine the Great initially pursued complete "Russification" of outlying estates of boyars and retainers at court, then French libertarian ideas proposing to recast Russian law, a plan stopped short by a hostile nobility and gentry living off the scree of serfdom. Tightening her hold, Catherine then acknowledged peasant labor the base of Russian land production and new industries, reversing Peter the Great's *ukazy* that serfs could make formal complaint against oppression and insist that prompt justice be made. Catherine's *ukazy* of 1767 thus "Russified" the heartland, making any petitioning serf subject to beatings (the *knout*), lifelong banishment at hard labor, and silence borne without appeal. True, serfs viewed as mere chattels often rebelled, but unity of the nation nonetheless required they be harshly put down by Catherine's imperial military.

The seed of a different future was also planted, for her encouragement of cultural pursuits helped push the gentry further out of touch with the peasants, the urban populace, and the need for peace. Restoring the Russian navy as a counterweight to British, French, and Austrian pressure on Turkey to make war, Catherine led a Russian naval and army pincer movement to victory—and eventual colonization of Turkish lands. This New Russia, as it was called, administered by Catherine's favorite lover,

Viceroy Potemkin, was then enlarged by Russia's 1783 taking of the Crimea, the Tauan peninsula, and the Kuban, winning the right for Russian ships to pass through the Black Sea and the Dardanelles. Thereby had Russia's new fleets completely defeated the Turks, breaking up their empire.

But as always, the costs came home. Corruption, a burdened peasantry, state monopolies controlling production, government borrowing and unfettered issuance of paper money, hyperinflation, foreign loans making Russia a debtor nation—these created conditions not unlike those in France that had already led to revolution. To stop this, Catherine enforced draconian measures and prevailed upon the Orthodox church to keep the populace passive. She repressed intellectuals opposing serfdom. She diverted critics at home by reconquering Poland, blotting it off the map by dividing the spoils with Austria and Prussia. And she left Russia hobbled by both popular burdens and unrest.

FREEDOM AND THE NEW RUSSIFICATION

Throughout the eighteenth century, then, Russians had tried to conquer non-Russians, establishing an empire that was again enlarged by taking Caucasian territory in the nineteenth century. Yet overall the cultures of different nationalities remained strong because there was either no attempt or weak and failed efforts to "Russify." With each zone holding its own historic customs, group ethnic identity and culture resisted Russia's official designation of geographic boundaries as the criteria of a nation. Ethnic identity, not identification with the tsar's foreign polities, was the dominant thrust in the zones of colonization.

"Official nationality" was nonetheless propounded by the next tsar of significance, Nicholas I. Building reactionary schools and armed forces, the new tsar imposed on his subjects an unswerving obligation to use their talents for the greater glory of the state—in law and science, technology and agriculture, architecture and war. Again taxing the nation's peasants as funding for such education and military training, the tsar created Europe's largest standing army, pressured landlords to fill its ranks from the peasantry, and used his military police to secure his goals. Deploying these forces under threats of war in 1854, Russia again took charge of the Turkish Empire, to be shared with other European powers.

Unification was once more carried through by Russification, now the pursued goal in controlling the German elite and in Siberia. And after the reign of Nicholas, Russification of the tsardom's education and legal systems was sought. Unifying Russia with the modern European system of markets and efficient production now also required emancipation of its peasantry.

At his 1856 coronation, Alexander II thus hoped to transform the underlying condition of the people, uplifting them from restrictions and serfdom. The tsar-liberator's initial *ukazy* reversed his predecessor Nicholas's harsh retrictions by awarding amnesty to all political prisoners, cancellation of taxes in arrears and other tax concessions, a three-year moratorium on obligatory military service, the abolition of military colonies, permission for those with wealth to travel abroad, expansion of university enrollment, and a relaxation of censorship.

His greatest step toward national unification was designed to offset the danger of a peasant revolution. In the first half of the nineteenth century there had already been nearly 1,500 peasant uprisings, and Alexander pressured the gentry to abolish serfdom as a security blanket for the landlords' future financial interests.

The deed was done in the Tsar's 1861 imperial *ukazy* submitted to a secret central committee, to be applied to a population of 47.1 million individuals divided into 20 million crown peasants; 4.7 million peasants of appanages, mines, and factories; 21 million serfs belonging to landlord proprietors; and 1.4 million domestic servants (*dvorovié*).

The lords were obliged to cede to the peasants or the rural communes the land actually occupied by the latter, with maximums and minimums to be fixed in each district. But in fact the landlords most benefited themselves by choosing one of two routes: to free their serfs and keep the most and best land for themselves, as happened in fertile southern Russia, or to extract exorbitant financial and labor compensation from the serfs when parting with their land, the case in less fertile northern and central Russia.

The peasants in general thus received less acreage (*dessiantines*) in the rich "black land" and more in less productive areas. To partition this seignorial land, the peasants were organized into communes by mediators of peace (*mirovyé possré dniki*) so that the commune, or *mir*, as the primordial element of Slavo-Russian society, acquired a new inheritance once held by the lord over his subjects, the right of police powers and surveillance of its members. And thereby the serfs were subjected to a new servitude under the "self-government" of local communes.

Since the crown peasants and the appanages were already practically free, they were subject to the payment of a rent or dues to be settled by state administrators of the domain or department of the appanages. And the *dvorovié* not attached to the land received only their personal liberty on condition of serving their master for two years.

Thus were the peasants either left without land or burdened by payments, the rest being subject to the new slavery of the ancient communes.

REVOLUTION AND SUSPENDED IDENTITIES

The obstacles to Russian unification remained formidable. England sought to keep the Continent balkanized, maintaining Turkish power in Constantinople, seizing Persia, and blocking Russia from the Persian

Gulf. England also allied with Japan to block Russia in China, Japan moving against Port Arthur and Dalny.

Yet in the last three decades of the nineteenth century, Russia strengthened its position, creating new alliances, building the largest standing army in Europe, and opening its borders to foreign culture, capital, and goods. Manufacturing seized the work life of its major cities. As foreign investors poured in, natural resources were rapidly developed, and an indigenous capitalist class challenged the ancient supremacy of the landed nobility.

Hitherto unopposed by an aristocracy bent largely on holding both peasants and the emerging class of capitalists in check, wage workers began raising demands without having to face heavy-handed state repression on a scale known elsewhere in industrial Europe.

Then, in 1905, a local "revolution" was followed by general strikes that paralyzed the nation until the Duma was established to balance contending party interests. But the intransigent tsar remained hostile, reducing the Duma to impotence, unable to resolve the problems of a Russia embroiled in a European war.

The infrastructure of the Tsar's government meanwhile weakened. The official bureaucracy of *tchinovniks* held secure posts in which they functioned poorly, if at all, in looking after production, tax collections, and popular needs. Liberals and capitalists backing the Constitutional Democratic party (*Cadets*), the main liberal party led by Pavel Milyukov and Prince Lvov, tried but could not wield the scepter of crown or power. And Kerensky ruled a Duma that could not touch the real base of strength in the hands of local councils of workers and soldiers' deputies.

Revolution then brought on the collapse of the Duma. Yet the Bolshevik Revolution was more a workers' coup of Alexander Kerensky's moderate and democratic-socialist provisional government than a movement extending beyond the urban domain. And even after seizing power, the Bolshevik-called elections for a Constituent Assembly brought the voters' overwhelming mandate for democratic parties in an assembly the Bolsheviks then disbanded by force. Proclaiming a dictatorship of the proletariat, Lenin's formula was soon reduced to the dictatorship of the Communist party, then the Central Committee, and thereafter its head, Stalin. Stalin then used Lenin's conception of the "Red Terror" to crush not only the defenders of tsarism and the Left opposed to the Bolshevik dictatorship but "dissidents" within the Communist party, who were assassinated or tried and sent to labor camps, the first gulags being Lenin's and Trotsky's camps on the White Sea's Solovetski Islands.

The Tsar's multiethnic empire had now been undermined. Political discourse began on the issues surrounding the population's identity. But during three years of encircling warfare, intervention, blockade, and mass starvation, this discussion was cut short by the Revolution's formula that identity was based solely on social class rather than ethnicity, the traditional *mir*, or nationalism; by the political prescription that the concept of "nationalism" was itself a protest against liberating "internationalism"; by the ideological conception of private land and industrial capital as means of existence and labor opposing the principles of egalitarianism and Soviet power; by the preconceived idea that the new "social contract" to build the nation required a multiethnic union, but above all a *union*; and by the unrelenting drive to create a centrist state following principles of Soviet federation.

The ethos of a "Great Russia" respecting ethnic or constituent republics' rights was thus subsumed under the idea of a federal unity dominating the geography of Russia. The Bolshevik conception of class struggle and proletarian solidarity demanded a supranational federation that rejected the concept of secession held by intellectual nationalists or ethnic groupings. The latter were to be awarded only institutions that gave deference and were responsible to the federal structure and party hierarchy in Moscow. And after the bitter Civil War, the bureaucratic structure was purposively molded to weaken the hold of ethnic groups. For this, Lenin recognized the necessity of a directing army of centrist bureaucrats, and the independent Soviet state strove to displace any new nationalist moves in the Baltics, Armenia, and the Caucasus. Stalin, though from Georgia, pursued his own derivative of "internationalism," aka "Great Russia" chauvinism, to repress traditional cultures in the republics.

From the center of the nation, then, efforts were made to prevent the formation of a popular and egalitarian multiethnic union. For more than seven decades, the rights of identification by ethnicity and culture were suspended yet not destroyed, acting as a foundation for these ethnic and nationalist identities to reemerge. And by the late 1980s they had reappeared with a force that would one day lead the Asian, Slavic, and Baltic peripheries to attempt to secede from the Union.

The heart of the European republics might be all that would remain of the Soviet Union.

GREAT RUSSIA CENTRISM

Both the old and new ideological stance of tsar and Soviet identity rested on unresolved conflicts: differing nationalist sentiments and the self-identities as ethnic communities; different regions and republics following traditions and habits of community solidarity; different methods of self-selection, identification, and emancipation; and various rewards as tsarist or Communist theoreticians, apparatchiks, bureaucratic followers, and Great Russia centrists.

Soviet society had matured by means of a dictatorial central plan under a bureaucratic oligarchy directed by a handful of Communist plutocrats determined to perpetuate past deprivations of civil society—

withholding meaningful political involvement, participation, and democratic mutuality from its republics and ethnic regions. Such Great Russia chauvinism was also a product of thought developed over hundreds of years of boyar and tsarist rule.

Yet regional, community, and ethnic sentiments were deeply embedded in provincial survival, fed by traditional lore, culture, and rights to land, herds, water, and living room. Ethnicity and provinciality defined the polity for most, power foci that were partly neutralized by Soviet power after the Revolution, yet still requiring the Soviet center to accommodate ethnic languages, mores, and hereditary rights. To stop self-determination or its ultimate expression through secession, the Soviets established lawful rights and procedures. So a new national identity emerged in the Soviet era, bringing a falsified sense of unity of national purpose when in fact the Russian Republic had a different self-image and different goals than the other republics.

Without doubt, the 1905 and 1917 revolutions drew on the tradition of the prerevolutionary *mir* of self-governing peasant communities. But Lenin and his heirs treated the peasants as a passive element in making revolution, to be held in check by slogans and promises ("Land, Peace, Bread") while the tiny industrial work force and conscripted military created grass-root soviets with self-governing bodies for limited goals within their economic, military, and political ken. Even the 1917 revolutionary soviet in Petrograd did not govern by taking immediate state power but by bending its organizational goals to undermine the provisional government's efforts to create a democratic forum along Western lines. The real power that emerged after the collapse of the provisional government resided with the inner sanctum of the Bolshevik party, its tightly bound circles of one-dimensional theoreticians creating a practical if limited path to transform the social order.

Over the next seventy-odd years, *bureaucratic centralism* emerged as the source of authority over Soviet territories, peoples, and republics. The center's criterion was one of controlling authority, not of emancipation of provincial rights—much like Ivan the Terrible's centrist quest and attempt to undermine the hereditary privileges of the executive council of boyars in governing the nation's feudal domain. The Soviet basic lesson plan had also come from Tsar Ivan IV, who had actualized Russia's heartland as a nation and emporium, strengthening serfdom and the *mir* while reducing the boyars and nobility to his villains and making them completely subject to his authority. For sovietization also transmogrified old identities and attempted to turn traditional mores and rights into historic icons, keeping them alive to pacify ethnic communities and republics, not to emancipate them.

Under the Soviet system, traditional communities retained their ethnic identities but often lacked state support for their cultural rights. And their striving for these rights was met with the arrogance of the

Soviet's Great Russia mentality and KGB military forces determination to stamp out any signs of self-assertion interfering with the central dictatorship, this being carried out in the name of an "all–Soviet peoples' democracy." Ivan Grozny had once done the same: justifying his central controls, punishing supposed traitors by establishing the *aprichnina* as an independent civil and military domain within the tsardom, and mobilizing the first assembly of the land representing all classes except the peasants to propose major reforms that did little more than ratify Grozny's centrist policies.

The central Soviet Gosplan also stressed a national perspective on production and allocation of resources, using lock-step ministries and growing bureaucracies to mobilize units of raw materials, energy, machines, labor, and output. As the state organization then consolidated its apparatus, it also promoted the division of labor by republics, specialization by communities and workplace, and thereby ultimate dependence of each region on others for its essential needs. The resulting interdependence effectively atomized the social structure and production, preventing traditional ethnic communities and local organizations from fully sustaining themselves, thereby also weakening their solidarity at key points for social opposition.

This centrist-directed demise of community self-sufficiency was promoted in the name of efficiency, though in Western terms there was little cost or input-output efficiency. Rather, the criterion of the centralized command economy was the need for rapid industrialization in the thirties and in the fifties and sixties.

For six decades, the nation was regulated by this central command apparatus. Under its hierarchical management, each director of production became a local dictator, a Stalin-like despot who without laws or prohibitions could do almost anything, even use terror controlling the life and death of subordinates, to maintain uninterrupted output sustaining and reproducing the system. The logic of such control was that regardless of scale or complication, the central Gosplan could regulate large-scale operations linked by transport, region, people, agriculture, mines, and factories.

Yet the emerging industrial society proved difficult to control. By the early fifties, the technological revolution was powerfully under way; space technology put Russia first, and the complexities of the technocratic economy signaled the weakening of the system of despotic management. A massive influx of information and data flowing to the central authorities could be neither interpreted nor used, the central planners sometimes blindly directing the system, leading to an open breach in rational production.

This breakdown in the command economy also appeared in the way work and communities were organized. The production structure that might have sustained itself as a vertical hierarchical order designed by the central plan weakened, and impending crisis and necessity stimulated community self-action and cooperation, often sustaining and reinforcing earlier social, ethnic, and communal ties of solidarity.

Soviet production and distribution were clearly facing centrist impediments by the late fifties. Slow growth rates were evident by 1958. By 1965, lower-echelon central planners were conscious of the need to change to a management system emphasizing the rational realization of knowledge and power for making basic production decisions. They even attempted to decentralize controls, with local management ordered to regulate production and to accommodate local markets. But this was a political question to share power differently, interfering with the authority of the top bureaucracy, which quickly put an end to the scheme.

The command economy and its bureaucracy that were supposed to stabilize the system then limped along, making a poor showing throughout the sixties and early seventies. In the sixties, self-emancipatory community survival was already being organized horizontally by locality and region, dispersing control and acting as a centrifugal force weakening the centralized command system. To correct the imbalances of center and periphery, the Brezhnev regime then resolved to award resources to every production center by distributing the power at the center to an enlarged number of ministries with regional bureaucracies in charge of resource allocation. As the centralized command economy then became an uncoordinated, dispersed grouping of unnumbered local helotries handing out favors to compliant Communist functionaries, power at the peripheries corrupted its bureaucratic operatives, led to the misdirection of resources, blocked these necessities from inter–Union commerce, and created national scarcities. Outwardly, it still appeared that living standards were rising through the mid-seventies. But by the late seventies, the process of provincial autarky and economic balkanization had slowed the growth rate for living standards to 1 to 1.5 percent a year.[1]

To correct these obvious impediments, the central planners next moved to control the hundreds of provincial ministries with their thousands of functionaries who held guaranteed jobs and other nepotistic sinecures that awarded them special access to housing, food, and other benefits. But it was too late. The command economy had already been fractionalized, atomized by spatial location and authority that spelled tremendous resistance to any reassertion of central direction.[2] The self-emancipation of the provincial bureaucrats had begun.

Under their newly asserted command, a recipe for economic disaster and regional conflict was also alchemized. As each provincial ministry and local authority directed its own labor force to the full, the shortage of workers gave local Communist directors ever more power. For now they locked workers into particular production operations in the local domain, which emerged as the new *mir* of Soviet society, inadvertently pushing up wages and creating a cost-price spiral that often outran incomes of those retired or in other limiting circumstances. Millions of people experienced a falling standard of living. Though their need for services then enlarged, tax collections to provide for them declined, with local and republic state budgets rapidly going into deficit. Infrastructures of roads, railways, and water delivery systems failed and were not renewed. Angry provincial populations, legally immobilized and locked by bureaucratic mandate into ethnic and other local communities, were now only bridled by local leaders, implosively building a force that might be released with future explosive power.

The multiplicity of ministries meanwhile became lobbies pressuring the central planners for increased allotments for their particular regional projects. The Kremlin lacking adequate resources, this bureaucratic "pluralism" then led to the disbelief in, total disintegration of, the authority and rationality of the central plan. And by the late seventies and during the eighties, the Kremlin authorities could no longer govern the economy.

A new emancipation was afoot. Society itself was restructuring by communities, factories, bureaucracies, and ethnic heritage. Reorganization at the lower reaches had undermined the old totalitarian centrist directorate.

PERESTROIKA AND THE NEW BUREAUCRATIC STATE

To regain control, the modern authors of *perestroika* were necessarily in search of old and new identities as well as legitimacy. Ethnic, regional, and religious ways that fed nationalist and secessionist sentiments could no longer be summarily repressed, dismissed, or chauvinistically disregarded by either the Communist party or state-educated intellectuals. For there were inherent differences of ethnicity, religion, regions, and republics that the Kremlin could not again meld in forced unity.

Legitimacy was also in question. The official lie that the nuclear disaster at Chernobyl was under control and posed no radioactive danger to Soviet citizens was seen as an absurdity that undercut popular belief in state competence and authority. Shattered by Andrei Sakharov's incisive warnings about the dangers of nuclear energy and the emergence of thousands of radiation victims, the bureaucracy had remained inattentive to growing popular awareness that the real catastrophe lay in the Soviet apparat, not elsewhere.

Thus the republics, communities, and public at large no longer believed the Communists or their government had a legitimate mandate to rule.

As head of the party, Gorbachev at first tried to control this spread of unrest by promises of openness, democracy, ethnic rights, and consumer satisfaction. He also attempted to create the infrastructure to deliver on these promise by consolidating hundreds of dispersed ministries under a hierarchical superbody called the Agricultural and Industrial Ministry. Naturally, the bureaucrats in the regional ministries resisted, and some, like Moscow's bakers, used their crucial position as provider of a daily necessity to threaten to withhold their services, effectively having themselves excluded from control by the central ministry. But the latter retained power to disperse individual dissidents, sending them to work in the various local agricultural ministries where, because there was no way to rectify agricultural imbalances, they were sure to fail and could be dismissed. Yet overwhelming ministerial resistance was now only too obvious to the central leadership.

Heated debate in the Central Committee and Politburo followed in 1987 as a concentrated attempt to save the economy from the impending disaster in production and distribution. While this led to a "voluntary radicalization" supporting Gorbachev's reforms and demands to create a democratic forum, almost nothing was done to alter the economy. The democratic movements in formation then exploded with titanic power in 1988. But the Central Committee misread this as anarchy, attempting to stop the population from using the democratic rights just awarded them.

Outwardly, it did appear as anarchy. Movements in different regions and republics were attempting to restructure their communities and economies using their traditional lines of horizontal organizations based on family, locale, culture, ethnicity, and nationalism. Using these venues, regions were soon battling with one another for scarce materials and food. Sectors of industry were consolidating locally to do battle with other regional sectors. And as this growing fragmentation spread, each informal community organization or other group made plans to add to its number, striving to become a mass grouping controlling resources and production at the expense of others. The balkanization of Soviet society was moving forward.

This partitioning also empowered local bureaucrats to bring the dissidents under their leadership, so that regional movements fell under the hegemonic control of new despots. Mikhail Gorbachev had at first encouraged the new local autocracies to undermine the old centralized bureaucracies, but soon he also feared they might become the source of self-assertion that could endanger the Soviet Union itself. Thus he tried to harness and ride the provincial emancipation movement, using fine words about the rights of self-determination of peoples and secession while also deploying traditional armed forces and KGB to keep ethnic nationalities and republics within the union's frame.

To unhinge these ethnic, provincial, and secessionist efforts, though, would now take a new form of organization, one that was democratically organized by autonomous communities and independent republics along the lines of social class, caste, and work. But that would be the future, for meanwhile a middle stratum of bureaucrats and professional workers first pressured, then allied with, the central government in the name of democracy to stop secessionist movements and the creation of independent republics.

CENTRISM, THE MIDDLE STRATUM, AND THE DENIAL OF POPULAR RIGHTS

These pressures would ultimately act as a prop to the disintegrating Kremlin bureaucracy. For middle management held solidarity not by tradition or community habits but only by self-interests. Their emancipation would thus appear as an elitist formation that while remaining chaotic was destined to play a conservative, structured role in 1990–91.

The Soviet origins of this middle stratum were different than in the West, making it open to alliances with various sectors of the professional "class" and black-market operators. In the West, the middle stratum of functionaries had historically been based on the technological need for managers and experts in production. But in the Soviet Union, the central bureaucracy had traditionally separated expertise from management, thereby preventing the middle stratum from consolidating. In 1987, these barriers began to fall; in 1988, they were swept away; and by 1989, the middle stratum had powerfully linked itself across the lines of production, distribution, black-market operations, academic institutions, sports organizations, and government bureaucracies.

The common denominator was less a demand for control than this stratum's quest to emulate the Western consumption of goods. Collectively, this stratum was the historic personification of Tsar Peter the Great, who had transformed the nation into a great European power looking westward for its values rather than only to the East.

For like Tsar Peter, the middle stratum wanted to transform the nation into a commercial power by autocratic mandate. As a revanchist sector supporting its own variety of *perestroika*, it also initially enlarged its control over the old bureaucratic ministries that were already collapsing under the weight of impotence. Yet this middle stratum was not necessarily a democratic force, for in attempting to ally simultaneously with the old bureaucratic ministries, it sought to use the tried systems of management and subordination to establish new relations of domination over the rest of society. In effect, this stratum's goals were little different than Tsar Peter's centrist-directed initiatives enforcing domestic reorganization.

What now might follow? *Perestroika* under the middle stratum was pitted against the worker with a guaranteed job who would not work, the nationalists and ethnic communities grasping for self-determination, and the "demagogic" intellectuals demanding pure democracy. Their brand of *perestroika* meant reorganization of the economy under local monopolies, where prices would be set in each particular region by a "laissez-faire" system where there were no competitors. An elite of local managers would be emancipated from outside controls. And joint-stock companies would issue shares to these same self-managers, who with state resources to support their enterprises would take personal profits for successful operations. Local soviets and labor collectives could fight for their share, though only at a disadvantage. And the new centrist policies would be balanced against the demands of republics and regions.

Russia would thereby again fracture into two nations: a Europeanized middle stratum and an ethnically culture-bound, impoverished periphery. Yet again this discrepancy could never last. A new revolution, a form of *perestroika* organized by independent republics, was destined to undermine all existing Soviet institutions save those rooted in community traditions—this last force to lead towards the minute balkanization of the former Soviet system.

There would be no return to the past bureaucratic incompetence now. For the middle stratum that had once been controlled by the central ministries had seen the failure of these bodies to reassert control at the top and the self-saving move of these same ministries to ally with the middle stratum against the masses organized by ethnic and national groups and republics.

The middle stratum was now caught between two worlds of power: the old centrists and the new democratic forces. It still faced the neo–Stalinist centrists demanding *perestroika* from above, with the next logical attempts being their centrist efforts to stop short-term inflation, pull out of the recession, monetarize the economy with Western capital that would award the nation "Third World" debtor status, and as a protest against this, community moves for self-management, possibly socialist democracy. Thus both the old bureaucracy and the middle stratum opposed, aligning with the party centrists advocating *perestroika* in a renewed Union, moving against popular democracy, session rights, and ultimately a Commonwealth of Independent Republics.

PERESTROIKA AND THE ETHNIC QUESTION

Perestroika failed in August 1991. To succeed by logic, principles, and semantic nuances, all political tendencies would have had to hold an egalitarian place, to be openly encouraged and allowed. Yet once more in Russian history expanding the Kremlin's centrist controls had a dual character: Russian occupation and coercion shaping the republics' institutions, cooperation with obedient local elites allowing retention of indigenous institutions, systems of legitimation, and culture.

Thus the Kremlin sought to reconstruct blindly the system of Catherine the Great to colonize and Russify the heartland—by making any secessionist-bent petitioning republic subject to political, military, and economic abuse; to isolation from the rest of the nation; to "self-sufficiency" without centrist-controlled access to essential resources; and to political silence without fair appeal. Republics viewed as mere Kremlin chattels rebelled, but unity of the nation nonetheless required they be harshly put down by the party-directed military, which itself influenced and bridled the power of the *prezident*.

The seed of a different future was also planted. For Gorbachev's encouragement of *glasnost* and *demokratia* helped push the middle stratum and the ministries further out of touch with the peripheral republics, the urban populace, and their need for a decent standard of life.

The costs of the Soviets' abandoned eastern empire and military machine had meanwhile come home. Official corruption, a burdened periphery of republics, state monopolies controlling production, government borrowing and unfettered issuance of paper money, hyperinflation, foreign loans making Russia a debtor nation—these created conditions not unlike those in the times of Catherine the Great that had threatened revolution. To stop this, both Catherine and Gorbachev were pressed to enforce draconian measures. She prevailed upon the Orthodox church to keep the populace passive; he, the Russian bureaucrats assigned to oversee the republics. She repressed intellectuals opposing serfdom; he, intellectuals opposing communism. She diverted critics at home by reconquering Poland; he, by closing down a foreign empire and promising *perestroika* at home. She left Russia hobbled by both popular burdens and unrest; he did the same.

For the Soviet system to survive now, neither the Armenians nor Azeris could be viewed as unessential to the nation's reorganization and, where it was fact, common destiny. Yet in the ideological, political, and cultural purview of the both peripheral and essential republics, all agreed that the decline and fall of the old centrist Soviet state were both necessary and inevitable. Thus the system would have to be replaced.

How, though, might a new order be brought forth? One ideological base might be a resurgent Orthodox church. Another might be the revival of Roman Catholics and Jews, requiring official protection and permission to emigrate freely. The state would have to deinstitutionalize anti–Semitism, anti–Catholicism, and anti–Armenianism, and eliminate all biases against the fifty ethnic communities and regions. It would have to control the military and stop its repression of dissidents. The Kremlin would also have to allow secession of both republics and ethnic groups possessed of traditional territories. It would have to stop its antisecessionist terror in the face of rising political hatred of both Kremlin Communists and authoritarian bureaucrats. And if all republics seceded, there would be no central state and apparat remaining.

Emancipation also had its roots in the past. For "official nationality" propounded by Tsar Nicholas I, to build reactionary schools and armed forces, was not unlike Soviet Russification of the republics' educational and military systems. Both tsar and Soviets imposed on citizens an unswerving obligation to use their talents for the greater glory of the centrist state. Yet Russification of education and legal systems, pursued to unify Russia with the modern European system of markets and efficient production, now also required emancipation of its most oppressed, uplifting them from both restrictions and impoverishment. And for the Kremlin, that demanded unfettered self-determination for non–Russians.

Until now, the falsification of essential unity of the republics had been an act of force and violence, accompanied by centrist deportations and murder of ethnic and nationalist opponents. The new opposition had thus advocated independent republics and regions as separate nations, anathema to traditional Marxists and Communists, who largely ignored national questions, were biased in favor of great industrial states, and believed the proletariat with their common denominator of oppression had no country. Lenin propounded that in the quest to capture the domestic market to secure investments and capital realization, the bourgeoisie had set up geographic boundaries called nations, and that these were but temporary phenomena that would wither away under socialism.

Something was missing in the formulation, though. For nationalism and culture were stripped of political meaning in the entity of a *Soviet federal union*, with all political power at the center. True, nominal encouragement of local politics and ethnic ways was official policy under Lenin. But Stalin's brutal repression and deportation of nationalists soon created a warren of republics that the central authorities controlled by force. With the original economies crushed and ethnic and nationalist drives kept in check, the temporary mobilization of central rule meant reconquest would periodically be necessary as long as the Soviet system retained its authority. And that became the major historical factor when the centrist state, its ideology, its politics, and its culture were imposed on the Soviet republics and all of Eastern Europe — that more than a half century later was openly questioned by ethnic communities, republics, and regions lying on the Kremlin's periphery and at its heart.

The imperious system that had been imposed on these regions had been rationalized by ideological suppositions that themselves were implicitly transmogrified versions of the Great Russian Empire built by the tsars and a Russo-centric culture enforced by the Soviets. Yet this imperial system, so powerfully built and strengthened, collapsed in the coup of 1991, to be followed by the emergence of fifteen independent republics and a new balkanization of the peripheries.

THE COUP OF 1991 AND ITS AFTERMATH

President Gorbachev had initiated the turn away from one thousand years of Russian tyranny but had also destroyed the legitimacy of the presidential post — and his own security cover — by dismissing the constitutional, freely elected leaders of the Congress of People's Deputies.

He had had to face dissidents like Anatoly Sobchak, representing Leningrad in the Congress of People's Deputies and Supreme Soviet, using his legal professorial credentials to attack communism's old guardians of the state-directed economy and KGB repression — from Prime Minister Nikolai Ryzhkov to KGB chief Viktor Chebrikov and CP theoretician Yegor K. Ligachev. The polarization of central party controls and popular rights was further exacerbated with the Communist party loss of its "leading role" in society through the abolition of Article 6 of the Soviet Constitution and a new ideological formulation for production ("private property") and distribution ("market economy").[3]

President Gorbachev had meanwhile held the fragmenting Union together only because he deferred to the programs of the Communist party, the KGB, the army high command, and the military industries. When his deference was compromised by reforms demanded by the population and dissident republics, though, these centers of power revolted against their titular leader, the force of their coup meeting stronger opposition in the streets, quickly putting them in retreat and leading to the collapse of the Union, its center, and the authority of President Gorbachev. And the twelve high Soviet officials and other suspects who had conspired to seize power in the failed coup not only quickened the demise of the Soviet Union they thought they were saving but led to their arrest and trial.[4]

The conspirators had begun plotting the coup long before it began in the early morning of 19 August 1991 with the announcement that a State Emergency Committee had taken control of the country. Summoned by the signal "ABC" calling for the strictest confidence, the conspirators had met two days earlier, 17 August, at a secret place to work out a detailed plan that also proposed that Gorbachev be included in the conspiracy and if he refused, be isolated from the politics of the nation.

With the victory of democratic forces led by Russian president Boris N. Yeltsin on 21 August, however, the attempted coup became the pivotal end for the Soviet Union as well as public support for Gorbachev's compromised *perestroika*. For the people now understood that Gorbachev himself had created the milieu for the coup, although there was no evidence that he had done anything to encourage the conspirators to organize or to join the conspiracy to return the country to authoritarian rule.

"We can say categorically that Gorbachev gave no hint, either directly or indirectly, that he was with them," Deputy Chief Prosecutor Yevgeny Lisov summed up a four-and-a-half-month investigation compiled in 125 volumes of materials bringing charges of conspiracy to seize power, carrying a sentence of ten to fifteen years in jail or the death sentence. "However, his long relations with members of the conspiracy, who were his closest associates, and some special features of his character, gave them, in our view, the right to think that sooner or later, after one, two, three days, they would be able to draw him to their side."

Prosecutor Lisov argued that the chief conspirators had opposed General Secretary Gorbachev's reforms since 1985. They included three of Gorbachev's confidants—Defense Minister Marshal Dmitri T. Yazov, KGB chief Vladimir A. Kryuchkov, and Interior Minister Boris K. Pugo— and had known each other a long time, enough "not only to talk over many things, but also to look each other over. There was no need for any special additional agreement to take decisive steps," Lisov continued. "All that was needed to take extreme measures was a sense of real danger," that appeared as the proposed Union treaty due to be signed the week of 19 August 1991. "The treaty would have brought considerable changes to the structure of the union and to their well-being and they decided that the zero hour had come," the prosecutor concluded.[5]

The failed coup was quickly followed by the declaration of independence of the Union's constituent republics, the pillage of the property of the old Union, the republics' clinging to old institutions, and bold if blindly untried declarations concerning free enterprise, a union of sovereign states, and common economic and military policies.[6]

And after the failed coup, President Boris Yeltsin of the Russian Republic, the lightning rod warring on party privileges and corruption, called for a level of self-determination of republics that made dismemberment of the Union unavoidable.[7] This was finalized by the Ukrainian independence referendum,[8] the Russian Republic's peremptory move for fundamental economic reforms ahead of other republics, and the disastrous collapse of production and living standards.[9]

BALKANIZATION AT THE PERIPHERIES

Unanswered questions followed the collapse of the central dictatorship. Would the old oligarchy of well-paid apparat and pampered apparatchiks try to seize or otherwise secure new powers for themselves? Would the military-industrial complex accounting for 60 percent of Russia's industrial production, more than 1,000 factories and some 7 million workers allow a 30, possibly 70 percent cut in production and displacement of vanguard technological labor when retooling had only converted assembly lines for 23 of 120 promised consumer items, with a mere 5 reaching world quality standards by December 1991?[10]

Would unfavorably situated ethnic communities go for the jugular of others holding traditional advantages? Would the words of democracy uttered by Russia's Yeltsin and his followers be sustainable in the milieu of crisis and looming famine? Would timely foreign aid be forthcoming for all the newly independent republics? Or without resources to sustain the millions, would the likes of Russia's Yeltsin, Ukraine's Kravchuk, Kazakhstan's Nazarbayev, and other republic leaders trained as Communist party autocrats move toward authoritarianism rather than the building of mechanisms to protect the people from their leaders?[11]

Popular mandates held by leaders in the major republics would certainly stop short the old Communist bureaucrats and party functionaries from immediately reasserting command posts. To quicken the Soviet end, the Russian Parliament had blocked an emergency request by the failing central government to issue an additional 92 billion rubles, leaving the State Bank with sufficient funds for only two or three days, and empowered Yeltsin to agree to finance the Soviet payroll, making Russia the nation's political paymaster for the national economy, the military, and the scientific community. But even President Yeltsin's susequent plan to let the ruble fall, prices rise, and living standards plummet made life harsh for the average denizen and provoked powerful and massive political opposition.

Output plummeting, unemployment escalating, a 28 percent value-added tax levied on Russian goods (to force business reporting to realize Government rebates),[12] inflation spiraling without ceiling, millions facing hunger in the winter of 1991–92, dangers lurked ominously in the unhinging of the enmeshed economic ties that had bred Union industrialization, technological arms production, nuclear preparedness, and dispersion of ethnic populations to worksites beyond their home territories.

Russia now required at least $30 billion in aid a year for five years, the funds to be allotted almost equally between (1) those to stabilize the currency to finance production and subsidize markets and (2) those for emergency imports of food and consumer goods during the initial burst of inflation. Realizing this, the Western powers and Japan had planned billions in aid, and the United States endorsed membership for Russia and five other republics in the International Monetary Fund and World Bank, the first to impose disciplined programs for economic stabilization, the second to subsidize loans for investment in specific infrastructural projects.

ALL NOT WELL IN THE NEW COMMONWEALTH PARADISE

But all was not well in the new Commonwealth paradise cutting the former Union into slivers of independent republics lying at the periphery of the old Kremlin. For the Commonwealth was not a nation-state that could dilute the sovereignty of its members but only a voluntary agreement between separate nation-states, each of which held the power to withdraw if its sovereignty was compromised.

No surprise, then, that fundamental cracks in the new Commonwealth accord emerged as struggles loomed over questions of Commonwealth centrism versus ethnic, language, border, military, and economic rights in the peripheries. As Russia advanced its claims to be the inheritor state of the former Soviet Union, other republics blanched, then made demands of their own, with Ukraine asserting equal rights with Russia, especially over control of the army and Black Sea fleet at

Sevastopol.* An outline of the future was emerging, for, as Alexandr Solzhenitsyn had foretold, "only by separating will we have a clear view of the future."

Political Centrism vs.
Regional, Ethnic, Language, and Border Rights

Decentralization of the old Soviet system immediately led to a new centralism within each republic. The old Communist apparatchiks who largely took over leadership in each republic had not discarded their corrupt ways of the past, again acting as a sort of "mafioso" grasping for central control, military puissance, and economic rewards superior to those held by those they dominated.

Coercion was as much the new modus operandi as the old, though the new leaders' rationale was a future for smaller central government with market forces to bind sections of the republic and self-determination to suffuse both government and economic affairs. The goals were contradictory, though, for centrally enforced austerity reduced living standards and led to mass downward mobility in each republic, while popular resentment at having no voice in decisions regarding their own destiny would necessarily lead citizens to view the government as illegitimate and unworthy of popular acquiescence and demands for conformity.

By January 1992, the supply system linking the republics and the cities had completely broken down. Under the former Communist command economy, supplies were centrally regulated and enforced, favoring the apparat and those staffing the government's bureaucracies. But under the strain of Gorbachev's failing *perestroika*, as the apparatchiks revolted and scrambled to secured their own interests, the command system had already begun disintegrating. By the time Yeltsin assumed power, the command supply system had ceased to exist. Though Yeltsin's government could try to free prices to induce a new supply, that was impossible in the short term as enterprises were either still state-owned or lacked raw materials and fuels.

Former Soviet president Gorbachev handily warned that the price reforms he delayed introducing during his six years in office would waylay Yeltsin's reforms, the former president waiting in the political wing, advising that the Yeltsin government had best "respond to economic and military signals coming from the various regions" of the new Commonwealth. The centralized Soviet state, he insisted, could have dealt

---

The fleet created by Catherine the Great was both symbolic of Russian and Ukrainian nationalism and legendary as the core of the early eighteenth-century Russian Imperial Navy home-ported at Sevastopol, a port besieged by the Turks and their allies in the nineteenth-century Crimean War, the Crimean only later being made part of the Ukrainian Republic in the 1950s.

with these problems, but the disparate, uncoordinated Commonwealth republics could not.[13]

His was a double message too, for it was easier to lack political power and advise Yeltsin what measures to take, knowing that as long as the former Communist leaders and apparatchiks remained in charge of the economic shock reforms in each republic, the masses would view their authority and measures to be sidestepped.

The old Communists, now "populist" leaders of the new republics, were caught in a bind. They could not force their reluctant bureaucracies efficiently to implement orders. "But if they [the apparats] do not act," said political analyst Vladimir Bokovsky, "the country will turn into a Weimar republic, marked by economic chaos and chronic political instability," with the old Communist coterie the wrong people in charge at the Commonwealth's critical transitional stage.

Populism republic-style would not stimulate production, raise living standards, or provide jobs, *Izvestia* thus argued in mid–January 1992, for "now, when power belongs to them fully and totally, the populist games demonstrate their helplessness [to act] and irresponsibility" to take needed measures.[14]

Bokovsky also thought Russian history was rolling backward as "the Yeltsin Government looks more and more like the Provisional Government in 1917, with its inability to solve main problems, lack of political support structures and dwindling popularity. . . . Frustrated multitudes already feel themselves robbed of the fruits of their revolution and deceived by former Communists (for whom they have coined the new and very expressive name 'commutants'). Before long, they will fill the streets again."[15]

The future thus boded either a revolution from below led by demagogues playing to the lowest popular sentiments or by reunited Communists, "commutants" who would ensure democratic forces remained dispersed and unable to present a realistic alternative program for local self-determination.

Even the revolution from below would necessarily be Communist-led, for the Communists were the only "reformed parties" with tight organizational ties and structures able to swindle the cities and republics of supplies. With commutants creating party substitutes for the defunct Communist party,[16] their posturing as democrats was calculated to legitimate the claim of each "to be the legal heir of the Communist Party, at least where its assets and property are concerned," Bukovsky wrote. "Each expects to unite in its ranks millions of former party functionaries across the country. But, somehow, there are no quarrels among them. . . . They all will form a cozy coalition of commutants. . . . They will be waiting in the wings, exploiting Yeltsin's every mistake—or even creating them because, like their forefathers at the beginning of this century, they can only hope to be accepted by a desperate population as a lesser evil than chaos, typhoid, hunger and marauding gangs. They need chaos and hunger to succeed at the next elections."[17]

Lacking a Foundation for Change

The material foundation for change was not yet present; 1991 average monthly outlays for food and other essentials were roughly 1,300 rubles in the cities (1,800 rubles in Moscow) and 400–500 in the countryside. But the average worker earned only 800 to 1,000 rubles a month for a forty-hour week, the shortfall being made up in part by some 180 rubles a month earned from moonlighting in the expanding private sector. With families pooling earnings from regular work and moonlighting, including the pensioner's meager 342 rubles a month, the population was just treading water, living worse than before, but still not starving.[18]

Then, on 12 January 1992, the initial resurgence of several successor organizations of the Communist party brought between 10,000 and 50,000 Communist supporters to the streets of Moscow angrily protesting rising prices and demanding the resignation of the Yeltsin government. Portraying the former Soviet president Gorbachev and President Yeltsin as responsible for the crisis, Vladimir Shebarshin of the Russian Communist Workers party railed that "only a true government of the people, not presidents, can rescue the country from crisis." And the Union of Army Officers had its spokesman, Lieut. Col. Aleksandr Terekhov, insisting that "patriotic-minded forces will not allow the Army to be disintegrated. They won't let our nuclear forces be placed under NATO's control."[19]

The Great Party Battle

The coup that led to the rise of Yeltsin in a new "provisional government" reminiscent of that of Aleksandr F. Kerensky in 1917 led to the outlawing of the Communist party. Yet the party retreated to the underground. And the old Communists, bureaucrats, apparatchiks, and corrupt opportunists reformed themselves into "democrats" ready to resume power in the wake of hunger, chaos, and protest.

The Union was replaced with a formless "Commonwealth." Though the army had sided with the people and the KGB seemed momentarily doomed, a weakened centralized Russian government was beset by conflicting city, prefect, district, and regional powers and duties, fighting one another to gain control over former Communist party property yet unable to replace central structures and positions with an oppositional political structure, a new ruling party of democrats, and a comprehensive alternative program.

In the aftermath of the coup, the Russian republican "government" was hardly better organized [than the conflicting government structures of the city of Moscow]. To the old Council of Ministers, Yeltsin had added a Council of State, and no one could tell whose power was superior. Then there was the Supreme Soviet of the Russian Federation, elected under an old balloting procedure concocted by the former Soviet President, Mikhail S. Gorbachev, and still dominated by former Communists who, legally, could block any initiative. (In fact, they proceeded to block two enormously important measures: a new Russian constitution and a law on private ownership of land.)[20]

With all these centers of governmental authority locked in constant fighting, incapable of properly functioning for three months after the coup, Yeltsin's later reorganization of the two councils into one administrative body under his control was unable to supply or distribute adequate food during the winter of 1991–92. Moreover, the disorganized revolutions in the great urban centers like Moscow, St. Petersburg, and the former Sverdlosk (now Yekaterinburg) hardly touched the provinces where democratic forces were weak, 70 percent of the local bosses were in sympathy with the 1991 coup, and these provincial "mafias" won time to regroup and plan a new strategy while operating the bureaucratic machinery Yeltsin depended on to implement reforms.[21]

Renewed conflicts of center and peripheries within and between republics began almost immediately too. Ruslan Khasbulatov, speaker of the Russian Parliament, demanded the resignation of Prime Minister Yeltsin and his cabinet for having enacted "uncontrolled, anarchic, nonregulated price increases" and economic reforms, a charge answered by Yeltsin's legal counselor, Sergei Shakhrai, that less than two weeks had passed before these unfair charges to bring down the government for its program of price increases to stimulate new production. The new price policy was both ineffective and politically dangerous, parliamentary speaker Khasbulatov added, insisting that the flawed economic measures might lead to a new Communist dictatorship.[22]

But would state-controlled monopolistic enterprises suffused by the old bureaucracies increase production in response to increases in market prices? Not until these monolithic enterprises were first privatized, two reform-minded news agencies insisted, for only then could price increases be effective to cover production costs and stimulate enlarged output.[23]

By mid–January 1992, as supplies to cities and countryside plummeted and prices skyrocketed to the upper limit of the new government pricing policy, Yeltsin attacked the "provocateur" serving old Communist apparatchiks better than free-market consumers: "These swindlers are doing this on purpose to frame us!" he roused one crowd on a provincial tour at Bryansk. But the real swindlers were the old apparatchiks in charge of factories, warehouses, and the means of distribution—refusing to fill contracts for deliveries and waiting for government incentives raising market prices and cutting their costs.

With the oligarchs in command of the economy, the republic

governments found themselves shadow-boxing with an opponent they could not touch. The mayor of Moscow, Gavril Popov, complained that Yeltsin's rising-price reforms had not introduced competitiveness into industry, nor could it so long as the old monopolies withheld output and supplies. And as the national supply networks broke down and raw material deliveries between republics slowed, popular backlash was predictable.

In the Moscow of mid–January 1992, most enterprises had raw material supplies for only two or three weeks of work. With the breakdown of contracts by republics and enterprise in the last years of the Gorbachev era, Moscow's first deputy premier, Boris Nikolsky, said the city had signed up fewer than one of five needed suppliers for 1992 construction of prefabricated concrete housing.[24]

And the picture was similar in most of the newly independent republics, as in Armenia, where food and fuel shortages halted industry, undercut public welfare and put the army in crisis because higher food prices were not covered by increased budget allocations.

The Ruble's Decline: Work More, Save Nothing, Eat Less

As the value of ruble savings fell and work could no longer provide sufficient income to survive, individual avariciousness and aggression surfaced.

Facing an annual 1991 inflation rate of more than 300 percent, the population had scrambled for ways to increase wages by working more hours, holding two jobs, starting a business, trying to get a hard-currency wage from a foreign joint venture. Speculation in foreign currency was also seen as a way to keep up with inflation as the ruble tumbled in value on the black market from 100 rubles to the dollar in December 1991 to 150 rubles in mid–January 1992, continuing to fall thereafter. Even legal purchase of dollars at banks was envisioned, which would act as a popular hedge against some inflation and make the ruble convertible. But savings would nonetheless erode.

Real estate investments would not keep pace with inflation either. For with 7,000 rubles equal to about $47 dollars in January 1992 and the cheapest dacha costing 150,000 rubles, a highly paid 2,000-a-month ruble income would require seventy-five months of savings, even if one had no other outlays. Few could make that investment, though the government permitted such purchases as well as buying apartments.[25]

And should the Yeltsin government repeat Gorbachev's currency confiscations, making hundreds of millions of unbanked outstanding ruble notes worthless, the populace would be further impoverished. The mere rumor of a new confiscation to prevent the collapse of the ruble brought thousands lining up at banks on 14 January 1992 trying to deposit their excess rubles so their savings would be accounted for under any currency reform. Denying such confiscation was envisioned, Russian Secretary of State Gennadi Barbulis took to national television asking the population "to not panic and trust the Government."[26] But trust was a rare commodity in the bleak winter of 1992. And President Yeltsin, himself bred to the old party apparatus he overturned to seek democratic reform, said it best in his 30 December meeting with British Prime Minister John Major: "The only thing that can impede our progress will be general unrest, and general unrest will happen if our reforms fail. Should the reforms fail, we shall face a new leadership and Russia will fall into the habits which tortured us for 74 years."[27]

Military Rights and Claims

Tsar and Soviet tradition had awarded the military a whip hand for aggression and enforcement. So it was no surprise that the newly liberated republics sought their own military and control over what were Soviet personnel and combat infrastructure.

Control over Crimean territory, its ports harboring the Black Sea fleet, and other military remnants of the defunct Soviet Union sharply pitted Ukraine against Russia, the battle initially being fought by words and broken agreements, imaged by the Russian Bear, Yeltsin, and Ukraine's Fox, Kravchuk, crossing swords.

President Kravchuk had outmaneuvered Yeltsin in the creation of the Commonwealth, which President Yeltsin thought would preserve a measure of economic and military unity among the old Soviet republics yet was undercut by Ukraine's preparations for its own currency and army as well as its claim to the Black Sea fleet. But Yeltsin struck back, relying on popular acceptance, asserting the primacy of Russia among heirs to the Soviet Union, reassuring the West by assuming responsibility for the nuclear arsenal, the bulk of the military, and commitment to Soviet agreements for arms reduction.

Yeltsin had hoped to keep the issue of the fleet to arms control, excluding the territorial question of ownership of the Crimean peninsula. But using its voice *Pravda,* the defunct Communist party sought to stir up Great Russian nationalism to make Yeltsin's term as president both short and fitful.

Ukraine then took over the instantaneous military communication network (along with various land and nonstrategic air force units), leaving Yeltsin's Moscow with conventional telephone backups that required hours to disseminate Russian orders. "The Army is now in a very ridiculous position," television viewers heard Gen. Vladimir Lobov expound. "The Army does not know to whom it is subordinate."

The republics also rivaled to establish command over the Black Sea fleet under central command, Yeltsin initially being committed to a centrally controlled Commonwealth defense force with the Black Sea fleet an "indivisible" commonwealth property, "subordinate to the joint command."

Since the 1960s, the fleet had been designed to take on the U.S. Sixth Fleet near the straits linking the Black Sea to the Mediterranean. A formidable force of 300 ships and 69 major combat ships, its inventory included 3 carriers, 6 missile cruisers, 29 submarines, 235 combat planes and helicopters, scores of support and supply ships, and 97,000 men.[28] Since thousands of ethnic Russians were the traditional backbone of this Soviet navy, Yeltsin's political wedge was their January 1992 protest in Kiev, adding fuel to Adm. Igor Kastonov's rebuff of the Ukrainian official demand that servicemen and women in the Ukraine swear a new oath of allegiance to Ukraine by 20 January 1992. Besides, Ukraine had neither the technical nor fiscal resources to assume control, the admiral hotly told reporters in Sevastopol.

Ukraine president Kravchuk countered in Kiev that once the Black Sea fleet had been disarmed of nuclear weapons, it should no longer be considered part of the Commonwealth strategic force and could be fairly claimed as part of Ukrainian territorial properties in Ukraine's Crimean port of Sevastopol.

In the next round of polemics, President Kravchuk laid out the logic of future Ukrainian control, arguing that

> the status of the Black Sea Fleet will determine the future not only of the fleet but will have great importance for the future status of the Ukraine. I think that no one doubts that Ukraine should be a maritime state. It has all the basis for it: Scores of kilometers of sea coast. More than one-fourth of Ukrainian citizens live in the Black Sea area. It has huge economic potential. Ukraine has a genuine desire for a maritime military force.[29]

The lock-step defensive posture of Ukraine envisioned an independent navy, air force, and army using central Soviet units already stationed in the republic, conflicting with Yeltsin's commitment with seven other commonwealth nations to structure a new central military command of responsible generals.

"In my division, I have more [nuclear] buttons than the President, so you better be careful of me," strategic air force commander Maj. Gen. Vladimir Bashkirov warned Ukraine president Kravchuk. But the president nonetheless demanded that all military personnel in Ukraine take a loyalty oath to his republic, and if they refused and took an oath to Russia, they would have to go there to serve.

Fleet commander Admiral Kastonov was outraged, recounting that any insistence on loyalty oaths could only damage the fleet comprised of forty-six different nationalities, with some ships alone staffed by sailors of twenty-five nationalities. "This is a mine that will slowly explode," he foretold. "Right now, we are having a sharp crisis with the Ukrainian Defense Ministry, with which we have collaborated and solved many problems in a civilized way. The ruin of the [Commonwealth] Union could bring about the ruin of the crews of the ships if we force them to take the oath to one of the sovereign states."[30]

And so the turn of words brought Russia's Yeltsin to militarily reposture, declaring that "the Black Sea Fleet was, is and will be Russia's," following this by a message to Admiral Chernavin putting the fleet's commanders under the protection of the Russian president, urging them not to swear allegiance to Ukraine.[31]

The admiral responded in kind, criticizing the Ukrainian leadership for its "hasty attempts" to take charge of the Black Sea fleet, warning of "chaos, strife and destabilization." Political figures should not toy with the army, he intoned the rights of the new Commonwealth command.[32]

Yet the dual claims of Russia and Ukraine were incompatible, contradictory, and unworkable for survival of the new Commonwealth. For it was still unknown how the old Soviet military establishment would be parceled out to the various republics and paid for.[33]

Both Russian and Ukrainian officials agreed to set up a working group of experts to deal with the dispute, their joint statement confirming "all earlier adopted agreements between Russia and Ukraine," both sides pledging "not to take any unilateral actions." To resolve the problem, the eleven members of the Commonwealth could still form armies but would have to define which were "strategic forces" to remain under their joint command. For while Russia called the Black Sea fleet a strategic force, Ukraine saw it otherwise, to be incorporated into its own emergent armed forces.

If Ukraine failed to comply, Yeltsin had meanwhile prepared a decree subordinating all former Soviet armed forces to Russia during the transition to a stable Commonwealth alliance.[34] "In two or three years, the fleet would simply die or, rather, it would sink at its moorings," the fleet's deputy commander, Admiral Ivan Kapitanets, elaborated on the Ukraine's dependence on Russian military savoir faire and industrial support. "I am inclined to think that this [contest to control the fleet] is a form of childhood illness of sovereignty and state independence. Like all such sicknesses, it will pass with time."[35]

But tempers flared in Kiev, some 3,000 Ukrainian nationalists rallying to denounce Russian "imperialist" calculations. In Kiev, President Kravchuk then backpedaled, saying that military experts would decide which ships were in fact nuclear-armed to remain under Commonwealth joint control and which ships, to be stripped of nuclear weapons by 3 June, 1991, would be divided between the Russian and Ukrainian navies.

Nationalism had to be tempered too, Kravchuk hedged. "There are 12 million Russians living in the Ukraine, an army with many Russians, and Russia is our neighbor from whom we get much gas, oil, wood. So we must have a policy against arguing with Russia, but not to abandon the interests of the Ukraine."[36]

Yeltsin took the cue, on 28 January visiting the fleet at Novorossisk, the only major Russian port on the Black Sea, reassuring the crew of the *Moskva* that the fleet would come under the unified armed forces of the Commonwealth and rejecting Ukraine's claim to the fleet. Yeltsin promised that if necessary the fleet would be supplied from Russian ports by sea and air, making it an indivisible force protecting the whole Commonwealth. But Yeltsin also built fear of great Russian might, signing a decree placing under Russian jurisdiction all land and sea forces stationed in the Baltic states.[37]

Defensively, the Parliament of Belarus* also voted to transfer all former Soviet army units on its territory to Belarussian control, returning Belarus officers serving outside the republic for comparable positions in its own army.[38]

Thus, in the competitive surge for republic defenses, the future of Commonwealth navies was uncertain.

Economic Autarchy

Shutting down the old central command system and replacing it with the dispersed, decentralized, autarchic jockeying of independent republics were also untried and chaotic.

Under the banner of Commonwealth and free markets, each republic freed reemergent bureaucracies to try to manage the production and distribution apparatus. These groups were interested in each republic's self-sufficient production by mobilizing adequate resources to fill consumptive needs, which fell far short of expectations, leading to a desperate government battle to upgrade output in each republic and efforts to protect domestic supplies from consumers in other republics.

The autarchic self-sufficiency of each republic at the expense of the others undercut any opportunity for cooperative economic life in the Commonwealth too. Isolated economic activity did not accord with the pledge of the eleven participating Commonwealth republics to bolster their common economic life and honor the ruble as the interrepublic currency.

Russia and Ukraine were the initial battle stations in the contest for material survival. Each planned to forward production at home, stop outsiders from purchasing their output, and limit large-scale dealings with other Commonwealth members. As the next line of defense, they sought Western aid from European "stabilization funds" and from the International Monetary Fund and the World Bank. As a condition of such help, the latter sought to impose austerity reducing popular living standards. And the IMF designed an economic recipe that would deprive Russian consumers in order to enlarge exports to be paid in hard currencies to repay Russia's $65-billion foreign debt.

---

*The new English-language version of Byelorussia.

The logic of such repayment would be that the future export of goods could command hard currencies that could then be spent on importing Western or Japanese goods, ultimately making their equivalent in rubles a currency acceptable as payment to foreign exporters. As the IMF also sought to impose exchange uniformity in rubles as a common currency between the republics of the Commonwealth, future market integration envisioned cooperation, not autarchic self-aggrandizement.[39]

Yet such self-accumulation went forward as thousands of vested groups from the old party, apparat and bureaucracies took charge of once public assets. These new centers "privatized" public holdings. "Former Party functionaries— the most clever of them who were smart enough to jump off the Party train before it crashed—turned to 'private business,' grabbing more than a fair share of desirable state-owned properties in this de facto 'privatization,'" one commentator insists. "Black-market operators and outright criminals got the rest. Thus, most profitable enterprises appear to have been 'privatized' even before any law was passsed, leaving law-abiding citizens only the least profitable leftovers. This, of course, is bound to generate a considerable public resentment and give a bad name to the whole idea of market economy."[40]

The keystone was Russia and its most valuable mass-produced product, oil. To force up its price to the January 1992 global cartel level of $18 a barrel rather than the equivalent of less than 70 cents in U.S. currency, the IMF pressured Russia to raise the consumer price to Russian commuters and truckers from 1 ruble (about one U.S. cent) on 4 January 1992 to 5 rubles (about 4 cents in U.S. currency) on 10 January to 25 rubles ($1)! At that price, heating oil and gasoline would be unpurchasable by millions of Russian families and commerical truckers, cutting off populations and delivered goods from markets, the IMF reasoning that popular discontent could then be pacified by republic subsidies to the needy. Combined with IMF efforts to cut government spending, thus eliminating the safety net of subsidies for enterprise, employment, and popular services, desperation might stalk the republic, making the government appear illegitimate in the eyes of the many—with unknown consequences.[41]

As privations cut living standards, each republic advocated self-sufficient production and narrow nationalism. Thereby exhibiting nationalist fears and xenophobia, both Russia and Ukraine planned to provide for their own citizens at the expense of others.

On 10 January 1992, Russia proclaimed border embargoes on most basic consumer goods, calculatingly blocking a "raid" on its limited retail supplies by neighboring republics. The logical enforcement methods of border guards would be impossible beyond surveillance of railroads and highways, though, for the vast frontiers could be crossed on foot or wagon without body searches to confiscate anything beyond bare necessities of the moment.

Ukraine simultaneously introduced its own protectionist measure in the form of a coupon system of payment for work, to be spent at state stores for vital food purchases at exchange rates set by the republic. The logic of this quasi currency paid as salaries would be threefold: to stop Russian control of rubles that could be used to enforce the Ukrainian currency shortage, empowering ruble-rich Russian shoppers and black marketeers from raiding limited Ukrainian supplies; to tempt Ukrainian citizens to cross the Russian border to dump their rubles for Russian goods; and to increase the ratio of Ukrainian wage payments in coupons from 25 percent to 100 percent, establishing an entirely new Ukrainian currency, thereby gradually replacing the Russian-controlled ruble regulating the Ukrainian economy.[42]

Ukrainian food and basic goods scarce, the government began printing millions of rubles of coupons for use in buying scarce goods. And President Kravchuk called on his chief economic advisor, vice president of the state bank Alesandr Savchenko, to plan the introduction of free markets, a Ukrainian currency (the Canadian-printed *brivnia*) within six months and to work with the president's advisory group of Western experts to promote changes in banking, finance, economics, and government operations.[43]

By the first week in February, the coupons were being used as a national currency, the Russians selling merchandise in Ukraine for rubles that were taken home, flooding the Russian economy, to be spent on the same quantity of goods, thereby fueling inflation. Both Russia and Ukraine then tried harder to secure their economies from each other. Russia reduced gasoline and timber shipments to Ukraine for rubles. The Ukrainian government no longer used the coupon as a rationing ticket for goods, allowing state stores to price food and other products in coupons, inducing merchants to accept coupons for nearly any product and state services, empowering the Kiev black market to make the coupon a medium of common money exchange. By early February, 16 coupons purchased a dollar, each coupon being valued between 2 and 7 rubles. And the future might see the coupon overshadow the ruble, contrary to Western advice that a common Russian-Ukrainian currency would promote trade and economic ties.[44]

Toward the end of January 1992, Belarus and Moldova had also been planning to issue their own forms of currency, while governments in several central Asian republics moved to seal trade borders to conserve their supplies and reimpose price ceilings in the face of popular discontent.

If the republics did not set a plan under existing trade agreements for the large-scale exchange of resources and goods, their assorted routes to the same autarchic end would erode any hope for near-term trade, undermining economic unity and discarding any illusion of a "common economic space." As living standards teetered precariously in each republic, even greater pressures would make autarchic solutions seem more necessary. For without resources to buy high-priced goods, production would fall away; without new investment in production, unemployment would escalate; without work and wages, hunger and homelessness would spread; without adequate government resources and unconditional foreign aid to sustain millions,[45] the legitimacy of the leaders of the republics would be eroded, and the republics themselves might fracture into smaller national and ethnic territories[46] — with unknown social and political consequences.

Part II:
The Great Leap Forward

Does Russia's revolutionary past offer any current guidance for the Soviet Union's, then the Commonwealth's, great leap forward—to transform the economy and decentralize its structures? Were concepts of the "free market" and labor incentives at issue in the past as they are under the new definition of creating a viable economic system? These questions were only partly resolved in the Soviet and Commonwealth debates and struggles of 1989-92.

Yet the centrifugal forces that threatened, then tore the nation to pieces and undermined its forced national unity had roots in earlier conundrums faced by both tsar and Soviet. In each case the rules of the Kremlin confronted discordant pressures and stresses, different demands from nationalist regions and cultures, different economic ways of surviving and prospering in different climes and geographies, different understandings of the purposes of life and community.

Free markets and labor incentives were measures proposed by the leaders of the 1917 October Revolution. In the early 1920s Lenin had already recognized the need for labor incentives to produce and introduced a hybrid market-socialism called the New Economic Policy (NEP). The old-guard Marxists saw it as a return to capitalist incentives, associating labor efforts with rewards, but Lenin railed against their supposed "infantile leftist" stance, which, he said, did not take account of the realities of Soviet technological and industrial backwardness.

An ideological battle ensued. In January 1921, Lenin recognized that discord in the Communist party itself could not "be fully cured and immunized in a few weeks." But was his fear that the party's illness was "chronic and dangerous" justified? Stalin was certainly part of the danger Lenin foresaw—witness Stalin's subsequent grasp for central dictatorship—but the other part was a vast "nation" that lacking economic incentives associated with work, the party could not control and oversee without regional military enforcement and bureaucratic surveillance. Six years later, in 1927, Nikolai Bukharin, Lenin's ally and chief ideologist designing the NEP, was thus avidly encouraging the peasants to enrich themselves by developing their own private plots of land.[1]

But collectivization was to follow shortly as Stalin stylized Bukharin's posture as a right-wing tendency, then moved to "solve" both labor incentive and output problems by immunizing his rule from party influence and criticism, accusing NEP supporters of "rightist deviation" and scheming to build communism in one nation by forceful methods.[2]

Rather than follow Lenin's lead that had relaxed the rigors of war communism, Stalin thereby reversed Lenin's New Economic Policy, moved the nation into isolation from the world system, and took a confrontationist stand, awaiting, he said, the future arrival of socialist revolution in other nations.

In Europe, that future never arrived. There was no revolution in a Social Democratic Germany or Western Europe.[3] In Eastern Europe, only a Fascist occupation, once routed, was replaced by a Soviet one. Stalin's system was put under attack after his death when Nikita Khrushchev demanded reforms (portraying Stalin's heirs as reactionary enemies of change).[4] And in our moment, as Soviet occupation of the East had been unhinged in the social revolutions of 1988–1991, the Soviet Union and Commonwealth sought détente and commerce with the West, partial demilitarization at home, and the eventual deployment of released resources to build domestic production — to offset infrastructural decay, stop stagnation, and build up the nation's technological base.

GLASNOST AS FORUM

Glasnost was the forum to discuss how this new system would emerge. Opposition to the Communist party coalesced in clubs, fronts and associations. Though the party did not officially offer its permission, opposition parties in Lithuania and Latvia moved to end the party monopoly and take charge of their national legislatures. During 1990, other republics then imploded, the June midpoint seeing Boris Yeltsin, demanding grass-roots reforms and using expert guidance,[5] elected as president of the Russian Republic. The republic then declared its sovereignty, affirming a "500-day" program to build a "market economy." And the fourteen other republics followed Russia's lead.

A multiparty system also emerged, and the Communist party became a minority force in the great city councils like Moscow, Leningrad (renamed St. Petersburg), and Stalingrad. The wheel had begun turning away from the centrist command system. Though Lenin had viewed the party as necessary to make the revolution and reorganize the nation under the NEP, Gorbachev saw the party as needing popular legitimacy as a ruling party within the strict framework of the democratic process by giving up any legal and political advantages. The resulting *demokratia* was the seeming footing for the transformation of the Soviet Union's political power base and the nation's reorganization into balkanized autarkic regions and republics.

Gorbachev was later to lose control of the process he began, yet in 1990 moved strategically to regain the initiative. At the center of the Soviet government, and controlling the party Congress from which he had exacted reelection as the secretary, he undermined the power of the Politburo and Central Committee with a "Presidential Council" that had no administrative apparatus to implement its policies, hence had to rely on the emergency powers of the president, or on the very republics and local administrations that opposed the central party! "Hence this brilliant [Gorbachev] performance was a hollow victory," says Martin Malia, "for it left Mr. Gorbachev somewhat in the position of the Empress Dowanger of China amid rival political warlords."[6] As we will see, Gorbachev's Soviet Government had become a power broker with weakened or nonexistent means for implementing local political programs, yet was positioned to use its emergency powers to maintain the status quo for several months.

This led to the chasm between planned change and its implementation. Under the plan for 500 days, to establish an economy ruled by markets, not bureaucrats, socialism and communism would allegedly be altered. The *New York Times* was ecstatic:

> The plan, to start Oct. 1, calls for a lurch toward private enterprise. The major Moscow ministries in charge of the economy would be abolished. That's crucial, because reform can't work as long as Moscow bureaucrats strangle economic initiative. The plan calls for selling state property, distributing land to farmers and transferring state-owned factories to private ownership.
>
> The proposal would bring monetary and price reform. For years, Moscow had run huge Government deficits that were financed by pumping money into the economy. Inflation was suppressed with wage and price controls. The combination of excess money and low, controlled prices has created severe shortages of consumer goods. If Moscow tried to decontrol prices swiftly, Soviet citizens would take their bushels of rubles and chase after scarce goods. Prices would skyrocket.
>
> The 500 days planners know that, so first they would end the need to print rubles by cutting spending on the armed forces and foreign aid. A banking system would be created to provide unsubsidized credit to private enterprises; a stock market would be created to facilitate private ownership. Only then would prices be freed.
>
> ... What's lacking so far are the all-important details. For instance, even if Moscow bureaucrats are eliminated, how would bureaucrats in each republic be prevented from taking over? How would state enterprises be privatized? ... No matter how Messrs. Yeltsin and Gorbachev answer these questions, their plan is a watershed. It commits the Soviets to capitalism. If this plan succeeds, it will bring 500 days that shake the world.[7]

WHY CENTRIST REORGANIZATION FAILED

But the plan would not bring success so swiftly. Though the party's agenda set out the limits on others as well as the party itself, the program set the frame for the eventual undoing of the centrist reorganization the party proposed. For the program called for the Kremlin apparat to remain in charge!

The party was also split into large and small factions. The conservatives of the apparat fought to keep the industrial ministries in control of resources, and the KGB and the army in charge of violence to offset any impending democratic takeover. The leading figures at the party's center sought to centralize party control in their own hands, trying to regulate the economy through the central plan, allegedly to promote democracy *outside* the party. The politically well-connected bureaucrats, wanting to retain their autocratic mandates, never stopped making decisions, refusing to truck with peasant and worker slowdowns, demands for improved benefits, or further falls in the quality of output. The farmers, workers, and local oligarches, slowing production, hoarding goods, held another vision. Regardless of escalating market prices, they could withhold their output.

The disappointed left the party in droves, as did those leading the democratic opposition in the major cities: Gavril Popov in Moscow, Boris Yeltsin in Sverdlovsk, and Anatoly Sobchak in Leningrad. In the cities and provinces, these reformers organized democratic fronts and sought a civil social order rather than a politically controlled Communist state. They also sought a federated commonwealth of independent republics, planning to do away with the monolithic Union.

The party stiffened to secure its positions. Party recommendations were allegedly designed to stop violent and Fascist oppositional movements. But their application to all oppositional forces was envisioned, one party proposal to the Supreme Soviet providing: "The formation and activity of organizations and movements that expound violence and ethnic strife and that pursue extremist, unconstitutional aims should be prohibited by law."

Yet responding to unrelenting popular pressures, the party's own legal agenda was altered, providing for "the separation of legislative, executive and judiciary powers" as "fundamentally important to the Government's efficiency." Citing Lenin's words, the party noted that "we should combine the advantages of the Soviet system with the advantages of parliamentarism."

Their grandiose, "ideological" formulation sounded like a rerun of a tract from Thomas Jefferson. "The Party's policy proceeds from the recognition of the sovereign will of the people as the only source of power. The rule-of-law state of the whole people has no room for dictatorship by any class, and even less for the power of a management bureaucracy."

Inexperienced with using a democratic forum, the party's language was still rawly hewed. But it nonetheless saw the way ahead would now involve conflicting political parties, a venue for fair elections in self-governing republics, and law and order, elucidating its provisos:

- The development and strengthening of the political rights of citizens: Participation in running the affairs of society and the state, freedom of speech, the press, meetings and demonstrations and the formation of public organizations.
- The electoral system should be brought in line with the principles of universal, equal, direct suffrage. We wish elections to become an honest competition between representatives of all the sections of society, of individuals and ideas submitted to the judgement of voters by the party, public organizations and movements, and individual candidates.
- The principle of the self-determination of nations in a renewed Soviet Federation presupposes the freedom of nation-state entities to choose forms by which to structure life, institutions and symbols of statehood. Our ideal is not unification, but unity in diversity. The Party reaffirms its commitment to Lenin's principle of the right of nations to self-determination, including secession, and favors the adoption of a law on a mechanism for the exercise of this right.

The logic of moving from Communist rigidities to democratic mobilization was not easily negotiated, though, and there was no fail-safe path, as Prime Minister Nikolai Ryzhkov and President Gorbachev discovered in 1990–91. Both within the party and among liberal-leaning activists, utopian economic solutions demanded instantaneous success rather than years, perhaps decades, of waiting. And meanwhile none of the contending protagonists would silently bear their cause.

"Law and order and requirements of Soviet laws" were nonetheless to be strictly observed, the party mandated through the Supreme Soviet. So any republic's withdrawal would be opposed by the party if based on "separatist slogans and movements that would lead to the destruction of the great multi-ethnic democratic state." With the party opposing the secession of republics, insisting that this was some sort of alteration of democratic-centralism, the party reasoned these republics should not be allowed "to implement barrack-room, hierarchical discipline."

Andrei Sakharov had foretold the rationale they would use.[8] And such party language was itself a clue to how removed its Kremlin ideologists were from popular sentiments and movements. The party reasoned in terms of centrist reform, not popular rights and needs. So the party's thinking about economic reorganization would thus evolve by tiny steps, lacking the holistic transformative sense inhering in popular demands.[9]

Chapter 2

The "Success" and Failure of the Soviet Economy

There is no revolution. There are just boys and girls who run about the city and shout that they don't have bread.
— Empress Alexandra, 1917, asserting
the central Czarist government was secure

I don't know about anyone else, but my tongue has trouble saying that edifying phrase "Man does not live by bread alone." It is true. But he lives by bread, too.
— M. Vershovsky, "Drawing the Line"

For complaining like this [about the lack of meat in the state stores], I may be arrested and get to eat in the labor camps," Miss Novikova said, pointing out that all the candor of glasnost cannot put sausage on the table. "But of course we have such a free country now."
— Francis Clines, *The New York Times*, 30 September 1990

When I criticize the Government program in terms of its compensation for rising prices of bread and meat, it is because it is the subversion of the market principle. People should not be paid because they eat bread and meat but because they work.
— Nikolai Y. Petrakov, assistant to
President Gorbachev on economic affairs

Still, for now, there was little direct hostility for Mr. Yelstin, and for many people it was still a chance to glimpse and hear "Czar Boris," as many in the crowd called him. And many gave him credit for taking to the streets, especially in a city as traditionally militant and divided as St. Petersburg. Public opinion polls showed that Mr. Yeltsin still held a 40 percent approval rating in St. Petersburg, but it also showed support for the far right.
— Serge Schmemann, *The New York Times*,
15 January 1992

Even the Moscow Circus could not summon the magic to save Masha, a mistreated zoo elephant. She died today after two weeks

65

of extraordinary rescue efforts. Much of her food had reportedly
been stolen by hungry zookeepers.
—Associated Press (Moscow), 28 January 1992

In the era of Soviet dominance, the logic of central government and its economic plan meant the Kremlin controlled the rest of the nation and "peripheries"; the cities regulated the countryside; the republic governments ruled over their citizenry; the co-ops and communes watched over their constituencies; the factory bureaucrats lorded over their workers; and the common people looked after their immediate needs.

These inequities in wielding power led to other inequities—greater incomes, benefits, and prosperity in Moscow and the secondary urban domain than in the rural areas. And from ships at seaports and landlocked countryside, an infrastructure of roads and rail lines carrying the nation's material wealth—foods, raw produce, and crudely processed materials—led to urban factories and great cities, not vice versa.

Receiving the nation's surpluses, favored cities were also the settings of gangling bureaucracies that held sway, offering their apparat the sinecures of long-term employment. Besides personal security, these chosen positions bred an attitude of authority, a way of thinking that one's functional line of performance depended for its permanence on "regulating" an underlying system that in turn was supposed to employ the nation, deliver its output to satisfy industrial and human needs, and accommodate the Kremlin's power elite.

But here the system broke down. For lacking a true democratic mandate, the hierarchical order revealed a fatal flaw. For too long it had heralded a national unity that the people now rejected outright. They had come to understand that the inadequate and skewed distribution of social benefits was glued to the bare ribs of industrial backwardness, inefficiencies of the bureaucrats in power, and the military's overarching puissance. The Soviet councils in which democratic participation was supposed to allow popularly voiced demands to regulate the nation's decisions were now seen as a miserable political sideshow, a shadow of the real powers held by the party Central Committee and the core actors of the Supreme Soviet. There was neither popular political participation nor adequate output to quiet the many. There was simply too little national surplus to reinvest simultaneously in extended industrial technology while oiling the military machinery and raising living standards to anything approximating the poorest capitalist nations of the West.

Few indeed besides the bureaucratic apparatchiks were ever entitled to the nation's full bounty. A well-rounded diet with sufficient calories and protein was a rarity for the underclasses, who also lacked other amenities, to say nothing of access to the elite's dachas, dollars, and special government stores stocked with Western goods. These elevated amenities went to the apparatchiks and the party's ranking members, while the common people unceremoniously had their cruder fare grown and made in Mother Russia.

This system was named socialism, but its real nature was bureaucratic centralism, centrist controls over monopolistic enterprises, caste preferences, an impoverished state, and privations for the Union's varied populations. And its tortured apparatus for distribution was negotiated through state mercantile monopolies that directed the extraction of raw materials and food and fiber in the various republics and peripheries, their shipment to the industrial centers, the distributive flow of manufactures from the center back to the peripheries, the shifting of labor from the urban domain and ethnic communities as the state directed, and from these centrally commanded processes the extraction of commodities and surplus to benefit an ever-enlarging bureaucratic maze under party control.[1]

THE CORE OF GOVERNMENT POWER

Throughout the Soviet era, these centrist bureaucracies were located at the Kremlin. And uncannily for seventy years, their directing plutocrats held at least one thing in common: They were unable to control the same social and economic structures they politically planned!

In part they had inherited the failed hierarchical orders of the Russian past. Earlier tsarist rule had also relied on a lavishly rewarded coterie, an educated group of the autocrat's advisers who decided the course of the nation. Yet neither the skewed system of primogeniture designating the autocratic lines of leadership nor imperial conquest characterizing the ties between regions was an effective means to mobilize populations of the peripheries for extraction of maximum revenues. The tsar's administrators were powerfully positioned to implement the extractive process—allowing local rulers to maintain traditional ways and mores so long as material wealth and revenues were paid to Moscow. Yet these administrators also generated conflicts and competition between regions. And during the early spread of technology, they set the South and the Urals at loggerheads over the assorted output of the metallurgy industry. They also ensured that the power-producing regions were in unbridled competition, with the Donets coal fields waging battles against the oil industry of Baku. In this sense, the late tsarist period helped bring Mother Russia together in a way that placed local authority in the hands of individual owners who developed resources and other means of wealth, subsistence, manufacturing, and distribution—means that ultimately came under the control of the Socialist state.[2]

When the revolutionary government became the guardian, it was supposed to look after these means for the good of the people. Yet the new Soviet center created a social and geographic division of labor that specialized the functions of work, quieted protest from the periphery by designating how resources would be used, controlled the geographic movement of labor, and designated how each region would fulfill production quotas that were part of the overall general plan set by the Kremlin's dictatorship. The resulting territorial organizaton of labor was in part based on regional specialization, in part on bureaucratic entrenchment that brought the centrist apparat special accolades and material benefits, and in part on the extraction of surplus which the Communist party took for its own organization and members.[3]

Later, during the Great Patriotic War against fascism, the Kremlin directed the defense industry in the Volga basin and the Urals, western Siberia, Kazakhstan, and central Asia—simultaneously evacuating industrial plants from the West and promoting new construction in the East, linking these and other regions while tying each of them to the party's leaders linked to Moscow.[4]

After the war, party-guided developments ensured that Moscow and Leningrad would remain the premier industrial centers, with other cities and zones kept in a lesser stage of technological update. Each stage of farming and industry thus reflected the regional standing of dependence designated by the Kremlin. And what emerged was comparable to the classic design of mercantilism: the center as manufacturer of the means of production; the outlying peripheries as importers of manufactures and machines and producers of raw materials, foods, and lesser manufactures; the metropolis as controller of the transport of material values between both center and peripheries as well as the nationwide movement of labor.

The dominant contours that emerged were seen both industrially and spatially[5]:

1. Moscow was the industrial center of the nation, the Kremlin controlling interregional production, distribution, values, and prices.
2. Moscow was also kept the most technolgically advanced. Whereas Moscow and the nearby regions of Yaroslavl and Ivanovo had been the seat of 80 percent of the Union's textile industry before the war, the postwar period witnessed Moscow's planned elevation as the machine-building center specializing in precision technologies while partly retaining its place in textiles and establishing its absolute hegemony in the production of the basis for Soviet "knowledge"—technocratic studies, self-serving propaganda, and patriotic literature.
3. On a second tier, the technocratic information coming from and machines made in Moscow were distributed to most of the republics, their ancillary regions, and territories. This spread industrial production, albeit keeping Moscow, then Leningrad (specializing in chemicals and industrial equipment), a technological giant's step ahead. Behind them were the Urals and Ukraine, supplying

these two industrial centers with fuel and metals while the Caucasus also provided fuel.

The cotton-growing regions of central Asia and Transcaucasia meanwhile imported textile machinery from Moscow, building their own textile industrial centers in the eastern regions, so they no longer had to import textiles from Moscow. Later, when Brezhnev turned these cotton regions into near-slave camps for child and female field workers, moreover, the region's textile mills thrived under—and were the source of tremendous revenues going to—the Kremlin and Communist party apparats.

4. Moscow, Leningrad, and other major cities effectively made up the nation's "urban domain," not only requiring the import of tremendous quantities of raw materials and foods but also in need of nearly unlimited supplies of fuel. From central Asia and Transcaucasia came cotton; from the Caucasus came oil; from the Donets Basin emerged metals and coal. The Black Earth region, Ukraine, the Volga region, Kazakhstan, and western Siberia sent meat products, livestock, and grain; fish came from the Lower Volga; timber products from the northern territories; fruit from southern climes.

The dominant flows of grain from south to north and timber from north to south had a deeper significance, too. For grain was moving from the hinterlands—from Ukraine, North Caucasus, Middle and Upper Volga—to the industrial centers, to the Northwest and Northeast. And from the granary and forests of the steppe in the south of western Siberia and in the north of Kazakhstan distribution moved to eastern Siberia and the Far East; south to central Asia; and west to industrial centers.

The regional division of labor in farming made Kazakhstan the supplier of livestock, meat, hides, and wool for Moscow; western Siberia, the European Northeast, and the Volga Forest area the source of dairy products; Ukraine and the Black Earth area the source of sugar (which later was supplemented by sugar-beet planting in other regions). Central Asia and the Transcaucasus specialized in subtropical crops, flax, hemp, sunflower, and cotton.

5. So too, new zones for mining, such as Kirovsk, the Karaganda Coal basin, the Vorkuta coal fields fell under central planners, who ordered out a labor force and delivered the raw materials to strengthen the industrial heartland. The apatites of Kirovsk were sent to the chemical industries in Leningrad and other cities as far as Ukraine; the coal of Karaganda went to Magnitogorsk, Dzhezkazgan, and south Kazakhstan. And the new railroads extending across republics, besides the building of hydroelectric stations, brought both materials and power to the industrial centers.

6. Such a relation of industrial centers and their peripheries could be directed only by viewing the worker as a source of power without taking account of the internal life of labor itself. Wherever local labor sources were inadequate to operate a mine or plant, the state directed a migratory work force. This was the history of recruitment for large industrial sites in Kuzbas, the Karaganda, and Magnitogorsk; for building hydroelectric stations on the Volga; for breaking virgin land and bringing old agricultural areas back into production; for setting up the vast complex of tractor stations and state farms.

And yet the industrial and skilled workers sent under Kremlin orders also subjugated the republics. As technically educated cadres indoctrinated in schools concentrated in Moscow and Leningrad, they became the new missionaries of skill — the foremen, engineers, and technicians — sent out to direct and control provincial workers, to create new towns drawing in populations from surrounding areas, turning the old *stanitsa* with a few thousand inhabitants into giant frontier settlements with several hundred thousand inhabitants. Hundreds of new towns thus drew migrants to the East and Southeast to ship their output and mineral resources to the great industrial cities.

FROM ONE-PARTY GOVERNMENT TO SQUEEZE ON THE SOVIET CENTER

Given this system directing labor division for production, farming, and distribution, equity might have prevailed. But the Soviet state was based on a one-party government ruled by a Central Committee that itself was under the commanding influence of the Communists. Its inner sanctum was controlled by a handful of ideologues, with a single leader like Lenin or dictator like Stalin or Brezhnev. Such a state held to the concept of a central plan under which *values* were placed on all goods and services, and purportedly following the labor theory of value, the planners developed a way of placing low values on raw materials and agricultural products, slightly higher values on semimanufactured goods, fractionally higher values on textiles and other early-stage industrial goods, still higher values on machine building and chemical processing, and the greatest value on "services" rendered by state bureaucrats and party functionaries. Such prices of production (as they were called) and value allotments for the apparat were then translated into the revenues each set of workers and bureaucrats would receive for spending on essentials, so that those with greater resources were able to command more benefits than others.

This was the Soviet logic of valuing production and distributing output. Yet no central force was ever able to unify its economic frames and systematize the methods of labor, production, and use or the allocation of what they created. The ideological ascendants of the Gorbachevs were not necessarily proficient, competent, or able in dealing with the congeries of republics, nationalities, and ethnic communities that were forced and drawn together in what was allegedly a single economic system. In this respect, just as the tsars failed, so did the centrist Soviets. The heirs of Lenin simply did not comprehend the depths of despair felt by those enclosed in a Soviet system directed and ruled by the party and its Central Committee.

"Everything is terrible in our economy and everything is stagnating [weeping] in our economy," Aleksandr Solzhenitsyn later wrote from U.S. exile in 1990. "There is no life without it. It is necessary to develop the people's sense of labor, and this has to be done as soon as possible because for half [a] century no one has found any reward in work. There is no one to grow wheat for bread, no one to take care of cattle. Millions are living in conditions that can not be called dwellings, and they spend decades in stinking hovels. The elderly and invalids are poor as beggars. Roads are in terrible condition, and nature itself is taking revenge."

Speaking to his compatriots, Solzhenitsyn further polemicized:

> Who of us does not know our troubles, covered as they are with mendacious statistics? Having been dragging in search of the blind and malicious Marxist-Leninist utopia for 70 years, we put a full third of our population upon the executioner's block during the incompetently conducted, self-annihilating "patriotic war." We have lost our abundance and destroyed the peasant class and its villages. We have driven away the very instinct for growing wheat for our bread.
>
> We have destroyed the perimeters of our cities, poisoned our rivers, lakes and fish with the waste of primordial industries. Today we are poisoning the last remaining water, air and soil with the additives of atomic death, and purchasing radioactive waste in the West. Ruining ourselves for the sake of grand invasions under insane leadership, we have cut down our rich forests, robbed our incomparable natural resources, the irreplaceable property of our great-grandchildren. Without mercy we have sold everything abroad.
>
> We have exhausted our women by forcing them to do laborious work. We have torn them from their children. The children were left to suffer from diseases, lack of discipline and corruption of education. Health has been completely neglected, and we do not have medicines. Even healthy food has been forgotten, and millions do not have a place to live. Lawlessness reigns over all depths of the country. And we cling only to one thing: not to be deprived of stupefying drunkenness.[6]

It might have been easy for the Kremlin to dismiss Solzhenitsyn as a fanatic out of touch with Russian realities. But the editors of *Consomolskaya Pravda* printed his words, understanding that philosophically he sought to raise the critical question of unrequited human need under seventy years of Soviet party hegemony. There was still no equitable distribution of land, too little bread, or even assurances of lasting peace, as the Bolsheviks had originally promised. And Solzhenitsyn's impatience with puerile elections and parliamentary machinations—his anger at seventy years of exploitation, crimes of state, and the gulag—were classically articulated by his refusal to compromise with evil in any form.

His political solutions might seem utopian, even reactionary, as he wildly called for a paternalistic autocracy founded on Great Russian nationalism, religious orthodoxy, and a Russian domain rooted in a common culture. And dissident in his own right, Andrei Sakharov thought Solzhenitsyn romanticized the patriarchal way of Russian life, putting it at odds with science, elemental democracy, and mistrust of Western concepts of freedom, pluralism, and respect for the individual.[7] President Gorbachev also railed against Solzhenitsyn's "Great Russian chauvinism" that looked only to the welfare and purposes of Russia, Ukraine, Byelorussia, and the Russified portions of Kazakhstan, and would exclude other republics and the Soviet Union's other nationalities. Gorbachev spoke of the many nationalities as part of the same country, with a heritage stemming the centuries. But this in part was conscious distortion, for the Union of Soviet Socialist Republics had been in existence only since 1924; the practical ideal of the soviet as a "council" had long been discarded (though it had been the rallying cry of the Bolsheviks from their formation), and the very concept of national destiny was nothing other than the Russification of the other territories, nations, and republics by subjugation, not by democratic and voluntary adherence.[8]

"As a Russian, I fully share concern for the destiny of the Russian people, for the destiny of Russia," said President Gorbachev, voicing another half-truth. "But at the same time, as a Russian, I cannot agree at all with Solzhenitsyn's attitude toward other ethnic groups, which is disrespectful—to be put mildly."[9] Using this as a platform and metaphor to appeal for tolerance among the nations of the Soviet Union and of the Russian Republic, Gorbachev attempted to associate Solzhenitsyn's idea of Russian self-determination with the populist thought of Gorbachev's nemesis—Boris Yeltsin, head of the Russian Republic.

And yet Gorbachev had to bow to the thoughts of both Solzhenitsyn and Yeltsin, and come to a similar logic by half steps. For though Gorbachev was a party man with no qualms in using blackmail to stifle democracy if a squeeze on Kremlin rule was overwhelming, the massive demands of "independent" republics still placed limits on any draconian measures he might take.

BLACKMAIL 1990

In the year 1990, Gorbachev repeatedly threatened to use his powers to maintain central authority in the face of political opposition and too little food to maintain living standards. Under the law that established the post of president in March 1990, the president was already empowered to impose martial law by declaring an emergency, either with the Supreme Soviet's two-thirds supporting vote or the approval of local authorities. Where the Communists held local power, approval was foregone. "In some places," added a threatening Gorbachev, "we may have to impose [presidential rule and] halt the activity of all institutions, including elected ones. The situation has reached the point where if this is required, we must do it."

"I must exhaust all other means at the President's disposal for a political solution," Gorbachev offered on 21 September 1990 as his public rationale before asserting such controls. Yet he also opposed any change in Soviet governmental power and administration, telling the Supreme Soviet that his government would definitely not resign and force the country to choose a new government, that if "we begin to overhaul the entire system across the land, this will be a gift to all manner of claimants of public office, an ambitious lot prepared to exploit the country."[10]

Gorbachev had meanwhile prepared for the worst-case scenario. Eleven days earlier, on 10 September, the president had put the troops on alert to surround Moscow, mobilizing detachments from the Ryazan airborne division to clandestinely travel 125 miles along the deserted road to Moscow at 3 A.M. Landing at the Ryazan airfield later that day, the troops that had left were replaced when thirty Ilyushin planes arrived carrying two regiments in battle gear with equipment.

Moscow rumors of a plan to enforce Gorbachev's will were rampant. For the troops were not headed for the Kremlin parade grounds, as the government contended, and they did not go off to help the farmers dig potatoes, which Moscow insisted would be lacking by winter, as "nowhere in the Ryazan district was there any such agreement for the harvest," said Col. Sergei Kudinov, a former chief of the political instruction department at the Ryazan paratrooper academy and then member of the Ryazan regional council.

Observing at the air base, opposition members of parliament floated other rumors, claiming regiments from the Pskov Division (then recently deployed in the Kirghizia republic strife) were landing in full gear. And on Moscow radio, Andrei Kurtinov of the U.S. and Canada Institute said: "The more feasible explanation is that it was an attempt to flex muscles, to show that the army is able, that they are ready. Probably, it was a kind of blackmail to show the liberals in Moscow and Leningrad that they are not the masters, not the only people in charge, that their powers are limited and could be limited further."[11]

The deeper purposes behind this talk and troop deployment were party demands placed on Gorbachev as a willing captive, for he had moved to make national production more efficient and politics more permissive only within the boundaries of Kremlin control and under the direction of the Communist party. He had opposed the popular rise of Boris Yeltsin and Yeltsin's demands to dissolve conquered regions and free nationalities from Kremlin rule. He feared Yeltsin's calls not for reform but for rejection of Soviet statism and the dissolution of the Soviet Empire. And though Gorbachev could not win *openly fighting* Yeltsin's platform,[12] he found more devious ways to accomplish the same goal.

PERESTROIKA THAT WAS NOT

Gorbachev's brand of *perestroika* had been centrally planned and had not promised to weaken the apparat—the skein of ties between party bosses, enterprise managers, and Gosplan bureaucrats beholden to the Kremlin. As the plan had no specific provisions for a new set of directors to implement market forces, the already crumbling Soviet economy could only further break down in the spheres of production, currency controls, distribution, and consumption.[13] And by the summer of 1990, there were severe bread, meat, and other consumer goods shortages.[14]

The economy seemingly moribund, the only logical alternative was left undone—to empty the government warehouses of things in short supply by selling them to consumers—thus absorbing their surplus 3.5 billion rubles, stopping inflation, and boosting popular morale. And to offset the decline and stimulate output, private ownership of the means of labor and decentralized individual economic initiative would be the next logical steps. But all these steps Gorbachev tried to delay.[15]

Instead, the president publicly procrastinated, initially proposing that a national referendum would have to decide the question of the privatization of some means of existence and production. "Private owner-ship of land—to be or not to be? To make this decision is the sovereign right of the people, and it can be taken only through a referendum," he said, adding philosophically:

> We pin the solution of the socialist revolution's fundamental concern, the elimination of man's alienation from the means of production, on the formation of multiple kinds of ownership. Thereby socialism will be brought in line with the private interests of people. . . . In essence, we are returning to the slogan "Factories and plants to the workers, land to the peasants!"

As alienation of "man by man" was not composed in this formula, delay at implementation meant the centrist bureaucratic control of the means of production, which had long alienated Soviet peoples, was not to be directly dealt with. Yet by making it sound as if he proposed taking the property away from the state these apparat controlled, Gorbachev tried to sidestep thundering public demands for change, proposing more delay:

We have to take the path of denationalization and create a mixed economy in which state-owned and joint-stock enterprises, cooperatives, rented enterprises and a definite proportion of private business would operate on an equal footing. . . .

One must not force the people into new forms of economic life, into shareholding enterprises, co-ops, lease holding or into private property without taking into account the realities of the society, the objective development of the economic processes, the main interest of the people, their moods, their psychology. . . . In reforming ownership relations we are creating realistic and healthy grounds for true collectivism, not the nationalization of everything, but the creation of free associations of producers, shareholding societies, producers' and consumers' cooperatives, associations of leaseholders and entrepreneurs—all this is the high road to true socialization of production on the principles of voluntary participation and economic expediency. . . . Private property would play a substantial role only in some domains, but only a rather limited role in society as a whole.[16]

Theoretical talk was talk about the future—without mentioning datelines. The argument: With the means of production in hand, the work effort of each person would determine the individual rewards the market distributed in material terms. "Only a balanced market can provide for realization of the main principle of socialism—distribution according to the work done," Gorbachev said.[17]

With work efforts the basis of earnings, the next logical step would be to stop inflation of prices above pay. "Cash income is depreciated when shop counters are empty," Gorbachev concluded of rising prices. Taking the availability and price of bread, food, and housing in relation to the price of labor as a determinant of living standards, it was clear that for seventy years these standards had periodically risen, often fallen, under the central dictatorship of party government, then been undercut in the late eighties by producers failing to bring their goods to market, as well as by consumers spending pent-up savings to inflate the price of an inadequate supply of goods remaining on the market.[18]

Theory aside, Gorbachev was playing with an opposition that wanted the immediate freeing up of markets. "President of the Russian Republic Yeltsin had," the *New York Times* editorialized, "taken the lead in freeing the economy from the apparatchik's grip and moving perestroika to privatization and regulated markets. And he seems more in touch with the emotional pull of nationalism than does Mr. Gorbachev, a cool rationalist who tries to reason with secessionists in the republics."[19]

DEEPER FORCES

The deeper dimension was that Gorbachev was tied to the Communist party and could not move without its approval. With the tide running in favor of Boris Yeltsin's populism, Gorbachev had not dared to face a contested election in 1989, taking instead a "safe" seat on the party slate, which made him a virtual captive of the party. As the party then swung to protect the positions and elevated benefits of its members, Gorbachev would have lost their support if he moved to undermine them, thereby eroding his original power base.[20]

And ideologically accosting him was Yeltsin, who had severed his own party ties, used the Parliament of the Russian Republic to end the tradition that allowed local party bosses to preside simultaneously over local governments, and asserted that the laws of the Russian Republic outranked those of the Union. Yeltsin sought governance over a republic twice the size of the United States, with 147 million people and most of the Soviet Union's oil, gold, diamonds, and ballistic missiles. Soviet decentralization and loosening the party's grip, he insisted, would eliminate the parasites of the apparat. Free markets and the wholesale privatization of the economy would of itself unmask the old bureaucratic "communism." Its operatives would be without work.

Yeltsin's logic was clear: Just as the Russian Republic had proclaimed the sovereignty of its laws over the national legal code and would delegate only limited authority to the Kremlin, so each ethnic homeland and community should prepare to run its own affairs. The ministries that then ran both industry and agriculture on a command or barter basis, requisitioning output and setting prices, should be replaced with free markets. To raise living standards, production would have to be raised and the workers rewarded for their efforts. The local factories would thus produce at a volume they set, sell in markets and at prices they chose, keep the revenue flow to themselves for reinvestment to cover costs and pay wages. But to install such a system would first require, Yeltsin said, "Denationalization of property, decentralization of everything — politics, economics, culture, everything."[21]

ON THE QUESTION OF HUNGER:
PARLIAMENT COULD NOT AGREE

Food, and the potential lack of it, was an historical counterweight in tsarist and Soviet politics,[22] momentarily tipping the balance in Gorbachev's favor in 1990.

"If in the next two or three weeks we don't rectify the situation, many cities will be left without potatoes and vegetables — and potatoes are our second bread," Prime Minister Ryzhkov told a rapt audience in a TV interview on 23 September, citing "cruel and unpleasant" facts about the pitiful attempts to collect the 1990 harvest. Despite a bountiful crop, as of midweek, he bemoaned, only one-third of the potato harvest had been gathered. September 18 had arrived, said he, but only 2 percent (12,000 tons) of Moscow's required winter stock had been gathered for storage, while Leningrad had put away only 10 percent (28,000 tons) of its needs.

To bring in the rest of the harvest, he insisted, the government had no choice but to rely on "administrative measures"[23] — that is, the *diktat* of the old command economy. Thus, he explained, "some institutions" might be closed, the army reserves called in as the labor force required for the final effort, local interests subordinated to national needs. Cities like Moscow, he added, were now beset by new liberal city governments that no longer helped bring in the harvest for themselves as they once had, lacking "mutual understanding."[24] It was a mean little political trick. But the prime minister insisted that President Gorbachev needed emergency powers to save the nation from economic collapse.

As Gorbachev had already gone before the Supreme Soviet, repeatedly requesting *special powers* to carry forward plans to switch to a market economy, he was now also fulminating that "in some cases" he might have to invoke his presidential powers and override local institutions. Yeltsin immediately mobilized the Russian Republic's parliamentary presidium to call the idea of emergency powers "inadmissible," vowing to challenge their validity on Russian territory.[25]

Yet Gorbachev won the moment, demanding and receiving emergency powers from Parliament on 24 September 1990 in the name of a more effective functioning of government. Approval by an overwhelming vote of 305–36 gave the president authority to effectuate policies on wages, prices, budget finances, and the "strengthening of law and order." The former meant continuing the old central economic plan; the latter, the potential mobilization of troops.[26] The Supreme Soviet's advance approval would not be required, but afterwards it would have the right to challenge the president's directives.

Still, this was not exactly the old mode of central planning and the KGB system, now lodged in the hands of a single man, not a Stalinist but also not a democrat. For Gorbachev would attempt to enforce a compromise between rival plans for economic change and redistributing power — between the central government and the republics, between the presidency and the republics' legislatures, among the newly emerging political parties and factions.[27]

The deeper logic was that the Kremlin would control mercantile operations between republics, siphon off revenues for the bureaucratic and party machinery, impose a renewed centrist administration on provincial communities, and face off with local efforts to decentralize control over barter trade and labor resources. It was the command structure pitted against regional autonomy, without a clear line of demarcation.[28]

Yet Yeltsin was firm: Any attempt to undermine the Russian Republic's sovereignty would be powerfully met by countermeasures.[29]

Using Gorbachev's executive order to approve the economic status quo, Ryzhkov immediately requested to keep in force the long-discredited ministries' central economic plan — and thus the Union intact — for another fifteen months. Gorbachev decreed that separatist-minded republics and insurgent localities would immediately have to live up to the central plan's contracts for the delivery of goods and other commodities across the nation. Yet almost immediately compliance presented a problem as the various republics asserted their autonomy and pursued their own decentralized economic agendas. Still, there would be neither full republican sovereignty nor a switch to "free market" economics in the near term.[30]

Gorbachev's status quo meant attempts to continue the command system and short-run stability: the bureaucracies directing the plan, the railroads delivering goods, the army enforcing order. The old apparatchiks would try to rule over an economy they could not control, forcing them to make new impositions the people and republics would resent—and surely organize to oppose.

National unity would also be delayed. Battle lines would be drawn between Kremlin *diktat* and republic nonconformity. Privatization of means of production would momentarily become an unreachable goal. The myth of a workable economy would be transformed into the reality of decentralized production, hoarding of surpluses, deprivation in the urban domain, and impoverishment in the countryside. Workers would delay or hoard production for fear of Kremlin confiscation of their output . Shoppers would hold government issue of coupons for commodities that would never be produced or ever reach the market. The candor and freedoms of *glasnost* would neither lead to arrest nor put bread, potatoes, sausages, on the table. And the only seeming way out was to attempt to build a productive and marketing apparatus on a decentralized foundation.

PARTY APPROPRIATIONS

Meanwhile, to cover lack of Russian supplies, the party spent hard currencies on imports and declared that Soviet resources had to be exported to pay the bill.

In the past, such a system of extraction of wealth and destruction of natural resources had been disguised by government statisticians, theoreticians, and would-be political magicians.[31] Communist property was the only item on the rise so far as relative wealth was concerned, Solzhenitsyn railed in 1990:

> They have looted lots of people's wealth, used it for 70 years. Of course they will never return all that has been wasted, thrown about, stolen. But you Communists should return at least what you still have: buildings and sanatoriums, special farms, and publishing houses. And you should live on your party membership fees.
>
> And for purely party work you should pay pensions on your own, not from the state treasury. All this nomenklatura bureaucracy, millions of parasites of the administrative apparat, paralyzing all public life with their grand salaries, privileges and special shops—we must put an end to feeding them! They must be involved in a socially useful labor and live on the money they earn.[32]

The party still refused to face up to its extortion. As President Gorbachev thus spoke of major economic change without "the luxury of getting involved in a reshuffle of political structures,"[33] it was almost too late for the public to believe he would ever voluntarily relinquish central rule. For the battle lines were clearly formed, with populations in revolt demanding economic improvements confronting party apparats and bureaucrats seeking continued control and undisturbed personal securities.

The bottom line, if party control was ever in jeopardy, was the military directed by the KGB. "Towering above us," Solzhenitsyn pointed out, "is the granite monolith of the KGB, blocking our access to the future. Their tricks are as transparent as their claims that they are especially needed today for international intelligence. Everybody sees this as the opposite of truth. Their only goal is to exist for themselves and suppress any movement by the people. There is no justification, no right for the Cheka-KGB to exist, with its 70 years of bloody history."[34] The Cheka had been the tsar's hidden enforcers; the KGB, the Kremlin's.

FAILED PROGRAMS FOR REFORM (1990–91)

Reforms were obviously required. There were at least two basic viewpoints and many programs and compromised solutions offered in 1990–91, with three distinct proposals emanating from three different social alliances:

> 1. The bureaucrats' proposal for continued state subsidies, price controls, central direction of the economy, which gauged consumption not by individual efforts but by right.
> 2. A completely free, decentralized market economy advocated by the breakaway republics that largely represented rural society and deprived urban masses.
> 3. A centrally directed economy using ruble subsidies to slowly introduce market relations, advocated by party centrists who feared decentralization spelled the destruction of their jobs in regulating the Union.

The first plan represented the past. Its tenet was that even without work for those who could, the state would provide. Everyone might have a job, but no one would be required to work to capacity. That was the situation that emerged after 1945.

Yet the last two alternatives were just as fallible, more hope than a scientific plan: utopian in the sense that the Soviet Union had nearly no experience in implementing anything like them. But that mattered little in the great party battle for control.

Plan One: Building Battle Lines

The first plan conception was that work benefits are only partly related to work effort and the state will look after everyone falling below a state-set standard of consumption. All able-bodied might have a job and might work, but if pay fell short, the state would remunerate the difference in welfare subsidies.[35] (It was the old English "Speedhamland System" given a Russian context.)

This old-guard program, propounded by Prime Minister Nikolai Ryzhkov in 1990, was more a negative shielding than a set of actual steps to be taken to bring a new order to fruition. For its core provision was across-the-board ruble compensation to society at large in the event of unexpected price rises, which everyone had already expected. This meant the central authorities would be pressured to expand the future money supply, both encouraging inflation and discouraging worker productivity.

The opposition took joy in belittling Ryzhkov's self-defined "moderately radical" plan to be put in place over a five-year term. "Such a 'radical' plan could only have been proposed by specialists 'radically' freed from the need to wait in line at the shops," Moscow mayor Popov intoned, to the laughter of some of the 30,000 protestors outside the Kremlin walls, referring to the fact that ranking officials like Ryzhkov and his aides were exempted from the ordinary Soviet citizen's daily duty to line up in search of ever-scarcer food supplies.

The logic of scarcities the public knew. The quality and availability of most meat had already fallen by September 1990, while prices had escalated. Government officials offered the vagaries that the price increase due on 1 January 1991 for meat procured by the state had already encouraged farmers to refrain from slaughtering their stock until the higher price would be paid and meanwhile had fed their herds from the cheap grain emerging from the nation's bumper harvest. It was also a cheap government shot because the public was then already paying the elevated price.[36]

Plan Two: The Great Party Battle

"If the economic plan is presented by the Government now in office, the people will not believe it," regardless of its substance, corroborated insurgent mayor of Moscow Gavril K. Popov in early September 1990 of the failure of Gorbachev's economic reforms under the controlled go-slow approach of Prime Minister Nikolai I. Ryzhkov.

Behind the advocacy of quickened reorganization of the economy along commercial and wage-labor lines was the populist Yeltsin, who opposed both centrist planners and the Communist directorate of economic affairs. He viewed the Communist ideologist Ligachev and President Gorbachev as unrelenting slaves to old Communist formulas about work efforts being unrelated to state-awarded benefits and the spoils system favoring Communist party members and their nepotistic allies.[37]

He had neither a capitalist mentality nor a socialist bent, but he understood the linkage of popular welfare to personal effort and the future production potential of the republics. He seemed beholden to no bureaucratic contrivance, thus freed to offer a plan for ethnic, republic, and personal liberation. With the many he was popular; toward his opponents, arrogant.[38]

Cabalist by nature of its organizational structure, the Communist party assailed him as an enemy of the state. Yet due to the jaded mood of a public preoccupied with economic survival in the face of Communist party loss of central control over the economy, Moscow and Leningrad leaders held powerful influence, even proposing to call off the public celebrations on Revolution Day, 7 November, Popov arguing, "Some people want to protest on Nov. 7 the Red terror of 1917. That is why we call on all political parties to abstain from political actions Nov. 7."[39]

But the Red Terror was now economic. Production had gyrated from 1981, reached a momentary high in 1986, backed off, reached greater heights in 1988, then crashed with a falling gross national product into the negative zone (minus .25 to 2.5 percent by 1990). As GNP had dropped, too few goods on the market had then sent prices up from a little less than 2 percent in 1984 to 10 percent in 1990.

Living standards were plummeting, and with production flagging, unemployment rose from 4.2 percent of the working population in mid-June 1989 to 4.9 percent a year later. To maintain the populace, imports would need to be enlarged. But as the net export on the trade account went from a surplus in hard currencies of about $35 billion between mid-1981 and 1985 to a small deficit from 1988–89, the Soviet inability to harvest a bumper crop meant grain imports would continue to eat up valuable hard currencies.[40]

No surprise, then: By early September of 1990, the political mood in Moscow was nasty. President Gorbachev had displayed the tragic flaws of centrist logic, bred of consensus among the traditional ruling Communist party and its apparatchiks, loyal ministers and bureaucrats demanding a compromised version of any plan for far-reaching change.[41]

By contrast, the loyalists behind Russian Republic president Boris Yeltsin had propounded a 500-day recipe for free markets, but Gorbachev insisted that he remain in charge of its reformation under one of his top advisors, Stanislav Shatalin. For indeed, in Gorbachev's vision, the surrender and dismantling of central controls and the start of one hundred days of stabilization measures would lead to a loss of the controls held by the Communist party and Gorbachev's loyal government, as well as lead to the disintegration of the Union under the pressures of mass unemployment, uncontrollable inflation, and civil conflict.[42]

The second plan expressed, then, that without work of the able-bodied, there should be no consumption. Everyone able must hold a job and must work. Otherwise, they would not eat.

The Hybrid Plan: Compromise

The hybrid proposal by dissident Gorbachev advisor Nikolai Petrokov was as much a psychological as an economic plan. "Soviet citizens would prefer to stand in long lines rather than confront a rise in prices," he criticized the Ryzhkov centrist plan. "The Government must enjoy popular support and confidence as we go over to the market economy." The state, that is, would stabilize prices for too few goods sold in government stores.

Like both Gorbachev and Yeltsin, Petrokov focused on taking from each worker according to ability and effort and remunerating each only in proportion to such labor. That, he argued, would regenerate the Soviet work effort, as those who refused to work would not eat or otherwise survive. Thus the government should not subsidize consumption or amenities, though during the first three months of his proposed 500-day plan prices should not be allowed to be set by market pressures.[43]

There was also urgency to move forward, Petrokov insisted. "We are witnessing the disintegration of the Soviet monetary system," he warned, accusing the central, command system of worsening the condition of the many as the daily downward spiral of the economy led individuals to take deliberate measures to protect their own positions.[44]

Joining together to back the Yeltsin-Shatalin handbook, numbering 224 pages, Petrokov and others explicated its essentials for the first one hundred days of dismantling the props of the state-directed economy and introducing private enterprise and initiative. "It's society's right to start living better today and not in some far-off tomorrow," the plan propounded. "Our sad experience [with seventy-two years of Bolshevik central direction and misrule] demonstrates how dangerous for society and normal life is the man who has nothing to lose."

To provide incentive to work, apartments and small land plots would be awarded to those who had earned them by hard labor under communism. But an inventory of the rest of the nation's resources and properties would be for marketing them to those accumulating sufficiently to buy them, the reformers emphasizing, "The state must not give away its property free. People [who do not compete for economic resources and self-improvements] will not believe in free property or value it adequately."[45]

The Basic Reform Program

Thus the basic reform program[46] was approved by almost all factions, each looking for its favored provisions:

1. freeing prices from state controls, except for some one hundred basic consumer goods, but setting wage and price controls in the early stages and protecting the living standards of low-income people

2. immediate slashing of government spending, including an end to Soviet foreign aid, a 20 percent cutback in appropriations for the KGB, and a 10 percent reduction in military spending

3. strict controls on the printing of rubles to prevent an excess of currency above the market value of goods available and to prevent consumers from unloading their weak rubles bidding up the price of scarce goods

4. creating a banking system and stock market to channel capital but preventing advances of credit by the government regulation of interest rates, again limiting the rubles available to compete for scarce goods

5. importing essential consumer goods to increase the supply, thereby stamping out the inflationary spiral

6. dismantling the central bureaucracy under the Gosplan, abolishing most ministries regulating industry, stopping subsidies to both industry and agriculture—again slashing the central state budget and freeing up resources for other needs

7. eliminating all regulations impeding the initiation or expansion of private enterprise and privatizing farmland, housing, and businesses by sale to the public of state and party properties, including cars, factories, and homes

8. selling off all state-held property—absorbing the publicly held 500 billion excess supply of rubles, thereby halting inflation—to promote private ownership, enterprise, and a spirit of personal accumulation linked to work

9. offering full powers to the fifteen constituent republics to set and regulate their own economic policies, allowing each republic to claim all the raw materials and property within their borders, set up their own banks, impose taxes, and send residual "dues" to the Kremlin to cover national needs such as defense and natural calamities

10. cooperation between all republics to impose emergency programs to stabilize the economy through austerity measures, even including a potential freeze on wages and other measures to control inflation.

This plan sailed through the Russian Republic's Parliament with only one vote opposed.[47] But the legislative quickness of Russia—with three-quarters of the nation's land, more than half the population, and most of its natural resources—nonplussed the members of the national Parliament.[48]

Then, on 12 September 1990, Prime Minister Nikolai Ryzhkov offered another program that used the structure of the Shatalin Plan yet provided a fundamental difference from the more sweeping 500-day program. President Gorbachev announced that there must be "one program on the basis of the two" rival plans, with the Ryzhkov Plan differences, by item number:

1. Central state price setting emanating from Moscow's bureaucracy would remain in place, so there would be no free-market level and allegedly no inflation.
3. Currency controls should be eased slowly.
8. Strict limitations should be imposed on private ownership and this initiative.
9. Central state controls should continue to preserve the federal government, limiting the power of the fifteen separate republics to set their own economic policies.

Adherents to the different platforms now fought a pitched parliamentary battle.[49] "No government in the world has voluntarily given away power and land," Shatalin offered as Gorbachev's—and now, ex officio, apparently Yeltsin's—chief economic advisor.

"They [President Gorbachev and Prime Minister Ryzhkov] are both afraid of finding themselves out of business," added Sergei N. Krasavchenko, chairman of the Economic Reform Committee of the Russian Parliament. "For Ryzhkov the danger is much closer. For Gorbachev, less probable, but not excluded."[50]

Thus the party agenda spoke of

• stronger guarantees to realize the right to work, including payment according to the quantity and quality of work done and its final results
• the formation of a mechanism to maintain employment, training, and retraining of personnel and adequate material support for those who are forced to change their trade, profession, or place of work.

GORBACHEV'S FATAL ERROR

The absurd and shocking extent of the apparatchiks' ignorance, incompetence, pretensions, and inflexible controls was the foundation for the atavistic malaise that made *perestroika* under Gorbachev impossible, forcing him to momentarily swing backwards to pick up their support, then unsuccessfully to try to go forward to bring *perestroika* to fruition. Gorbachev's fatal error was that he miscalculated how the party, the apparat, the army, and KGB would react to his renewed effort to undermine the traditional bureaucracies of party, government, security, and military force.

Gorbachev had deployed his personal authority and power in the party and among the apparats favoring *perestroika* between 1985 and 1990.[51] Yet as the party had been the power behind the state, Gorbachev thought he could not openly confront it without fomenting a revolt.

As *Izvestia* later detailed an investigator's testimony, "The Soviet state during the 70 years of Communism was turned imperceptibly and easily into a mechanism for the feeding of Party interests." Facing powerful party opposition to proposed changes, then, Gorbachev had momentarily swung to the side of the apparat in 1991, appointing its leading members as his closest advisers, even authorizing the party to put its capital into small enterprises, joint-stock companies, private banks, and other capitalist ventures, a Russian parliamentary hearing later disclosed. By summer 1991, party functionaries had thereby scurried to shelter themselves and their money from a conversion to a market economy, perhaps calculating that the party itself would have to go underground.[52]

Gorbachev even brought Shevardnadze back to appease the democrats, illusory though it was. "It is perfectly obvious that by returning to his job as Foreign Minister . . . Mr. Shevardnadze is helping the center maintain its respectability in the eyes of the West, as is Mr. Yakovlev, who returned to the Kremlin earlier," human rights advocate Yelena Bonner wrote, parenthetically adding: "Their return to government confirmed that their Democratic Reform Movement, an elite club that excluded representatives of workers, independent republics and democrats, was democratic in name only. Its aim was to preserve a unified state and its military-industrial complex."

When Gorbachev decisively moved outside the frame of the traditional unified state and complex directed by the party and against its wishes to proceed with *perestroika* unfettered, he provoked the poorly planned military coup discussed in Chapters 1 and 14, leading step by step to ever new schemes to create a market economy.

POSTCOUP PLANS: CREATING A MARKET IN RUSSIA'S IMAGE

Postcoup Russian market plans were framed by Western financial precepts of austerity fostering declining living standards. These plans largely ignored those in charge of, and profiting from, the Russian economy: the old party functionaries, apparats, oligarches, mafias, and provocateurs in controlling centers of production, storage, and distribution of goods.

As post–World War II bureaucracy had thickened the complexities for the distribution of goods and services, corruption of its intermediaries and bribery by both buyers and the public had become an essential ingredient for maintaining personal living standards. The official legitimate economy was a barrier to survival, thus followed by few in government or private life, giving rise to a massive catch-22 of underground trade in necessary and surplus goods, actually draining from one-third to one-half of all Soviet output. "Historically," Lydia Rosner documents,

> every Soviet official controlled a sphere of influence that allowed for a life of privilege: access to a network of special stores, hospitals and service establishments. But it was not only the official who was involved in

such "crime"; the ordinary citizen participated through a system of
shabashnichestvo (freelance work) that moved consignments of stolen
materials from construction sites into a private industry of home
building; from clothing factories to a private industry of independent
seamstresses, and so on.

The system allowed the average citizen to accumulate some income
by negotiating to provide special goods and services outside the state
system. Parents bribed teachers to "look after" their children. Taxi
drivers bribed supervisors to assign them to cabs and gas. Butchers accepted bribes for meat. From top to bottom, socialization of Soviet
citizens included acceptance of a nonlegal system of self-help and free
enterprise.

With the Soviet citizen understanding well that the consequence of
honesty was deprivation, foreign-made technology and other goods
bought from returning travelers by middle agents and entrepreneurial
"mafia" and sold under the table at inflated ruble prices followed the laws
of supply and demand. Yet the people's ideological supposition was that
these selling activities were illegal, as was turning a profit, thus requiring
the millions engaged in underground activities to seek means surrep-
titiously to secure and store their accumulated wealth, to hide their ruble
earnings in mattresses, hoard dollars in foreign banks. Any plan to reform
the new republics' economies, then, would require a clear redefinition of
legal economic affairs, "free enterprise," and selling goods and services to
make money and profit.[53]

Yet the new Russian plan did not clearly distinguish the underground
activities of the past from the new reign of legal economy. Rather, crudely
formulated by Russian Deputy Prime Minister Yegor Gaidar and un-
tested in January 1992, the proclaimed scheme concentrated on several
practical components that did not take account of the rapid downward fall
in living standards:

- improvement in Soviet economic expectations held by Western nations, to be facilitated by four sources: the central bank's stronger ruble; Parliament's tighter budget; the Yeltsin government's practical
  economic plan; and some $20 billion in temporary foreign aid, in-
  cluding $6 billion in emergency food, $5 billion in currency stabilization funds, and $6 billion in balance-of-payments aid
- government implementation of a free market, with prices to assume a
  level based on supply and demand
- stimulation to production and delivery centers to supply the market of
  supposed ruble-rich buyers
- central bank controls preventing printing excess rubles, regulating interest rates and turn to the ruble's floating rate of exchange with the
  dollar
- parliamentary tightening of the national budget, curbing spending and
  raising necessary taxes

• drastic revision of the military-industrial complex and a switch of government and industrial resources to civilian production.

In part, this plan was designed and was to be guided by Jeffrey Sachs, a Harvard economist, who viewed demand-led supply in the context of a free marketplace. Though Sachs argued it would take time for higher prices to elicit adequate supplies, the doubling of prices in the single week 7–14 January, had not yet brought forth new goods, and consumers were critical.[54]

For it was more a crisis-designed program that created its own political dangers than a scheme for social renewal, Deputy Prime Minister Gaidar, reporting to Parliament on 16 January 1992 that the "panic" among consumers and the populace had become "the most serious threat we face now." Price reform had led to an initial burst of 200 to 300 percent price escalation and bitter hardship, he admitted, yet some stores were being supplied with meat and dairy products.[55]

Still, that would not solve the basic dilemma. Both Gaidar and First Deputy Prime Minister Gennadi E. Burbulis were warning on 24 January that without Western credits, the country would not be able to buy the grain it needed to keep bread on the table by spring. President Yeltsin told a meeting of the Russian government that the country's ordeal could be compared only to the dark days of hunger of World War II.[56]

Domestic solutions seemed increasingly unlikely, for the chairman of the Russian Central Bank and Parliament would not cooperate, as Gaidar-Sach's model called for.

Bank chairman Georgi Matyukhin complained that Yeltsin's "shock therapy" had already brought soaring prices, no new production, and higher risks of spreading social unrest. Gaidar's program to float the ruble against foreign currencies, he argued, was a bad prescription designed by the International Monetary Fund and World Bank, allowing Russian assets to be purchased dirt cheap by outsiders as the ruble plummeted and would "allow our whole republic to be bought for a dollar!" The only path to establishing convertibility with the dollar was by internal stabilization of supplies of needed commodities and fostering exports earning hard currencies. Parliamentary speaker Ruslan Khasbulatov said nearly the same, calling on Yeltsin to dismiss his cabinet.

The logic of moving from the old command economy to a foreign-directed one and then to a free-trade system based on falling Russian living standards was the frame for foreign advice. Yet such advice was not designed to deal with either social chaos or the Russian-bred character. Fearing hunger and deprivation, the population could not long survive on the hopes of Western technocrats. Sachs baited the Russian Central Bank and its parent central bank of the defunct Soviet Union as "the main source of the hyperinflation that is now under way." He wanted its printing-press money excesses to stop. And he also wanted Parliament to stop setting central bank policies and to tighten the national budget and raise taxes.[57]

He seemed to be blind to, or wantonly ignore, the political possibilities that Yeltsin's government might lose popularity and give way to the old factions of the Communist party or others beholden to a centrist, authoritarian state. For the Russian people's resentment of Western institutions and capitalist calculations might one day center on their leaders' turn to foreign solutions and investments that impoverished them. "We are determined to prevent the government's policy from becoming the basis of dictatorship," chairman of the Russian Parliament Ruslan Khasbulatov warned of the Russian people's increasing disappointment with reform, making them open to, or victims of, a new dictatorial oligarchy.[58]

Western liberals and democrats took up this reasoning too, focusing their lens on the need for immediate foreign aid. "The West has got to be ready to take some calculated risks right now in supporting Yeltsin's imperfect, but nevertheless bold, initiatives," declared Robert D. Hormats, vice chairman of Goldman Sachs International and a former assistant secretary of state for international economics. "If Yeltsin does not succeed, he is not going to be followed by a combination of Thomas Jefferson and Milton Friedman. He is going to be succeeded by some Rasputin-like xenophobic nationalist." Thus, he said, the 22 January 1992, aid-giving coordinating conference in Washington, "which is being held at the foreign ministers level, has to go beyond mere coordination. Coordination can be done by technocrats. These ministers need to make some fundamental decisions, not just about coordination but about whether at this moment in history it is more important to support the Yeltsin reforms with a broad package of economic assistance."

The New York Times editorialized along similar lines:

> Mr. Yeltsin is surrounded by rivals and advisers ready to counter economic crisis and popular discontent with authoritarianism. Furthermore, most of the preconditions were not in place when Mr. Yeltsin freed prices, like banking and tax systems and tight money. And no economist knows whether hoarders and producers will move enough goods to market to halt spiraling inflation.
>
> No sooner did Mr. Yeltsin take the leap than his rivals began backtracking. Their distaste for the disorder of markets and democracy is exceeded only by a dangerous nostalgia for the strong hand.[59]

Other republics faced the same fears, Kazakhstan planning to offset crisis with timely reform programs. With its economy operating at 60 percent of production capacity, useless state factories laying off workers, and prices expected to rise more than sevenfold in 1992, the autocratic former Communist leaders of Kazakhstan moved to privatize 40 percent of its capital Alma-Ata's housing supply, privatize production, and set up an academy to train experts able to introduce a market economy. Rich in minerals and territory under a Muslim Kazakh majority, its incipient business class sidestepped heavy new taxes with off-the-book deals; its 11-million majority tried to accommodate its 6-million Russian minority; it contracted with the Chevron Corporation to develop its lucrative oil fields; and its property conversion authorities began distributing shares to workers in slightly less than 5 percent of its enterprises. Still, the chairman of the state conversion committee reported, most workers hesitated "to allow auction of their factories for privatization, because they know new private managers will demand harder work and efficiency and they could lose their jobs." For thus would be changed an old formula that everyone held a government-assigned job with guaranteed pay but no one had the incentive to work.

Reforms had to be quickly implemented in the face of the impending crisis too, Dr. Chan Young Bang, one advising U.S. economist from the University of San Francisco, insisting there was little time: "Within two years, there'll be fresh stagnation, and then big social unrest unless positive and very radical change can happen."[60]

RUSSIA'S IRON HEART AND SHOCK REFORMS: THE SPREADING BATTLE FOR DAILY BREAD

The Yeltsin government's "shock reforms," initially raising many prices fourfold between 2–15 January, could be effective only if the old *apparat*, oligarches, and unions relinquished control of production, distribution, and storage centers. Otherwise, there seemed no way to use price increments to elicit increased output and delivery in the short run.

If the old power centers were openly confronted, moreover, they might further withhold goods from markets, aggravate the crisis, and ensure that reform politicians would be turned out of office by the populace. "The market is being set up in difficult conditions," Yeltsin warned. In the wake of the collapse of the Soviet Union and the economic crisis, "mafia-like structures [were] striving to keep their dominance *in distribution,* [by] open sabotage and [through] ideological opposition."

These structures also dominated *production.* Yet in criticizing the slow pace of privatization, Yeltsin at first concentrated on a legislative program that by the close of 1992 would put more than 70 percent of Russia's *wholesale trade* organizations, *retail trade* stores, and restaurants in private hands.[61]

Some of the monopolies keeping food off the market were still under government ownership and control. The government, not having itself overthrown the archaic central command system of rules, the process of making and distributing key commodities like bread and milk made production slow, inefficient, below capacity, and incapable of generating enough revenue to upgrade technical methods.

The illogic of the old central planners had ensured the farmers and millers a certain level of income, building up Moscow's grain and flour reserves to carry 8 million people through the winter by allowing them to charge set "market" prices. It also set the income of bakers and workers in retail bread stores by allowing each to add no more than 25 percent to their costs of raw materials or bread-factory charges. But access to sufficient bread-delivery vehicles and the system's rules also empowered the retail distributors to limit bread-factory output 10 to 15 percent below capacity production. Not only was service slowed due to theft-protection procedures eliminating "self-service" as people fingered loaves or took chunks and put them back, but cashiers handling unsanitary money did not double as salesclerks handling hygienic bread. And the rules encouraged store managers to resist overordering by penalizing them some three rubles' credit for every loaf purchased at four rubles, meaning less money for store manager and employee bonuses and partially bare bread-store shelves that were exhausted before closing time.

Though the Moscow Retail Bread Committee rejected suggestions by economist critics, arguing the committee wanted to limit supplies to keep prices up, the Moscow city government offered stores subsidies for returned bread so they would be encouraged to order more. And more was needed* as the population substituted bread for more costly foods like milk, cheese, meat, and eggs; used cheaper black breads rather than more expensive high-quality flour in white bread rolls sprinkled with sugar; considered sale-priced day-old bread at 20 to 30 percent off; and were the object of older bread returned to factories being ground into crumbs for use as filling in meat.

Though there were sufficient reserves of flour for four or five months until the 1991–92 winter wheat was harvested in May, Russian farmers wary of rising prices were withholding grain supplies. Russia, lacking the hard currency to keep up purchases from the West, was banking on Western credits to buy the grain it needed to keep bread on the table in spring.[62] And the crisis of insufficient bread making and delivery loomed because the government had yet to jettison the impedimenta of the old command economy.[63]

Milk, meat, pajamas, shoes, and car production were similarly trussed by extortionist middle agents, where prices were neither set by the state nor dictated by a competitive market but set at levels producer-distributors demanded. If consumers refused to buy at inflated prices beyond their means, perishable goods rotted in the stores; others were sent back to producers, who then cut back production or closed down and fired workers rather than reduce costs. The still-monopolized realm of

---

*Daily bread production in Moscow ranged upward from 2,300 tons in January 1992, having risen from less than 2,000 tons in January 1991; maximum capacity was 2,800 tons.

production had used state price liberalization as an excuse to extort higher prices. "Where there are monopolies, liberalization can only give the results that we have seen," Georgi Matyukhin, head of the Russian Central Bank, told the newspaper *Sovetskaya Rossiya*. "The monopoly begins with a cut in production, and then raises prices. Anyone can understand that."[64]

Under Siege from All Directions

Along all these fronts, the Yeltsin program was thus under siege from more cautious politicians above, the oligarchies in the middle, and the working class below. The juggernaut was the state budget. With the 24 January Russian Parliament budget approval of disarmament measures creating unemployment and welfare cuts certain to impoverish millions, the fuse was sparked for a future explosion if Western aid failed.

For that budget called for an 85 percent cut in government arms procurement, certain to cause widespread unemployment among the defense sector's 8 million workers in military factories who had sustained the bulk of the Soviet Union's defense industries by concentration in isolated regions and cities. Parliament voted to cut military outlays from what had been 25 percent of the entire Soviet economy to 4.5 percent of Russia's gross national product, carrying 62.3 percent of the new Commonwealth burden of a single joint army. Parliament also offset the impact of the cuts by authorizing the central bank to give $10 billion in credits to aid military factories in converting to civilian production, and Deputy Prime Minister Gaidar said the government was prepared to set aside half of the budgetary savings from cuts on arms procurement as social assistance to these displaced workers, the cuts nonetheless rippling through the economic system, raising unemployment from 60,000 in January to a government-estimated 7–8 million by October.

If unemployment did not break the back of government legitimacy, the inability to stabilize the ruble might. As the central bank had pumped some $600 billion of loaned rubles into the economy in 1991, the population barely kept up with prices. But 1992 government attempts to control the central bank's printing-press money were sure to take away the essential means of survival for those without work or on fixed incomes—the old, young, and enfeebled.[65]

And prices would be increased again under the government's 28 percent value-added tax on producers, who tried to pass the tax on to consumers, raising prices beyond their means.

Would the government bend to the demands of various segments of the population? *From above*, price increments were the obvious excuse to wage battle against Yeltsin's cabinet, speaker of Parliament Ruslan Khasbulatov openly attacking Yeltsin's taking personal control of the cabinet and its price increases. Opposing Yeltsin's appeals to St. Petersburg's dockers to take possession of their enterprises from the old guard, Mayor Anatoly Sobchak also took cover, arguing that "nowhere in the world does a major port belong to a workers' collective."[66] A coalition of the old *nomenklatura*—the still avid Communists, neo–Communists forming new parties, the Soyuz coterie, and party-linked generals and conspirator–Kryuchkovite KGB believers—stood at the right wing ready to support Vice President Aleksandr Rutskoi and deposed Mikhail Gorbachev.

Seeing the danger, Yeltsin calculated to upstage them by appointing as head his own revanchist Russian minister of security, Viktor Baronikov, who was to direct the undiminished strength of the former KGB under the watchful eye of reform-minded Minister of Justice Nikolai Fyedorov, whose mission was to cleanse the Ministry of Kryuchkovite generals, colonels, and apparatchiks, dateline 1 July 1992. But that proved impossible when the Yeltsin economic plan faltered, foreign aid was not forthcoming on the scale he envisioned, and the population questioned the legitimacy of his government.

From the middle, the oligarches of production, distribution and extortion kept goods off markets, leading Yeltsin to vow to crack down against the "mafia-type structures" trying to divert economic reforms off course. These privateers and public monopolies were able to use the lack of legal rules and market coordination in Russia and between the republics to their own advantage. Yeltsin's government thus announced on 23 January that it would move to eliminate state trading organizations acting as price-setting monopolists.[67] For black-market commerce cared not for official regulations over domestic or interrepublic trade.

The latter also was closing down. "Each republic has begun to act on its own and has been putting up barriers in the way of traffic of goods and establishing various quotas and licences," Nusultan A. Nazarbayev said, explaining the decline of trade endangering reforms and the advantages for black marketeers.[68] For each republic was now raiding the others of their material wealth, both goods and resources. Russians raided Ukrainian markets; Ukrainians bartered in Moldova after Ukraine introduced coupons, leaving its citizens with a cache of increasingly worthless rubles; and Moldovians looked to a future union with Romania to exchange goods and share their markets.

As the Russian price escalation worked its way across the former Soviet republics, those with narrow market economies were drained of food supplies by ruble-rich buyers. The internal economy of Moldova had traditionally linked its more than half-rural population to the urban domain, with virtually every family having relatives or friends on the farm with whom to exchange food and processed goods. Even during the Soviet era, the marketplace was bereft of much quality goods for sale, but thereafter the sudden rise of prices brought in both ruble-rich Ukrainians and Moldovian farmers with pigs and cows or basic goods like sausages, milk, and noodles. The resulting double drain on farm supplies—from the traditional urban-rural exchange and now Ukrainian-rich buyers—threatened domestic survival for the first half of 1992. "These Ukrainians' rubles are emigrating to Moldova, where they are buying our cows at 20 to 30 times the normal price," criticized Mihai Patras, chairman of the parliamentary committee on finances. "Our peasants who have saved maybe 1,000 rubles over the years, now think they can become millionaires overnight. They don't understand that it's just paper."

The Moldovian Parliament had not acted for two years to stem price escalation in the wake of what was already a supply raid from the outside. Farm fodder prices alone had risen 55 percent from January to September 1991, causing agricultural production to drop 16 percent and gross national product to drop 23 percent. Then the Russian price war began, those in Moldova multiplying as high as a hundredfold in January 1992 alone. Recoiling in the third week of January, Parliament replaced the ruble with the leu, still neglecting to set a date for its introduction and value yet foreseeing that the Romanian leu might someday find a parity for exchange. The government also set up customs checkpoints on its borders, though holes in its iron curtain found Ukrainians crossing at a ratio of ten routes for every one covered by a post.

As Parliament then struggled to defend the internal market in the wake of the loss of food supplies, other supplies were no longer being shipped into the republic, so that the rising costs of raw materials for farming and factory meant producers lagged in turning out goods Moldovians could afford to buy. Raw materials and spare parts for Moldova's industries were in such desperately short supply that tractor assembly in Kishinev, unable to get supplies delivered from other republics, closed.[69]

The old interdependence of republics was almost gone, displaced by a new, avaricious search for food and materials. Historical borders were also breached in the search for food, security, and economic advantage, Finland mobilizing its frontier guards along the 816-mile border in watch for smugglers, con men, and weary refugees fleeing toward their prosperous Nordic neighbor.[70] And in the frontierlike market lacking legal rules, properties still technically owned by the state became the subject of privatization by Western and Russian lawyers negotiating contracts, payoffs, and promises of fast profits.[71]

Republic Autarchy, Underlying Discontent, and Privatization

The Commonwealth of Independent States was failing by the end of January, and since the West was too slow with aid to keep it together, the Russian intelligentsia began thinking in terms of Gorbachev's conception of a Union treaty. The still-small Fascist parties backed the *nashi* movement, and the turn to autarchy in each republic spelled defection. "We should perhaps be thinking already of the second Commonwealth because this one is not working," thought prominent Russian economist Andrei Fedorov. "I believe the Ukraine will soon defect."[72]

Yeltsin, reading the political weather vane, knew Russia could not alone stop the Ukraine exit. But he was adamant that Russian autonomy and land mass would not be infringed or partitioned by Tatar or other nationalities seeking independence. Only so many presidential ukaz decrees could hold the population in limbo, check, or awe, though, for price reforms were not bringing forth production, unfettered markets, inexpensive food—or the democratic forum the liberal intelligentsia demanded.

In each republic, meanwhile, populations grumbled, complained, protested, Russia providing a crystal case of the crisis-laced cracking of the government's façade reinforcing the turn toward autarchy.

From below, there was discontent from the Russian trade unions representing 60 million members. On 17 January their protest against higher prices was called a warning "action" to the government, supporters of the Federation of Independent Trade Unions demanding more generous social benefits, picketing government headquarters in Staraya Ploshad, but not yet initiating strikes.[73] As living standards worsened with January's price escalation of 300 to 350 percent, Russia's gross national product dropped 16 to 18 percent, and the government's pacification program began with a reduction in the new sales tax from 28 to 15 percent, cutting anticipated government revenues by $208 million, to be made up by printing money,[74] fueling more inflation as more money chased the falling supply of goods.

To enlarge output, Russia began a crash program to sell off 25 percent of state-owned shops, factories, and other property by the close of 1992, reserving 25 percent of shares in individual enterprises for current employees. Though the Russian Parliament had adopted the law on privatization in July 1991, it had lacked regulations, allowing managers of state companies worth 2 billion rubles to form their own joint-stock companies in 1991. These self-serving takeovers allowed the companies to lease out premises for private profit and sell assets on privately run exchanges. But as the government's 89 local state-property committees around Russia began implementing the privatization plan in February 1992, the state sought to raise 92 billion rubles (about $840 million at the current exchange rate) and to allow Russian entrepreneurs to compete by placing administrative regulations on foreign investors to stop dirt-cheap bids (the ruble had fallen from 32 cents in November 1991 to less than a penny by the first week of February 1992). Foreign companies would be limited to owning shares in certain defined categories, such as the building materials industry, bankrupt firms, and enterprises cutting production for lack of imported equipment or materials. "We intend to change the nature of the process," Yeltsin's chairman of the state property committee, Anatoli B. Chubis, said, "and to move away from the theft of state owned property."[75]

With the Yeltsin schematic in jeopardy, two significant factions surfaced among former Yeltsin supporters: those protecting the old power centers and those in the Yeltsin cabinet and entourage wanting to undercut them by curing Russia's ailments with foreign aid—and autarchy.

The revanchists were led by Russian vice president Aleksandr V. Rutskoi, an air force general and hero of the Afghanistan War, who with the support of army officers and managers of budget-cut military industries was elected as Yeltsin running mate in the spring 1991 election. Not only had Rutskoi created an offshoot of the old Communist party, but he had broken with Yeltsin over the president's repeal of a state emergency ukaz to control nationalists in the southern Caucasus Muslim enclave of Chechen-Ingushetia. An opportunist, Rutskoi played to the extreme patriotic forces of Mother Russia, using both old Communist party papers like *Pravda* and the old Soviet government's *Izvestia* to call for the preservation of the unity and dignity of the army; the rejection of Western solutions, products, and utopian economic plans that imposed economic pain—warning that the Russian people were headed for "economic genocide" under the course chosen by the government and its Western advisers. While Yeltsin warned of the threat of dictatorship made up of the "Red" former Communists and the "Brown" neo–Fascists, Rutskoi tried to unite them through the Congress of Civic and Patriotic Forces, telling their 3,000-strong 8 February 1992 gathering that the government was pursuing a Bolshevik strategy of "revolution at any price," as in the 1917 revolution; that an "economic state of emergency" and the creation of a separate Russian currency were essential; that speculators and "biznesmeni" were ruining the economy. While tactically trying to unite the patriotic "Great Russia" Right and Communist party Left, Rutskoi still supported the popular president and shared his goals. But as one curious Congress attendee and research physician intuited, "This smells of national socialism."[76]

AILMENTS, AID, AUTARCHY, AND
NEW SPHERES OF INFLUENCE

As the battle went forward and intensified, both Western and Asian nations bred to trade and investments saw the danger of the republics' return to the old centrist command system if commercial credits, grants, and investments were not offered. For autarchic republics might resurrect centrist command economies and compete to close their borders to trade to protect resources and output, balkanizing their Eurasian territories in a way incompatible with Western transcontinental market designs.

To offset such steps, Western nations sought an increase in global trade as the best means to stimulate economic growth in Eastern Europe. "Keeping markets open does not cost money, it just needs political energy," the former chairman of the Federal Reserve Board summed up the February 1992 meeting of the World Economic Forum. "And nobody feels they have much money to spare" in the milieu of a 2 to 3 percent growth in Western economies in 1992–93.[77]

Yet each grantor nation reacted differently, generally trying to implement the traditional departmentalization of foreign policy, infrastructural development, direct government aid, and overseas commerce. Rapprochement between the United States and Russia was initiated with President Yeltsin visiting the United States with a political agenda to put the footing of U.S.-Russian relations on a new plane. Under U.S. tutelage, infrastructural aid and loans were to be provided by the World Bank and International Monetary Fund after experts devised a plan for rigorous austerity to stabilize Russia's economy and back the ruble. Only with inflation controlled, inefficient enterprises closed, and workers reoriented to new industries would industrialized member nations financially support the IMF program.

In providing timely survival resources, donor nations sought to bring Russia and the other republics into the global market, reasoning that *aid grants* in food and commodities were essential to fill human requirements, lessening the need for the republics to seal their borders; *commercial credits and guarantees of payment to exporters* would help granting nations extend their spheres of trade; and *foreign investments* would stimulate production and employment within the various republics, becoming a factor in future interrepublic trade and commercial relations with both Eastern and Western Europe. Yet direct government aid for Russia would become a domestic political decision by each nation. And commercial trade, loans, and investments would be based on the calculations and fears "about political, economic and social instability in Russia," as President Yeltsin said after his meeting with some eighty leading U.S. bankers, executives, and economists in February 1992.[78]

Though each grantor nation worked out its own formula for humanitarian and technical assistance, all agreed on one factor: The race for government legitimacy in Russia and the other republics would be calibrated by the pace at which these foreign awards could be consummated. "Look, the West is afraid of a social explosion in Russia, and they say, 'We will tell you where it is likely to be,'" criticized Gennadi A. Zhukov, deputy chief of the Russian Commission for Humanitarian Aid. "The European Community decided it is going to be in Moscow and St. Petersburg, so that is where they send 200 million ECU's of humanitarian aid."[79] The United States was even more cautious, unable to provide Russia's needs for billions because of America's domestic economic recession, also fearing KGB mischief at its Moscow embassy and confining Foreign Service professions in dealing with the newly independent republics and Russians.[80]

Between September 1990 and January 1992, some $80 billion in government assistance was pledged to the former Soviet Union, though delivery was to take months or even years. "The Russians think we can produce $30 billion for them," commented Richard Pipes, Harvard expert on Soviet affairs, "but they do not yet understand the imperatives of democratic politics."[81]

Most (48.1 percent) of the aid was export credits (that required repayment) and guarantees tied to exports from donor nations. Other credits (14 percent), strategic assistance (13.8 percent), and balance-of-payments support (10.6 percent) were largely loans that also had to be repaid. Nonrepayable aid grants took the forms of food and medical support (3.9 percent), technical assistance (2.3 percent), and other supportive assistance (7.5 percent). So the lion's share of foriegn help was offered on a debtor-creditor basis.

The aid was also designed to solidify ties between donor and recipient republics, acting as an entrée of possible future commercial relations or spheres of mutual influence. German aspirations for a trilateral, transcontinental sphere led to its provision of 57.1 percent of all aid during this period. The other European nations trailed far behind, Italy providing 7.4 percent, the rest of the European Economic Community 11.1 percent, and the European Free Trade Association only 3.1 percent. The United States (6.5 percent), South Korea (3.6 percent), Japan (3.1 percent), and an assortment of smaller nations (8.3 percent) were relatively minor actors in the joint aid effort.[82]

The politics of aid held to both short- and long-range goals. France was concerned with on-site mechanics to deliver emergency aid to those in need, with the new republics "the practical actors" in joint efforts. And most Western programs began to insist on tracking deliveries of goods to the door of the hospital, orphanage, or other designated recipient in the emerging welfare system, ensuring that pharmaceutical drugs were not diverted, disappearing onto the black market of the "mafias" or the kitchens of the old Communist party *nomenklatura*. True, chocolate, U.S. dried army rations left over from the Gulf War, and similar processed foods were deliberately sold commercially for high prices, but the proceeds were to be funneled back into aid projects, covering transportation and organization in getting aid to other Russian cities beyond Moscow and St. Petersburg and into Ukraine.[83]

Germany was interested in longer-term ties yet also cautious that Western European labor could not be forced to pay the price. "Labor in Western Europe is thinking in terms of the first half of this century," declared Volkswagen chairman Carl H. Hahn, underlining the preoccupation of many Western European industrialists with domestic affairs, costs of production, and government budgets. "We have to shed the trace of certain socialism that exists in the West even as it has gone under in the East." Speaking just after German steelworkers represented by the powerful I.G. Metall union had obtained a 6.4 percent negotiated wage increase, he understood that profits could be secured only by increasing prices, so that its inflationary effect would stop the central bank from lowering interest rates to stimulate borrowing and economic growth and thereby provide the capital aid Eastern Europe required.[84]

Germany also wanted the United States to provide more nonrepayable assistance beyond the United States–provided $5 billion in repayable farm credits for the republics to import American grain and other foodstuffs. The United States might be willing to offer $645 million in new 1992 humanitarian and technical assistance, but its role as leader in the coordination effort was in question despite President Bush's fine words about building and sustaining democracy and economic freedom in the former USSR. "Let us help the people throughout the independent states to make the leap from Communism to democracy, from command economies to free markets, from authoritarianism to liberty," he said to the foreign ministers of 47 nations at the State Department meeting on 22 January 1992.[85]

The United States was seeking the cheapest route to rebuild its economy, cut its military outlays and CIA investment in covert action,[86] and hold future influence in Eurasia. Director of the Defense Intelligence Agency Lieut. Gen. James R. Clapper, Jr., had testified to the Senate Armed Services Committee on 22 Janaury 1992 that the Russian federation's military procurement for the first quarter of 1992 "appears to have been cut by about 80 percent," reflecting reductions in virtually all classes of equipment. As well, he said, 1992 spending on military research and development might fall by as much as 30 percent from 1991, and there was only a low likelihood that unauthorized personnel in the republics might seize and use the 30,000 nuclear weapons. "I see virtually no likelihood of premeditated Russian or commonwealth military aggression against the U.S. and its allies," he reported. "The intentions of the new commonwealth states towards the West have clearly changed, and overall, the military capabilities of Russia and the successor states are in profound decline."

"The threat to the United States of deliberate attack from that quarter has all but disappeared for the foreseeable future," CIA chief Gates echoed, citing the elimination of new Russian weapons production.[87]

From the Rusian side, Foreign Minister Andrei Kozyrev wrote in Izvestia on 2 January 1992 that the aim of Russian diplomacy was "to achieve radical reductions in nuclear weapons and curtail the arms race."

The military policy of Russian leaders will be to "no longer consider the United States our potential adversary," President Yeltsin told BBC News. "We want to change our military doctrine, turn our intercontinental ballistic missiles away from all cities of the United States."[88] "Russia believes that the time has come to considerably reduce the presence of means of destruction on our planet," he told the UN Security Council on 31 January 1992.

I am convinced that together we are capable of making the principle of minimum defense sufficiency a fundamental law of existence of contemporary states. Today there are real opportunities for:
- Implementing deep cuts in strategic offensive arms and tactical nuclear weapons;
- Resolutely moving towards significant limitations on nuclear testing and even towards its complete cessation;
- Making ABM defenses less complicated and costly and eliminating anti-satellite systems;
- Considerably reducing conventional armaments and armed forces;
- Ensuring practical implementation of international agreements on the prohibition of chemical and bacteriological weapons of mass destruction;
- Enhancing the reliability of barriers to the proliferation of weapons of mass destruction.[89]

The central matter for Yeltsin was to reduce to 2,500 the number of nuclear weapons each nation deployed,[90] the conversion from arms to civil production, from an Armageddon bipolar world into an alliance with the United States:

> Russia considers the United States and the West not as mere partners but rather as allies. It is a basic prerequisite for, I would say, a revolution in peaceful cooperation among civilized nations. We reject any subordination of foreign policy to pure ideology or ideological doctrines. Our principles are clear and simple: supremacy of democracy, human rights and freedoms, legal and moral standards.
>
> I think the time has come to consider creating a global system for protection of the world community. It could be based on a reorientation of the U.S. Strategic Defense Initiative to make use of high technologies developed in Russia's defense complex. We are ready to actively participate in building and putting in place a pan–European collective defense system.[91]

With Russia, Belarus, Ukraine, and Kazakhstan moving to carry out disarmament treaties earlier negotiated by President Gorbachev, the United States could now retire its own missiles, save resources, and use a small part to aid Russia. For a corresponding U.S. elimination of its own older long-range nuclear weapons systems with more than one warhead would significantly cut the Pentagon budget.[92] As the Pentagon planned to suspend production of most new weapons after developing test models, 35 to 45 percent of total costs would be saved, with 20 to 25 percent spent on research, design and development of the test models. Some $50 billion would be saved over the five years 1992–96 by a production cut of the B-2 bomber and the Seawolf submarine—some $6 billion to $8 billion in savings in the Pentagon budget for fiscal year 1993.[93] And a future agreement was possible to rid the United States and former Soviet republics of multiple warheads on missiles (MIRVs, or multiple, independently targetable, reentry vehicles).[94] The government's nuclear and hydrogen bomb industry at Rocky Flats, Colorado, actually stopped production in early January 1992, the last products being the submarine-launched Trident II missiles and their plutonium triggers, though some 400 of these weapons were still being carried by four Atlantic fleet subs.[95] It would only be a pittance to reallocate the $645 million President Bush asked of Congress for 1992–93 humanitarian and technical aid to the Commonwealth republics.[96]

The Pentagon meanwhile tried to sidestep the fact that the cold war was over, ending the forty years of Soviet threats against which the military chiefs planned Pentagon doctrine, weapons, and training. With a minuscule cut of $10 billion from the previous 1991–92 fiscal year, the Pentagon wanted to retain the rest of the military budget. Defense Secretary Dick Cheney and Chairman of the Joint Chiefs of Staff Gen. Colin L. Powell together outlined for the Senate Armed Services Committee the Defense Department's proposed $281-billion budget for the fiscal year beginning 1 October 1992.

Atavistic, their arguments accounted for neither the total Soviet collapse nor Russian disarmament plans. For past Pentagon plans for missiles and a standing army had at best assumed a gradual decline of the Soviet threat, and maintenance of strategic nuclear forces was predicated on an unrelenting Soviet nuclear offensive. Despite these now invalid presumptions, the two Pentagon officials objected to eliminating budgets completely or more than 4,000 warheads that would remain after the Yeltsin-Bush cuts in long-range land-based nuclear missiles. "Strategic nuclear forces will continue to play an essential role with respect to countries other than the Soviet Union," Mr. Cheney rationalized. "Other countries threatened to acquire them. This requires us to maintain a secure retaliatory capability to deter their use." Both Pentagon men also objected to cutting uniformed personnel any faster than a 25 percent planned reduction from 2.1 million to 1.6 million by 1995, foreseeing a need for smaller, more mobile, and flexible armed forces deployed on short notice for regional conflicts. "This is a reshaping, not a demobilization," General Powell advised, warning that cutting the armed forces too swiftly could undercut the morale of the all-volunteer military and hurt future recruiting.

Planting such fears, their budgetary logic was convoluted, devoid of an historic frame, as Senator Kennedy proved, showing that the Pentagon budget would be roughly the same in constant dollars as during the J. F. Kennedy and Nixon administrations, the senator adding, "Either the Cold War is over or not!"

Cheney, wanting his Pentagon budget, backed down, first noting that the Soviet Union's demise had permitted the Pentagon to introduce a new weapons-buying strategy, then admitting the Soviet "threats have become remote, so remote that they are difficult to discern. Even if some new leadership in Moscow were to try to recover its lost empire in Central Europe or to threaten NATO, the reduction of its conventional military capabilities over the past several years would make the chances for success remote without prolonged force generation and deployment."[97]

That would mean a Eurasian land mass no longer under the threat of a major war, a reconversion of military industries to civilian production, a new opportunity for transcontinental and transoceanic commercial and investment ties, and before the onset of a new authoritarianism, a race to create Western spheres of influence in the republics of the former Soviet Union and Eastern Europe.

With President Bush's 1992 proposal to reduce military spending by 1.8 percent of GNP (from 5.2 percent to 3.4 percent), U.S. savings could go in three possible directions: aid to the Soviets, domestic budget cuts, or new industrial investments. For every dollar on government outlays on weaponry some $2.30 extra GNP was generated from auxiliary industries, also reducing imports of military raw materials and components. But public investments in infrastructure like road building or bridges would generate an extra $2.50 in GNP using domestic materials and helping to increase productivity by reducing transportation delays and costs. New investments in plant and equipment would produce output for the life of these assets, something a weapon as product could not do, creating more permanent jobs than those lost in military industries. And switching from military research to civilian research and development by a proposed 7 percent and a 23 percent increase ($803 million) in that going to supercomputers would keep the U.S. technological edge.[98]

The future of a relatively pacific U.S.-Russian relationship would not necessarily mean vast sums for aid to Russia, though. For America's old brand of anticommunism that was common from 1947 to 1991 could no longer win public endurance, even in peace, for deprivations at home. Programs such as national health care and broader trade-union rights had nearly vanished from the scene of American politics, and almost every successful national politician had stood in the center or on the right. The cold war had "made 'national security' the justification for everything—the interstate highway system, the National Defense Education Act, the Vietnam War, the foreign aid program," former assistant secretary of state Richard Holbrooke explained the defining issue in political discourse and public policy. "J. William Fulbright used it to sell his scholarships and J. Edgar Hoover used it to sell his wiretaps."[99]

Some released U.S. funds could now go to the Commonwealth of Independent States as aid to eliminate the foundations for Soviet totalitarianism. "Perhaps for the first time ever there is now a real chance to put an end to despotism and to dismantle the totalitarian order whatever shape it may take," Yeltsin told the UN Security Council summit. "After all, an economy mutilated by ideological diktat and built contrary to all common sense forms the principal material basis for totalitarianism. A profound awareness of this causal relationship has led the Russian leadership to embark upon a most difficult economic reform. We have taken that risk in a country where an all-out war was waged against economic interests for many decades."[100]

Russia was committed to democracy and free markets, Yeltsin told a rapt private gathering of eighty executives from government, business, and banking at the New York Federal Reserve Bank on 31 January 1991. Economic reforms, he said, were a continuation of the battle against communism and the failed coup in August by Soviet apparats. "Today the fight for democracy continues, not on the barricades, but on the economic front," he said, adding that among the decisive steps to a free market would be a presidential decree "granting concessions, along with a law on mineral resources which, in particular will create great opportunities for attracting foreign capital and technologies into the raw-materials sector."

His checklist also set the path for "most-favored-nation treatment" for trading partners, concessions for individuals and possibly group enterprises, and the creation of "joint corporations" in automobile manufacturing, energy production, farming, and highway construction. Yeltsin wanted "reciprocity" in these areas too, as well as removing U.S. limits on technology transfers, a U.S.-Russian agreement on investment protection and a Russian-American international insurance fund for private investments in which other nations could also participate.

The key framework would be stabilization of the ruble, with the industrial democracies setting up an assistance fund—something yet to be done after seven months of Russian pleading, Yeltsin pointing out the great danger to defending democracy. If the effort failed, he warned, "once again there will be mass repression, once again we'll have the arms race and the world will be put into a completely new orbit."[101]

The U.S. government understood the message, leading with foodstuffs sold on guaranteed credits and freight covered by loans. The republics bought on the American grain markets starting 24 January, pushing up corn and soybean prices. "They didn't have the money to pay for freight before," Vice President Fred Soneson of Chicago's Linnco Futures heralded the U.S. Agriculture Department's shifting of aid to cover freight charges.[102] American farmers and their lobbyists were also elated at the emerging guaranteed Commonwealth markets. And beyond emergency food and medicine, the West would pressure the Commonwealth republics to adopt reforms by withholding long-term loans until applying International Monetary Fund–type austerity—no large government deficits due to subsidies to production and consumers, no central bank money growth allowing mass consumption and employment until outdated factories were renovated and workers reemployed.[103] Russia and some of the other republics agreed, but Ukraine refused to follow IMF reforms for a balanced budget, strong central bank control over inflation, and thereby a stable Ukrainian currency that could be used to pay foreign exporters of goods to Ukraine.[104]

The Japanese, meanwhile, focused on horse trading to rebuild its sphere, offering an initial $2.6 billion mostly in export credits and $50 million additional to the Red Cross for humanitarian aid to the Commonwealth but making it clear it would not make larger contributions until Russia returned to Japan the Kurile chain of disputed islands the Soviet Union occupied at the end of World War II.[105]

And Nippon reeked of a new martial conservatism, an expansionist future militarism, first deploying Japanese troops as part of the UN peacekeeping forces envisioned by the Liberal Democratic party allied to the still small Komeito party, itself financed by the 8 million members of the Buddhist Soka Gakkai (Value Creating Society), which with billions of dollars in assets and enormous political leverage had gone against its pacifist principles in supporting Prime Minister Miyazawa's militarist parliamentary bill.[106]

Germany, meanwhile, focused on both the Commonwealth and the rest of Eastern Europe, particularly Poland and Czechoslovakia. "This region is the German sphere of influence," offered economist Laszlo Lang of Hungary at Budapest's Central European Research Center. "What Poland cannot accept and Czechoslovakia is beginning to resist is well understood here."[107]

The new republics in the Commonwealth were also the object of German economic assistance, though export assistance to German industries was based on a triangular transcontinental scheme. The government of Germany West would subsidize private industry located in Germany East and, to stimulate its production and employment as well as stop emigration from East to West, offer credit guarantees for payment on Germany East's manufactured goods shipped to Commonwealth republics if these republics defaulted.

The financial and political stability of all three zones was essential to the plan. For Germany West had extended $94.3 billion in worldwide export credit guarantees, was footing an enormous cost upwards of $400 billion in rebuilding eastern Germany, and had financial limits that might destabilize its own political structures if too much aid was offered to the Commonwealth. Yet West Germany had also been the former Soviet Union's principal trading partner in the West, and its aid was motivated in part by the desire to maintain those trade links to prevent large-scale emigration from the Soviet Union to the West.

Also, Germany East had been one of the former Soviet Union's main trading partners, pressuring Germany West to offer denationalized companies in Germany East export credit guarantees of $6.1 billion (1991) for trade with the new Commonwealth republics. Cutting back such credit guarantees to $3.1 billion for 1992 might force many eastern German factories to close, adding to the surge of eastern unemployment from

11.8 percent in December 1991 to 17 percent in January 1992 and leading to a further exodus of eastern workers to the West where rising unemployment accompanied workers' demands for 6.8 to 10.5 percent wage increases, rising inflation, and the Bundesbank's defensive move, the highest interest rates in the postwar period.[108]

The western German government would thus increase its aid of $34.4 billion and export credit guarantees of $18.5 billion (October 1990–December 1991) only if the Commonwealth republics exhibited both political and financial stability. Using the criterion that a given project could help the Commonwealth state to earn foreign currency as well as the survival necessity of the applicant German company by exporting to the Commonwealth, German Economics Minister Jürgen Mollemann looked to long-term Commonwealth stability. "It will all depend on whether the Commonwealth of Independent States can develop new structures fast enough, in which one can transact legally and technically complicated financial credits," he said. With the "appearance of disintegration" of the Commonwealth, another German official offered, Bonn was reluctant to extend fresh credit guarantees.[109]

Nor should currency stabilization funds be provided until currencies actually operated as units of account, Federal Reserve governor Wayne D. Angell explained. For the Russian ruble had already lost all its value and had been replaced by barter. "Until Russia and the other Republics have a unit of value there is no point in talking about a stabilization fund."[110]

Chancellor Kohl's deeper logic also ran true: It made no sense for the West to provide humanitarian aid while the old Soviet republics were moving to build new armies that would breed internecine warfare among them, effectively building defenses against the unification of Europe and upsetting Europe's balance of military forces. But Kohl coyly neglected to mention the subtext: their fear of pan–Germanic aggression.[111]

To offset this, Germany attempted to bring the old Soviet republics into the 35-nation Conference on Security and Cooperation in Europe and to mobilize the Group of Seven industrialized nations to sidestep the inability of the 105-nation General Agreement on Tariffs and Trade (GATT) to open Western markets to Eastern European trade.[112]

This fit into the schematic of Anders Aslund, a key adviser to the Yeltsin government, viewing the privatization of stores as the focal point for domestic and foreign trade. "In all countries, privatization starts with trade," he said. "The marketplace is the essence of the market." Yet such a non sequitur had its elemental reality: Privatization of retail stores and wholesalers was to be 75 to 100 percent consummated by the end of 1992, with foreign investment welcomed. The 92 billion rubles in payments to the government might be quite worthless, as Western investors knew, but the stabilization of the ruble was critical.

"Until we have a stable convertible ruble, we cannot do anything and we need perhaps $5 billion to $6 billion from the West to accomplish that," recounted Antoly Chubais, the minister in charge of Russia's privatization program. He added that another $5 billion was needed for balance-of-payments support to get foreign trade going again, and sought a few billion in emergency and technical aid.[113]

Thus foreign aid, trade, and investments became the purported basis to move away from new government-enforced rigidities in the Commonwealth states, though conditioned Western commercial ties might become their cause in establishing market economies and new investment spheres. Would not these external pressures come to bear on the centrist controls and bureaucracies already reemerging in each republic, trampling on ethnic, community, and popular rights? The answer depended in part on comprehending the past of such inequities that were becoming stepping-stones to momentary discontent and future change.

Part III:
History Without End

*What we may be witnessing is not just the end of the Cold War,
or the passing of a particular period of postwar history, but the end
of history as such: that is, the end point of mankind's ideological
evolution and the universalization of Western liberal democracy
as the final form of human government.*
— Francis Fukuyama, "The End of History"

Propounding the thesis that the West has accomplished its
ideological goals in a bipolar world, Francis Fukuyama presents the notion
that the highest stage of geopolitical and socioeconomic development is
in the process of being reached. The theoretical framing of socialism, he
argues, has been moving toward, and is succumbing to, a democratic way
of thinking, expressed in its parliamentary forum, market, possibly even
future calculations of capitalist investment. With ideological liquidation
of Marxism-Leninism, future reforms and socioeconomic reconstruction,
a great transformation will eventually produce a near equitable system
and human satisfaction.

It will also produce anomie, Fukuyama guesses, as the material fulfillment of needs leaves an empty ideological space: a lack of the one's social
purpose. The fetish nature of the marketplace and its elements — commodities, amenities and other material things available for sale — will thus
produce and be based on a grim human boredom.

When, then, will history end? For Fukuyama, it is based on socially
satisfying a tripartite division of human nature. Besides *reason* and *desire*
infused into Western conceptions of human nature, Fukuyama views
political history in terms of the human drive for *recognition* (Plato's
thymos), which engenders pride when it is satisfied, anger when frustrated, and shame if unasserted.

Throughout history, he argues, some men have asserted mastery over
others, the process taking the highest form in the quest for freedom that
reached its apogee in the age since the American and French revolutions,

107

bringing forth universal satisfaction through common, shared democratic citizenship. The historical mastery of such freedom placed no man above others, so that this freedom quest fulfilled itself, came to its term, ending "History" (capitalized to signify consummation and closure by establishing a "meaningful order" to the hitherto broad sweep of human events).

As each nation has achieved its own liberal democracy (negotiated by fully satisfying Fukuyama's conception of the "three parts" of the human soul), its History will also end, leaving a world in which (so far) most in Eastern Europe, Eurasia, and elsewhere are still in History, and the End of History is the condition of people only in Western Europe, the United States, Japan, and a handful of other nations.[1]

This argument is capped by equating autarchic nationalism of the new republics with the foundation for democracy, based on the assumption that mobilization of the forces for production forwarding economic development within each new nation will have to precede or be coterminous with changes in those social relationships that will make democracy a reality.

"It is wrong to generalize about the prospects of democracy or nationalism in the new Eurasia," Fukuyama says. "But it will co-exist, often within the same country, and many states will walk a fine line between assertions of legitimate national identity and intolerance. The consolidation of the liberal form of nationalism [i.e., democracy] will depend on the ability of the new leaders to manage the daunting task of converting controlled economies to market-based ones and on the help they get from the outside world."

To evaluate this thesis—to show that it is part logically self-evident, part factual, part bizarre chimera, part metaphysical nonsense, and another part nonanalytical empiricism—a review of its historic and ideological frame is required.

For as long as humankind walks the earth there will be human historical development (prospects of democracy or nationalism among them) regardless of the way humankind perceives or records the steps. Nor can history of these steps *simply* be identified with the notion of idealist purposefulness or a preconcerted universal plan: the day-by-day turn of events unfolding and realizing a preconceived "Idea" or destiny, as propounded by Hegel, Schelling, and other European sages, and long before them by tribal shaman and religious thinkers envisioning the manifest end for a chosen people or revelation at a second or future coming of a particular deity, or a millennial Last Testament or Final Judgement.[2]

Chapter 3
Centrist State, Social Theory, and Market Economy

Transition to market relations and their effective functioning are possible only under conditions of a strong and clearly organized state power. The experience of all countries which have achieved a developed market economy and high living standards is indicative of this. . . .

A resolute transition is necessary to the new structures of state and economic management aimed at formation of the market-type economy and providing for the effective interaction of union, republican and local bodies. This goal demands that the development and implementation of economic reforms and of programs of transition to market relations should be singled out as a special function of state management without any further delay.

In the first instance, it is necessary to use to the maximum the special powers granted recently [to myself as] the President of the Supreme Soviet. In this regard it would be advisable to elevate the role of the Council of Federation so that it works out and implements through the union and republican organs of power those decisions approved by the republics. Accordingly, an inter-republican economic committee is to be created at the Council [of Federation] that would consist of the representatives of the republics, experts and scientists.
. . . . .

It is urgent to restore the vertical chain of subordination of the executive bodies [I head] so that the governments and executive committees at different levels [of republics and local communities] would be under double subordination—to the corresponding local councils of the People's deputies and to superior bodies of executive power [I head or control]. The decisions taken by superior bodies within the framework of their competence are binding on subordinate bodies. Such a law [awarding Boris Yeltsin power] was adopted recently by the Supreme Soviet of the Russian Republic. A similar law [awarding me power] is under consideration in the national Parliament.

—President Gorbachev's proposed program submitted
to the Soviet legislature, 16 October 1990

109

At critical historic moments, most of Russia's tsars and Soviet dictators have similarly viewed centrist hierarchical controls as the main ingredient to social, political, and economic stability, reorganization, or transformation.

In the name of tranquility or revolution for some greater end, they have centralized control in their own hands. And in the closing months of 1990, the Soviet's president and party loyalist Mikhail Gorbachev followed tradition's past, arguing that under his executive authority, overarching a hierarchical order, the greater good of the Soviet people was at stake in overthrowing what had been nearly seventy years of Communist doctrine opposing competition and the fetish qualities of the marketplace.

POLITICAL ECONOMY AND MARXIST LORE

Ideological evolution of Marxist-Leninist political economy was part of Gorbachev's program for change, questioning the relevance of its earlier precepts. For Bolshevik theory held that the wage system bred the early Communist drive to overthrow rather than to accept and reform its capitalist framework.

In the West at least, Marxist theory preached that labor struggles to secure "a fair day's wages for a fair day's work" were reformist because they sought secure jobs at wages that would provide only subsistence to sustain the work force (and support the family through procreation) and reinstate its energies, as well as moderate the workers' level of exhaustion, which in turn would allow labor to return full strength for the next workday.[1] Labor was thereby locked into the system of production not only as a wage earner but a wage slave, Frederick Engels discerned.[2]

Over time, the capitalist system also posited expansion: As more capital was drawn into production and the demand for labor expanded, there might be a general rise in *total wages* that in turn would fuel the extension of the marketplace.

But there were three possible success scenarios and/or barriers: capital accumulation might initially breed an extension of the wage system; momentary stagnation of the market or a financial crisis might result in a cut in employment and the general wage level; and a period of capital disaccumulation might lead to massive unemployment, wage cuts, and a speedup so that to survive, the reserve army of jobless would join the overworked and underpaid to seek control over the product of its labor and/or the means of production.

True to this logic, as the wage system developed and faced crises, three historic movements emerged. The first, led by *petty commodity producers* trying to protect their handmade output from being undersold by manufactures in the emergent market, attempted to *destroy* the new mode of capitalist production—a system that *reformers*, backing the second historic movement, wanted to *expand* by mobilizing earlier forms of capital,[3] technology, and an enlarged wage labor force. And the third was led by the *utopians, Socialists,* and *Communists* seeking to *capture* the new means of production to put them under the control and at the service of labor.

Theoretical Foundations

The foundation of these movements and the rewards — or losses — for emergent social classes were elaborated as theories propounded by Adam Smith, Karl Marx, David Ricardo, John Stuart Mill, Thomas Malthus, Frederick Engels, and Nassau Senior among a host of others.

Smith had argued that labor should have subsistence as a share of new output, sustaining the theory that workers were entitled to a fair portion of the value of the commodity they produced.[4] But Marx said such a fair share was only better pay for the slave of capital. For the wage system was based on the private appropriation of the social means of production against the interests of labor's control over both these means and the product labor created.[5]

Holding another view, theorists following Ricardo supported the wage system, reasoning that labor should receive subsistence, capital should take surplus, and the landlords should get nothing as land drained both capital and labor. Ricardo's logic was that the natural price of labor was subsistence to cover essentials established by customary habits, for the relations of production established both the level of wages and labor's exhaustion during the workday.

But land that yielded output (making up the means of subsistence) at rates of diminishing returns caused higher prices for both food and ground rents (reflecting the land value on which it was grown), in turn fueling labor demands for higher wages to cover these costs; hence capital's payment of permanent increments in wages to buy *the same quantity* of labor power, so that the worktime required for labor to produce value to cover its own subsistence rose while the time to produce surplus for capital fell, cutting profit rates.

Through the market, the landlords thereby absorbed an enlarged share of capital's entitlement to surplus.

Ricardo's solution was simple: If England's Corn Law tariffs keeping out cheaper foreign wheat were overturned, the costs of imported subsistence, competitive English grain, and thus English wages and land rents would fall, reinstating the capitalists to their fair share of surplus.[6] Others took a position siding with the landlords or either capital or labor, based on their own theories about the source of profits.

Malthus appeased the landlords, insisting that they alone took up excess commodities when manufacturing produced more than the market could absorb. Excess production, he argued, caused a fall in capital's employment of labor and the production of commodities, creating a double blight: an unemployed surplus population that would also procreate faster than enlargement of the food supply, and idle capital, limiting employment, production, and profits. The problem could be solved, he said, only by the landlords' rents being used to consume the excess manufactures, while the surplus population that outran food supplies would succumb by starvation, pestilence, war, and other causes, depopulation also quieting the spread of revolutionary thought and action.[7]

By contrast, Marx sided with labor, arguing that capitalism transformed all things into exchange value, rooted in subsistence wages or less, and the brutal exploitation of labor power to create salable commodities. Thus only revolution could rectify the proletariat's position, to take charge of both the means of labor and the product of their effort.[8]

Engels similarly favored labor's consumption of the total value of their output, both subsistence and surplus. He theorized that though labor deployed the forces of production under capital's direction, labor was paid only subsistence and could not fully purchase the very commodity it had created. Consumption by the class of laborers was thus limited by the availability of wages for subsistence under the existing relations of production, a condition that revolution would transform.[9]

There was thereby a wage fund for subsistence, argued Adam Smith, Marx and Engels, Ricardo, and Malthus. Ricardo said capital justly received its share of surplus above labor's subsistence through the production process, Nassau Senior arguing that capital took its share during the last hour of the workday, so that hours of work must not be reduced to accommodate labor taking away capital's profit.[10]

By contrast, John Stuart Mill believed labor's reward from output should be enlarged by concentrating on the sphere of commodity distribution, arguing that alteration by redistribution in this sphere, not by altering the wage system, would rectify social injustices.[11]

With variations, all these theories were to resonate in the political territories that first made the Revolution and became part of the Soviet Union, building Soviet theory, yet nonetheless generating implosions from their disregard or unfair application.

IMPLOSION AND SOVIET THEORY

For seven decades Soviet theory followed the Marx-Engels prescription that under communism, capital would not exist and thus would not be entitled to any part of social output.

The peasants and collective and state farmers were to become both efficient and the Soviet source of a cornucopia of nourishment, thus receiving the full value of their output, as distinguished from Ricardo's concept of the landlord's extortion—exorbitant prices above unfettered market value based on the diminishing returns on the land.

Workers would also be rewarded with the full value of their labor efforts, not having to sacrifice surplus to employing capitalists, as Ricardo demanded, or to landlords, as Malthus hoped, or to capital for working the last extra hour to produce a surplus for the employer, as Nassau Senior had proposed.

Bureaucrats would exist only to aid fair distribution of commodities and state services, à la John Stuart Mill. The state, its apparat, and armed forces would eventually wither away, and the complete rewards of education, technology, science, human labor, and social services would be available to all.

All these benefits were to be diametric opposites of anything that might ever emerge from capitalism and its system of exchange value and integrated markets.[12] And all these principles were supposedly applied but in practice were distorted in the course of seventy years of Soviet history,[13] ending in an implosion that led to the rejection of their substance in the late eighties.

THE STATE AS "BENIGN" OVERSEER

Even in the sixties, though, it was questionable that the Soviet Union could continue to propound concepts of equity and equality while denying its own citizens the substance of fairness and a decent life.[14]

Yet three decades later, in 1989, Mikhail Gorbachev was openly advocating that the state act as benign overseer of private capital to employ wage labor and open the market to commodities that, facing labor as things to be bought and meeting consumer demands, would assume their own price levels based on the demand of buyers earning various rates of wages or with access to means of exchange.

The Blind Eye

Though this was seemingly designed to stimulate hard work and consumption, a blind eye was turned to the inequities and inequalities that would again ripple through the hierarchical relations of the Soviet system of rewards and the fetishes of the Union's undeveloped market. There was still no vision of rebuilding the nation on the basis of genuine soviets — involving grass-roots democracy, workers' control on the job, and an egalitarian system for regulating the quality of what was produced in relation to community needs. Using these touchstones of equity, it would take new political philosophers and theoreticians to construct a future egalitarian system out of the dissolving relationship of republics and center, and the confounded evolving recipe for a mixed economy.[15]

Still bogged down by the late eighties in Brezhnev's nine-year genocidal war in Afghanistan — leaving over a million Afghan dead, involving hundreds of thousands of Soviet soldiers, expending 15,000 Soviet lives—billions of rubles of Soviet resources and manpower went up in agony and smoke.[16] The domestic economy had flagged, budget deficits loomed, and these flaws were disguised with mendacious statistics, the cumulative drain appearing as an absolute decline in domestic living standards.[17]

A Cracking Façade

In 1987, the façade of what appeared to be a powerful economy cracked, revealing its irreversible fallibility in the next four years. True, in response to worker demands, creating the illusion that they were somehow winning improved living standards, Soviet wages rose sharply (6 percent of workers earned more than 300 rubles a month in 1981, 15 percent in 1989). Yet 1990 overall production fell, and the output of consumer goods hardly changed, leaving Soviet citizens with hundreds of billions of rubles in savings but little of value to buy on the government-controlled market, resulting in a hyperinflated "free market."

True again, adjusted for weather variations, grain yields rose sharply during the Gorbachev years, with the 1990 output of 240 million tons the highest ever. But some 40 percent of the grain either rotted or was eaten by pests, estimated the Soviet's highest-profile agricultural economist, Vladimir Tikhanov. And once more, short supplies drove up many food prices in the urban domain.

But the main causes of shortages were linked to an oversupply of means of exchange and the appearance of a new social stratum in charge of the fast-emergent laissez-faire market.

The logic of this market was based on extortion. For those who controlled food supplies reasoned that there was little sense in taking rubles in payment when the currency was sure to be worth less, or practically worthless, by the time one found something on which to spend them. And as government food supplies were diverted by tens of thousands of petty merchant operators, it became increasingly difficult to find staples at price-controlled stores. The denizens of Leningrad, Moscow, and the gritty industrial cities of the Russian heartland had become fair game for extraction to benefit the private centers of newly accumulated wealth. However fleeting, socialism would have an emergent petite bourgeoisie.

For the door to the free market had been opened a crack, and Soviet output was now being *redistributed*, as both producers and merchants slipped through, taking charge of marketing in their own interests. "Some of the food is being withheld by producers and local governments bent on bartering for industrial goods," a reporter noted the turn to self-aggrandizement. "Some is being sidetracked by old-guard bureaucrats eager to discredit *perestroika*. The rest is being diverted to the black market by criminals who no longer worry about ending up in the gulag."[18]

By early February 1991, the scene again changed, Gorbachev reopening a new gulag for "market extortionists"—another means of political repression.*

For in fact both farmers and local governments were withholding food *to assert their independence from the Kremlin*. This political weapon, not the failed production of food, was the fulcrum, focus, and cause of deprivation in the urban domain, merging political protest with empowerment of the new middle-agent sellers to extract their price.

Their sources of supply dovetailed with growing consumer demand, regardless of the price they set. For now masses of people were clamoring for butter rather than guns, unfettered access to consumer goods of their choice, and the social expression of these—political and human rights to decide their own destiny.

False Promises

As almost every adult Soviet already knew in the late eighties, the Soviets simply had not made good on their earlier promises of social and economic equity—and now would do so by default. Ex-party member Roy Medvedev (who had once been in the Gorbachev inner circle and with Gorbachev's help, made public KGB chief Adropov's secret files) intuited there was no other way for the reformers to keep a mass following, that the party itself would be blamed for the escalating malaise, with "too many people demanding an explanation from the party for having led the country into the unprecedented crisis that was violently shaking it."[19]

For in the first half of 1989, the downward spiral had been both sharp and politically explosive, Medvedev outlining the ongoing struggle— material rewards, taking the form of ethnic and religious warfare:

> The politicization of the masses in the most progressive areas of the country led to an increase in separatist movements. But to this alarming fact was added a new element, caused by the decline in the real standards of living of broad masses of people: social revolt. The Fergana massacre in Uzbekistan, whose victims were the Meskhet Turks, resulted from an explosive mix of elementary social claims, religious activism, and a subversive political *Jaquerie* made up of organized mafias, state powers, and party fringes. The Novy Uzen revolt in Kazakhstan showed even more clearly the social consequences of glasnost, even if everywhere— from Central Asia, to the Caucasus, to the Baltic—all the social and economic demands were triggered by national claims. The Novy Uzen Kazakhs rose up against the Caucasians, the Uzbeks against the Meskhet Turks, the Azerbaijanis against the Armenians, and the Georgians against the Abkhazes because *they could not distinguish between the*

See Chapter 14.

> *violation of elementary needs and the violation of their traditions and their history.* The Soviet Union was a container holding dozens of similar latent conflicts that were ready to explode.[20]

Violation of needs was rooted in the Kremlin's past schematic, violating its own alleged principles of equity, either distributing or withholding benefits. But this itself was a function of the geographic and social division of labor, based on historic Russification designed to destroy the traditions of different nationalities.*

President Gorbachev, recognizing the "nationalities problem" was bound up with faulty distribution (lifting a thought from John Stuart Mill), offered the Kremlin's delayed response:

> The situation in the people's economy is growing worse. The volume of production is decreasing and economic ties are being disrupted. Separatism is growing. The consumers' market is devastated. The budget deficit and solvency of the state have reached critical levels. Anti-social phenomenon and the crime rate are on the rise. Life is becoming increasingly more difficult. People are losing interest in work and confidence in the future is disintegrating.
>
> The economy is at a very dangerous stage: The old administrative system of management is being destroyed, but new incentives for work under free market conditions have not yet been created. Energetic measures, based on public consensus are necessary for stabilization of the situation and for speedy progress on the road to establishing a market economy.[21]

Such progress, we shall see, meant centrist state *diktat* under the hierarchical rule of President Gorbachev and the Politburo.

Squeeze from Above and Below

In 1989, Medvedev had already sounded the alarm: "The economic reform itself would inevitably cause a new series of unprecedented social and territorial imbalances. From 12 to 15 million jobs would be 'gotten rid of' by the end of the century as a result of the projected development of productive technology, adding to the already serious tension in the labor market in areas with high rates of growth."[22]

With such potential mass unemployment due to imbalances of technology and labor, regional conflicts would threaten reform programs as well as central rule. And without a leader of their own, moderate conservatives and reactionary forces supported by the army would foment their own revolution *from above*.[23] Yet under either a left- or right-leaning

*See Chapter 1.

state, conceivably in the name of market economy, the shares for farmers, labor, and the state would be preset by the Politburo, the central apparat, and starting in 1990, the president and his cabinet. Gorbachev was caught between the revolution from above and below.

From below, the questions raised were "Can and will Gorbachev abruptly accelerate reform, toward the market, toward a definitive opening of the country, toward a confederation of autonomous states, and at the same time, toward a drastic reform of the political system, which shifts the center of power to the new parliament, and sanctions the separation of powers?"[24]

In part, Gorbachev answered in the Soviet legislature in late 1990 that "the choice" had already been made. But this implied pressure from the oligarchy of army, apparat, and Politburo on the right and the new Parliament, mass movements, and dissident republics on the left. And Gorbachev politically balanced rightwards, deftly pirouetting along a razor's edge to stop total alienation of the Left:

> There is no alternative to the transition to the market. The whole world experience [has] proved the vitality and efficiency of the market economy. The transition to it in our society is dictated by the interests of the people. Its goal is to create a socially oriented economy, to turn production to the satisfaction of consumers' demands, to overcome the shortages and the shame of the shopping lines—in reality to provide for the economic freedom of citizens, to establish new conditions for encouraging their diligence, creative abilities, initiative and high productivity.

Under this formula for new conditions, Gorbachev nonetheless reasoned, there could be no grass-roots democracy securing economic freedoms, no independent republics, despite rhetoric about their "sovereignty":

> Through the nationwide market a unified economic space will be created, which will integrate all republics and all regions of the country. Transition to the market will allow for creation of an economic basis for voluntary unification of the sovereign republics within the framework of a renewed federation and strengthened union.[25]

This sophistry convinced no one, *voluntary unification* being increasingly unlikely, as the president relied on the widely discredited existing power structure, based in turn on the Communist party and central decision making chained to traditional power and privilege. As he dodged the key point of the Shatalin plan* for radical free-market reform and decentralized public participation, he completely lost the historic moment for change.

---

*See Chapter 2.

A Chance Missed for Democratic Freedom

"The plan would have destroyed the old power center and replaced it with a new one that could have gained popular allegiance," said George Soros, Wall Street financier and supporter of Eastern European democratic leaders and movements.

> This was to be accomplished by transferring economic powers to the republics and concurrently delegating those powers to a newly created central organ: the interregional economic committee.
> . . . .
> On Oct. 1, Mr. Gorbachev was given emergency economic powers. If the 15 republics voted similar powers to their representatives, the interregional committee would be able to create an *economic federation on a new basis*. This was a brilliant idea. The committee would have gathered popular support by battling the hated bureaucracy. It would have severely curtailed the government budget and spearheaded privatization.[26]

The West could no longer look to Gorbachev as advocate and liberator to overturn the apparat, the state bureaucracy, the army, the KGB, that through the government budget together absorbed as much as one-third of total Soviet output! There would be no new structure to replace immediately this oligarchy or to operate as an interregional committee between republics.

The rift of the central authority absorbing revenues and regional republics starved for benefits continued, leading to such a crushing failure in feeding and supplying the nation that out of desperation the people turned toward making war on the center. Though they attempted to seize their independence, the republics they inherited were locked into the Soviet crisis, and once more in Russian history they might be pressured to accept reluctantly a dictatorship of the heirs of the party, again mandating which groups would receive subsistence and which would absorb the social surplus.

CONSEQUENCES OF UNDERMINING THE CENTRIST STATE

With the disintegration of the Soviet Union, the fifteen separate republics were without a common ruling party able to foster interrepublic cooperation in production, trade, and military affairs. It would take years, possibly decades, to resolve the differences between republics either separately or as part of their Commonwealth of Independent Nations. Food and material shortages, public protests and riots, government repression and police controls, would stud the landscape of the republics. For as inheritors of the Soviet division of labor, production, and distribution, none were yet self-sufficient or able to reallocate internal resources, renovate production, reassign the workforce, rebuild distribution systems and provide adequate social services.

3. Centrist State, Social Theory, and Market Economy   119

What would appear as violent chaos of deprived and displaced populations, then, would be a harking back for the relative securities of the past, an unwillingness and fear to face a future promising only further risks and desperation. Vulnerable populations of the new republics might ultimately view the reformers who overthrew the Soviet system as barriers to their own well-being, calling on the army, the party, the KGB, and other surviving organizations to save them from the new leaders and bureaucratic apparat imposing deprivations and the decline of living standards.

Failure to Create Conditions for Production and Distribution

As the new regimes could not alone reconstruct the old conditions essential for production, distribution, and survival, they held momentary power but not public trust.

The old Soviet command system had ensured that each republic would be interdependent with the others, that none would be self-sufficient, that the Kremlin would assign detailed functions to each, effectively making each dependent on the central authority to keep it in a state of prosperity and dependence, unable to survive by itself.

On the eve of each republic's declaration of independence, it proved impossible to create self-sufficient industries, resurrect old ones, or create new ones. Thus the separate agonies of the new republics dogged the heels of the nationalist drives of both Communist and populist politicians. For each republic now required a political center to replace the old one in Moscow. And the separate parliaments soon replicated the old Supreme Soviet, presiding over factional animosities, endless debates over raising revenues, designating budgetary priorities, and allocating too few resources to satisfy too many needs.

The difference, though, was that the old Soviet interdependence was gone and each republic was on its own. And fueling production by mobilizing energy supplies, raw materials, machinery, and parts came to depend on new industrializing formulas and old authoritarian connections and habits of thought. Russia's Yeltsin could try price increments to induce new output, but new capital was required, the infrastructure for production and markets still lacking. Economic activity was calculated to shrink a catastrophic 40 percent in 1992, inflation to rise 700 percent, linked to a government deficit amounting to 25 percent of gross national product and a defense budget of 30 to 40 percent of all government outlays.

To prevent a coup, the budget could not be slashed carte blanche laying off the armed forces without providing former military personnel an assigned place in an expanded economy, one that neither existed nor was privatized under the Yeltsin government plan.

It was nearly impossible for the new and former ministers to mobilize resources quickly and develop skills, knowledge, and production to accomplish this. For in early 1992 no one could define which authority centers owned which state industries and facilities for production, thus ensuring that privatization would be a laborious long-term project. The underpinnings of a market economy were also practically nonexistent. Central economic planning had not developed the efficiencies of accounting, management, distribution, and regulatory systems, so few Russian factories produced competitively priced products. Any new efficiency measures oriented toward the market would also require mass layoffs — and unacceptable political risk in the early nineties.[27]

True, the Baltic states had traded with Scandinavia, had knowledge of some operations of privately held enterprises, and had harbor access to the sea, but they too lacked personnel to direct private enterprises. True, Estonia might proudly reject all Russian controls and refuse to join the Commonwealth, but it was nearly barren of fuel the winter of 1992. Also true, Ukraine held a rich agriculture that could be reorganized into private plots, strips, or farms, but President Kravchuk's central authorities offered little help fearing such measures might reduce output, instead concentrating on controlling the Black Sea fleet for trade and might. And though Russia held extensive resources that could be turned over to private mining enterprises, they would require huge infusions of capital and skilled management teams to negotiate exports.

In the crazed quest for self-sufficiency, the republics tried to keep resources within their boundaries, broke barter agreements made with former East-bloc nations through their defunct common market (Comecon), and exported to the West for payment in hard currencies. President Boris Yeltsin had decreed that Russian companies could keep part of their foreign currency earnings. And oil companies then categorized countries reliant on Russian gas and oil by those promising goods and those paying dollars, marks, or pounds sterling. Poland, able to pay for half its 1992 oil needs by the exchange for $500 million of food, pharmaceuticals, and coal products, thus found itself playing second fiddle to Western oil companies promising hard currencies. And Russia reneged on a trade arrangement, cutting pipeline deliveries to Poland by 40 percent in December 1991.

As Poland's subzero temperatures increased energy consumption in January, there was just enough to burn to save machinery from damage in the nation's steel mills, glass and ceramics works, fertilizer plants, and auto factories. Without essential Russian gas, on 23 January industrial Poland thus ground to a halt. Poland's daily *Gazeta Wyborcza* tried to rationalize that Poland was reliant economically on Russia but was looking to Western Europe as a priority, seeing the Russian riposte as getting even.[28] But in fact it was more a question of Russia earning hard currencies to import Western machinery and goods.

The future path was similarly set upon autarchic survival of each former Soviet republic and each nation of Eastern Europe—the self-assertive turn to nationalism and the resulting pattern of balkanization expressing itself as a way of thinking, socially, economically, politically, and militarily.

Failure to Unify the Military

In the Soviet era, the main branches of the military and KGB had been the force mobilized by the party to threaten or wield against dissident populations to maintain internal security. But in the transition from Soviet to Commonwealth, both military and KGB lost place as centralized bodies and were threatened with elimination or dispersal among the republics and their hundreds of subdivisions.

For self-preservation as an elite caste handed down from the Union, military officers in all branches of the armed forces quickly used their common bonds in local assemblies to create a lobbying network to cope with the new Commonwealth's political and ethnic subdivisions. Meeting in the Kremlin's Palace of Congresses 5,000 strong on 17 January 1992, military officers of all ranks vociferously demanded that the old Soviet armed forces remain intact, that their status be preserved, that the divisions by republics and ethnic communities not divide them by political calculations or jeopardize their security. "I have but one concern," interim Commander in Chief Marshal Yevgeny I. Shaposhnikov declared, bringing the officers to their feet, "to lead the military forces with minimal losses out of the plight in which our country and armed forces find themselves."

Appealing to President Yeltsin and Kazakhstan's President Nazarbayev, the vast majority of officers held no nostalgia for a return of Communist Soviet power or domination. Rather, they warned that politicians might use them for a "civil war" as they had in the Baltic states and Georgia, that they might be claimed and divided by various republics requiring allegiance and loyalty oaths, that they might be economically impoverished with low pay and housing shortages, that their uncertain future would breed a lack of purpose.

They called on Commonwealth politicians to maintain momentarily a common security system, a unified military command within a single strategic military arena. They thus pleaded that the republics not divide the army and navy during the transition period when Commonwealth leaders were to decide the future of the army's 3.2 million men and Soviet naval and nuclear forces. Forming an Officers' Coordinating Council to lobby for and represent their interests in defending all the people of the Commonwealth, they resolved that their battle stations were not to be mobilized to fight against each other yet required a legal foundation under state patronage for their survival, albeit as a privileged caste in a post–Soviet democracy.[29]

This plea was not acceptable to either Ukraine or Russia, both battling to put the joint armed forces and military equipment under their control.

THE ILLUSION OF POST-SOVIET DEMOCRACY

Post-Soviet republican governments spoke of democracy but lacked the socioeconomic infrastructure for a new beginning in fairness, equitability, and egalitarianism. For these governments neither destroyed the old mechanisms of political and bureaucratic power nor planned the future direction of strategic industries, production, and trade—necessary conditions to sustain the various sectors of each republic's population. Yet without such foresight and planning, post–Soviet democracy would remain an illusion, and governments ruled from the upper reaches by the new elite would attempt to design and enforce makeshift, unformulated programs.

Dangers to the stability of the new regimes also pressed. For there were at least two avenues to a return to centralized rule: material entrapment leading to the fall of legitimacy of the leaders of the various republics; armed usurpation by disgruntled parties, military leaders, and apparats.

Thus a broad sketch of the dilemmas and the frailness of momentary measures point to a probably unstable Russian future.

Economic Entrapment vs. Privatizing the Economy

Democracy in the republics was not stillborn but in its political infancy during late 1991 and early 1992. It was supposed to survive in the milieu of unregulated price inflation and an unresponsive obsolete industrial infrastructure that required imported technological replacement at an ultimate cost of perhaps 2 trillion in hard currencies.

Political stabilization in the form of viable popular governments also required social services and near full-employment policies that would not be undermined by inadequate state budgets and rapid privatization dislocating millions and creating joblessness.

Past Soviet subsidies to industry and consumers had maintained production and payrolls, even when facilities were technically outmoded and workers were inefficient and unproductive. But in the new milieu, there was little immediate prospect that private entrepreneurs or workers could obtain ownership rights to state-owned facilities, raise capital to finance the introduction of new technologies, secure delivery of needed materials, pay salaries to maintain living standards, upgrade labor efficiency in production, stock inventories, and deliver goods to markets where consumers had sufficient resources to buy. Yet all these steps were necessary to restore production, employment, living standards, and distribution.

Not even the first step could be smoothly negotiated, for government policies and commercial extortion had together sent prices soaring. Government provided an inadequate safety net to care for the desperate, young, and old, and the incidence of economic crimes escalated. In Russia alone, a state budget deficit of 15 to 20 percent of the republic's national income in early 1992 made reform plans for its rapid reduction a recipe for uprooting populations, creating an army of unemployed homeless people in need of welfare the government could not provide. More than 40 percent of industrial capacity lay idle by late March 1992, output declining by 10 percent a month and tax revenues falling and haphazardly collected.

With insufficient government revenues, the "right to survive" was no longer a government obligation. So-called price liberalization allowed the Russian government to sidestep the old command system's budgetary costs of subsidizing food purchased from state and cooperative farms at high prices and then sold through state stores at low fixed prices to maintain living standards. And at the new high prices, government purchases from farms and middle agents were remitted in still higher prices, giving the Russian state a cut in the surplus extracted from consumers.

As the Russian government in January 1992 still adhered to the old command economy that had set rules to provide for food workers' salaries by limiting bread factories and retail outlets to price increments of 25 percent above their respective costs, the new troika of beneficiaries from increased consumer prices were thus the farmers, the hoarding middle agents, and the state.

The allotment to the state from surplus food prices and a new 28 percent value-added tax also became the salary fund for a new body of bureaucrats to join the remaining apparatchiks. Coalescing as a social caste might take time, but the material rewards of the government remaining in charge of food processing and distribution set the new bureaucrats against privatization of these economic centers. Yeltsin was creating a line of defense against his own policies to sell government-controlled enterprises.

Privatization of communications, oil, and other industries also faced barriers, for there were inadequate governmental lines of authority over production, personal savings, and management know-how to fuel renewal of the industrial system, even in the form of joint-stock companies. Russia's key oil output had steadily fallen, with an expected drop of 20 percent between 1991 and the end of 1993. This was the consequence of confusion about the proper agencies of government responsibility, the decline of the economy, the consequent fall in capital investment, and the shortage of equipment. To offset the decline, in January 1992, as the first of many, the Russian People's Oil Industrial Investment Euro-Asian Corporation (Nipek) attempted to combine large and small domestic and foreign capital (keeping the participation of state-owned enterprises under 25 percent to avoid regulations that would cost the new company its independence). Under a board of directors chaired by the former Communist party first secretary of the Khanty-Mansi region, the first 25 million rubles in capital were provided by ten founding investors, including Siberian oil and commercial firms, a Soviet-Lebanese joint venture, and local governments. For the balance of a hoped-for 3 billion rubles, Nipek set low share prices of 1,000 rubles (about $10) to raise funds from small investors, offering vague statements about its plans to use its capital to bring western Siberian idle oil wells back to life and fill up refineries then working at an average of 75 percent of capacity. Under a general director, Anatoly S. Gumenyuk, whose last job was the same in the state Komineft oil concern, plans were laid to have 2 million tons of oil at Nipek's disposal by the end of 1992, Gumenyuk refusing to say which fields would be tapped. "The oil is there, the fields are there, the people are there," he ticked off the essentials. "Until now, the system did not allow us to work properly and now, for that, we need time and money."[30]

Government impediments still remained, Nipek announced in *Izvestia* on 25 December 1991. "At this time the Government has still not defined the general direction of its policy for privatization, taxation, the rules for the use of mineral wealth, the regulation of foreign economic activity."

Privatization of land in the republics would also require careful planning by new centers. As the Soviet absence of land records could not be the basis for distribution, evaluation of the variations of the quality and quantity of land might enable its equitable subdivision. The cooperative use of tractors and combines too large for small farms would also be necessary, as would the eventual redesign or import of new tractors and heavy farm equipment.[31] But as land redistribution would take time, food imports would still be essential in the 1990s.

Price Riots, Economic Strife, and Political Legitimacy

In each republic, variously situated sectors of the population held quite different perceptions of the legitimacy of their rulers, and these largely turned on the leaders maintaining popular living standards and sustaining the hope of a more democratic, secure future. In Russian cities, downward mobility and widespread hopelessness quickly led to the government's loss of support from various segments of the working class and intellectuals. "Yeltsin may lose the support that has made him strong so far—that of liberal-democratic intellectuals, highly skilled workers and engineers," said *Komsomolskaya Pravda*, pointing to his common, didactic, and backslapping ways appealing to "the least educated section of the population."[32]

But besides loss of support, when crowds became unruly, traditional methods were used to repress them. Thus military power was loosed in the early months of 1992, datelines from St. Petersburg to Georgia and Tashkent recording civil price riots and political-economic strife, parlaying in part a broader struggle of sectarian autocracy and regional autarchy.

Autarchy in the name of market economy had spread price increments between republics to prevent supplies being raided by competitive states. Russia began unregulated price increases to encourage new output, followed by Ukraine, Uzbekistan, and the other former Soviet republics, each trying to secure home supplies and output. The problem was compounded as some stores unable to afford to stock the more costly output of food and manufacturers began leaving their shelves bare; and because their warehouses were full of goods consumers could not afford, they stopped ordering, forcing meat, produce, and candy factories from Moscow to the Russian Caucasus to cut production.

In St. Petersburg, members of the revanchist Russian Communist Workers party and the United Front of Working People mobilized 3,000 protesters with banners sloganizing "Give Us Bread!" "Down with the Democrats!" To keep up with prices by securing higher wages, the city's subway workers also threatened to strike.[33] But higher wages spent on a constant supply could only force prices still higher. And with January 1992 price rises from three- to thirtyfold causing a sharp decline in living standards, citizens hotly complained, sought price cuts, struck for higher wages, sometimes rioted for bread.

Complaining of higher prices, food shortages, and a new apparat of "democrats," 15,000 Communists allied with the Fascists on Moscow streets on 9 February 1992. Communist forces, marching, waving the hammer and sickle and displaying pictures of Lenin, Stalin, and Castro, mobilized their members and other chauvinist parties, including the anti-Semitic nationalist Pamyat, the old monarchists, and the army, calling for return to the old securities provided by the Communist central bureaucracy.[34]

"The paradox of our time is that they have done all they could to end Marxism and now right-wingers are coming out to demand its return," a schoolteacher reported. "This is a tough winter, no hunger yet but heavy shortages and long lines, and people are getting meaner," another denizen depicted the anti–Yeltsin rally. "It's as if people actually want to be slaves again."

The crisis was also eroding liberal belief in the Yeltsin program. "Let's back our Government on condition that if radical reforms don't take hold in the next few months, we'll have to join the red-and-brown crowd," a leading insurgent, Father Gleb Yakunin, said to the crowd, smiling grimly and using the color code for the Communist-Fascist alliance.[35]

As the crisis bit deeper and new production was not immediately forthcoming, moreover, each republic had tried to appease popular demands. Russia was critically short of vaccines for serious childhood diseases like measles, diphtheria, tetanus, pertussis, and polio. Cases of diphtheria rose 54.7 percent in 1991; pertussis increased 25.1 percent and measles by 12.2 percent—with two of every one thousand children contracting it expected to die.[36] Polluted drinking water had brought a sharp increase in dysentery and gastroenteritis because of breakdown in water purification plants in parts of Siberia.

And with Russia's 1992 inflation at 350 percent between 2 January and 13 February, with retail trade only 63 percent of a year earlier, with industrial output falling 15 percent, President Yeltsin backed down from his economic plan, increasing state subsidies for pensioners and the poor, trying to stabilize collective farm output and the wheat supply. "Everything necessary must be done to ensure the normal sowing of crops," he reassured, assigning his chief critic, Vice President Aleksandr Rutskoi, to reorganize Russia's distress-ridden agricultural domain "in order to occupy his time to the limit."[37]

In other republics, rationing existing supplies sometimes caused delays in issuing coupons and other allotments, leading to riots jeopardizing old and new political powerholders. In Tashkent, for example, the government of President Islam Karminov made the unforgivable error of lifting price controls, introducing food coupons to allocate existing supplies but not distributing them to students and not raising their stipends to keep pace with rising prices. The happenstance of truck drivers late in delivering bread to shops put students afoot on 16 January 1992, some vandalizing food shops, overturning cars, throwing rocks at police officers, others marching toward the presidential palace to demand Karminov's resignation, only to be met with police firing blanks, then live ammunition, killing 6 students, injuring 103 others. And as thousands of students gathered the next day in the student quarter, troops and the Interior Ministry police blocked all roads leading to the area and fired to contain continued student protest.

Reacting to the protest, Uzbek officials then sent students home, arrested fifteen students on a hunger strike protesting the shootings, and tried to pacify the rest by promising to subsidize their food and increasing student grants from 170 rubles ($1.50) a month.

Accusing Karminov's People's Democratic party (formerly the Communist party) of ruling by "dictate and terror," the nationalist Uzbekistan Popular Movement (aka *Berlik*, unity) then threw its support behind the students and their delegation to press Karminov for their demands and an investigation of the shootings.[38] And the next day some 3,000 university students marched peacefully through Tashkent to protest the shooting deaths of the 6 students.[39]

As riots spread from republic to republic, some governments stiffened, others backed down, stabilizing prices or even lowering them. Parliament in Muslim Tajikistan on 18 January passed stiffened legal penalties for taking part in demonstrations during the workday.[40] On

19 January, Turkmenistan president Saparmurad Niyazov decreed a ban on price increases for basic consumer goods. Azerbaijan president Ayaz Mutalibov also ordered bread prices be cut 30 percent, though higher prices for vodka and other high-demand commodities were to compensate for the revenue lost.[41] And though tactical responses varied, the underlying problem of inequitable distribution of too little food for too many people remained.

Conflicting Claims to Power

Autocracy was also a failing in former Soviet republics become independent amid conflicting claimants of power. And in at least one instance, in former Soviet Georgia, the would-be autocrat was replaced by former Soviet Foreign Minister Shevardnadze, promising a future democratic state.

Georgia's popularly elected president, Zviad K. Gamsakhurdia, had become increasingly autocratic in the closing months of 1991. The opposition mobilized. And as a military battle between Gamsakhurdia's faction and a new Military Council led to a two-week siege of the Parliament building that destroyed the Georgian capital, the president fled the country to Armenia, then returned to Zugdidi, the western stronghold of his Megrely homeland, calling on supporters to march to retake the capital.

Responding with an emergency declaration, the ruling Military Council then mobilized 400 militiamen to move into western Georgia to establish a battlefront.[42] And on 18 January, claiming they controlled 90 percent of the republic and preferred not to shed blood, the Military Council then asked the president to depart or suffer the consequences. By the end of January, he was thus driven from office.[43]

As soon as the civil war ended, U.S. Secretary of State James Baker III and other Western powers pressured the Military Council to find an intermediate resolution, calling back Baker's political ally, the old head of Georgia's Communist party, Eduard A. Schevardnadze, to assume the chairmanship of the State Council of Ministers, effectively making him Georgia's leader. The new government then committed itself to restore civilian rule, to begin discussions on national reconciliation, and to hold parliamentary elections in 1992. Western recognition and loan supports immediately followed. On 23 March 1992, the European Community opened relations with Georgia, the next day the United States preparing to establish full diplomatic relations as the last of the fifteen former Soviet republics so recognized, and to support Georgia's membership in the International Monetary Fund, the World Bank, and other international organizations.[44]

As in other former Soviet republics and non–Communist Eastern

European states, though, it was an open question whether these lending agencies would impose conditions of austerity and require new government rigidities, setting parameters for and limiting the decision-making rights of any future democratic parliament.

Chapter 4
In the Land of the Blind

*Then he wept without intention, for he was very weak and ill
now, and they took that as a favorable sign.
They asked him if still thought he could "see."
"No," he said. "That was folly. The word means nothing—less
than nothing!"*

. . . .

*He expected dire punishments, but these blind people were
capable of toleration. They regarded his rebellion as but one more
proof of his general idiocy and inferiority; and after they had
whipped him they appointed him to do the simplest and heaviest
work they had for anyone to do, and he, seeing no other way of
living, did submissively what he was told.*

*. . .And blind philosophers came and talked to him of the wicked
levity of his mind, and reproved him so impressively for his doubts
about the lid of rock that covered their cosmic casserole [in this
sealed off land] that he almost doubted whether indeed he was not
the victim of hallucination in not seeing it overhead.*

*So . . . [he] became a citizen of the Country of the Blind, and
these people ceased to be a generalized people and became indi-
vidualities and familiar to him, while the world beyond the mountains became more and more remote and unreal.*

> —The prisoner Nunez, with eyes to "see,"
> in H. G. Wells, *The Country of the Blind*

*If we do not break out of this foolish system of wage leveling,
we will ruin everything that's alive in our people. We shall suffo-
cate.*

> —President Gorbachev, April 1990

*People do not learn respect for work by having their noses rubbed
in "the work ethic," as if they were stable boys being given a respect
for horsemanship by having their faces shoved into manure.*

> —Jonathan Kozel, *Rachel and Her Children*

FROZEN INTO TIME

Frozen into time, handicapped by the state in the land of the blind,
the multitudinous populations making up fifteen Soviet republics had

129

been bred to bureaucratic tutelage. They had lived through centrist Stalinist direction from a higher reach and the repressive, feudallike overseers of the military state. They had survived by government subsidies, price controls, and wage leveling. They were pressured to work. But the state and its apparat had suffocated their human ingenuity and initiative, trying to motivate them with threats for thinking, the folly of seeing another way of living.

For the masses to view the underbelly of Soviet power had been nearly impossible through the focused lens of the entrenched Communist bureaucracy and Stalinist apparatchiks,[1] steadily growing and making up a gangling body of 18 million bloodless automatons by the last decade of the twentieth century.

For seventy-odd years, the soul of the people had been crushed by these would-be demigods: anomie became their lot.[2] And the resulting "qualities of the Russian character" ostensibly "tended to make public life intractable and pose formidable obstacles to reform: their escapism, their impracticality, their lackadaisical attitude towards work and their vicious envy of people who try to get ahead."[3]

To strip away the mental handicaps imposed by the state, to liberate the populace in thought and fact, was no simple task. For the Soviet past bred fear, the army, KGB, and Stalinists enforcing repression. Their miscalculations had led to internal repression and defensive war, costing the nation 40 million dead since the great October Revolution, and they again stood ready to displace any Kremlin leader who might reach beyond his grasp, encouraging democracy either by guidance or by initiative from below.[4]

So rather than dismantle the centrist state that bred repression and purposelessness, the Communists in power blamed the populace for the apparat's failures and mindless ways. The path for change was clear. But until the many gained awareness and cut the chains of the bureaucratic centrist state, they would live more as helpless charges than the vibrant people they might become.

CENTRIFUGAL DISINTEGRATION

The opposition had calculated that centrifugal disintegration would mean balkanization of territories and states. Yet given Moscow's enforced division of regional labor among republics and ethnic communities in both the Soviet Union and Eastern Europe, economic self-sufficiency might be delayed or appear impossible.

Limits on Freedom from the Centrist State

Only by agreement could unified regional markets become ancillary regions linked to the integration process in the Soviet Union and, later, in the rest of Eastern and Western Europe. The republics and their subdivisions would thereby fit in the missing pieces of the puzzle, integrating markets across the entire European continent. To elaborate this speculation about future possibility, the Soviet opposition posited that local production and markets would be extended.

Similarly, a freed Eastern Europe initially foresaw national independence and consolidation of each nation-state. National government seemingly would ensure political pluralism, democratic rights, and freedoms for all citizens. The central government would unify domestic markets through stimulation of production and employment, unification of monetary and fiscal policies, and other reforms that touched the ownership and use of property, production facilities, and land. There would be no internal tariffs or other barriers to the movement of goods, labor, or capital.

There were material limits to the logic of such integration. For freedom from the Soviet helotry beyond its borders and the centrist state within demanded resolution of historic regional and ethnic problems that remained unsolved for more than four decades of Socialist rule. Questions of the equitable use and distribution of land, resources, means of production, and output continued to be raised spatially and by ethnic regions. Regions that sought to protect their equitable share opposed the old centrist methods of government planning and impositions, seeing the federation of many regions under a national government as anathema to material equity.

By contrast with centrist federation, they viewed regional or ethnic control as the critical element of freedom and self-determination. Once these elements were secured, it would then be up to each area or community to enter a larger cooperative body or confederation of independent states. The cooperative unification of a wider trade area or market would take detailed negotiations and expend much time. Yet there seemed no other way to widen the area of commerce for eventual unification with other zones or custom unions.

These were the planned steps toward future market integration, still blocked by enforced conditions of unfreedom handed down from the past.

THE SOVIET CONDITION OF UNFREEDOM

Freedom from control over their labor by others, freedom to participate fully in the political labor process, was absent for the Soviet people during most of the seven decades after the Bolshevik Revolution.

Though workers sought self-direction on farm, in factory, and at most assigned posts, they were manipulated and made the means to an end they neither controlled nor fully comprehended.[5]

Under the Kremlin's central plan administered by a powerful and growing bureaucracy, mass production using old and dangerous technologies had led to the extensive socialization of labor but also to the regulation of the work force as objects from whom maximum endurance and production were expected. Such alienation was framed by a *nationalist mission to accumulate*, to upgrade one day the condition of the population, and to best Western competitors.

A future cornucopia was the projected Communist goal setting the momentary relations between bureaucrats and the mass of workers. And based on such heralded promises and fear of opposing Communist *diktat*, the workers conceded to their position, momentarily giving up both individuality and freedom.[6]

Nonetheless, there remained the paradox of a central plan implemented by bureaucrats and an army of workers carrying out orders. For both order giver and order taker had their roles prescribed and defined, making them as mechanical as their tools of work.[7] Both understood the functions and techniques of their respective roles, but neither had a definitive idea of the goals for which they labored. They moved machinelike in a blind for decades on end. And rather than pursue the Socialist aim of production of *useful values* that might have bettered their condition, they found themselves turned into automatons making more and more machines, implements, and military paraphernalia, objects quite useless to improve the immediate quality of their lives.[8]

The producers of these commodities, absorbing their life energy, were all treated as objects, estranging them from the conditions of labor, from work effort, and from the things they created. As production became increasingly complex, they could not identify their specific labor in these objects or often acquire them, as these things also appeared as useless to them, going elsewhere as missiles, machines, and exports. In this sense, they lived as serfs from whom the direct product of their labor was extracted.

Bureaucratic centralism, forwarding this accumulation of the means of production, war, and foreign exchange, thus bred the fetish of phantom consumption, making its mark by alienating the very populace it promised to liberate.[9]

Losing Faith

The many nationalities that had once hoped to direct their labor efforts communally and enjoy the fruit of their work lost faith when the overarching state designated the parameters for their existence and spread its bureaucratic flank to mediate how they would work and live day by day.

And though they had never formally delegated powers to the Supreme Soviet or any other body for such purposes, the falsification of their mandate left them helpless, isolated individually, "unconcerned" with problems they could not resolve.[10]

In this sense, the common people developed the pathology of master-slave, a split personality, thinking one thing, doing another: secretly seeking freedom yet working as object at the command of circumstances, external needs, defined by this or that bureaucratic functionary. Such individual pathologies raised to the level of social neurosis allowed free speech on questions of equality for all, not personal aspiration for betterments above one's coworkers, neighbors, friends.

Yet speaking lies in irrational ways sometimes allowed truth to emerge, though usually only in tight family, ethnic, nationality, or social circles through the mediums of humor, oppositional tracts, and metaphoric parody; signifying the universality of the pathology of oppressed communities, their hundred nationalities with divergent interests and many thoughts held at least one common theme—freedom from Moscow.[11]

The common people and many nationalities no longer identified themselves by conforming to the political or other mandated beliefs of the functionaries of the apparat. Why should they follow political prescriptions without the means of real control in their own communities?

By the late eighties, group submission to powerlessness was no longer dominant among the "minority" peoples of the Union. The tables had turned, and millions among the various nationalities now realized they were no longer, if every they were, the authors of their own destiny.[12]

FAILINGS OF APPARAT DIRECTION

Soviet centrist direction of the economy ideally posited an apparat that was competent to allocate resources and labor power to produce useful commodities and services, to alter output in response to popular needs and requirements, and to keep close account of the relationship between production costs, revenues, and subsidies from the state.

In all these tasks, the apparat had failed miserably if not completely. For the central plan neither required technical innovation nor the full use of productive forces, so there was no way to calculate labor's comparative productivity over time.

The quality of labor was itself disregarded, so that the incentive to work was absent and unrewarded. Rather than use labor for its varied skills, the central plan calculated output by volume, so that a speedup of all workers regardless of function would meet the preset goal.

And these objective plans could not be varied without each factory or production center mediating through the central apparat to approve repairs, alter investments, change the balance of skilled and unskilled labor, find alternative suppliers, ship output to other designated locations, and so forth. Such a centrist-peripheral linkage made production efficiency, labor policies, and equitable distribution unworkable in supplying the population's needs.

Central bureaucratic direction also failed to link the sphere of production with that of distribution. There was no coherent central calculation of the quantity of quality goods required to meet popular needs. The "law of value" was arbitrarily fixed by setting prices on commodities using some vague notion of a socially averaged remuneration for work, but distribution through the mechanism of prices neither guaranteed required output nor quality goods.

The result was a system that worked backward: rationalized on the basis of the prices set on commodities but actually put in motion by the central plan to invest so much in means of production and materials, so much in the production of particular consumer goods, so much in wages to enable the population to buy those products, and so much in shifting labor from one production location to another.

There was absolutely no scientific way production outlays – rubles spent – could be compared with the average socially necessary cost of production that under the best of plans would have represented the optimal efficiency of labor using existing technology and materials. Balancing supplies between industries and commodity output on one side with the availability of funds in the hands of the public on the other took the form of experimental markets that reflected guesswork about the availability of assorted quantities of shoddy goods – supply – and pent-up savings rather than genuine demand: there were simply too few quality goods produced in the Soviet Union and too many printing-press rubles in circulation to define what demand might be in the future.

WRONGED AND UNBRAIDED

Unbraiding Soviet workers' lack of a sense of responsibility – and resisting wage reforms that would reward good work – in 1990 President Gorbachev sharply rebuffed the public that the culture of envy could snuff out any spark of worker initiative and daring, crippling hopes of economic progress in the nation.

This glib casting of blame was historically misplaced. For the times were out of joint, rooted in the Kremlin's backward exploitation of labor to accumulate capital, the workers' movement for things economic and democratic freedoms being a natural expression of seventy years of deprivations.

The truth was that the Soviet Union had not yet entered the twentieth century by comparison with the freedoms and mass consumer markets existing in the West and parts of Asia.[13]

Soviet people also had no illusion about their purported rights and freedoms. They had not been conditioned with an abundance of consumer goods that made them either willing wage slaves or entrants to markets with money of their own. Like their Western brethren, moreover, they were not happy on the job, in their government-controlled unions, in their position as charges of the state, or in (or under) the purview of the army. They certainly sought to be mass consumers, but they were not good soldiers on the production line, in the factory, or in the field. They felt satisfaction neither at work nor in the marketplace.

Jobs and Pay Without Work

Holding jobs, they pretended to work and to be paid, but they were unhappy workers who produced far below their capacity. The persona of worker did not comport with the condition of direction from above, managers manipulating them as things, unconcerned with their creative abilities and active participation in and direction of output, blinded to the potentialities of their technical knowledge, foresight to plan, and abilities to control the pace and skill of the labor process. Soviet labor was not master of its destiny or circumstances, then—to share work and experience, to remain free from exploitation, to participate in meaningful production, and to create a humane community without seeking selfish self-aggrandizement. And yet the Soviet worker—not the Communist party, not the state bureaucracy and apparat—was blamed for these failings.

As an act of political vanity elevating his stated mission, in 1990 President Gorbachev spoke glibly of the need for hard work, comparable remuneration, personal acquisitions, and well-being—unwittingly, he lamented, begetting envy of others. The pot had called the kettle black. For rather than a generalized personal failing of its people, the Soviet Union had institutionalized state subsidies that discouraged work and kept personal possessions at a minimum. One might work hard yet never establish a standard of life and personal security worth much at all. The nation's workers had no reason to work hard and did not.[14]

Rationalizations about a common fate, with all putting in the same or their best efforts, simply did not approximate what had taken place or, from the point of view of its genesis, the primary forces behind the general situation where everyone held a job, no one worked full force, and the state supported the population by running up ever-enlarging deficits.[15]

The linkages were more complex, of course. A few of them, points in the uphill climb Soviet ideologues must one day make to begin to understand the results of seventy years of failures:

1. *Linking money supply and output levels:* To reach future stability, control over the Soviet production of high-quality goods by well-paid, willing workers will have to be balanced against the supply of money. This remains critical to provide adequately for the population, protecting real buying power by stopping inflation, normalizing consumption patterns, and creating incentives to produce and trade:

- The state will have to stop shifting resources by printing money used as subsidies for producers, consumers, and the military.
- An independent central bank will have to replace the state function of creating and borrowing phantom fiat to finance their deficits, artificially massaging the numbers to make it appear that no deficit exists.
- The creation of such fictitious statistics will have to be replaced by irreproachable fiscal and monetary policies, converting the ruble into a convertible currency against the hard monies of the West, so that both internal and global trade can proceed.

2. *Linking unfettered trade and the movement of goods, capital, and labor:* Today's basic demands of the separate republics are aspects of a common historical process that other nations have experienced in the past: Moscow permitting the barrier-free movement of people, goods, and capital within the nation and across national borders — without central direction.

STEPS TOWARD CENTRIST SURVIVAL

Fear had taken hold of the party and the apparatchiks in the Kremlin when a key provision of the "500-day program" promised to devolve almost all central economic powers to the nation's republics.

As President Gorbachev got political cold feet, he pushed an unworkable, vaguely worded sixty-six-page document through Parliament. As a phantom plan to nowhere, the Kremlin center would hold against the forces of dispersion.

Seeking to preserve his position between the demands of the party apparat and the military on one side and the mass movements and republics on the other, President Gorbachev worried that independent republics running their own economic affairs would demand equally sweeping political powers, leaving him as a figurehead president with real power transferred to his nemesis, Boris Yeltsin, and other leaders of the republics.

Against the 500-day plan, he had powerful bureaucratic and military backing. The apparat, the KGB, and the military flexed their muscles, sending squads of military paratroopers marching to the capital.* Directors of the giant military-industrial complex, accounting for as much as 30 percent of all industrial output, also worried that a radical reform would drastically cut production and subsidies, possibly causing shutdowns of entire plants. Managers of military factories in the industrial Urals started grouping together to create an "anti-reform bloc."[16]

---

*See Chapter 2.

This was both deadly serious and expected. Ever since Peter the Great had set up a cannon factory in Perm in the eighteenth century, the region remained a center for the Russian armament industry. In 1990, one defense-industry plant after another lined the streets of the town, turning out everything from howitzers to fighter engines. As the Soviet Union had cut back on military spending in the late eighties, however, the unanswered question was how to pursue conversion to civilian production. But still the system largely remained in place. The defense plants, even the ones undergoing conversion, remained in the monopolistic hands of Moscow ministries, which continued to take almost all military production at fixed prices, centralized management of Perm's industry acting as a powerful break on free-market efforts.

Even conversion, gobbling up resources, boded ill for the government's attempt to reduce its budget deficit. And the government fixed prices so that consumer goods rewarded less factory "profits" than producing military hardware, so the government had to subsidize civilian workers' pay and plan to make future capital investments it couldn't afford.[17]

It would be difficult, then, to extend the "free market," undermining the ministries of Moscow, contesting the rights of the party, the apparat, and the army. They made demands the president could not refuse.

CENTRISM IMPLODES: THE PERIPHERIES' GRASP FOR INDEPENDENCE — FALLING INTO NEW SPHERES OF INFLUENCE

With the failed coup of 1991 and Gorbachev's resignation in a huff, preferring a federated Union to a Commonwealth of Independent States, centrism imploded. Russia and Ukraine moved apart over questions of territory, the Black Sea fleet, insular trade, and autarchic production. The Baltic states, Kazakhstan, Belarus, Kyrgyzstan, and Armenia established direct diplomatic relations with foreign countries, envisioning aid, mutual trade, and Western investments. Rigidities on armed preparedness, centrist authority over production and distribution, and suppression of popular rights became the order of governments in Azerbaijan and Georgia in the Caucasus; Turkmenistan, Tajikistan, and Uzbekistan in central asia; and Moldova on the Romanian border. And as the Westernized republics looked west to Europe and North America for help and commerce, the Muslim states of Azerbaijan, Kazakhstan, Turkmenistan, Tajikistan, and Uzbekistan looked south and east, to Iran and other Muslims of the Middle East. Thus were opened new possibilities to establish emporiums throughout the former Soviet republics.

Establishing New and Joint Spheres of Influence

The new spheres of influence, different from past practice, were designed to deal with a "war" of sorts, an all-encompassing economic, political, and military balance of power in the newly independent Muslim states, the Middle East, and the U.S. client state of Turkey.

The old cold war had called for multilateral "containment" of communism so that it could not spread rather than demanding its overthrow or weakening, foreseeing it would eventually collapse from its own internal pressures and decay.[18] In contrast, the new Western spheres of influence were both separate and joint efforts, each nation seeking the least burdensome and least costly path to generate commerce and investments within a sphere of multilateral policies calling for tranquility, austerity, aid, and disarmament—creating a general diplomatic and material sphere in which the individual spheres could securely expand.

This double-edged emporium was designed to be cost-effective in the new post–Soviet republics as well as in the Middle East, Latin America, and East Africa, allowing the Western nations (and Japan to a lesser degree) to maintain a semblance of political legitimacy in the eyes of domestic populations at home. But the balance of unmet home needs in the face of burdensome outlays abroad nonetheless strained the national consensus in most Western nations, raising questions whether foreign policy served national interests or any domestic social policy.

To offset these domestic political pressures, foreign outlays had to be cut. One way was establishing a joint sphere of influence in the old Soviet republics, using multilateral diplomacy and collective resources for building democratic institutions that could quiet the separate republics' nationalist forces and stem their introduction of autarchic economic, political, and military policies.

The logic of combining budgetary funds from the United States, Western Europe, Japan, and rich Middle East states to pursue national interests and overlay them with the seeming common destiny of all had its basis in the mutual need for control over the spread of armaments and the quest for unfettered access to foreign markets and investment spheres. For each participating nation hoped to sidestep being isolated by domestic social and political pressures that might demand withdrawal from foreign involvement, using the defensive arguments that security at home required NATO defenses, the United States–Japan Security pact, a peaceful Middle East, the creation of stable Eastern European economies fostering the extension of trade without protectionist barriers, and/or the curtailment of the spread of nuclear weapons and missile delivery systems to irresponsible Third World nations.

These joint efforts had become feasible with the end of the cold war because the U.S. sphere establishing a "new world order" was linked to multilateral cooperation for aid, arms, and protective security essential in various troubled regions—from the old Soviet republics to the Middle East, Latin America, and Africa. NATO, the Pentagon's central command, and the Japanese self-defense forces thus divided their functions and resources for surveillance and outlays to aid or police the former

Soviet republics, the Persian Gulf, the Indian Ocean, East Africa, and East Asia.

National Action Within the Collective Sphere

By early 1992, each participating nation had more or less begun acting within this collective sphere. Yeltsin had pushed hard with appeals for funds to save Russian reforms, using threats of impending political disaster, telling the French of his faith in these reforms. "But if they fail," he warned, "I can already feel the breath of the red shirts and brown shirts on our necks."

"If Russia fails in its reforms, especially of the economy, a dictatorship will appear," he said at a reception in the Paris City Hall. "That is why the international community must contribute to a solution. Its delay is becoming dangerous."

Businessmen hesitated to invest in Russia despite Yeltsin's critical three-month dateline warning, insisting, "Perhaps you can save a franc today, but if there's a return to the cold war, you will have to spend thousands of times more."

Knowledgeable politicians of Gaul understood that Russia had historically been a French ally, acting as the counterweight to any Teutonic aggression. With a united Germany again swinging its heavy political weight in Common Market and Eastern European decisions, France was quick to seize Russian friendship, on 6 February 1992 granting a $370-million credit to import French grain, a $22-million line of credit for technical assistance, and a $405-million barter agreement. France would also send emergency food supplies and medical assistance, Prime Minister Edith Cresson assured Yeltsin, to soften "the social costs of the transition to the market economy for those who are most vulnerable — pensioners, children and the sick."

France and Russia would also keep technically advanced, small-scale nuclear arsenals encircling a unified Germany should any future revanchism become *politik*. President Yeltsin thus promised Russia would reduce its nuclear weapons stock to "a minimum force sufficient to deter terrorism and irresponsible leaders."[19] President Mitterrand clearly understood, and as a security measure against a future bellicose Germany, Yeltsin did not press him to reduce France's nuclear *force du frappe*.

Japan was the most cautious, carefully picking its markets and investment zones. It had spent $1.2 billion in bilateral commercial aid in Africa to promote trade in fiscal 1991–92. But as far as the Commonwealth republics were concerned, Japan would provide the former Soviets nothing beyond $100 million for food, drugs, and aid to Chernobyl victims; some $50 million in humanitarian aid to post–Soviet Russia; and another $2.5 billion in the form of credits and insurance to ease eastern Russian purchases of Japanese products — thereby concentrating on the

region closest to Japan where future investments in gas and oil exploration were envisioned. These would follow the Mitsui Corporation consortium securing $8–$10 billion in loans and insurance from the Ministry of
International Trade and Industry to explore oil and gas reserves off
Sakhalin Island. But any other Japanese aid would depend on softening
Russian opposition to handing over the Russian-seized islands and group
of islets in the Kurile chain north of Japan.[20]

The U.S. State Department had meanwhile prepared for the new
world order, strengthening the "Soviet Desk" so the old task of "containment" of the spread of communism was sharply switched to offering help
in reorganizing former Soviet institutions to make them comport with
those in the "free world." Its Office of Independent States and Commonwealth Affairs now concentrated on the needs of individual republics,
placed linguists speaking local languages in its missions, and tried to train
the various nationalities in the steps required to set up Western legal and
political institutions.

In February 1992, embassies were established in five of the newly independent republics—Ukraine, Kazakhstan, Armenia, Kyrgyzstan, and
Belarus, envisioning others in Azerbaijan, Turkmenistan, Tajikistan, and
Uzbekistan.[21] The Baltic states were not only recognized, with $18 million
in aid, but the United States urged the swift withdrawal of Russian
troops.[22]

The West would also help to eliminate and or shift certain social
elites and technological workers away from reliance on arms and warfare
to socially or commercially useful tasks, setting the frame and conditions
for democratic civil society and Western advantages.

True, Yeltsin might be able to alone dismantle and retire with pensions the general staff that was still riddled with hand-downs from the old
Soviet guard, military men who had secretly backed the 1991 coup and
only gradually realized that the centrist Soviet system would not again be
mobilized as a superpower.

But alone, Yeltsin could not reduce the Soviet military-industrial
complex to the pursuit of small-scale military nuclear research necessary
to keep up with weapons breakthroughs by other states poised to possess
unknown nuclear weaponry in the coming decade.* The United States
thus sought to draw Russia into peaceful research, knowing that this
might still free up Russian funds for military research.

Nonetheless, some $400 million in congressional appropriations were
used for assisting the new republics of Russia, Belarus, Ukraine, and Kazakhstan to remove and dismantle all strategic nuclear arms, to store
plutonium, convert enriched uranium for civilian fuel reactors, and

---

*By the year 2000, at least six Third World countries will possess intercontinental ballistic
missiles, and eight others will have developed nuclear weapons.

employ nuclear scientists to dismember and renovate nuclear technology or work for the U.S. "star wars" program.

A Western-financed clearing house was envisioned in militarized industrial cities to convert their arms industries to civilian use by finding jobs in foreign-financed, privatized, commercial projects for 100,000 Soviet nuclear scientists—to stop them from selling their expertise to hostile nations by pairing the talents of those holding the most advanced nuclear knowledge with the needs of foreign investors, universities, private research organizations, or governments willing to pay for commercial nuclear research. The elite 2,000 to 3,000 nuclear scientists with sophisticated technological and theoretical knowledge were to be redeployed; the 8,000 to 12,000 secondary scientists and technicians in the nuclear military industry were to draw on U.S. congressional appropriations to dismantle and destroy nuclear weapons or be employed in the United States on study and work grants. The rest of the 85,000 to 90,000 nuclear and military workers would be transferred to civilian production or employed to dismantle weapons to the 9,000 level, as provided by the Strategic Arms Treaty, or perhaps to the 2,500 level Yeltsin proposed.[23]

The United States also planned to buy critical technologies (from prototypes of a nuclear power system for space orbit to electrical propulsion rocket components) from the counterpart Soviet missile program, speeding up the U.S. deployment of the antimissile defense system, hiring about 1,000 Soviet scientists and engineers. Some $50 million was to be used to buy Soviet space hardware, a small fraction of the $5.4 billion the United States sought in fiscal 1992–93 for the antiballistic missile defense program. The purchase, *Aviation Week* recounted, could save more than $4 billion in star wars development costs and bolster the troubled economies of the new republics.[24]

Spheres in the Central Asian Republics

Would such measures alter the balance of power in the central Asian republics?

In the nineteenth century the major powers had used military force in the "great game" to establish spheres of influence over central Asia. Replaced by the Soviet state in the twentieth century, the 1991 independence of the separate central Asian republics made them vulnerable again to becoming part of the spheres of other states.

Iran had seized the opening, sending capital, trade missions, and preachers into the five central Asian republics from 1991–92. Libya also offered large sums to buy uranium from Tajikistan mines, President Rakhman Nabiyev's government being strapped for revenues. But Nabiyev was both the former head of the Communist party and opposed to the Islamic Renaissance party, the fundamentalist slate he had outflanked in a 1991 58 percent–38 percent presidential vote. Under U.S. pressure for potential recognition and financial aid, he still saw the necessity for good relations with neighboring Iran but in February 1992 said he was unwilling to sell uranium to accommodate the hope of the Islamic world to build atomic armories.[25] "It has been a long-standing dream of the Islamic world to have its own nuclear arsenal," the weekly *Moscow News* had reported in January. "After the defeat of Saddam Hussein, Rakhman Nabiyev may be the leader who could help them meet their atomic ambitions."

Alive to the new intrigue, Washington had moved quickly to align its Turkish ally, to mobilize CIA recruits, and to open embassies in the central Asian republics, securing pro forma promises that they would honor human rights, arms control, and free markets—none of which they had done or planned. Turkey and Egypt, both U.S. client states, were to be deployed to help draw Azerbaijan, Kazakhstan, Turkmenistan, Tajikistan, and Uzbekistan into the Western sphere of influence—away from Iran and possibly Iraq.

Muslim Turkey was to be the role model of a secular state integrally tied into the Western alliance, itself devoid of respect for human rights, free markets, and arms control. "There is now a struggle for the soul of Central Asia—and Turkey, Iran, Saudi Arabia, Pakistan and the United States will all play a part," explained Graham E. Fuller, former top-ranking CIA analyst for the Middle East. "These Central Asian states are now asking themselves, Are they Turks? Are they Muslims? Are they just individual Uzbeks and Tajiks? Or are they part Westerners because they were part of the Soviet Union? We are present at the creation again and we can't just sit back and say that until they have a better human rights record we are not going to deal with them."[26]

The U.S. State Department was willing to establish diplomatic ties with Azerbaijan, accepting its promise of respect for human rights despite its blockade and brutal escalating attacks against Armenian villagers in Nagorno-Karabakh.[27]

Yet such simplistic fears of a potential pan–Islamic bloc did not account for the need of these former Soviet republics to diversify their economies through trade with Iran and other Islamic countries. Still, liberal papers like *The New York Times* saw dangers to be remediated by U.S. actions, editorializing that

> Iran continues to pursue a worldwide campaign of assassinations, death threats and support for terrorism. And it is actively shopping for missiles and nuclear bombs.
>
> Iran hopes to draw the former Soviet republics into its orbit and has been aggressively wooing several of them. But Teheran's efforts face major obstacles. Most of these countries are Turkic in language and culture, not Persian, and many of their Muslim inhabitants are Sunnis, not Shiites.
>
> More important, all have just emerged from foreign domination and are scarcely eager to rush to any other country's exclusive embrace.

It is reasonable for these countries to wean their economies away from distant European centers and develop new rail and trade links with Turkey, Iran, Pakistan and China. Such steps would fortify their independence and their economies, goals Washington has an interest in encouraging.[28]

Islamic diversity among the new republics along Russia's rim continued to evolve, trying to maintain their independence while looking to Turkish, Korean, and Western aid and advice for economic progress in building either theocracies demanding uniformity or future democratic secular states.

Part IV:
The Eastern Europe
That Was

As centralized states topple across the 6,000-mile breadth of Eastern
Europe and Asia, the monolithic national identities formed under Communist Party leadership are vanishing everywhere — and to many people,
history appears to be moving forward and backward at the same time.
   Ahead lies a new internationalism, with its chief allies in a dynamic,
globalized economy that knows no borders at all.
   Behind lie ancient, unresolved conflicts, some dating back 1,000 years,
that fermented in a closed system for half a century and are now exploding into bitter tribalism.[1]

   Having destroyed European Communism without acquiring a single
grey hair, [the still-20-looking, 40-year-old Wonder Woman] is prepared
to pit her bulletproof bracelets and Lasso of Truth against the ruthless
demons who seek to re-enslave the liberated lands.[2]

Set free from Soviet control in 1989–90, Eastern European states
were stirred by old ethnic battles, expressing themselves as claims to territorial, civil, and religious rights. As the struggles intensified, they devolved into narrow battles promising to balkanize nations that had been
consolidated under Communist domination for half a century.
   The revolutions from below roiled governments once exploited by and
dependent on Moscow largesse. While officialdom delayed assessing the
realities of the new stage of history, the redefinition of rights, liberties, and
the quest for independence raged at the lower reaches of the social pyramid.
The logic of governments trying to maintain economic ties with Moscow
was being questioned in the streets and in communities. And the obvious
escape for some governments was aid, trade, and investments from the
West; for others, an extension of indebtedness to creditor states.
   Populations meanwhile were on the move, skilled workers looking to

145

emigrate for a better life. "The golden dream of this labor force is first Western Europe, then the United States, then Australia and finally Latin America," analyzed Jorge Mora of the multilateral International Organization for Migration. Their quest for El Dorado threatened to break wage levels and unions in the West, though, and to provide South America with replacement of skilled labor and capital that had been fleeing the continent for a decade.[3]

APPEAL TO THE WEST

Appeal to the West was politically imperative as Moscow cut benefits and imposed new hard-currency charges on the entire Eastern bloc. The Soviets had bitten off more expenses than they could chew in supporting an armed empire in Stalinist Eastern Europe and now undergoing expensive digestive surgery at home, were leaving the unconsumed scraps for others to support.

At a more confident moment in 1989, President Gorbachev had insisted that communism would have to absorb the best the West could offer for new opportunities in moving toward its "just and noble goals" for releasing the enormous humanistic and democratic potential contained in the "socialist ideal."

Abandoning the claim to have a monopoly on truth, Gorbachev looked forward to a world "on the threshold of an entirely new era" and a new Europe that would be "a commonwealth of sovereign democratic states," based on spiritual values, pluralism, religious tolerance, and mutual understanding.

For religion, individual conscience must prevail, he said, and foresaw that "the moral values that religion generated and embodied for centuries can help in the work of renewal of our country, too."

Exactly how the new order would be established in each republic, nation, region, or community came to be based on the population's demands and material resources, though. And how these resources were and would be mobilized depended on political organization, traditional mores and beliefs, and sense of purpose, knowledge, and skill.

Section A:
Patterns Past and Present

The illusion of a rapid transformation of former Soviet republics and Eastern European economies into commercially viable production centers accommodating many millions of people is today evidenced by a lack of capital and technology for investment; an educational apparatus steeped in ideological formulations that have little to do with organizing the forces for production; and deep political and ethnic divisions within each nation-state, region, and locality.

Politics also remains primary in such reorganization. Likely there will have to be political coalitions bringing divergent interests and parties together to support a common program to unhinge old technical linkages in production, rearranging the use and locale of resources and labor mobilized for output. So long as such coalitions are lacking, the realignment of production forces will face human barriers—lack of cooperation, periodic protest, or revolutions anew.

Without political consensus for the future, moreover, technocratic government policies are bound to fail and make matters worse. It would be folly, for example, to follow traditional Western economists' dismal recipes for rebuilding Third World markets: imposing austerity, cutting production and employment to shift resources to other purposes, or in the case of state-controlled economies, phasing out subsidies and removing price controls, simultaneously causing a fall in living standards and driving out inefficient production centers that employ millions.

Using such cookbook prescriptions, a neat little circle of cause-effect is supposed to shift resources to more efficient producers and motivate workers to upgrade their skills to gain employment in the new enterprises. But it has not smoothly functioned that way in the past and will not likely do so in the future.

The reasons are obvious enough. Starting with state-encouraged increments in prices, those that occupy the production and distribution spheres abandoned by the state are positioned to raise prices, reaping greater revenues at public expense. But what they do with these enhanced revenues may never be known unless there is a state oversight that free-market specialists wish to eliminate. They may distribute them to their own favored workers while others outside the production or factory circle reap no rewards. Acting as merchants, they may form a new social class of "extortionists," recycling revenues by repeatedly buying low and selling high. Or they may privatize factories, expanding their investment base, hence production, employment, and private profits. But without input costs and output values known, these possibilities are strictly conjecture.

It will take either careful central planning or an unusual combination of state direction of private enterprise to make sure there is an expansion of investments, the introduction of new technologies and materials, fairness to the labor force, volume production of quality output, and marketing at affordable prices. How else could a "market economy" be created? Converting state enterprises to private ownership and encouraging some firms at the competitive expense of others and their workers do not guarantee this sequence.

Nor does creating an unemployed body of laid-off workers who feel abused and suddenly become politically aware. Will the state provide a security net and blanket for them until they can learn anew, retread their skills, or secure new employment at comparable wages?

In the early nineties, these steps had yet to be taken, raising still another question: Would the government enlarge its supply of housing so that displaced workers could move with their families to potentially expanding sectors of the economy? The Communist state had never been on the *qui vive* in building workers' homes in Eastern Europe, so there was neither available housing nor a potential housing "market" on the horizon. Either this lack of adequate living accommodations or constructing look-alike state-owned apartment complexes in the grimy monoliths of mining and factory districts had been a Communist method to preset levels of remuneration to prevent the mobility of labor, maintain surveillance over the many at work, and segregate populations by social caste and geography.

To change these narrow designations of times past will take years, perhaps decades. But the critical linkages in the dynamics of change will remain *political*—both internally and from without.

Finance Western-style may be the mother of exchange relations, but the inducement to locate in the new Commonwealth republics and Eastern Europe will have to guarantee its security and profitability. By contrast, equity Eastern-style has been the popularly demanded assurance of the right to life, however badly those in the East may have lived over the last five and a half decades. Given these needs for both capital and human security—though it may be useless to preach morals, comparative or otherwise, in forwarding social transformation—the fact remains that *both capital and popular equity are required for the political recipe that will facilitate the reconstruction of the Commonwealth republics and Eastern European economies.*

In 1992, Russia plotted the path, hiring the investment banking firm Goldman Sachs as its chief adviser for inducing foreign investments to counterbalance post–Communist economic chaos. "We want to create a new image of Russia for foreign investors," Deputy Economics Minister Leonid Grigoryev declared, while Goldman Sachs officials vowed to encourage "greater comfort and greater optimism" among foreign businesses looking for trustworthy prospects, Goldman focusing on a "short list" of changes in burdensome government practices to attract these investors, lining up individual major clients for specific deals yet keeping Russia's fair interests uppermost.[4]

Assume, then, that Western investments arrive with management savoir faire; that grants of aid and trade come on the scene expecting the infrastructure to be transformed and the labor force to be both cooperative and compliant. It could happen if daily life and labor are made equitable. But exactly how social equity will be calculated, designed, and negotiated is not yet known.

What is known is that the initial step for equity is putting people into jobs at pay high enough to eliminate poverty and maintain living standards. Neglect this, and any program will probably fail politically sooner or later. For without buyers, production and employment will turn backward. Thus in early 1992 Russian shoppers refused to buy high-priced goods, dipping more than ever into their rainy-day hoards of food supplies, waiting for prices to drop and wage increases to keep pace with price rises.[5]

Tearing down the old "command structures" that directed resources and labor also requires that *new ones* replace them. But few of these existed in the Commonwealth republics and Eastern Europe in the early nineties. In some countries, the old apparat with "skills" and "knowledge" was back in the saddle. In others, continued Communist-style management over state-owned enterprises using backward technologies ensured labor's inefficient production of low-quality goods. In still others, managers took charge of the majority of shares in factories, directed these facilities as their private fiefs, and expanded both production and employment.

Though new governments elected to bring about change were in place in most of these states, they could not equitably transform their economies without the constant participation of populations and communities affected, secured or harmed by each change in policy or structure. Hence the situational dilemma experienced by each republic, region, community, workstation, job position, and living unit to be here detailed, analyzed, and reviewed.

Chapter 5
Captivity and Breakaway
in Eastern Europe

*The end of history? The remarkable uprisings in Eastern Europe
are more like a resumption of history. As Hungarians plan for
their first free elections since World War II, demonstrators in
Czechoslovakia quote Thomas Jefferson and chant the name of
Alexander Dubcek, who failed heroically in 1968 to bring reform.
And now, astonishingly, Prague's hard-line rulers have agreed to
form a new coalition government.... These events add up to
something the experts insisted could never happen: a revolution
from below, tolerated if not encouraged by the Soviet Union. But
it would be equally mistaken to assume that the renewal of history
in Eastern Europe will lead inexorably to democratic triumphs.*
— Editorial, The New York Times,
29 November 1989

*In Europe, a new era of German-Soviet détente in Mitteleuropa
may be opening, but without the balance provided by a continuing United States commitment, the British and the French, not
to mention the Poles, Czechs and Slovaks, could see it as a
destabilizing threat.*
— Graig Whitney, The New York Times,
16 September 1990

POSTWAR EASTERN EUROPE

With powerful revolutions from below in Eastern Europe building
the foundation for détente in Mitteleuropa, the U.S. military presence in
Europe is coming to an end and economic and sociopolitical history opening new horizons for a transcontinental system — dreamed of for centuries
yet never before consummated.

Still the battle for unity is not over, for the great power struggle
among Western nations — within their various alliances, and each of them
with Eastern Europe and Japan — is again being shaped by earlier en-
counters culminating in the postwar order, requiring an historical retro-
spective to make sense of the present.

Looking back toward the end of World War II, in late 1944 and during 1945 Russian troops had advanced forcefully to replace retreating German armies. There was desperation as the German SS elite troops sought to finalize Hitler's solution to eliminate the rest of the Jews, Poles, Gypsies, and other "dissidents" in the hundreds of concentration camps and prison factories.[1] The forced march of these inmates back to Germany left in its terrifying wake millions maimed and dead. Fascist *barbarosa* and earth-scorching policies everywhere left devastation, community and village life disorganized, millions of homeless, farm and factory production dissolved, people terrified, living nearly helplessly in a state of unrelenting anomie.[2]

But German evacuation also left a vacuum. And the Russian troops, viewed as liberators, empowered Eastern European peoples to pull communities together, to attempt to build coalitions among members of various democratic parties working with Socialists and Communists. There was genuine, if momentary, freedom of movement and political organizing, sometimes allowing free elections establishing independent governments. Yet these conditions of freedom were soon systematically replaced.

The dissolution started in 1946, intensified in late 1947, and was finalized in 1948, East and West immersing themselves in a bitter competitive grasp for territory and power. Both the U.S. State Department and Kremlin warned of potential war of the Western Allies and the Russians in the spring of 1946, and early the next year President Truman offered military aid to Turkey and Greece to offset Greek Communists supported by neighboring Soviet-controlled states.

One-party rule in Eastern Europe once established to accommodate Soviet goals, Stalin's diplomacy subserviated this zone to Russian geopolitical needs and economic requirements. Western influence was also blocked by Soviet-pressured Eastern European governments rejecting U.S. Marshall Plan aid in mid–1947. Backed up by the presence of Soviet tanks, world Communist parties linked through the Cominform enforced the communization of all East European governments.

The last remaining borders to the West were sealed with the February 1948 Communist takeover of Czechoslovakia and the likely murder of the Democratic Socialist foreign minister Jan Masaryk, pushing the Western European powers into the Brussels defense treaty in March 1948.

The anti–Communist front then expanded into a unified defense system, supported by a U.S. Senate vote in July 1948, taking form in March 1949 as the North Atlantic Treaty Organization, which linked the U.S., Canada, Britain, France, Belgium, Luxembourg, Holland, Denmark, Iceland, Norway, Italy, and Portugal. Later, in 1952, Greece and Turkey were added.

The cold war realigning boundaries, Germany was partitioned in

1949 between the Western sphere, called the German Federal Republic, and that of the East, the German Democratic Republic. Both sides re-armed their ally, the West moving decisively in 1950 under the pressure of the Korean War dividing that nation; the East more slowly in 1955 with the formation of the Warsaw Pact. Europe was now divided territorially, economically, and militarily, with the line of demarcation severing Germany.[3]

FROM THE DIVISION OF GERMANY
TO THE FIRST SIGNS OF FREEDOM

The division of Germany began with the Allied powers demarcating occupation zones in 1945. It was followed by Russia's year-long blockade of land routes to the Western enclave in Berlin at the heart of the Soviet zone, the establishment of the Federal Republic in 1949, and the creation of the Democratic Republic a few months later.

The Berlin blockade spelled not only an American airlift but efforts to rearm Germany through the European Defense Community, a European army, and, after the French undermined this effort in 1954, West German adherence to the Brussels treaty of 1948 and then to NATO.

By 1955, German soldiers were fully armed, and a decade later they were the backbone of NATO's ground forces, equipped with nuclear weapons tipped with warheads under U.S. control, faced off against a Russian arsenal of equal or greater weight. Both sides saw war as a possibility, thus requiring a balance of nuclear terror.

West Berlin remained the focal point of tension and probable conflict. Governed by the 1945 Potsdam Agreement, it attracted East Germans longing to partake of its personal freedoms and capitalist successes, some 3.5 million crossing to the Western zone from 1950 to 1961. As the flow increased to 30,000 East Berliners in July 1961, Khrushchev drew the line, ordering the East Germans to seal the entire boundary throughout the city with barbed wire, soon to be replaced by the hated wall that communism built. And though Khrushchev relented somewhat after backing down in the Cuban missile crisis, the West's refusal to recognize the East German regime was offset by the latter's heavy armaments and a 127,000 standing army by 1968 under Stalinist Walter Ulbricht, undermining any chance for détente.

Cracks in Stalin's eastern empire threatened in 1948 when Marshal Tito's Yugoslavia asserted its national variety of communism outside the Soviet sphere, though other Eastern Europeans still lacked determination, terrain, and material strength to follow his lead. But with Stalin's death in 1953, the pent-up demand for elementary freedoms was suddenly released in powerful anti–Communist demonstrations in East Germany. Through repression, they came to little, but three years later in 1956,

Khrushchev's ascendancy and denunciation of Stalin before the Soviet Communist Congress questioned the dictator's centrist controls, methods of repression, and imperial legacy. The message was clear enough: communism would ultimately require an egalitarian base to survive.

Such liberties, though, were still not freely allowed in the Soviet helotry in Eastern Europe. The Poles, remaining as anti–Semitic as they were in facilitating the wartime German occupiers to decimate the Warsaw ghetto,[4] wanted freedom for themselves and rioted in the summer of 1956, threatening Soviet rule. A Russian delegation headed by Khrushchev was dispatched to Warsaw, and Russian troops were readied. But control and resolution lay elsewhere, first by returning to power the former Communist party secretary-general Wladyslaw Gomulka (who had been thrown into prison for "nationalist deviation" from 1951 to 1954), then by Khrushchev's sacking the Russian puppet defense minister Marshal Rokossovski, along with dozens of Russian officers holding key positions in the Polish army. Russia remained in charge by cosmetic change of Poland's political and military administrators.[5]

Deeper discord exploded in Hungary a few days later, Imre Nagy, a nationalist and Communist victimized by Stalin, proclaiming Hungarian neutrality and withdrawal from the Warsaw Pact. Advancing Russian troops and tanks did the rest: smashing the "revolt," dispersing the opposition, hanging Nagy with his collaborators.

So far, the alignments in Europe had shifted very little. Poland under Gomulka was locked geographically into the Soviet sphere; Hungary was held by armed occupation. Only Yugoslavia retained its independent socialism and acted as a buffer state for Albanians to leave the Moscow club and join China during the long Sino-Soviet dispute.[6]

In 1968, it was Czechoslovakia's move. Defying Russian tutelage, the Czech Communist party threw Antonin Novotny from office in 1968. But the new leadership under Alexander Dubcek demanded fast changes: a human face for socialism to emerge with greater democracy at home, a market economy, tighter relations with Western Europe. Soviet tanks again rolled, occupying Prague and the major cities, crushing the Dubcek regime, Kremlin forces arresting him, putting him in chains, forcibly sending him by plane to Moscow, stripping him of all power and authority.[7]

Yet Eastern Europe was imperceptibly moving away from strict central planning of output, distribution, and prices—toward exchange relations that one day might spell greater equity. True, COMECON had been established as the medium for the "holy" Soviet Empire's economic impositions on Eastern European states. But its 1949 policies of inequity could not long hold after Czechoslovakia demanded (but was stopped from implementing) decentralized planning to fill individualized consumer needs and demands for quality goods.[8] A universal model for rational use of resources for production and distribution had been presented,

questioning COMECON methods of centrally organized technical production and commerce at prices set by the Kremlin, promoting specialization
and thus dependence in the name of a morally vaunted "socialist division
of labor."[9]

For now Bulgaria resented selling its foods and raw materials at low
prices set by Moscow's apparat. Poles wanted their creditor trade balance
with Russia to be paid at least partly in gold so they could directly trade
for Western goods. And the 1962 Soviet-Polish attempt to award COMECON
supranational authority was seen by Romania as tantamount to stopping
its industrialization, to turning its sovereignty into a hollow dependence.
When Moscow relented with capital grants to promote bilateral "cooperation," the peripheries in Eastern Europe were already looking to Western
markets. Romania took the lead in foreign policy and trade, tightening its
relations with West Germany, siding with Israel (against Arab states) and
China (against the Soviet Union) for both politics and commerce.[10]

FREEDOMS IN WESTERN EUROPE
HERALD THOSE IN THE EAST

As the Soviet hold was being questioned in Eastern Europe, Western
Europe was confronted by the English drive to expand its markets and the
French demand for an independent policy that would one day unify the
European continent—without British or U.S. controls.

President de Gaulle foresaw a continental system under French
design, not unlike Napoleon's earlier vision of an industrial France piv-
otally importing raw materials and exporting manufactures.[11] Appealing
to Eastern Europe, de Gaulle also sought to weaken its resolve to remain
within the Soviet sphere. And though the Polish Parliament obediently
listened while Soviet loyalist Gomulka arrogantly disdained de Gaulle's
efforts, the Romanians saw the opportunity to pursue traditional links
with French education, language, culture, commerce, and investments.

Britain then skipped over France and the U.S. State Department to
set its own course in Eastern Europe—to keep the European continent
divided, continuing a British foreign policy that had lasted successfully for
at least two hundred years.[12] Despite State Department logic that a well-
provided Eastern Europe would strengthen communism and make it a
more formidable enemy, the British Foreign Office advised the government to offer the Eastern Communists five-year credits to buy its manufactures and stimulate the English economy.[13]

Germany, with its two wings, also accommodated British policy to
keep the Continent partitioned, undercutting the French challenge for
Continental unity. The Soviet Union unwittingly fit into Britain's scheme by
arming Poland, as did the United States in rearming West Germany. And
Poland helplessly became the territorial dividing line, for though the Poles

feared the reunification of Germany, they feared more that the United States would allow West German revanchism to proceed unfettered. Thus a proposed 1957 compromise (the Rapacki Plan) to reunite Germany — initiating military disengagement and advancing Continental unity — proved historically premature, for it called for a nuclear-free zone covering Germany, Poland, and Czechoslovakia.[14]

The Soviet Union, West Germany, and the United States all rejected the plan. The State Department saw Russian superiority in conventional ground forces. West Germany refused to give up its renewed military shield, sought reunification through all–German elections, and applied the "Hallstein Doctrine" that negated West German relations with all states (save the USSR) that recognized East Germany. Khrushchev then used the crisis in Berlin as a counterweight to détente, reaffirmed by Stalinist measures in Ulbricht's East Germany.

All that would end in 1990 with détente, steps toward disarmament, and a reunited Germany, making the forgotten Rapacki Plan reality.[15]

Western Europe's New Reality

A new reality for Western Europe also struck home: Continental raw materials and markets were required to accommodate national output in most Western states. Such supranationalism was only to accommodate half of Europe, though. For it was here that emphasis was placed: The $10 billion of U.S. Marshall Plan aid went to the Western wing; the European Council formed in 1949 remained a Western forum for debate, as Winston Churchill had planned for European unity against the expansion of Soviet communism; the Organization for European Economic Cooperation defined Atlantic patterns of aid under the Marshall Plan; and Britain's Attlee government rejected participation in the Monnet Plan to reconcile France and Germany and create a supranational Western European federation, emerging as the European Coal and Steel Community (ECSC).

Britain thereby revealed its true design to keep the Continent balkanized and Germany in subjugation. For Britain rejected the ECSC outright, the Foreign Office having notice that German chancellor Konrad Adenauer had secretly cleared the pact in advance so that France could negotiate the economic pact with Italy, the Netherlands, Luxembourg, and Belgium. Playing out Bonaparte's late eighteenth-century design for a "Continental System" under French control,[16] the 1951 treaty linked these six nations in the ECSC under a common High Authority establishing Europe's first postwar common market.

On German *military* subjugation, though, both Britain and France agreed, opposing U.S. military integration of Continental defenses. Though the 1950 French government had initially proposed a European Defense Community and European army, Britain's Conservatives, entering office in 1951, refused to join, and a year later France changed its posture. Though France initialed a military treaty in 1952 with the five other Continental nations of the ECSC, neither France nor Britain would join or ratify it. France then developed its own *force du frappe*, Britain successfully using the nationalist French assembly as a foil to forward its plan to keep the military forces on the European land mass at loggerheads.

Yet British economic policy would ultimately fail in the face of Continental needs. Covering the field of production and markets, the six nations proposed a common market, signed the Treaty of Rome setting up the European Economic Community in 1957, and planned to adopt by 1970 similar economic policies by means of a supranational commission, an overseeing European parliament, and a council of national ministers to make final decisions on the commission's policy proposals—to remove all restraints on competition and to permit the free movements of workers and capital investment; to adopt common transport, export, and agricultural programs; to eliminate tariffs within their customs union; and to put up a common external schedule of tariffs.[17]

Britain declined to join the EEC, floated a plan for a competitive pan–European free-trade area, tightening its Commonwealth and building its own European Free Trade Association in which it was the dominant industrial power. The Continent would thereby remain partitioned territorially, politically, and economically.

French Bombshell

A political bombshell then exploded in France in 1958 when Charles de Gaulle was reelected president, opposing the EEC's federalist scheme. Proselytizing that each nation-state formed by a common historical culture must be in command of power within its boundaries, de Gaulle viewed the Continent as a congerie of contiguous nation-states that might one day confederate but could never act as a supranational body through the ECSC, EEC, defense community, or any other fashion. He thus opposed the planned European political union during the years 1960–62, seeing it as the mingling of intergovernmental authority, refusing to accept concessions of the other five nations.

England then threatened to upstage de Gaulle by applying to join the EEC. With his usual firmness, the general vetoed its application in 1963, moving swiftly to ally with West Germany to seal continental unity against British interests. Exchanging visits with Germany's Chancellor Adenauer, de Gaulle spoke deftly in Bonn of "*das grosse deutsche Volk*," signed a 1963 mutual cooperative treaty for trade and tete-à-tete governmental and military exchanges, yet boycotted the EEC Council of Ministers that proposed its own levies on agricultural imports, which would have awarded the commission a huge revenue flow and thus puissance as a supranational force.

De Gaulle arrogantly disdained it as "a technocratic body of elders, stateless, irresponsible," angling by weighted majority voting in the Council of Ministers to impinge on France's national sovereignty. France then demanded and won maintenance of the council's unanimity rule, giving de Gaulle veto power, momentary control over the other continental members' joint economic policies, and position to maneuver to regulate the single commission and shape its presidency.[18]

Fearing America

De Gaulle nonetheless sought to create the Continent as an independent force between the superpowers. From 1954, when the French rejected the European Defense Community treaty, to the joint policy of Britain and France to tell the State Department nothing before launching the 1956 Suez War to protect their shipping interests, America was viewed with reserve and fear.[19]

In 1958 de Gaulle insisted on a joint French-Anglo-American directorate over Western strategic military policies, which the Pentagon condescendingly ignored. And de Gaulle responded by keeping U.S. nuclear warheads off French soil, withdrawing the French navy from the NATO command in the Mediterranean, and using anti–American propaganda to withdraw from NATO's integrated military system in 1966, forcing NATO headquarters to move from Paris to Brussels.

As Europe grew more powerful economically and the real threat of Soviet aggression subsided, moreover, nations of the Continent began to view the U.S. adventure in Vietnam as misguided—further reason to separate from the military bent of mind of Presidents Kennedy, Johnson, and Nixon. Only West Germany *demanded* a continual U.S. military presence on the Continent. Yet because the United States held predominant military power and overwhelming nuclear strength placing the control buttons in the oval office of the U.S. president, Europe sans the Federal Republic saw its terrain in jeopardy of American arrogance and possible miscalculations.[20]

Kennedy proved they were right after the Cuban missile crisis: He left Europe defenseless by withdrawing from its territories all land-based missiles capable of hitting Soviet targets! Later plans for Europeans, particularly the Germans, to share nuclear control were put aside in 1964, only to be raised again in 1966 to give Europe consultive, not decisive, powers in knowing how the United States would direct its nuclear force.

The United States double-crossed Europe again in 1967 by setting up its own antimissile system without consulting its allies. And the United States pressured Britain to foot the bill jointly to keep ground forces in Germany, then unilaterally withdrew 35,000 of its 225,000 standing army, leaving Britain to follow suit, withdrawing a full brigade, while Germany cut its military budget.

Europe felt vulnerable to American military whim and British slavishness. Anglo-Saxons were now seen in league following their own interests, which were different from those of the Western Continent.[21]

ANGLO-SAXON DEFENSE AND THE NEW FRONTIER

Britain, meanwhile, sought its own sphere of commercial influence. To secure its continental trade, in 1958 it joined Sweden, Norway, Denmark, Austria, Switzerland, and Portugal (and in 1961, Finland) in the European Free Trade Association, eliminating all intra-association protective tariffs by 1966.

The American Challenge

But the best Anglo defense remained the British offense in pursuing entrance to the EEC. Its application was categorically blocked on 14 January 1963 by de Gaulle's veto, for the *unstated reason* that the United States controlled the Atlantic community and was using Britain as its Trojan horse in European defenses and for the *expressed reasons* that Britain drew its food from its commonwealth and empire, had its own system of agricultural subsidies, and had obligations to the European Free Trade Association. If Britain entered the EEC, de Gaulle argued, it would soon become "a colossal Atlantic community under American domination." He feared that U.S. nuclear defense and a multilateral force would both fall under "the American command of NATO."

The American challenge also appeared economically and geopolitically. The most widely read and discussed tract in Western Europe, *Le Défi Américain*, by French journalist and later politician J-J Servan-Schreiber, warned in late 1967 that "within fifteen years the world's third industrial power may be American industry in Europe." But the so-called challenge in the EEC amounted to only about 5 percent of new corporate investment at the time (almost the same challenge based on the exact percentage of Japanese new investments in the United States twenty-three years later). Technological takeover was the basic worry, then and now, for as U.S. companies had increased their total plant and equipment investments in Western Europe from $1,750 million in 1963 to nearly $4,000 million in 1967, four-fifths of Europe's computer industry was controlled by U.S. subsidiaries.

The critical factor was the Common Market itself: intra-EEC tariffs were falling; there were still few mergers of European firms across national boundaries; and U.S. firms saw the opportunity to mobilize superior management skills, larger internal and external financial resources, and superior technology to advance mass production that could gain access to common markets without tariffs. In gaining this foothold, Servan-Schreiber was exercised that U.S. subsidiaries were not only receiving parent-company infusions of capital but were reinvesting revenues covering depreciation allowances as well as profits in new production. These subsidiaries were borrowing European capital to expand further and were benefiting from the United States exporting its balance-of-payments deficit by paying with U.S. dollars that Europeans were forced to treat as a reserve currency—as if they were gold.[22]

After America moved in January 1968 to reduce its negative balance of payments by restricting its dollar outflow, though, U.S. subsidiaries in Europe expanded largely by *borrowing* European finance.

Continental Repositioning

Western Europe then positioned to confront the United States with renewed industrial might, based in part on new technologies advancing high-volume production and in part on the absolute decline in the *capacity use* of competitive American technology from the mid-sixties to the early seventies.

A united Europe might have outflanked the United States economically, but France again vetoed Britain's application to join the EEC on 27 November 1967, again blocking the Continent from direct access to British nuclear technology, the largest aircraft industry in Europe, and advances in computer science. Drawing on Anglo-French history and Gaul's classical xenophobia, de Gaulle exercised his pathological fear of Anglo-Saxon domination despite British prime minister Wilson's offer of technological cooperation with the EEC and his portrayal of the success of these efforts in a future "industrial helotry."[23]

In part, de Gaulle's strategy worked to France's advantage. Under the Yaoundé Agreement, the Common Market drew on its established ties with eighteen African nations, largely former French colonies, to benefit France in acquiring needed raw materials and markets. France also wanted special arrangements with Spain, Morocco, and Tunisia. And the other EEC members acquired British technology through *bilateral arrangements* outside the community treaties. In these ways, despite itself, the Continental infrastructure for production and trade was fortified.

America's Imperial Overstretch

Over the next fifteen years, the material positions of America and Western Europe were reversed. America was periodically weakened from overproduction and a lack of markets; a shortfall in savings and neglect of new investments in the latest technologies; a pool of unemployed and a general lowering in the wage scale; worker inefficiency on the job and the manufacture of defective and inferior goods; the fall in America's competitive position in global trade; spiraling inflation, internal discord, and heavy military expenditures in Vietnam; an escalating national debt, increasing the tax burden on future generations; a fall in government educational support and social services, causing backwardness in work skills and unresolvable domestic conflicts; and a fixation on maintaining industrial output and employment through federal budgetary allocations for the production of conventional and high-tech armaments in the congressional districts of abiding politicians.[24] And as U.S. unemployment periodically rose, Western Europe was working at capacity, reflected in rising profit margins in Europe and falling margins in America.

As the productivity of U.S. workers fell, real wages declined 20 percent between 1965 and 1981. But in approximately the same period, the economies, real wages, and living standards improved in Western Europe and Japan. Even the worldwide recession of 1981–82 hit the United States hardest, reflected in the relative decline of economic growth, standards of living, and absorption of the accumulated stock of economic wealth.[25]

Competitive investment, labor, and trade patterns were now poised to change swiftly. Starting in 1948, the chief mechanism for institutionalizing industrial nations' commerce had been the General Agreement on Tariffs and Trade (GATT), pursuing gradual reductions in tariffs, nondiscriminatory customs procedures and duties, and methods to settle trade disputes.

But as the United States began its relative decline in 1969, GATT became the battleground for disagreements between nation-states. And given America's overstretch—concentrating on arms expenditures; investing abroad while neglecting technological production of quality output; refusing to retrain U.S. labor; and neglecting to secure its domestic population from inflation, unemployment, homelessness, and poverty—for the next three decades it remained so, with intensified economic bantering over trade dumping, market shares, and other trade rights.[26]

By 1989, the United States required new investment spheres for low-cost labor near resources and potential markets. It sought markets for grain, other food products, and high-cost domestic manufactured goods. It extended its sphere of commerce by special agreements with Israel, Canada, and Mexico. It sought greater market shares for agricultural and technological products in the European Common Market and Japan. Its policymakers and political power brokers realized military outlays had to be reduced to devote resources to solving domestic problems tearing at America's social structure. And the historic opportunity for fulfillment of these goals dovetailed with events in Eastern Europe and the Soviet Union—the potentiality for détente and disarmament, the new quest for freedom and the powerful, mass movements from the lower strata.

EASTERN CENTRIST "DEMOCRACY" AND WESTERN STATE CAPITALISM

Was it possible, though, that Eastern European social democracy and Western state capitalism might coexist without military threats in a milieu of moral, cultural, commercial, and technical commonality?[27]

Since 1985, President Gorbachev had thought so, calling this "a common European home." He understood that the pressures on the Soviet Union were internally unresolvable: a financially bankrupt Moscow had had to surrender its costly military and political ambitions for expansion beyond its borders in return for a plea for commerical admission to the "club" of Western industrial nations—lowering barriers to trade between the Soviet Union and the West, the United States ultimately granting Russia most-favored-nation status, food and technological aid mostly from Germany and the Western Continent, and some aid and trade with Japan.

As the *material basis* for Soviet *perestroika* was likely decades away from being reached, then, the Kremlin clearly depended on Western aid, trade, and investments. Yet the West hesitated, for the Soviet Union was slow to change its political hegemony or its command economy. Repression of republics like Lithuania was anathema to Western powers, and central-plan controls spelled phantom bookkeeping, production quotas, designation of the type of goods to be produced, and setting all-important "prices."

This was the source of the Soviets' "mendacious statistics": cooking the books. For such methods meant that if central planners set prices too low, goods would not be produced because costs could not be recovered, and factory managers would report losses, leading to their criticism or demotion at the hands of the central planners.

Managers and the accountants under their authority easily solved the problem: they lied. So the first plan of President Gorbachev was to turn the "big lie" back on itself, to use the central plan to promote the production of more consumer goods, reasoning that billions of hoarded rubles would thereby be spent without forcing up prices.

The solution was simplistic, though, because the problem ran deeper. The millions of privileged bureaucrats directing the system would never reveal true production costs or relinquish their power without a foot-dragging battle and organized rearguard sabotage. They could argue that they could not produce consumer goods, buy capital equipment, or hire labor because prices for their products were too low. The logic of central planners keeping prices too high would also cover real costs and salaries and keep the bureaucrats in key positions as regulators. The apparat thereby hoped to hold the moment.[28]

The moment might last years, a decade, perhaps longer. President Gorbachev had no intention of undermining centrist rule that would guide any planned modification of socialist principles by exchange relations. He sought to maintain socialism in the sphere of production, Kremlin control in finance, and exchange relations in the circulation of commodities.[29]

For as the preamble to his compromise plan offered to the Supreme Soviet enunciated, "The transition to the market does not contradict the socialist choice of our people."[30]

SECURING FUTURE DEMOCRACY
AND ECONOMIC WELL-BEING

In neither the former Soviet republics nor Eastern Europe was the choice of the people socialist, though. The quest for freedom of both Soviet republics and Eastern European states had redrawn the map of Europe on the basis of nationalism, ethnicity, religious regionalism, and autarchic interests. Through secession and political disintegration, states, principalities, and ministates emerged. The hope of future democracy within each politically autonomous region did not always square with the enforced mobilization of popular will for common economic well-being, though. And in the short term, both democracy and servitude might coexist in various degrees or one might override the other. For the call for national unity was bound to lock certain groups into plans not of their own choosing.

The concurrent division of existing states into smaller geographic units would not ensure either self-sufficient development or freedom. For the new self-proclaimed, autarchic democratic regions at first held back openness toward other regions requiring their cultural knowledge, labor, resources, and markets. Panregional or trans–European commerce might be stillborn or worse cut off from traditional exchange. So the unfolding of small unitary regions was no guaranty of their will or power to cooperate across their borders, despite utopian schemes, past or present.[31]

The Baltic states thus declared independent self-sufficiency, though none were self-sufficient in fuel or industrial goods. Georgian Ossetians and Abkhazians called for independence without a clue how they would survive in isolation from trade, farm machinery, and consumer goods they relied on the outside world to provide. Azerbaijanis made war on the Armenian enclave of Nagorno-Karabakh and vice versa, though each required the other for future commerce and political goodwill, the Armenians wanting to reunify with Armenia, Azerbaijan stopping them because 30 percent of the enclave was Azerbaijanis and as pressure, cutting off all food and energy supplies to Armenia proper—hardly the basis for sustaining either newly independent republic.

With former Communist apparats posing as reform leaders in most of central Asia, moreover, nationalist unification by repression of minority rights was common, fueling minority efforts to break away, often without planning a path for economic liberation.

Thus the Uzbekistan Fergana Valley would be free but still in need of resources from the outside. Uzbek president Islam Karimov might publicly adhere to Washington's 1992 strategic diplomatic-recognition principles—commitment to free elections, respect for human rights and minorities, and establishment of free markets. But the opposition leaders recounted that the president was a dictator, Abdul Rakhman Pulatov of the most popular nationalist movement, Birlik (Unity)—itself not allowed to field a candidate in the 85 percent vote for President Karimov— nonetheless calling for U.S. diplomatic relations to improve the situation "for those forces that do not have democratic freedoms. Politically we have no freedom at all, although officially we are registered. The totalitarian regime has been destroyed in Moscow, but in Tashkent it continues to exist." Yet no one then knew if Birlik or the Islamic Party of Rebirth (also not allowed to field a presidential candidate) would respect the population of 10 percent of Uzbek's 20 million that was made up of Russians, Ukrainians, Jews, and other Europeans, who tended to back Karimov, believing he would best protect them from Islamic fundamentalists and Uzbek nationalists driving to purge the nation of all Russian cultural influence.[32]

Moldavia's possible quest to reunify with its ancient motherland Romania bred independence efforts by minority Turkish-Christian Gagauz and Russians it required for skill and technology. Croatians moved to secure their independence and recognition by the West, though they needed Serbian markets and much else. Hungarians in the Ukraine, Slovakia, Romania, and Croatia sought protection from or reintegration with Hungary but sought their daily bread in the states that tied them.

Great Russian chauvinists too called for separation from Ukraine, wanting to take back the Crimea, Sevastopol, and the Black Sea fleet, neglecting the need for Ukrainian food supplies, resources, and overlapping populations, cutting to a fraction Russia's customary shipments of petroleum and natural gas, causing Ukrainians extreme hardships in the dead of winter. Ukrainian leaders also seemed blind to the fall in Ukrainian output in every branch of industry, a 1991 to February 1992 decline of 8 percent in labor productivity, reversion of coal production to the 1955 level, and severance of the vital economic links to the rest of the old Soviet Union, even the Russian part of the Donets basin.

Ukrainian and Russian miners in the Donets sought to awaken their brethren to the sorry state of the new nationalism, with its emphasis on national differences, cutting off interdependence and exchange under the newly elected old Communist leadership. "We don't like them to raise differences between nationalities," offered Mikhail A. Krylov, a copresident of the 35,000-strong, independent miners union. "We minors have no nationality. On this strike committee we have all nationalities: Russians, Ukrainians, Jews, etc. All miners are close to one another, regardless of nationality."

"We must show all the Ukrainian people who they elected," Krylov continued. "Former apparatchiks. It's useless to expect anything good of them."

"We have changed from one political machine to another, with practically the same people," Krylov said, denouncing the Ukrainian government of former top Communists President Leonid Kravchuk and Prime

Minister Vitold Fokin for excessive emphasis on rivalry with Russia, trying to break the union by individual rather than collective contracts; cutting pay under threat of shutting down unsafe, unprofitable, backward mines by provoking a strike; and imposing a dangerous work speedup by forcing labor violation of safety rules to earn better than mimimum pay.

"This was not our view of independence," Krylov explained. "Those who shout most about independence didn't support us then [when the miner strikes helped weaken the Soviet Union and undermined Communist power]." Krylov alluded to President Kravchuk. "Our view of independence was always the destruction of the center, the Kremlin, and getting the party out of economic life. We wanted to be left alone in the Ukraine to solve our own problems, economic and political."

But a new center in the Ukraine president's office had powerfully emerged, advocating a narrow nationalist view centering not on the people's survival by interdependent exchange with other republics but on competitive arms. "They don't talk about the economic future, about what we want now," said strike committee member Viktor Shumyatsky. "They want to talk about the Black Sea fleet. We don't understand why we need it. We think Kravchuk raises it to make people forget about the price of bread."[33]

Demagogic Russian president Yeltsin was at once a power broker issuing *ukaz* and a democratic driving to overturn the Communist apparat. The Communist hangers-on, like Vice President Alesandr Rutskoi, held no real power,[34] only potential appeals to the population over Yeltsin's failing program—for in early 1992 Rutskoi still had no organization other than his own small neo–Communist party, no electoral track record, and few allies except the neo–Fascists.

The lesson of ill-fated policies by central *diktat* was lost in neither the declaration of independence by Croatia, Bosnia-Hercegovina, and Slovenia, before the Serbs made war upon them nor in the Baltic republics when Moscow sent its repressive lockstep troops. Azerbaijan took no heed to secure the Armenians in the Nagorno-Karabakh when in 1991 it repealed the enclave's autonomy and demanded that the central government in Moscow transfer to it all troops and weapons.[35]

Yet disintegration of old power centers and the emergence of independent regions would one day lead toward building new alliances, perhaps reintegration in common zones for trade, political, and military cooperation.

Thus without the old Kremlin coordinating social services and directing production quotas and food distribution, each republic, though still unprepared, had to unify its population, often at the expense of minority rights; to compete to try to fill the void, creating their own centrist hierarchy, stopping food and resource deliveries to other republics and enforcing food prices, rationing, and so on. Yet from necessity for survival, the former Soviet republics might eventually drop barriers to exchange and come together in loose economic blocs, with an entrée to the West.

"Yesterday, as never before, we understood that the Commonwealth of Independent states is the structure without which we will never survive," Belarus president Stanislav Shushkevich said at the 15 February 1992 summit meeting of former Soviet republics, adding, "We realized that the ailments of the commonwealth countries are identical, and therefore we have to unite to solve them."[36]

Economic and political cooperation through the Baltic Council would also bind Estonia, Latvia, and Lithuania in future negotiated commerce with Russia for oil and other resources, Scandinavia for quality manufactures, and Poland for coal, heavy industrial products, and possibly consumer wares.

Some republics might also lose territory or go over to other states entirely: Tatar, Bashkir, and Checheno-Ingush loosening from Russia, Abkhasia and autonomous South Ossetia from Georgia, Moldova linking tightly or loosely with Romania. And from Vistula to Vladivostok, there would be future rumblings for self-determination and democracy.

Engineering a "New Order" in Central Asia and Beyond

The new central Asian republics would be divided between rich and poor, with some able to privatize agriculture, oil, gas, and minerals for export earnings, others mired in outdated industrial cities unable to compete, earn foreign exchange in export markets, and import necessities. Central Asia and the Middle East would meanwhile find the old Soviet Caucasus reliant on Turkey as a Near East fulcrum, backed by funds from Germany and the United States and maintaining both political and economic ties with Iran, Pakistan, Egypt, Saudi Arabia, and other oil-rich states.

An organizationl framework also existed in the mothballed 1963 Economic Cooperation Organization. Having been part of the Central Treaty Organization set up by the United States and Britain in the fifties to deter the Soviet Union from expanding southward, the cold war over, ECO now sought new impetus. Thus the leaders of Iran, Pakistan, and Turkey as founding members of the twenty-seven-year-old ECO welcomed Azerbaijan, Turkmenistan, and Uzbekistan and future membership for Tajikistan, Kirghizstan, Kazakhstan. Non-Muslim Romania also asked to join.[37]

An expected ideological split emerged between fundamentalist Iran and nonsecular Turkey. Insisting that the organization develop an infrastructure similar to the European Community, Turkish president Turgut Ozal sought membership for its vassal Cypriot state of North Cyprus and called for the ECO's "immediate steps to eliminate tariffs and non-tariff barriers, . . . to establish the free market system, the advantages of which are no longer contested," adding that "the relatively developed infrastructure of Europe is facilitating cooperation in that continent."

But Iran sought other, somewhat incompatible guidelines for economic development and trade cooperation, Iranian officials stressing the importance of safeguarding "common regional values" as people of the Caucasus looked to their neighbors for economic aid and guidance. "This is the meeting of a large Islamic family," Iranian president Hashemi Rafsanjani said, addressing the summit meeting, stressing "issues concerning Muslims," calling the plight of the Palestinians "a deep wound," and emphasizing the potential of the economic grouping, which he said could draw lessons from organizations like OPEC and ASEAN in Southeast Asia.

Reaffirmation from Pakistani prime minister Nawaz Sharif looked to his government's preoccupation with the role of religion in politics, "favoring a strong Islamic bloc" in the Economic Cooperation Organization, also attempting to win U.S. aid and military equipment by laying claim as a rightful partner of the new central Asian republics and blunting India's efforts to dominate south Asia.[38]

Yet there was commonality in ECO members' approval for a 10 percent reduction in regional trade tariffs, a common market for agricultural products, the training of experts, and the creation of a Common Development Bank, which according to Turkish businessmen would compete with the activities of a Saudi-based Islamic bank in the central Asian republics.

Still, a powerful contest for Turkish or Iranian spheres in the Caucasus might raise their ire and quest for self-sufficiency. "The fact that Turkey and Iran focus their attention on the Caucasus," said an experienced Iranian merchant operating for a decade in the old Soviet Union, "could make ECO an influential political and economic instrument. Both countries are important regional players and have enjoyed stability. But all the ceremonies and compliments they offer will mean little if the rights and dignity of people of Central Asia are neglected for strategic gain."[39]

The chain of command—from Washington through Turkey to North Cyprus, possibly through Pakistan and the Caucasus, eventually linked to the European Common Market—was designed to create a new framework for America's "new order."

As the logistical base for humanitarian airlifts and potential Western investors in the newly independent central Asian states, Turkey was at the focal point of balancing U.S. and European Economic Community interests in the region as well as in the Caucasus, the Balkans, and the Middle East. Though a negative model in mistreating, repressing, and torturing its Kurdish minority, U.S.-backed Turkey sought a wider commercial and political role in the "new order" in Europe and the Aegean as well as the central, Far, and Near East.

"Turkey's interest in eventual membership in the European Community would be best served by removing Turkish troops from Cyprus," former U.S. ambassador to Greece, Monteagle Stearns said, unlocking one corner of the puzzle. "Greece's interest in strengthening its security in the Aegean would best be served by supporting Turkish membership in the Community; and the Republic of Cyprus's interest would best be served by lifting the economic embargo imposed on the [Turkish occupied] north."[40]

The Future of Russia and Central Europe

Central Europe too would economically link Austria with a free Hungary, Croatia, Slovenia, and a Czechoslovakia possibly divided into Czech and Slovak states, not as a reversion to the pre–World War I Austro-Hungarian empire but as a new assertion of historical necessity.[41]

To create a common European market, mainly a German and U.S. sphere of influence, the most critical link in the whole chain would be Western finance backing the Russian ruble, creating a zone of monetary influence from the Urals to the Middle East, across Eurasia to the United States. Separate currencies in vogue in the newly independent Soviet republics in 1991–92 would thereby become interchangeable with the ruble as the central bankers' standard of value. Indigenous and Western investments in each autarchic "protectionist" republic would become the first step in capturing internal resources and markets, to be followed by exchangeable currencies facilitating trade between the republics and globally.

Center stage, then, Russian rubles would have to be made exchangeable with and stabilized against Western currencies. Otherwise, local and provincial markets of private *tolkuchka* traders and *kommersants* would remain isolated, reselling goods at higher speculative prices, suddenly released from the constraints of the immutable prices that communism taught.[42] Russian hyperinflation on the doorstep of its crisis in the 1991–92 production-market cycle could be offset by establishing an external stable exchange rate of the ruble with the dollar and other hard currencies, then fostering the equitability of exchanging rubles for the newly emergent currencies in the various republics. As the ruble went into a free fall with Russians scrambling to buy hard currencies in early 1992, the West lethargically moved to financially back a billion-dollar fund to assure speculators that dollars and marks would continue to be available. Yet stabilizing the ruble for foreign trade would be no easy or costless task.

The so-called Group of Seven wealthy nations could certainly mobilize resources to finance a multibillion-ruble stabilization fund to back up Russian gold and meager reserves — to maintain the ruble's value for international transactions, to promote domestic confidence in the ruble's value, allowing Russians to implement their domestic reforms, control their mania for printing-press money, and feed their population. But most of these resources might be lost—and Western politicians skewered at home—if the speculators went on the attack, paying cheaply acquired rubles for expensive dollars and marks, thereby forcing the fund to keep the ruble from plunging against foreign currencies. And what if the Russian reforms failed to comply with the lenders' prescriptions for speed and effect in reforming its central bank, cutting its issue of printing-press rubles, reducing its high inflation rate, reversing its large budget deficit, and promoting privatization of industry and commerce to stimulate production and distribution? International financial institutions might devise an overall economic program. But disciplined domestic economic policies might also induce a counterrevolution, and trade of oil and other resources at world market prices would take time to generate a trade surplus to strengthen the ruble.

Time was of the essence in creating the stabilization fund, said Russian government adviser Harvard economist Jeffrey Sachs, citing Russia's late 1991 to early 1992 reforms by slowing the printing of rubles and slashing the government deficit from 20 percent of gross domestic product (GDP) to about 5 percent—though he did not show its real effect, neglecting to say GDP fell by a greater percentage still. "This is a pivotal moment in Russian history," Mr. Sachs said, justifying the need for a ruble stabilization fund. "If the ruble starts strengthening, if goods come into shops, if the Government is bolstered to carry out further reforms, then they can succeed. If, on the other hand, sentiment turns negative, the ruble weakens and shops remain empty, then things can spin out of control."[43]

Yet the Russian Central Bank could not comply, its fiat printing press funneling newly minted rubles to the commercial banks for interest-bearing loans to state and private enterprises. With some 135 million rubles outstanding in loans in February 1992, much of it to commercial banks relending to farmers and state-owned farm equipment companies, the money-losing farm sector was unable to repay the commercial banks, and the latter had not repaid the central bank. To refinance the farm sector for spring 1992 planting so the nation could renew its food supply, the central bank would be forced to print more, not fewer, rubles, so that rubles would be less valuable, making them less easily converted into dollars, thereby staving off foreign investment, discouraging exports, and making imports harder to purchase. International Monetary Fund efforts to make the ruble convertible into hard currencies would thus be delayed until after the spring planting.[44]

True, the central bank attempted to shore up the ruble by significant cuts in bank credit and by selling its own dollars to weaken hard-currency demands against the ruble, causing momentary exchange rates of rubles to dollars to fall. But without central bank credit, production would fall, and once central bank dollars were exhausted, the ruble would again plummet. Only a foreign ruble-support fund could save the day.

"You can help us most of all if you help the Soviet Union on its irreversible but immensely complicated road to democracy," Czechoslovakian president Vaclav Havel had told Congress in 1990. That would have required the United States to come up with a small part of $25 billion, far less than the $100 billion a year (in 1992 dollars) the United States spent on European defense during the cold war era.[45]

But this want of a nail to bootstrap the failed Soviet Empire meant that it was conceivably true that belated Western aid would face further chaos, autarchy, and possibly counterrevolution.

Chapter 6
Entering a European Home

Before the 1991 attempted coup, the Kremlin had studied the situation in the West and determined that the U.S. economic decline and Western European strength could be mobilized to Soviet advantage. If the United States could be brought into a bargain for peace and Western Europe a bargain for trade, the USSR could switch its resources from readiness for war to industrial expansion and popular welfare. That would involve not only Soviet détente with Washington but massive arms reduction. And that would also mean liquidating the Stalinist regimes in Eastern Europe and replacing them with coalitions that would pursue both socialist and marketplace goals. Only thereby, reasoned the Machiavellian inner sanctum of the Communist party, could the Soviet Union itself be strengthened economically, politically reorganized, and socially reconstructed.[1]

There was one catch: The Continent and its market might be consolidated just as the Soviet Union disintegrated into squabbling balkanized republics, principalities, and regions bent on their own self-determination and autarchic sufficiency at the expense of the others. And that is what happened after the failed coup.

LOGIC OF A FAILED POLICY

This Soviet logic had emerged only after strained Kremlin attempts to rebuild the Russian economy after World War II, to manipulate U.S. arms negotiators, and to reorganize failing internal production.

Domestic and émigré opposition movements sped the Soviet breakdown. From the gulags in Siberia in the late thirties to the 1948 formation of underground anti–Stalinist organizations like the Communist Party of Youth, and the seventies opposition to the Brezhnev centrist bureaucracy with its rigid labor and slave policies and intellectual mediocrity, the foundations for resistance to the hierarchy's imposed servitude in production and literature were strengthened.[2]

The centrist structure still remained intact,

- though Stalin and his labor camps were exposed and condemned by the party as a whole in the sixties;

171

- though the dictator's body was removed from the mausoleum as a symbolic negation of his deeds;
- though semitruths about the bloodthirsty tyrant were detailed in the *Report to the 20th Party Congress*;
- though his surviving victims were released from the gulag labor camps;
- though Solzhenitsyn documented the terror in *Underworld* and *One Day in the Life of Ivan Denisovich*;
- though Khrushchev banned terror campaigns.[3]

The Stalinists and their stereotypical followers survived during the stagnation period, the safety of the noisy criticism of the anti–Stalinist effort never touching its roots in party, army, or apparat.[4]

Besides the censors, there was also a world of enforced social labor that turned on *bureaucratic centralism* in both the Soviet Union and Eastern Europe, keeping populations in order. And until 1989 there was no official democratic forum to effectively voice one's opposition, so that clandestine movements for freedom were the only path toward liberation from party hegemony.[5]

THE KREMLIN RELENTS

In Eastern Europe, lightning change struck Communist peripheries in 1989–90. The external events appeared as a battle for the streets, for the momentary control of government. But deeper forces lay in Moscow, the KGB and Politburo analyzing the breadth of discontent and the relatively weak position of the Stalinist regimes without sufficient Soviet military muscle to back them up.

The Kremlin was already under heavy economic pressures at home and sought to lighten military expenditures by pursuing détente and domestic renewal, *perestroika*. For it saw the potential failure of its long-range plan if it became embroiled as policeman in Eastern Europe, especially after the Soviet public outrage accompanying the withdrawal from Afghanistan. The Politburo was swayed that one way to quiet the anger at home and strengthen the Soviet economy was to withdraw its military shield from Communist-led Eastern European governments, leading the Poles to put Solidarity in power; the Hungarians to proclaim a republic; the Czechs to challenge the entire state, its Communist bureaucracies, and their control over the economy; the East Germans to force reorganization of the Communist party, the government, and relations with the West; the Romanians and Bulgarians to oust their longtime Communist leaders; Albanians to implode against their impoverishment, explode against Stalinist government, and seek escape by ship to Italy.

The mass movements would not truck with Communist government excuses either, pressuring the CPs to surrender their "leading role" both constitutionally and practically.

The Soviet-installed Communists were quickly eclipsed, though their past acts were not forgotten: suppressing the East German "uprising" in 1953, the Hungarian revolution in 1956, the "Prague Spring" in 1968, and Poland's Solidarity for a decade in the eighties. Now it was the opposition's turn to seek a separate peace and destiny in each Eastern European state, to redraw the map of Europe and participate in plans for production, distribution, and trade. The leaders of movements once repressed would be called upon to act as officials in the new governments, to negotiate with existing Communist states, all the while calling on the emerging forces of revolution to consolidate. For intellectuals were now setting the direction, defiant students using every conceivable method to organize, and newly emboldened workers ready to strike, to keep up the pressure for democratic elections and change, headed by new leaders they chose. The Communists were about to lose power to the dissident movement, soon to be transformed into the political opposition, so that shortly the Communist party and its heirs would become the failing opposition in mass-supported democratic governments.

The steps to broaden the movement were to emerge with this political force, some Czechs following the American credo "That all men [and women] are created equal, that they are endowed with certan inalienable rights; that among these rights are life, liberty and the pursuit of happiness." Following a similar quest, between summer and early November of 1989, 167,000 East Germans composing 1 percent of the population emigrated to the West. Four weeks after the Hungarian Communist party changed its name to Socialist, only 30,000 of its 720,000 members had exchanged their membership cards and registered anew, while forty-seven new political parties organized to take part in nineties elections for the people's democratic hearts, emphasizing a higher standard of living, the nation's heritage, and traditional European ways.[6]

Czechoslovakia providing a classic case, dateline 27 November 1989, a reporter said: "At many factories, workers responded to the students and formed strike committees that were aligned to organize today's work stoppage. The committees are now being asked to operate as Civic Forum representatives, passing along suggestions to the movement from the grass roots."[7] The scenario was set. As the "Civic Forum" leaders developed a democratic political and economic program to guide the nation pending free elections, the new democratic committees expanded the base of representation of the nation—to carry Czechoslovakia from Communist domination to democracy based on free elections, broad political party participation, a likely reintegration into Europe, and, one day a Europe without military blocs—so, in the best of worlds, neither NATO nor the Warsaw Pact would survive.

SUBSTANCE BEHIND DÉTENTE

The long-term possibilities for détente and arms reduction still remained unclear to the West, for it was hard for Western leaders to comprehend that the Communist world seemed determined to make itself into an equal member of the Western marketplace. Symbolic steps in this direction were unmistakable, though. In 1989 President Gorbachev offered official support to Poland's first non–Communist government since World War II. With the change of name of the Hungarian nation from the People's Republic to the Republic of Hungary came an epic recasting of the Hungarian Communist party as democratic and socialist, based in part on the fallibility of Soviet budgets to finance political-military intervention and domination. And with the breakdown of the central economic plan in both nations in trying (or not really trying) to promote production and the fair distribution of output, Warsaw and Budapest sought to transform their economies from central planning to domestic and foreign capitalized production for exchange in free markets.

Links East and West

The Soviet Union meanwhile hoped to establish a common Eastern European market, doing away with its military presence and thus compulsion as a means of establishing "new premises" for the development of economic cooperation.

To create Eastern-bloc economic coordination, Foreign Minister Shevardnadze explained, there was a need to alter the "system of mutual clearing of accounts, prices and the rates of national currencies"—a clear reference to the multistate bureaucracies that ensure an absence of freely convertible currencies impeding trade, loan guarantees, and unfettered investments.

For similar reasons, the balance of power in East-West relations began to turn in part on going beyond past mistakes and pursuing new arms negotiations and government concessions. Both France and the United States were outclassed (and morally wrong) in aggressions in Indochina, and the Soviet Union was immoral, corrupted, and outmaneuvered in Afghanistan.

These imperial aggressions had thrust both West and East into burgeoning social and budgetary crises and internal political diaspora, demanding a change of their domestic and international strategies.[8]

"History"—not those nations within history and those outside it*—"will judge us by whether we have taken the opportunities which

---

*See Francis Fukuyama's absurd delineation of the democratic West being outside history and the Socialist East still being within its confines.

have emerged from these reforms of the whole of Europe," said West German foreign minister Hans-Dietrich Genscher in late 1989, encouraging the West to pursue a united Europe by taking advantage of the new freedoms and reforms in Eastern Europe, potentially weaning Romania, Czechoslovakia, and East Germany to overturn their neo–Stalinist regimes.[9]

Body Blow to State Budgets

Bipolarity, dangerously balancing U.S. and Soviet military forces, simply could not outlast the escalating military burdens weighing on East or West.

Taking an historical snapshot, both the United States and the USSR were pressured to give up the cold war in favor of détente, arms treaties, and the peaceful resolution of conflict — not only because of moral renunciation of nuclear warfare but because neither economy could stay out of economic crisis without slowing the replacement of outmoded existing weapons and cutting costs for so-called missile defense.

Eastern and Western European military alliances should thus be phased out, Foreign Minister Shevardnadze insisted. "They did not always exist, and nobody treats them as a lasting factor of the future." Thus the North Atlantic Treaty Organization and the Warsaw Pact might be "political realities of the present day," he said, but the long-term goal should be "gradually transforming them into political-military organizations by developing civilian [oversight of] . . . their activity and simultaneously reducing all military elements."[10]

Security in the nineties was to come in the form of U.S.-USSR reductions in conventional and nuclear arms, dovetailing with the end of the Warsaw Pact and the conversion of post–Soviet forces and NATO from instruments of mutual deterrence into organizations of mutual reassurance, creating a zone of security from the Urals to the U.S. West Coast.

The military calculus might also rest on the common denominator of East-West trade, on 16 December 1991 Poland, Hungary, and Czechoslovakia becoming associate members of the European Community. Western aid and trade, loan guarantees, and investment capital in Eurasia were to follow.

Following this logic, in 1989 the United States cut military subsidies to Latin America, and Foreign Minister Shevardnadze declared the Eastern European nations would henceforth have "absolute freedom of choice" in forming or reforming their governments and economies.

Stalinist Czechoslovakia momentarily resisted, using police power against demonstrators demanding civil freedoms, chiding riot officers as "Gestapo!" and chanting "The world is watching!" — the slogan in Chicago when the police attacked demonstrators at the 1968 Democratic National Convention. And Czech Communist leaders at first insisted that economic and political change had to be orchestrated by their own Stalinist party, despite the self-condemnation by leaders and Communist parties of both Poland and Hungary for their countries' roles in the 1968 Warsaw Pact invasion of Czechoslovakia that put Moscow's Czech and Slovak puppets in power.[11]

But nonetheless, the logic for the new era of peace between great powers and their reduced military subsidies to lesser ones was leveraged by the body blow to their state budgets, which had already led to fraudulent accounting, hidden taxes, cuts in social services, and increases in national debt limits.

The spheres of influence held by East and West might fracture at their edges, then, with multipolarity going beyond the classic balance-of-power alliances of a few great powers parading raw military hardware as mutual deterrence. But multipolarity would also breed grim nationalist determination, perhaps weaker ideologically than the old bipolar commitments against the "evil empires" of one another, yet threatening by raising the number and level of parry and riposte through proliferation of nuclear arms.[12]

WAR, PEACE, AND IGNORANCE

The Union weakened and at odds internally, it seemed the Soviets had favorably repositioned their military forces in the seventies and eighties. Driving a hard bargain for the West to ratify Soviet claims to the Baltic states and a sizable slice of prewar Poland in return for a European-wide security conference treating then present borders as permanent, in 1972 General Secretary Leonid Brezhnev agreed to a reduction of U.S. and Soviet troops in Europe called Mutual and Balanced Forces Reduction. President Nixon hoped to sidestep Senator Mike Mansfield's pressure for the withdrawal of troops from Europe. But the Soviets apparently had no real intention to reduce troop levels (the talks produced no reductions) or to honor human rights pledges.

Two U.S. presidents and Henry Kissinger were outmaneuvered momentarily, and Kissinger led President Ford to sign the Helsinki Accord in 1975, albeit on the basis that the signatory nations would honor human rights at home and permit a follow-up conference to review progress ("Basket 3").[13] Brezhnev worked this double-cross, but grass-root pressures worldwide nonetheless pointed to Soviet violation of his human rights pledges and later imperial quest in Afghanistan.[14]

Indeed, for almost a decade and a half, détente was simply a holding action to stop war between the superpowers while both pursued, supported, and armed dozens of regional wars elsewhere. Then a new historical period opened at the end of the eighties. Peace for the United States, Western Europe, and the Soviet Union was now essential to solve their *internal problems.*

"We are still not exactly clear about our own health, ecological situation and culture," Natalia Ivanova wrote in 1990. "Every day we become aware of new gaps in our information on ethnic problems and territorial claims connected with them, be they 'the black holes' in the past or 'the blanks' in the present. Paradoxical as it may seem, the more we learn about the once forbidden or hushed-up issues, the broader our 'field of ignorance' grows."

It was obvious that Soviet communism was built on lies without end. Ivanova elaborated:

> The country's actual history was distorted, and current developments dressed up or ignored for the benefit of a particular "ruler" and his associates, or the multimillion stratum of the Bureaucratic-and-Administrative System. The public was suffocated by lack of information, and the grave brain damage caused by this will take a long time to cure. Only a meticulous all-round analysis will enable us to reveal the entire complex and comprehensive truth and gradually turn the country into a normally functioning, self-adjusting system. There is no other way out.
>
> We are now only at the very beginning of this process.[15]

Western Europe, meanwhile, required peace, unity, and transcontinental markets. "We must strengthen and accelerate the political construction of Europe," French president François Mitterrand concluded in 1990, with NATO and the Warsaw Pact momentarily continuing as overseers of stability and treaty compliance while also relaxing restrictions on technological transfers and other trade.

CUTTING COSTS IN EASTERN EUROPE

For the Soviet Union's survival, the Kremlin had moved quickly to remove all barriers to the mass movements emerging on its Eastern European flank. "During the last five years, dramatic changes have taken place in the relationship between East and West," announced the Nobel committee awarding Mikhail S. Gorbachev the 1990 peace prize.[16] "Confrontation has been replaced by negotiations. Old European nation-states have regained their freedom.

"The arms race is slowing down, and we see a definite and active process in the direction of arms control and disarmament. Several regional conflicts have been resolved or have at least come closer to a solution. The U.N. is beginning to play the role which was originally planned for it in an international community governed by law."

Though the steps to destroy Stalinism and toward democratization within the frame of socialism differed from nation to nation, the process was similar: Communist party–led governments that had remained in power for four decades had ruled through overt force or the threat of force against popular interests. The working population personally and collectively feared to stand against the Stalinist governments, giving a falsified credibility to the party-run state. But such legitimacy could not last as central control over the nation's supply of human freedom also limited production and distribution—and led to falling living standards, downward mobility, and grudging, inefficient efforts by the working class. Though street protest issued not initially from them but from intellectuals who had studied the relationship between unfreedom and economic failings, the intelligentsia were quickly joined by workers and families that had experienced an oversupply of deprivation.

At first, Communist governments dealt with these dissidents by arrests, beatings, and imprisonment. But before long, each government was unable to cope with the scale of protest, largely because it lacked foresight* as well as programs to ameliorate popular demands, thereby to legitimate itself. As soon as a party government offered token concessions, moreover, the opposition demanded more, to the point where the party itself could not keep its legitimacy in the eyes of the many.

Once the fuse was ignited, massive protest flashed the signal not only of deep disenchantment but open demands that the Communist-run governments step down. With millions moving into the streets, with urban mass transit halted and cities standing still, with the protest made in the name of the nation, nationalist flags unfurled or pinned to every lapel, a "general strike" would go on until free elections were held.

Stalinism and neo–Stalinism were soon to be no more, and even high-blown rhetoric of liberal-leaning factions within the Communist party could not stop the surge of humanity in the streets. Vain CP promises about future guarantees of political pluralism and cultural freedom were met with popular derision, protest marches, and new democratic demands. And the only moment of grace left to the Communists was to stop the use of force against their own children, who had powerfully spearheaded the opposition.

From Prague Spring redux to a reunited Germany, Communist Eastern Europe was soon to be no more.

Section B:
The Inner Reach

Eastern Europe, in the process of breaking free of the Soviet helotry in 1989–91, moved toward Western ties more or less, falling into either an

---

*Like the fabled Greek Epimetheus, without foresight they were not prepared for the possibility that from five decades of state-enforced immiseration and a lack of civil and political rights, an explosion of emotions would burst the façade of the dictatorship of the proletariat.

inner reach by way of German territory or an outer reach by circuitous paths that at first made it more difficult to cut commercial ties with the Soviet Union.

The consolidation of the two Germanys in 1990 promised to unify *Grossdeutschland* politically, economically, and potentially militarily. Teutonic unification also meant common borders with Poland and Czechoslovakia would provide a future opportunity for heavy commercial traffic, exchanging technology, labor, manufactured goods, and services. A united Germany might promise the territorial integrity of both Poland and Czechoslovakia, but such promise spoke to artificial boundary lines the military was never to cross, not the probable integration of their economies, not the political influences of one another.

Thus was established an inner reach locking a unified Germany to the Western Continent and enticing Poland and Czechoslovakia to use *Grossdeutschland* as a way station for commerce not only with Germany but with the entire Western zone.

Hereafter it would become impossible to speak of German unification in isolation from its immediate Eastern neighbors.

Chapter 7
Prague Spring Redux: The Eastern Europe That Is No More

We failed you in 1938 when a disastrous policy of appeasement allowed Hitler to extinguish your independence. . . . We still remember it with shame.
—Prime Minister Margaret Thatcher,
speaking to the Czechoslovak Parliament,
18 September 1990

I, Alexander Dubček, as the First Secretary of the Communist Party of Czecho-slovakia, was abducted by the KGB in August 1968, and by Soviet plane taken to Moscow in chains.
—Autobiography

In 1968 we did not only cross the border of Czechoslovakia with our tanks; we crossed the border of morality. . . . Recently we officially condemned our invasion into Czechoslovakia. How can we now plagiarize the old Czech schemes, with the meaningless creation of new so-called rescuers of nations—new Lithuanian Husaks and Bilaks?
—Yevgeny Yevtushenko, *The New York Times,*
19 January 1991

History has begun to develop very quickly in this country. In a country that has had 20 years of timelessness, now we have this fantastic speed.
—Vaclav Havel, Czech Civic Forum

The fall of Communism can be regarded as a sign that modern thought—based on the premise that the world is objectively knowable, and that the knowledge so obtained can be absolutely generalized—has come to a final crisis. This era has created the first global, or planetary, technical civilization, but it has reached the limit of its potential, the point beyond which the abyss begins. The end of Communism is a warning to all mankind. It is a signal that the era of arrogant, absolutist rea-son is drawing to a close and that it is high time to draw conclusions from that fact.
—Vaclav Havel, President of Czechoslovakia

180

CZECHS TO THE STREETS!

Vaclav Havel had again been arrested by the Communist regime in early 1989. A crackdown under way, it was intensified in the fall when on 17 November riot police intervened to crush a large demonstration in Prague, injuring dozens and electrifying rumors of fatalities. Those who had stood in opposition as members of the Charter 77 human rights group since the Soviets' crushing of the Prague Spring of 1968 suddenly had thousands of potential allies together under Charter 77 leadership, coalescing within forty-eight hours into a Civic Forum among the Czechs and the next day, the Public Against Violence among Slovak dissenters.

Organized demonstrators took to the streets daily, with 27 November the day of a massive general strike. Without the ominous shadow of Soviet military intervention, the opposition presented unalloyed pressure after ten days of tumultuous student-led demonstrations, then an immense general strike of fully one-half the population.

"How is it possible that so many people immediately understood what to do and that none of them needed any advice or instructions?" Havel asked of the Czech movement for liberation, answering that the hopes of the past had been shattered to

> pay for our present day freedom. Many of our citizens died in prison in the 1950s. Many were executed. Thousands of human lives were destroyed. Hundreds of thousands of talented people were driven abroad. . . . Those who fought against totalitarianism during the war were also persecuted. . . . Nobody who paid in one way or another for our freedom could be forgotten.[1]

Government legitimacy withered, forcing the Communist government to recognize and negotiate with the Civic Forum and the Public Against Violence. Another forty-eight hours later, the government had been forced to abolish the constitutional provision guaranteeing the Communist party's leading role, itself refuting the logic for crushing the 1968 reform movement under Dubček. "Life has shown it is not important what is written," admitted fallen party leader Milos Jakes of the constitution. "We must try to win the confidence of the people."

That confidence had been withheld for 346 years: 298 under the Hapsburg Empire, 7 under Nazi Germany, and 41 under Soviet guns and apparatchiks.

Transitional Government

The government now promised to create a broad-based coalition cabinet, to pass a new election law to hold free-ballot elections supporting multiparty democracy, to give up its hated monopoly under the one-party system. The transition to another way of operating came in view as the temporary prime minister Adamac appealed to the opposition Civic Forum for suggestions for potential cabinet members. For as Communist party chief Karl Urbanek worried, the Communists risked losing future elections and would have to reposture "to change into a modern political party that, in democratic and correct competition, seeks and finds its irreplaceable position in society."

The party thus moved to transform its image. Backed by the Communists still holding parliamentary control in the closing months of 1989, Communist prime minister Marian Calfa appealed to the nation, calling for a democratic state with a market economy.[2]

Then, in December 1989, a new government with a majority of non-Communists was formed, with Havel as president and the old Communist leader of the Prague Spring, Alexander Dubček, as chairman of the Parliament.

On the day of Vaclav Havel's inaugural reckoning, the legislature assembled at the medieval Hradcany Castle spiraling above Prague, Prime Minister Marian Calfa solemnizing:

> He has won the respect of all. He never accepted the suggestions of friends or foes that he go into exile, and bore the humiliation of a man oppressed and relegated by those in power to the margins of society. Your vote for Vaclav Havel will be a vote for insuring the human rights of every citizen of our country.

And then issued Havel's oath, a twenty-gun salute, a military parade, the new president addressing a joyous crowd thronging the castle yard:

> Dear friends. I promise you I will not betray your confidence. I will lead this country to free elections. This must be done in an honest and calm way, so that the clean face of our revolution is not soiled. That is the task of all of us. Thank you.

In what then seemed a symbolic post, Havel would serve only until a new president could be elected for a regular five-year term.

And so devolved the presidency of independent Czechoslovakia — first held by Tomas G. Masaryk from 1918 to 1935; then by Eduard Benes to 1938, as the Western Allies relinquished Czechoslovakia to Nazi Germany in the Munich Pact; then again from 1946 to 1948. But thereafter a Communist decree required that all presidents be members of the party, the edict lasting to 10 December 1989 when the Stalinist Husak resigned and Havel took the oath without promising loyalty to the cause of socialism.[3]

Hope and the Return to People's Government

Havel spread "hope," that gem held fast in Pandora's box after all diseases had escaped to plague hapless man. For in the great movement for social change, Havel demanded state tolerance of individuals and a people, jointly participating, sharing responsibility for their own destiny. Thus, said he as president, addressing the nation on 1 January 1990:

> The previous regime, armed with a proud and intolerant ideology, reduced people into the means of production, and nature into its tools. So it attacked their very essence, and their mutual relations. . . . Out of talented and responsible people, ingeniously husbanding their land, it made cogs of some sort of great, monstrous thudding, smelly machine, with an unclear purpose. All it can do is, slowly but irresistibly, wear itself out with all its cogs. . . .
>
> Let us make no mistake: even the best Government, the best Parliament and the best President cannot do much by themselves. Freedom and democracy, after all, mean joint participation and shared responsibility. If we realize this, then all the horrors that the new Czechoslovakian democracy inherited cease to be so horrific. If we realize this, then hope will return to our hearts.[4]

Hope, electrifying his every word: "Perhaps you are asking what kind of Republic I am dreaming about. I will answer you: A Republic that is independent, free, democratic, a Republic with economic prosperity and also social justice, a humane Republic that serves man and for that reason also has hope that man will serve it."

Hope for a government of people, he recalled: "My most important predecessor [Alexander Dubček] started his first speech by quoting from" a prayer by the 17th century Moravian churchman John Amos "Comenius. Permit me to end my own first speech by my own paraphrase. Your Government, my people, has returned to you."[5]

For the moment, though, the return to people's government was slowed. For Havel's hands were bound by Communist apparatchik holdovers, populating the state ministries, blocking reforms.

The old order would thus have to relinquish the material impedimenta sustaining the leading role of the party, framed in turn by Stalinist rigidities imposed across Eastern Europe, justifying the Communist monopoly on all aspects of Czech life from every enterprise and union to each building and theater.

Though the crime of opposing CP domination ground to an end, the old party momentarily defended its portfolios of control over the "socialist" economy, the military, and the sinecures of state ownership and bureaucratic positions.

TASKS OF THE OPPOSITION

The opposition's task would now be to ferret out these allotted benefits to the Communist elite and its party entourage. Even when the constitution deleted the words reciting the coveted "leading role" of the Communists, their apparatus loomed, directing factories, schools, courts, and government bureaus. The opposition made demands, but yet to be won were ministerial posts, free elections, and a solid place in economic planning.

Government concessions, though, first came in the form of state cultural ministries announcing a relaxation of censorship of books, films, and plays. A new cabinet of so-called experts and professionals was to include members of the Communist and other parties. But at first the Communists said voting was to be put off, leading the opposition to contest the Communist domination of the cabinet.

With 6–7 million people on the streets on 27 November 1989, the Communists already knew they would find their party in a minority, and the opposition agreed the leading role of the Communist party had come to an end, demanding free elections, freedom of assembly and association, freedom of speech and press, the abolition of government supervision of the churches, and change in the defense law. Those in office who had betrayed their oaths and not followed the will and interests of the people would be replaced in by-elections. And the movement held out the threat that the "results of negotiations [with the government] are sufficient for it to appeal to all citizens to continue their work while maintaining a permanent strike alert."[6] A call for a general strike could issue at any time.

Opening to the West

Future measures were still unpredictable, but the move to political egalitarianism and open markets could not be stopped. Finance Minister Vaclav Klaus announced on 5 January 1990 that henceforth Czechoslovakia would join Poland to overhaul the Soviet-designed COMECON's unequal trade relations and transform market dependencies.

Czechoslovakia also looked to the West to gain relief from Soviet hegemony that made the Czech steel, armament, and plastic industries almost completely dependent on Russian purchases. The famous Skoda Works and eight giant Slovakian gunsmith factories were still the armory of the Warsaw Pact, with credits used to purchase inexpensive Soviet raw materials and critical oil supplies, so any transition to a new order of trade would of necessity be calculated and gradual.

Havel then moved, asking Secretary of State James Baker for technical experts to help the government work around some of its own ministries. Viewing Washington as "a beacon of freedom," Frantisek Cardinal Tomasek, Archbishop of Prague, also thanked Baker for everything the United States had done for his country—at its 1918 founding, its 1945 liberation, its 1990 promise of aid.[7]

Who Will Defend and Control Whom?

Throwing off the yoke of Soviet domination, Havel and the Kremlin soon agreed to the withdrawal of Soviet troops, signing a treaty of cooperation between their security forces. "This is a treaty that is symmetrical and not directed against any third nation," President Havel declaimed, hailing the end of the cold war Security Treaty under which Soviet and Czech intelligence networks worked jointly against the United States and other NATO nations.

Havel refused to renew the treaty of Mutual Cooperation and Assistance that made Czechoslovakia an economic satellite of Moscow. "Our relations have a new character, a new quality now," the president reported.

And the border with Austria was meanwhile opened by the government and hard currency appreciated vis-à-vis Czech currency.

Double-Threat Military

Senior military commanders met dissidents to assure them no crackdown would halt liberalization, though Forum leaders remained on constant alert to the danger of military intervention and the CP, despite its insistence it was "interested in playing a full role in a multiparty system, to gain its rightful place in competition with others."[8]

The army and the party's militia were viewed by the opposition as a dual danger to both liberalization and past economic formulas. General Vaclavik rose in Parliament to support the Communist general secretary in his quest to use the army to defend the country and for construction, not to act against the demonstrating opposition, as the Civic Forum feared the army would, to protect "the interests of specific political groups."

Still, Communist chief Urbanek in Parliament rejected the Forum's demands for dissolution of the party's militia, its cells and enterprises, the sale of party-owned buildings and the dismissal of Communist heads of enterprises. These spokes in the Communist wheel of motion had been their power of state-planned economic affairs, with the party chief Urbanek arguing against abandoning the socialist economic system to prevent a situation "similar to that in Poland, where factories are being returned to private owners or sold to foreign owners. We resolutely reject views claiming that we must return to capitalism."[9]

Demilitarization and Civic Forum
Politics vs. Communists

As the Civic Forum pressured, the military was forced to withdraw from defensive operations. General Vacek called for the elimination of defense barriers along the German border, no longer fearing German reunification or a repeat of Hitler's 1938 seizure of Sudetenland borders with East Germany from Czechoslovakia—nor apprehensive of the return of millions of Germans forced out in 1945 when Czech lands were repossessed.

This was also a step toward the demilitarization of the Communist party itself. For the withdrawal of party groups and political officials from the military and police departments prevented direct Communist control over state institutions. Communists formed their Democratic Forum to urge changes in the running of the party, including the abolition of the dictatorial leadership at the center.[10] And as a next step, the CP disbanded the People's Militia units of armed workers that had played a crucial role in the Communist seizure of power in 1948.

Yet all these changes did not reinvest the party with power. At the party meeting in late December 1989, members remained blind to changing popular sentiments. "These delegates still have the illusion that we are still in charge of policy, when in fact real power is now somewhere else," judged Jaromie Sedlak of the Democratic Forum Communists. "Of course power is now dispersed. There are several points of power, but the main force is the Civic Forum."[11]

Any military coup to secure a neo–Stalinist state without calling on the Soviet Union to mobilize its 800,000 troops still stationed on Czech soil would now have to face the opposition on the streets, the pacifist factions within the party-run parliament, and the church.

The 1968 Soviet invasion had been an anachronism, as was Czech "normalization" under the neo–Stalinist Czech party. Yet any retrenchment after twenty-one years of power would be both fitful and powerfully opposed.[12]

And there was no letup. When the Communist deputies in Parliament demanded that Parliament not elect the president, delaying the program of the Civic Forum by a three-month wait for a direct popular vote, the Forum mobilized its 1,500 organizations to pressure Parliament for a quick election to put its leader, Havel, in power with Alexander Dubček as president of Parliament, and ensure one-fourth of Parliament, mostly old-line Communists, would be replaced by new deputies supporting change.[13]

As the Civic Forum viewed Havel's support to be weaker in the countryside than in the capital, and any other method would depart from the constitution, they argued that Parliament should elect the president, and Parliament wanted Havel.[14]

Solving the Economic Malaise

Czechoslovakia would face another type of crisis too: production on a scale calculated to lift the nation out of debt and create a new technological base to enhance the output of quality goods for widened markets.

The private sector was practically nonexistent with workers guaranteed jobs and income regardless of the quality of work, massive industrial pollution requiring environmental rehabilitation, and trade 80 percent directed toward other Communist nations. The way out for Czechoslovakia was to rely on its traditional industry and agriculture, using modern technological imports from the West.[15]

It needed to reduce its $6.9-billion debt in Western currencies in the face of the need for political and economic restructuring and competence in running the nation's productive apparatus. So the old industrial base of steel, coal, machinery, and chemicals would also have to be supplemented by specialized industries like electronics and advanced machinery. Decentralized planning and more autonomy for local workers and managers would have to stress capital investment, imported technology, and worker satisfaction.

In 1989, Czech machine tools were fifteen years behind in key technologies available in the West. Companies were starved for resources, parts, and hard currencies to import this technical equipment, and the lack of open markets prevented improvement in the quality of products and productivity. To make amends in these areas, the Western embargo on shipping sophisticated technology to Eastern Europe would have to end, along with impediments to Western aid and loans.[16]

In late 1990, plans had been made to use Soviet-built nuclear power stations, closing down eleven polluting, unprofitable state-run coal mines employing 9,500 workers to supply coal-fired electrical power stations in the Ostrava region some 240 miles from Prague. Unsure of itself, the government kept them on tap to be used if required.[17]

To elicit an enlarged output indirectly, meanwhile, the government allowed a one-time price hike that fueled 1991 prices 45 percent, but this was offset by government fiscal and monetary policies keeping it at 1 to 1.5 percent a month, foreseeing inflation at less than 10 percent for 1992.

Western capital was also elicited in the form of opportunities. The new government mandated that the size of private enterprises was to be unrestricted so that joint-stock companies could issue shares to foreign investors, who might also acquire controlling interests. Security for these investors might emerge through state agencies of foreign governments that would help teach the Czechs business methods and their languages and back their own citizen investors.

The key components creating the essential conditions for a market economy would meanwhile have to be put in place: restricting the money supply and slashing the budget deficit so prices would not soar out of control when these were scheduled to be freed on 1 January 1991. But as state monopolies remained in many industries, price increments were almost a certainty in the early nineties, running at an estimated 14 percent annual inflation rate.

Shock therapy, so-called, included the government's removing price controls on 85 percent of goods sold, closing inefficient state-owned enterprises, privatizing thousands of shops, clamping down on money-supply growth, and making the Czech crown convertible.

Inflation would lead to the devaluation of Czech currency at home, and on 21 January 1991, the country also started to pay for Soviet oil imports in hard currencies at world market prices, shifting an added $2.5 billion a year from potential investments in modernized factories and improved quality and variety of consumer goods—also leading to an estimated 5 to 10 percent drop in output in 1991.[18]

Economic Dilemma and Turn to the Right

Domestic and external shocks decimated the economy; politics turned toward the right, and both Czechs and Slovaks reaffirmed the need for personal survival above grand pronouncements about government democracy, socialism, or individual rights.

"Nobody can tell what the tolerance limit of the population will be," foretold the Czech republic's economic minister, Karel Dyba. "People voted for a Government that promised hardships, lower living standards and some unemployment. It's one thing to be for a market economy, and another thing to experience the not-so-nice side of a market economy."

"When the political consensus behind an economic program is lost, it can be dangerous," confirmed senior official Jan Fabianek in the Economic Ministry. "It might force you to choose second-best solutions or loosen up on controlling inflation. It could even threaten newly emerging democracies."[19]

The 1991 collapse of the COMECON trading system and the tailspin of the Soviet economy had devastated Czechoslovakia's exports to other COMECON markets and led to reorientation of industry toward the West, the privatization of domestic industry, and encouragement of foreign investments.

Privatization began with the 1991 Ministry of Privatization's return of 10 percent of all state property worth $10 billion, covering hundreds of thousands of state businesses and agency property or state bonds or vouchers, to original owners or their heirs. These had been confiscated in February 1948 by the Communists' seizure of state power and their brutal takeover of farms and factories, summarily expelling owners from their houses and sometimes sentencing them at trials to hard labor for the sole crime of belonging to the "enemy class."

On 20 February 1992, Parliament also voted to return land to people of Hungarian and German origin who were dispossessed by the Communist government after 1948, but not to the 2.5 million Sudeten Germans who lost their land when they were expelled in 1946 and 1947 for nationalist yearnings that had been the pretext for the Nazi invasion and occupation.[20]

This return did not cover compensation for seizures carried out between 1945 and 1948 when the democratic government nationalized big business, putting 60 percent of the economy in state hands, including the giant Skoda auto works and the Bata shoe company. These and other large firms became the subject of 1991–92 share distribution to the public.[21]

In the quest to turn state properties into privately held shares quickly, moreover, the government opened an unregulated Pandora's box: 600 offices across the country to give away 40 percent of the state-owned economy to citizens over 18 registering for coupons, at a cost of 35 crowns ($1.25) for a book of coupons to be exchanged for shares in privatized state companies at a per-share cost of 1,035 crowns ($35), the average real asset value being many times greater. As some 6 million of these coupon books were bought up by 450 private investment funds led by the largest, Harvard Capital and Consulting, prospective buyers were forced to come to them to "entrust" their registered coupons for the promised payback of 10 to 15 times the original $35 per share investment after a year.

But all was not fair in the maddened democratic stock market. Using aggressive advertising with TV commercials produced by a Czech-U.S. advertising company using a sexy female model, confusing the company's American name with Harvard University's investment trust, Harvard Capital and Consulting employed 22,000 commission-paid agents to canvass clients outside government registration offices to sign up between 20 and 30 percent of the 3 million people who had bought and registered coupon books by January 1992. Harvard effectively centralized control over the power to buy shares that would establish a controlling interest over major privatized industries in the nation.[22]

In the legal vacuum created by post–Communist economic transformation, regardless of the ability to honor the pledge, Harvard or any other fund could make guaranteed promises of a payback many times the original investment. Investors might lose everything, or companies might be stripped of their assets to make the promised payments. Harvard Capital's 500,000 investors could conceivably require promised payouts in a year of more than 5 billion crowns (about $165 million) while the fund's capital totaled only 1 million crowns, an infinitesimal equity. "The issues are so underpaid [i.e., below book value of company assets]," said Harvard Capital founder Viktor Kozeny, "that having calculated the actual value to be much, much higher, we were able to say, 'Look, if you don't want to remain an investor, then after a year and a day you can come back to us, and we'll pay you back 10 times what you originally paid in.'"

But what if equity remained minute and there were insufficient funds? Kozeny planned to use outside bank credit lines to secure repayment of an estimated 20 percent of redeeming couponholders, effectively reducing the fund's capital. He or other unscrupulous fund managers could then pay back by stripping the funds and the assets of the companies they controlled. Their get-rich-quick schemes might also raid Czechoslovakia's already undercapitalized industries and deprive investors of both their money and share rights.[23]

"The Czechoslovak program will produce a lot of abuses that are avoidable," said economist Andrzej Rapaczynski, commenting on the widespread distribution of shares that will be controlled by mutual funds set up to oversee the new enterprises, rip them apart, and reorganize purchased state companies, "but it will be more of a success in the long run."[24]

Once this period of frontierlike expropriation of small investors was over, industry would be set in place by both domestic and foreign infusions of capital and technology, and these privately owned corporations could then reorient production and markets under the new government's policy favoring peacetime output and sales.

Foreign investors quickly saw large-scale Czechoslovakian industry as a plum to be picked, ripened, and consumed. "Central Europe will be an important market in several years," judged Raymond Lévy, chairman of Renault, whose principal shareholder was the French government. "It's necessary to make an effort to invest there."

Both Renault and German Volkswagen had made bids for share partnership in Soda, the successful Czech auto giant making the best auto in Eastern Europe. Volkswagen offered to invest as much as $3 billion to build a second Skoda factory, doubling the company's output. Renault promised to help modernize the country's truck industry, push component suppliers to invest in Czechoslovakia, produce a car already on Renault drawing boards, uplifting Skoda's quality and image beyond its solid if simple Favorit compact car. But government approval in March 1992 went to Volkswagen, as Europe's biggest car company, to take over Skoda under the guidance of the Czechoslovakian Anti-Monopoly Office, a total of $6 billion to be invested in Skoda for Volkswagen's initial 31 percent stake, which was to rise to 70 percent by 1995.[25]

Other foreign investors calculated their chances to meet Czechoslovakia's government approval requirements. Still others counted customers, comparing Poland's 40 million population with Hungary's 10 million and Czechoslovakia's 15 million. But by early March 1992, foreign investments were nearly $800 million, up from about $100 million in 1990 and nearly $600 million in 1991, though most were concentrated in a few large undertakings.[26]

Breakdown of Authority Structures

Despite modest economic successes from late 1989 to early 1992, there was a breakdown of governmental authority and political uncertainty. The first undermined the ability of the government to direct and stabilize social relations centrally, the second to a potential splintering of the nation.

The introduction of democracy and incipient capitalism undermining the Communists' previous authority promoted the widespread attitude that freedom meant a "free-for-all to get rich" and undercut fear of the police, bringing on a crime wave in Prague.

This was fed by President Havel's decision in early 1990 to grant amnesty and early releases to two-thirds of thousands of prisoners, some subsequently rearrested and charged with new crimes. Police recorded a doubling of Prague crime and a fivefold increase in street crime in the two years from the Velvet Revolution to the middle of December 1991, also indicating that 80 to 85 percent of Prague street crime was committed by Gypsies, fueling widespread prejudice and attacks against Gypsies (and remaining Vietnamese guest workers) and engendering protests by Gypsy organizations that insisted that these crimes involved only a small number of repeat offenders recently coming from poorer eastern Czechoslovakia.[27]

National partition also threatening, in December 1990 President Havel had asserted that a breakup of the nation into Czechs and Slovaks would end both economic prosperity and democracy. Slovakia's parliament had demanded that the federal Parliament cede many powers to the constituent republics, seeking the division of major federal institutions like the railroads, the central bank, and pipelines bringing oil and goods from the Soviet Union to separate Czech and Slovak companies.[28] The nation was already divided economically too.

Collapsing Communist authority resulted in the end of the Warsaw Pact. Provision of heavy weapons and disarmament had cut Slovakian arms production and export to the old Soviet Union. Once one of the most efficient arms forges in the old Soviet bloc and the world's sixth largest exporter selling low-priced weaponry to Warsaw Pact nations and to the Middle East, the arms works either continued to make their own deals with buyers from Syria to Brazil, Nigeria, and Croatia or tried to convert to civilian production. Slovak and federal authorities had battled over the right of arms merchants to make deals, though in early 1992 the law required government licenses for companies exporting the arms themselves.

Yet the arms industry was in jeopardy, as the Economic Ministry revealed statistically. In 1987, under the old Communist regime, Czechoslovakia delivered $566 million to its Soviet-bloc allies, but by 1991 delivered only $50 million. Legal arms exports to other nations totaled $326 million in 1990 but only $186 million in 1991.

President Havel had told the nation that the continued activities of arms merchants in collusion with officials of the old military-industrial complex were dangerous and "jeopardizing" Czechoslovakia's "position in the world." Yet in February 1992 Economic Minister Vladimir Dlouhy tried to pacify angry Slovak managers and workers at arms factories, pledging a pragmatic new government arms sales policy condoning the limited sale of arms according with Prague's foreign-policy aims.

In all of the nation's twenty-eight arms factories located in separatist-minded Slovakia where unemployment was far higher than in Czech lands, leaders had accused the Czechs of doing little to save industry. The nationalist and Communist-affiliated Slovak leader Vladimir Meciar castigated the "irresponsible" government arms policy since Slovak arms factories "had such large orders we could live off them for seven years," hedging Slovak factories not to "supply to politically sensitive areas" but also not to halt arms exports since other countries would simply "step into the gap."[29]

In the wake of the loss of Soviet markets once absorbing 75 percent of production at factories like Dubnica's huge Heavy Machine Works, the reduction to 8 percent spelled soaring unemployment among the 80 percent of the work force in this town of 25,000 people. The linkage between arms production cutbacks laying off one-third of the plant's workers and the reduction of steel output at the town's mill put steelworkers on a four-day week as furnaces were shut down. So from being the Soviet gunsmith, towns like Dubnica became the locus of farming, small state-privatized shops, tourism — and waves of emigration, seeking work in Germany or Holland.

From the Soviet-imposed 1968 reintroduction of arms manufacturing that had brought prosperity to wean Czechs and Slovaks from yearning for freedom came giant arms factories that could be converted to peacetime production only by the expenditure of many millions — $500 million in the case of Heavy Machine Works. And the hope for foreign investors was the town's future, involving investors like Oaklahoma Reda Corporation's investment of Western technology, mobilizing skilled Slovak labor, and finding customers for drilling pumps in the oil fields of Western Siberia, to be bartered for Russian crude oil, creating a new triangular pattern of trade.[30]

Triple-Bind Economy

Though the Civic Action Forum had thrown out the Communist government, almost from the start the Forum was ideologically split into two wings. The fractured Forum that had won the first free parliamentary elections and controlled the government of Prime Minister Marian Calfa only tenuously supported the governing coalition. And in October 1991 its members elected Finance Minister Vaclav Klaus chairman of the movement, upsetting President Havel's candidate.

Klaus's faction stood for liberal faith in an economy free of government intervention, striving to create a "right-of-center party" in coming parliamentary elections. The other faction, Havel's so-called Liberal Club, stood for liberal social and political tenets and included his longtime associates and fellow prisoners of the Charter 77 dissident movement as well as the 1968 Communists, with Deputy Prime Minister and Foreign Minister Jiri Dienstbier the Liberals' leading personality.[31] And Havel straddled both groups, strongly favoring Klaus's far-reaching economic reforms, yet philosophically more attuned to the Liberal Club's conception of free thinking and personal ingenuity.

As the political split widened, the government was caught in the triple bind of needing to confiscate Communist assets, increase output, and close down money-losing industries. "We have an irrational, wasteful, nonfunctioning centrally planned economy," Vaclav Klaus explained. "The transition to a free-market system must be radical, immediate and irrevocable."[32]

December 1990 legislation had slated ill-gotten Communist assets for confiscation. The law looked to the Communist "mafia" composed of former government officials, corrupt bureaucrats, black marketers, and members of the disbanded secret police, who held vast sums of illicit wealth that empowered them to place high bids at the auction of hundreds of thousands of commercial establishments under Parliament's Small-Scale Privatization Act. At best, though, the law would be difficult to apply, President Havel citing the extent of past abuse with the example of the United Agricultural Cooperative of Slusovice, Moravia, which was transformed after the 1968 Soviet invasion into a massive center for chemical and computer factories, owned its own commercial airline, carried on its own foreign trade, and amassed huge hard-currency reserves laundering hundreds of millions of dollars for Communist cronies.

But what could be done to stop the old Communist elite from becoming a new political or ownership elite and upper-managerial coterie? By late 1989 when the Communists were forced from power, about 100,000 Czechoslovakians had been persuaded, coerced, or paid to spy on fellow citizens. Background screening of parliamentary candidates in the weeks before Czechoslovakia's first free elections in June 1990 had been badly flawed, and both the national Parliament and the legislature of the Czech republic moved to hold a new round of screening to review the background of suspected informers—parliamentary members, deputy ministers, and presidential aides—by comparing partly destroyed card catalogs and computer files recovered in Prague and the country's 108 districts. Thus, in February 1991, officials again began screening more than 1,000 top parliamentary members, government ministers, and their aides.

Though the Communist party complained that its members should not be discriminated against in securing important positions in economic restructuring, that it was a legal party entitled to hold property and to organize itself under the law, Czech film director Milos Forman did not sympathize with their deprivations. "For 41 years, the party not only discriminated against hundreds of thousands who didn't want to subscribe to its political and economic platform," he wrote, "but also put tens of thousands in concentration camps, and executed thousands, often without a trial."[33]

Forman was not alone, some 25,000 to 60,000 demonstrators jamming Prague's Old Town Square on 11 October 1990 to oppose the party's call to reorganize Communist cells at the workplace and to support the government's proposal to confiscate the party's property "gained in unjust ways, giving it an advantage over other political parties and movements in contradiction to democratic principles."³⁴

Yet confiscations and accusations were often unjust. In 1968 dissident student leader and Civic Forum parliamentarian Jan Kavan was accused of collaborating with the Communist secret police twenty years earlier because he had met with an agent diplomat in the London Czech embassy. And in a cause célèbre, the respected environmentalist Dr. Bedrich Moldan (who had worked for a geological institute dealing with air pollution problems and in a marginal though officially sanctioned environmental organization) was dismissed as environmental minister because he had met with secret police agents in the Communist era. "In the conditions in Czechoslovakia at that time," he said, "it never crossed my mind that I could refuse." The dismissal, criticized the Czechoslovakian Union of Environmentalists, "speaks more than anything about attempts to get rid of an able expert who would be a tough adversary of the growing industrial and economic lobbies."³⁵

In December 1991, Parliament also imposed a one- to five-year prison term for anyone "supporting or promoting movements such as fascism and Communism," supporters saying the new criminal law would not make membership in the Communist party a crime but only forbid advocacy of human rights violations. President Havel offered that the vague law had a wide range of meanings, and a federal prosecutor did not know how the law would be applied. Though right-wing critics said the sanctions were too weak, others complained that the law was too harsh because it punished large categories of people without providing any case-by-case examination of specifically alleged abuses. "In Czechoslovakia, as well as other post–Communist countries," said leading political commentator Jan Urban, "we're seeing a trend to oversimplify politics by trying to ban the enemy."³⁶

By early 1992, only a few top-ranking Communists had been unseated and prosecuted, not for perpetuating the Soviet system but specific crimes. Thus former chief of the Prague chapter of the Communist party was convicted of ordering the harsh treatment of anti–Government demonstrators yet was released from serving part of his prison term. Thus Frantisek Kincl, the last interior minister of the former government, and the former heads of the Communist secret police and counterespionage service were charged with abuse of power for having ordered the temporary detention of government opponents in 1988–89. Though they argued they were guilty of nothing more than having "strictly" fulfilled their duties as mandated by the Communist party Central Committee, sending instructions to the Interior Ministry and various security services insisting on severe action, and in accordance with laws of the times, both Alexander Dubček and President Havel planned to testify about harassments and imprisonment at the hands of those responsible for human rights abuses. The logic of the prosecutions, explained Martin Butora,

President Havel's human rights adviser, was to hold former Communist officials accountable, especially when thousands of them had repositioned themselves as part of the economic elite.

Testifying in defense of the actions of the former government, Czechoslovakia's last Communist general secretary, Milos Jakes, reaffirmed Central Committee instructions to the various ministries and security services, afterward stating that post–Communist "talk of devastation" was just "slogans," Communist power having promoted "constant development and people lived quite well," in sharp contrast to the subsequent transformation to a market economy, causing "unprecedented catastrophic consequences on people's lives."[37]

Even the treason charges proposed against eighteen Communist officials in connection with the 1968 Soviet invasion were dropped because the twenty-year statute of limitations had expired and some of the former officials had died. Crimes committed "against peace" were not covered by the statute, but a spokesman for the Interior Ministry, Martin Fendrych, said the authorities could not definitely prove that the officials had committed the suspected offense of asking Moscow to intervene in crushing the 1968 political reform.

Communist wealth in the process of being confiscated, the next step was to close down inefficient production. After forty years under a Soviet-designed command economy, most businesses operated through an inefficient alien plan that made them uncompetitive in world markets. Even Finance Minister Klaus had expected in 1990 that at least one-third of the Czech economy would remain in state hands. And government plans to close bankrupt industries also looked to state loans and foreign capital to rebuild existing plants and retool military factories for heavy equipment and consumer goods.[38]

To enlarge production directly, privatization of industry was accelerated, and competitive management, modern technology, and Western markets were sought. Both domestic shareholding and foreign investors were encouraged.[39] Yet as long as the economy remained dominated by state enterprises under management of former Communist party officials, they held the power and information to maintain their dominance and enrich themselves. Seeing that they held no interest in assisting the transformation to a politically democratic and capitalist system, Parliament passed laws banning former Communist officials from employment in high-level government posts and top management positions in state-owned enterprises for five years.[40] A so-called process of lustration was to ensure that public officials be evaluated by a high set of moral standards, thereby establishing individual responsibility. To fail the lustration process, an individual would not only have had to hold a position of power in the previous totalitarian regime, but positive documentary evidence of active collaboration with the hated secret police had to be produced, including the dossiers of the secret police, the main pillars of totalitarian control.[41]

President Havel himself sought to secure individual expression over centrist government formulations based on so-called objectivity, recognizing the need for both the personal sphere and the objective external sphere. "Many of the traditional mechanisms of democracy created and developed and conserved in the modern era are so linked to the cult of objectivity and statistical average that they can annul human individuality," he told the World Economic Forum in Davos, Switzerland, 4 February 1992.[42]

Meanwhile, as the economy lagged, both democracy and market economics pulled young Czechs and Slovaks to the right. Chairman of the Parliament Alexander Dubček came under heavy criticism for his lingering leftist views and legislative incompetence, and five of President Vaclav Havel's major legislative proposals were rejected, including voting reforms and a referendum on national unity that Slovak nationalists feared would endorse keeping the country together. The conservative leader of the Civic Democratic party and Finance Minister Vaclav Klaus set his free-market policies on a collision course with those of leftist Foreign Minister Jiri Dienstbier and the liberal president, foreseeing a newly installed Parliament electing Klaus, a Czech, as prime minister in the June 1992 national elections and refusing to reelect Havel, also a Czech, as president, opposed by Slovak leaders like Vladimir Meciar demanding equal Slovakian representation in major offices.

Democrats were again on the run, the most famous being Professor Eduard Goldstucker, who endured six-year imprisonment under the Stalinists purging the Communist party in the fifties, fleeing to England after the 1968 Soviet invasion and returning in 1989 to find Prague Spring denounced in 1992 as a botched fight between factions of the Communist party whose bitter consequences Czechs and Slovaks had borne for twenty years.

"The tremendous reaction to the horrors of the old regime is that the pendulum is swinging to the other extreme," the seventy-year-old professor said. "Noble ideas should be looked upon with great suspicion, it is now believed, because they caused great grief, so you have a deep distrust of intellectuals. This is a telling moment," he continued. "They say we must run away from the ideals of basic equality of man, in a society so traumatized by the past and so unstable. And such ideas are bringing about unsavory results."[43]

So the future economic, political, and military map was clouded. The nation's major tasks were to maintain democracy, create jobs, advance efficient production, supply the people with quality goods, care for those in need, and try to reduce dangerous levels of air, water, and soil pollution. Given the different regional, labor, and other interests, coalition governments would through political parry and riposte necessarily juggle state laws, election procedures, and administrative functions.

No one could see the future. Yet the moral imperatives of the revolution might keep the spirit of the democratic population alive to meet individual needs while transforming the material base of the nation—not only in the tradition of Tomas Masaryk in the nation's first democracy but that of Dubček in the second, Havel of the third, and many more to follow.

Chapter 8
Deutschland über Alles

Anyone who invests there takes part in the internal European market and in a region in which high growth rates can be expected in the next few years.
— Chancellor Helmut Kohl, 25 November 1990

There had been lawless order on the eastern side of the Elbe.[1] "Led by the working class and its Marxist-Leninist party," article 1 of the East German Constitution had declared, the nation was a Communist state of workers and farmers.

But the working class had not led, only followed the party mandate, and this formulation for undemocratic methods was out of touch with popular beliefs and demands. Mass protest and demonstrations had also been met with police repression in early October 1989, and the Party used Parliament as a rubber stamp and prevented it from convening to deal with popular outrage.

More important, the Stalinist "personality cult" of successive Communist party chiefs Walter Ulbricht and Erich Honecker was beset by "political arrogance" and "self-satisfaction," linked to a "special relationship" with Soviet generals who had commanded more than 300,000 Soviet troops stationed in East Germany since World War II, said Werner Jarowinsky, the Communist party leader in Parliament. Thus could they hold the population in awe.

"They thought that they held a special line to the Kremlin," reported a member of the Central Committee, "and that in times of stress they could count on the marshalls. They thought in the autumn of 1987 that the marshalls would join the conservatives in Moscow in dumping Gorbachev."

But when that did not happen, the Honecker leadership attacked Gorbachev's policies, even boasting that East Germany was so successful by comparison with the Soviet Union that its standard of living exceeded that in West Germany. "Coming as it did when hundreds of our young people were beginning to flee to the West by way of Hungary, that made the cup run over for many of us," a party official conceded.

Amid angry protests on the streets and hot criticism within the party, former president of Parliament Horst Sindermann was soon apologizing for having let the population take charge, waiting too long to call the legislature into session and the army into the streets.

Party head Jarowinsky rationalized: "Our party is determined to draw radical consequences from this bitter fact. We need change in the Constitution," he offered, looking over his shoulder at the threat of the democratic program of the New Forum, the largest opposition group. "It's time to come closer together."

MIGRATIONS EAST TO WEST

As the Communist-controlled cabinet came under popular fire, it had initially renamed its most feared institution of control, the Ministry of State Security (STASIS), the Office of National Security (NASIS), then announced its dissolution and resurrection under a new civilian administrator of "legitimate intelligence" controlling two separate organizations, each reporting to the Communist prime minister Hans Modrow. One, a secret police agency, was officiously retitled Office for the Defense of the Constitution, copying the name from the West German intelligence agency.

"When the pressure rose," said New Forum member Sebastian Pflugbeil, "they promised to dissolve the STASIS, but then they formed the NASIS: Same people, same offices, same tasks. The pressure grew again and they formed a commission to dissolve NASIS. But even while this commission was working they formed the Office for the Protection of the Constitution, even though we haven't agreed on a constitution!"

Prime Minister Modrow recoiled, promising to speed the dismantling of the security apparatus and agreeing not to form the new agency. Still distrustful, the New Forum immediately mobilized a demonstration at STASIS headquarters in East Berlin, to build a symbolic wall of bricks at the gate to the headquarters, then lost control as hundreds of protestors wildly raided the building, breaking windows, crushing doors, desks, and computers, and torching and shredding files. As expected, the Communist press defended its security systems and their right to spy, blaming the New Forum for the raucous raid.[2] The rest is known: The raided files and millions of other secret documents ultimately came under the control of the West German Office for the Defense of the Constitution, to be used against both East and West German Communists and the Left.

UPRISING

Popular dissatisfaction running high, East German migrations to the West during late 1989 accompanied massive demonstrations and protests, forcing the Communist-run government to turn from its traditional methods of brutal police repression to open meetings, never intending that genuine dialogue be implemented by the authorities.

"The main role of the Party will remain," Günter Schabowski, East Berlin party chief and member of the East German Politburo declared at the outset of a public meeting with dissidents. "This is not open to discussion. This dialogue will take place within these confines. The leading role of the Communist Party is the only alternative to decaying capitalist society. But the leading role must be a genuine consensus between the party and the broad masses."

Given the rhetorical rigidities, the opposition openly pondered if the Communist party would ever give up its traditional undemocratic ways: fixed elections, privileges for party leaders, enforced military service, deploying provocateurs in demonstrations, travel restrictions, the use of mines and guns to blow up or shoot those trying to cross the Berlin Wall or swimming the Spree River.

Party logic focused its blind spot in the Politburo, which seemed unable to cope with demands of the popular uprising. Party leader "Krenz had no chance to be accepted until he dealt with the real burning issues," insisted the leader of the largest oppositional group, New Forum, demanding political change. "So far there is no change in structure. He could perhaps gain some credibility among the people if he convenes independent commissions to investigate the demonstrations and the elections. It is difficult to say concretely what Krenz must do, but he must do something to win back the trust of people. The demonstrations will continue until Krenz makes changes," he concluded of the party government's fall from legitimacy. "But it's very difficult to expect that they [the party leaders] can make a 180-degree turn. An entire change of leadership is needed to bring about reform."[3]

"The *Politburocrats* denounced the uprising of the people as a counter-revolution and wanted to repress it with violence, but in reality they were the counter-revolutionaries," Academy of Science member Professor Schumann told a special session of the Communist party Congress. Stalinism, he explained, linked to "Prussian-German authoritarian ways of thinking and doing things," was partly to blame. But as East German leaders themselves had had little choice in taking over administration of the Stalinist system, that system absorbed them, then took them over. The party held a monopoly on power, and absolute power corrupted absolutely. When members tried to object, they were punished, expelled from the party—7,000 until 1987, 11,000 in 1988, and 18,000 to October 1989.

The CP was fighting to make itself appear legitimate, to drop the hypocrisy that it was "the conscious and organized shock force of the working class." It hoped to change the image that its military units resembled the Nazi *Wehrmacht* with their military parades of goosestepping troops. It now portrayed itself as steering between stopping anarchy and preventing annexation by West Germany, which would change borders, weaken the Left, and encourage West German business takeovers of East German industry, land, and state structures.

"The German Democratic Republic is in the midst of an awakening," declared the Central Committee's prologue to its newly adopted November 1989 program. "A revolutionary people's movement has brought into motion a process of great change. The renewal of society is on the agenda."

The program included "free, democratic and secret elections," a "socialist planned economy oriented to market conditions," separation of party and state, parliamentary supervision of state security, freedom of assembly, and a new law on the press and broadcasting.[4] The revolution in the streets had forced their political hand.

The legal opening to many parties would also pit the CP's "Socialist Unity Party of Germany/Party of Democratic Socialism" against the "East German Christian Democratic Union," which was sworn to socialist goals, as well as against the "Democratic Awakening," advocating a free-market economy and against an alliance of the two mass opposition movements, "Democracy Now" and the "New Forum."[5]

STEMMING EMIGRATION

Still the great migration went on as East Germans flowed westward and the West German state allocated social-service budgets to aid them, engendering a dual crisis: a shutdown of essential production in the East, and an overburdened budget in the West. Both led to a political crisis, and each was resolved by calling for the same remedy: stem emigration.

With East Germans now guaranteed full West German benefits if they settled in the West, including pensions based on the work they did in the East, some 340,000 had arrived in 1989, along with an equal number of people of German descent from Eastern Europe and the Soviet Union, adding to West Germany's unemployment rolls and aggravating a severe shortage of low-income housing.

With the prospect of another 500,000 settlers in 1990, the premier of Saarland, Social Democrat Oskar La Fontaine, polished his bid for chancellor by calling for curbs on state benefits for immigrants to encourage them to stay home.

Not to be outdone, Chancellor Kohl declared in January 1990 that the priority was to stop this "loss of blood" of 1,000 East Germans a day that threatened to undermine the East German economy and overwhelm the West German social welfare system. "Stay home!" he told Germans seeking a unitary state. "Together we will get the country going again."[6]

As the 1990 daily exodus increased to 2,000 East Germans and continued to disrupt industrial production, it also reduced the marketing of goods to disappearing customers, led to more joblessness and a cycle of homelessness. Too few goods also fed inflation. Crisis impending, the way widened for the right-wing Republican party, still banned by the East German Parliament from participating in elections, to move to the streets, fighting bystanders, shouting "Sieg Heil!" "To hell with the Jews!" "Germany united Fatherland!"[7]

But the center parties did not react; the economically insecure looked westward; and only the Democratic Forum fought the right-wing skinheads in the streets.

THE AWAKENING

As the crisis deepened, it looked as if German partition were nearing an end in late 1989. "Europe, though Europeans did not always appreciate it, has been a haven of order these past 44 years," the *Economist* of London reflected on 10 November 1989. "For Eastern Europeans the price of that stability has been high: a lifetime wasted under a government you loathed. For West Europeans the stability has been marvelous. They could get rich, and start to build a new unity, within a clearly defined zone which ended at the river Elbe and the Bohemian forest."

The Communists still clung to the past, though. "If the border between both German states falls before a European unification," warned Communist chief Modrow, "then discussions about changing borders will start all over Europe. Peace would be seriously threatened."[8]

The warning was both too late and historically misplaced, for down came the wall the Communists built in Berlin. People chiseled it away, danced upon it, and there was no longer a reason to risk swimming the Spree to the West. For the East to stop the economic and political merger of the two German states now, there would have to be an alternative to West German solutions for the crisis in the East.

West German capital was meanwhile angling for economic annexation. "West Germany had the highest rate of savings in Western Europe," bragged Bonn consultant Ulrich Pfeiffer in December 1989. "We have enough capital to finance the reconstruction of the East German economy all by ourselves."

With talks following among dozens of West German firms and East German state enterprises to build joint ventures and enter other forms of contractual cooperation, East Germany held a political edge to open its western borders without consulting the Soviet Union, and West Germany pursued an economic plan to affiliate with the East, without informing the United States, Britain, or France as the Western Trilateral Powers holding peace treaty rights. The West's revanchist economic plan would come first.

"The catastrophic situation in our plants can only be cured by very high investment of capital from Western countries," foresaw Lothar de Maiziere, the new chairman of the East German Christian Democratic Union, at a party conference in December 1989.

As the party proceeded to drop a commitment to the socialism it had supported for forty years, the only answer to East German backwardness seemed to be the marketplace for capital, technology, and goods. "This isn't blackmail by Western monopolies. It's not a sell-out of the East German economy. It's just the logic of the market," de Maiziere explained, seeking "the most far-reaching adaptation and integration" of the economies of the two Germanys.

The path of market logic was being spun with a metaphysics the Communists had never known. "The Protestant Churches have worked very closely together for a long time, while recognizing each other's independence," new Communist party chief Gysi said. "Here is experience that could also be useful to others."

On this slender reed joyfully swung the West German Social Democratic party, which in its heyday of government power in the seventies had all but recognized East Germany as a separate state. Now its spokesman called for "conditions of peace in Europe in which the German people achieve unity in free self-determination." It thus called on the four World War II Allies—France, Britain, the United States, and the USSR—to give up rights over Berlin and all of Germany by signing a peace treaty with the two German states, separately or together.

"Unity is a question of time," said the timeless Willy Brandt, former Nazi opponent, German chancellor, and senior statesman for the Social Democrats.

Unification was also supported by "Democracy Now," although in stages in order to keep East German sovereignty intact. And the East German "Democratic Awakening" called for complete German disarmament to facilitate eventual German unity.[9]

Such politics and economic support were quick to merge as Chancellor Kohl announced a multibillion-mark package of assistance to East Germany. Tactically this offended both East German governing parties and opposition movements, which together sought economic cooperation in the frame of the soveriegnty and state identity of both Germanys.[10] But their quest was not to be.

SCENARIO OF UNIFICATION

East German democratization laid the groundwork for unification under capitalist West German political structures, financial power, and markets. The pressing 1989 reality of "human unity" between East Germans crossing the border to the West was undeniable, but beyond this, to speak of the reunification, confederation, or any other form of merger between the two Germanys was thought to "anticipate history unnecessarily," advised former chancellor Willy Brandt.[11]

Unification, though, was not simply a political gesture. Implications struck deep when Chancellor Kohl proposed a "confederative structure" joining the two Germanys, East German prime minister Hans Modrow retorting: "If we went on the path of Kohl's plan, we would end up as a 'homeland' of West Germany like the homelands for black tribes in South Africa. We would get all their pensioners and they would get all our young workers."

But Modrow was outmaneuvered and was to lose influence and power as Kohl's political machine poured West German finance into the East German political campaigns waged by Kohl's Christian Democratic Union and his liberal checkmate, the Social Democratic party, both undercutting Modrow's Communist-led interim cabinet, with its expanded membership of opposition groups in a self-described "government of national responsibility."

The cabinet losing control of the state, Prime Minister Modrow helplessly conceded defeat in Parliament: "East Germany is no longer governable except through broad responsibility." Broadly responsible, the opposition in the government also sped the moment of West German takeover by making the West deutschmark the standard currency of the emerging monetary union.[12]

It was now obvious there would be West German annexation of the East and eventually a capitalist GDR, but not necessarily neighbors or equals.

BIG-POWER DECISION MAKING

As the West German elections made clear, on 3 October 1990 Kohl became the first chancellor of a reunited Germany positioned to guide rapid economic consolidation and monetary stability. Yet East Germany was relatively undeveloped, so there could be neither economic equality nor universal social justice in the initial phases as a single nation.

West Germany taking the lead, all other nations were easily outmaneuvered. Britain, France, the United States, and the USSR, the Big Four postwar Allied authority, were now to deal with external security issues.

By secret negotiations unknown to East Germans, the United States and the Soviet Union followed the West German political prescriptions for unification on the condition that German discussions with the Big Four would deal with "issues of security of neighboring states," meaning Poland, Czechoslovakia, and the USSR itself.

The other European states were simply cut out of the decision. Save Poland, Eastern European states were not even consulted, and the Western NATO ministers were presented with a fait accompli. Questions of the text to cover the security of specific states neighboring Germany and in the rest of Europe were *not* included, and the requests by incensed Dutch, Italian, and Belgian ministers were rejected.[13]

"They were told in no uncertain terms that this was a matter for the Allied Powers with legal rights in Germany, and no one else," a U.S. administrative official said. "That is why the deal was cut this way, we told them; and if you don't like it, I'm sorry, but you have no legal rights."[14]

While Chancellor Kohl stumped East Germany calling for a common fatherland—one Germany, one people—during the first free election campaign since 1933, to take place 18 March 1990, Poland and the Soviet Union had second thoughts about German revanchism. Bronislaw Geremek, Solidarity's leader in the Polish Parliament, had been railing that "the only way to change the border along the Oder and Neisse rivers between Poland and Germany is war, and Germany knows it." Putting heavy pressure on Moscow, Geremek demanded that Poland be allowed to take part in talks to be held by the two Germanys and the four postwar Allied powers, about *both* German reunification and the security of Europe.[15]

Gorbachev then became conciliator, trying to assure Russians and Poles that German unity was based on years of agreements, that Poland would be included in the evolving formula for German reunification, that a united Germany would *not* be part of NATO.[16] "We rule out an approach when three or four nations will initially arrange things and then tell the other participants the already agreed upon position," Gorbachev insisted. "This is unacceptable."

Gorbachev himself was to instruct his foreign minister to violate this promise.[17] But nonetheless, his grand design was disarmament and the elimination of military blocs. "The process of German unification is organically linked and must be synchronized with the general European process," he explained, "with its core—the formation of a fundamentally new structure of European security which will replace the one based on blocs."

Ultimately, Gorbachev hoped, an "international legal act" would guarantee borders, peace, trust and cooperation. He proposed that by 1995–96, all troops would be recalled within their respective national boundaries, and that by 2000, all foreign military bases would be eliminated.[18]

So as Europe itself was more tightly linked, West German revanche was momentarily to be forgotten and a single German state emerged, with fears yet uncertain consequences for the rest of Europe.[19]

Chapter 9
Poland's Democratic Step

We want democracy and civil liberties. We have no capital and therefore are not capitalists, but want to encourage foreign invest- ment to employ our unemployed at good wages and thereby build a domestic consumer market to meet people's needs.
— Lech Walesa, Solidarity spokesman

They want debt forgiveness. That is their position, and they just won't move off it. But we aren't a government. We have to write off our bad loans. Then our stockholders start screaming. The Poles have yet to grasp how Western banking works or what write- offs mean for creditworthiness. Simply put, we loan you money and you don't pay it back, you never see another damn cent from our bank. That's just how it is.
— Director of Eastern European operations for one of Germany's biggest banks, February 1992

As we know from history, the sequence has always been dif- ferent. Capitalism first, mass democracy second. We're trying to combine mass democracy and capitalism, and it's never been done.
— Former Finance Minister Leszek Balcerowicz, 1992

Solidarity leader Lech Walesa commanded a mass following in the early nineties yet faced an economic crisis requiring massive infusions of Western investments, aid and goods.[1] Such resources were not available simply for the asking, however. The Western infusion of capital had barely begun, so by the early nineties, Eastern European nations were savagely competing against one another for too little available capital and aid.

POLAND'S IMMEDIATE NEEDS

Prime Minister Tadeusz Mazowiecki had prepared the nation to meet Western requirements in 1990, calling for the population to negotiate "landmark changes unique in history." Poland, he said, would have to leave behind its outmoded system, "based on 19th century doctrines and embrace one based on market mechanisms." Under the auspices of auster- ity, added Finance Minister Balcerowicz, "skills, knowledge, able hands, talent and willingness to work all count." Together they called for the swift implementation of a new program to shore up the "catastrophic" state of the economy.

Economic Plague

With crisis at hand, Poland had experienced a severe drop in 1989 production, massive unemployment, homelessness, a sharp increase in the crime rate, and 900 percent inflation. This economic plague demanded a social cure, but seeking foreign aid to correct these failings meant bowing supinely to those demanding classical "austerity"— withdrawal of subsidies to state enterprises, effectively driving the weakest out of production, hence more unemployment in inefficient industries; control of inflation by cutting consumption, yet removing regulations on price levels to reflect real production costs, again forcing out enterprises with above-average expenses.

By these standards, the International Monetary Fund demanded a heavy price for their loans of some $3.9 to $4.2 billion and the rescheduling of Poland's $40 billion in foreign debts.

By meeting these conditions, though, no revolutionary government could have long held power. Nonetheless, Solidarity tried, driving a hard bargain—and a wedge into the hearts of its supporters—ensuring its future transformation or downfall.

TAKING POWER TOO SOON

Since they took power too soon, the political deck was stacked against Solidarity idealists. Not only did they lack experience in the methods of bureaucratic administration, but they lacked knowledge of the entrapment that awaited those reliant on conditioned foreign loans.

They were soon to find that great popular sacrifices accompany such foreign-imposed requirements. With Solidarity performing the motions of government rather than those of an opposition movement, they initiated a legislative program designed to break the old socialist state monopolies, cut government subsidies of all kinds, and transform government enterprises into private ones. Now Solidarity could award only limited social programs from the mighty helm of state, its government program,* demanding

• the immediate balance of the deficit-ridden budget through strict "austerity," thereby cutting off most state subsidies to state enter-

---

This program was largely designed by economist Jeffrey Sachs, Economics Department, Harvard University, 1989–90. The reader can judge its effectiveness.

prises and other institutions (including the increasingly unpopular Communist party);
• unregulated price increases as the market allowed, but limited wage increases imposed by employers;
• an end to state monopolies run by managerial apparat and bureaucrats, beginning with the orderly sale of state properties to the prviate sector;
• immediate turn of the zloty into a currency convertible with the world's hard currencies, ensuring its lessened domestic worth and devaluation in international exchange markets;
• cuts in subsidies for goods and services, running at about 31 percent of (1988) public spending to some 14 percent (1992), in order to maintain at a lower level those living in government housing, using public transportation, and receiving subsidies for coal, bread, low-fat milk and cheese.

It was a fine program for isolated budget analysts and bloodless foreign leaders, but not one that dealt with the grinding reality of daily living conditions. The expected results would be real income cuts of up to 20 percent in the early nineties, a 25 to 30 percent drop in industrial output, some 400,000 to 1.25 million jobless, a 4 to 18 percent fall in gross national product—but immediate price increases of 25 to 50 percent each month in the early stage for some products as enterprises lost their subsidies and raised prices to survive. Although the figures were forever changing, 500 to 1,000 percent inflation a year was expected in the short term.

Only the neediest—retirees, the disabled, low-income families and displaced workers—would be helped with inflation-indexed aid, so "nobody should feel his existence is endangered," Finance Minister Balcerowicz blithely assured. But no one was soothed into belief, and the nobodies making up the great majority of Polish citizens feared the worst to come.

Nobodies and the Status Quo

Although the Communists had lost control of the Polish Parliament to the forces of the Solidarity movement, they maneuvered to take charge of the economy. Acting as the middle agents between producers and consumers, they presumed that such a rearguard defense would award them revenues and keep them in effective control over the Polish population. One day, when living standards had been widely decimated, they thought the population would ask them to take charge again.

The small, private, economically vulnerable farmers were a potential constituency for both the Solidarity government and the Communist opposition. As a large group of political "nobodies," each with only a few acres, these farmers made up 75 percent of Poland's agriculture. To improve their own condition by bringing more produce to market, they sought to raise their per-acre output to above the traditional 50 percent of that in Western Europe.

Yet having lived relatively well on the government dole of fixed farm prices ensuring profits for the most inefficient, they had opposed the government's 1988 measures forcing them to sell their output to the Communist-dominated food and processing cooperatives that acted as monopsonistic buyers at set prices and monopolistic sellers in the urban domain. The small farmers reasoned that their selling prices would thereby be lowered while the middle-agent Communist food and processing cooperatives would secure the profit by forcing food prices upward — 1,000 percent by the closing months of 1989!

Why had they, the small farmers, not reaped the benefit of this surge in prices? Small farmers thus sought yesterday's relations with the state, demanding the status quo that guaranteed minimum prices rather than risk the free market that would throw them into the hands of the Communist-controlled food distribution system.

Could the Solidarity Parliament and cabinet protect them when their costs were rising and prices of produce — paid by the profit-absorbing intermediaries — were sinking? Agricultural Minister Czeslaw Tanicki said the government could help by intervening in the market as buyer if farm prices fell too low, curbing the food-processing monopolies and increasing the distribution of farm marchinery, fertilizer, and other agricultural supplies to improve production in the countryside.

But the rural members of Parliament wanted direct state intervention, guaranteeing prices and government farming investments. With Solidarity running the failing free-market agricultural policy, moreover, the government became the Communists' scapegoat, turning the rural half of the population against it. "Farmers' incomes are going to be left without any protection," argued Communist deputy Ryszard Smolarek for maintaining minimum guaranteed prices. "Opinions are getting more and more radical in the countryside," reaffirmed Deputy Jacek Szymaderski, calling for greater state intervention in agricultural development.[2]

The farmers might openly turn against the Solidarity government at any moment.

Offsetting the Decapitalization Process

Other potential opponents hurt by Solidarity hovered in the wings of Parliament. Decapitalized by the central Government's plan in the past, both farming and industry required new infusions of capital to keep the population at work earning an adequate income to maintain living standards. But as new investments were not forthcoming, the population worked neither at full tilt nor efficiently. The nation was disaccumulating capital, consuming the proverbial "seed corn" that would be the basis of next year's production and harvest.

"The Polish system has been eating up people who have tried to build something," Jan Bednarek, one engineer venture capitalist, complained of the centralized planning straitjacket he hoped to untie. His became a success story of recapitalizing an entire city of 70,000 people, Tomaszow Mazowiecki, questioning if the same could be done nationwide in a socialist framework.

His methods were decidedly capitalist, however, for he took the earnings of an old state-owned textile company, Wistom; shifted people from this overstaffed factory; pledged start-up money for new enterprises they initiated; guaranteed these enterprises a partial market by selling to "Wistom"; and picked key industrial products, including factory automation and industrial processing equipment, to sell in a wider domestic market.

Bednarek's goal was to maintain the town's employment level, to switch to nonpolluting production in high tech, to guide the excess work force into new enterprises humanely without state wage controls; and to ensure that the workers would ultimately own the factories and tools they worked with.[3]

The rest of the nation would require like employment by the infusion of new capital, either self-created or borrowed.

Something Borrowed, Something Blue

There were two aspects of borrowing great sums of foreign capital, though: ending old controls and imposing new ones. To unravel forty-five years of authoritarian controls, the Solidarity government needed hard currency to buy adequate food supplies, technology, and manufactured goods — to guarantee against reckless monetary policies and assure workers that their wages would neither erode in value nor be useless to buy newly available goods.

The old Communist regime had already submerged the nation in a foreign debt that it could not repay. Western financial lenders were suffering a corresponding loss as the market value placed on Polish bank debt plummeted from 38 cents to the dollar in 1989 to 19 cents by 4 January 1990, with expectations that the new Solidarity government would do more to feed the people and devote fewer resources to paying the debt.

Initially the Solidarity government had moved to slash interest payments on bank loans, thus devastating prices placed on the loans in the secondary market. So though the previous Polish government had paid its interest on bank debt in full to the "Club of London" until October 1989, it had not met all its obligations to other lending governments and international institutions known as the "Club of Paris."

The British bankers, always cautious, recognized that their Club of

London's private banks were losing some capital and that Western tax-payers, backing the Club of Paris, were losing their shirts. Promises to pay were justifiably disbelieved by global bankers. "The market is anticipating more debt service interruptions from Poland, followed by Western government pressure on commercial banks to offer substantial debt relief," said a Shearson Lehman analyst. "Banks are reluctant to be holders of Polish debt when these concessions are required. Therefore, they have begun to dump it."

The buyers of this discounted defaulted debt were largely Austrian and West German banks, coalescing as a new financial *Anschluss*. If the Poles defaulted, U.S. banks with a third to half of the outstanding loans would be heavy sellers to the Austro-Germans, offsetting the losses suffered against bank reserves already set up.

German-Austrian inroads were also more likely as Poland was caught in a web of making political decisions not to pay the Western banks, imposing austerity on its citizens, yet seeking ultimately to improve living standards through increasing finance by the West.[4]

Hat-in-Hand Borrowing

With the Solidarity government in place by early 1990, new foreign borrowing was thus sought on stringent terms. Lech Walesa went to the United States to whip up congressional and private support for an infusion of new loans and capital. The U.S. and Polish visions were almost eye-to-eye, for trade unionist Walesa spoke of Poland's need for a working economy, with America investing money in a democratic nation to, Walesa said, "make business deals of the century."[5]

With a bumpy political terrain ahead, Walesa addressed a joint meeting of Congress:

> [O]n our path there looms a serious obstacle, a grave danger. Our long subjection to a political system incompatible with national traditions, to a system incompatible with rationality and common sense, coupled with the stifling of independent thought and disregard of national interests. All this has led the Polish economy to ruin, to the verge of utter collapse. The first government in fifty years elected by the people and serving the people has inherited from the previous rulers of the country a burden of tremendous debts they incurred and subsequently wasted, of an economy organized in a manner preventing it from satisfying even the basic needs of the people.

Then came Walesa's fiery pitch for Western aid:

> Stalin forbade Poland to use aid provided by the Marshall Plan, the aid that was used by everyone in Western Europe, including countries that lost the war. It is worth recalling this great American plan, which helped

Western Europe protect its freedom and peaceful order. And now it is the moment when Eastern Europe awaits an investment of this kind – an investment in freedom, democracy and peace – an investment adequate to the greatness of the American nation.

The economy we inherited after more than five decades of Communist rule is in need of a thorough overhaul. This will require time and means. . . . Today all the countries of the Eastern bloc are bankrupt. The Communist economy has failed in every part of the world.[6]

Hard Currency Borrowed

With hard currency borrowed, however, came new regimentation by the twenty-four nations making the International Monetary Fund loans. "The muscular economic package announced this week by Poland's Finance Minister is designed to stamp out rapid inflation," said *The New York Times.* "It may, instead, stamp out the Solidarity-led Government. The Plan boldly seeks to create a market economy nearly overnight. But along the way, prices will temporarily soar and hundreds of thousands of Polish workers may lose their current jobs."[7]

Would Solidarity's government now waiver? The government plan for "austerity" ensured inflation, unemployment, and downward social mobility for almost the entire working population. The litany of evils might include a million jobless, an expected reduction of real earnings from 20 to 40 percent, hence new rounds of protest, possibly government restoration of some subsidies, certain political changes, either to the left of Solidarity or to the right-leaning, Communist populists demanding a less stringent program.[8]

The only solution seemed to be building new factories that would offer jobs to the unemployed, getting private Western capital to take advantage of 50-cents-an-hour wage rates for production not too far from the distribution centers of Europe. Promises of low wages would more than offset lower production volume per worker – the use of more labor that was neither well-disciplined nor self-motivated.[9]

Hanging Time in the Balance

Time now hung in the balance: Would austerity be accepted by the supporters of the Solidarity government, or would the populace turn from office the preachers of new relations of work, community, and distribution?

The ossified order of the past would undergo a crash economic program, yet such strong medicine might kill the patient, requiring the doctor to water down the cure before recovery was complete. "We elected these people, they chose experts to develop these policies, and we have to trust them" was one early expression of belief of the faithful at work. "It would be wrong to go on strike against a plan put together by a government that we elected."

Yet in the struggle to survive, not everyone was so inclined. Expecting prices to soar, people stripped store shelves of chicken, Kielbasa beer, and other essentials of seeming luxury. People rushed to spend all their wages and more, so no savings remained. Savant foreign consultants then infused added apprehension, technicians calling for work layoffs, 40 percent in some cases.

A Catholic people, many Poles felt only faith in God would somehow get them through hard moments in the march toward an uncertain future.[10]

Farmers and workers who created Solidarity and supported its early economic programs now questioned their faith. As far as they were concerned, this was no time to cut state subsidies, end price controls on consumer goods, stop wage increments, lower living standards, bankrupt enterprises, and create more unemployment. There was no social safety net large enough or brimming with sufficient subsidies and protections to care for them. If workers went on strike, the entire program would collapse; if they went along but required substantial state subsidies, they might keep jobs and maintain incomes regardless of how often they appeared on the job or how hard they worked.[11]

CREDITS AND COMMUNISTS

Poland was soon to double-cross foreign creditors, Germany to begin economic revanchism, and the Communists to level criticism at the Solidarity government. The Government had allowed Polish companies to exchange their zlotys for state-borrowed foreign dollars to buy capital equipment abroad. As Polish industrial capital was effectively upgraded at the expense of its foreign financial creditors, this scheme led to a plummeting market value of Poland's outstanding loans rather than bolstering Poland's credit rating. And this enticed German investing revanchists to buy portions of the discounted Polish foreign debt, sharpening Communist criticisms of the Solidarity giveaway!

The initial critique of the Communist-controlled Trade Union Federation (OPZZ) also spoke to labor's living standards. "We cannot agree to the policy of free prices and of frozen incomes of working people [that would lead] to further impoverishment of a considerable part of society," OPZZ railed, arguing that a comprehensive system of social protection was being replaced by a free market "in which the stronger win and only charity is left for the weaker."[12]

Hard work, less consumption, more unemployment, halfhearted state benefits—these were the components of the state program and widespread disaffection. From 1 to 4 million might be jobless, with no rights to future work or security, as the Polish legislature moved to allow enterprises to lay off workers unconnected to basic production. Bankruptcies pushed up joblessness too. And unemployment insurance that kept former workers 70 percent alive was based on the percentage of their most recent wages for three months—50 percent for bed and bread in the following six months without work, 40 percent thereafter. They could starve increasingly faster as time progressed, waiting in the unemployment lines.

In the round-robin system of employers laying off the most costly workers, then other employers rehiring them more cheaply on their willingness to accept a speedup, there would be only momentary benefits available at the unemployment office. Candidates had to prove that jobs seemingly offered them were nonexistent. They could not turn down twice-offered tasks appropriate to their skills; but if they entered job-training programs, they would receive their old salary level. Yet the deeper logic was that the employers running the ever-cheapened labor auction could review those layed off by skill level and potential fortitude.

"Now we can take our pick, while before we had to take whatever came in the door," reported a pleased hiring official at the state car manufacturer FSO. "Now I am getting skilled men who really want to work. Before we got the dregs of society."

The Catch-22 of Work and Welfare

The "Catch-22" was that the so-called dregs would go on state welfare, the Solidarity government's safety net. Some who couldn't find work were not that, of course. Special state provisions were made for men over 60 and women over 55 who were laid off and program-designated to receive 75 percent of their last wages until normal retirement age of 65 for men and 60 for women.

The other half of the package was already known: There would be too few jobs, so new "capital formation" was encouraged by state subsidies that might better have been *directly invested* in current production to employ the jobless.

The way the program functioned was that the government effectively made two promises: first to lend, second to subsidize, both leading to tremendous potential losses and fraudulent enterprises. The first promise was state lending to employers if they guaranteed to use the funds to hire jobless workers. If the company kept the worker for twenty-four months, the government would then cancel 50 percent of the loan. But thereafter the worker could be fired, and the employer could start the same process again, using the new state loans to pay off the debt outstanding, every repayment of loans effectively putting off any outlay from internally generated capital.

Because such loans could amount to 1.5 times the unemployed person's former annual income, the loan sum allowed the employer to pay the salary for 1.5 years; then pay from capital for a half year; next lay off the worker; hire a new worker, getting a 1.5-year salary loan; and pay off the first debt (for 1.5 years' salary times one-half the original loan outstanding, equal to three-fourths of a year's salary) and have one-fourth of a year's salary left over![13]

The No-Job, Price-Rise Squeeze

The second government program was subsidization of new capital formation, itself dependent on austerity at popular expense. Skating on the cracking ice of joblessness, the government pursued a policy of supply-demand, pushing higher prices to elicit hidden surplus goods, more production, greater investment, and employment.

Closing unprofitable factories and enlarging unemployment in one locale were to be offset by profitable production and more jobs in another. And by early March 1990, the hidden surpluses of food had hit the market: Fresh meat, sausages, butter, sugar, coffee, and exotic fruits were being brought to market by farmers, merchants, and other middlemen buying cheaply in bulk in Poland and wholesale in West Germany, selling at markup yet often below the prices charged in government stores.

By elevating prices, the government also drew out personal savings, devaluing the zloty to 9,500 to the U.S. dollar. Those who had kept dollars hidden suddenly brought some of the $3 to $6 billion to the market, and prices in zlotys scaled skyward to pay for more imported goods. This ironically leveled prices as a barrier below the stabilized zloty-dollar value, establishing a so-called "demand barrier" that might even lever prices down.

But once these savings were gone, the only source of funds would be employment or government subsidies under the safety net. For the old state subsidies to enterprises had now evaporated, so plants that closed and fire workers would have to cut national income perhaps by one-third. Momentary downward mobility could be offset only by activating new production, employment, and wage-spending for goods.[14]

To accomplish this, it would only be a matter of time until new State subsidies would be offered.

All Is Not Well in Paradise

As the squeeze on real incomes surfaced, though, property crimes became a way for many to survive, punctuated by increased break-ins for basic foods like flour and sugar. A sharp surge in crimes in November 1989 came shortly after the government had removed price controls on goods. Home burglaries moved up to 171,156 in 1989 from 103,769 in 1988, a 65 percent rise, while store break-ins rose 30.43 percent to 47,452. There was also an epidemic of battery and car radio thefts, partly because Communist central planners left the nation with a shortage of spare parts and post–Communist authorities lacked enforcement mechanisms.

The Solidarity government had reorganized the police from riot and security forces to civil patrols. But the lessened fear of the state's security apparatus led to a rise in criminal activities and victim complaints. For now economic upheaval and disparities in employment and income could not be controlled by police who were unprepared to fight crime, leaving citizens to protect their own homes and cars with burglar alarms, better locks, and bars.[15]

SUCCESS AT A PRICE

Looking back to the 1 January 1990 initiation of state shock therapy under the Solidarity reformers, Communist methods were jettisoned and new experiments in cutting subsidies and budgets tried at the price of unemployment, reduced living standards, crime escalation, and incurable anger — and Polish jokes about plenty of worthless money, a plethora of excellent goods no one could afford to buy, and everything to lose but one's obligations.

By the close of 1990, the Solidarity government had changed its leadership from Prime Minister Tadeusz Mazowiecki to Lech Walesa by a national election; moved from a foundering state sector in favor of fast-growing private production; gone from a deficit to a hard-currency trade surplus of $2 billion; and lowered the 50 percent monthly inflation rate under the Communist government to 4.5 percent.

But there were now more than 1 million unemployed, 5 out of every 100 workers; industrial production was down 20 to 30 percent, returning to 1975 levels; and a groundswell of uneasy protest issued from consumers throughout the nation.

The shift to the market system that produced unemployment, wage controls, recession, and too little money to buy high-priced goods also produced an unsalable surplus of high-priced food and other items in over-stocked stores. The conversion of Polish zloty to ratios of hard currency meanwhile meant that higher prices for oil and other imports payable in dollars could not be paid, so there was a sharp drop in debts for trade with the Soviet Union as well as with East Germany, then going through its own fall in production, employment, and regional trade.

Yet at the start of 1991, Prime Minister Walesa was promising a new era of prosperity to be earned by the sweat of people under his personalized state authority. Millions of Poles recalled that benevolent authoritarian leaders of the past had not always done as promised; again the future of the Solidarity government could not be viewed with equanimity.

1991–92 Plans Gone Awry

The economic policies initiated in January 1990 had gone bust by March 1992. Government-owned industrial output had been devastated, sending unemployment to 10–15 percent. Inflation had been 70 percent in 1991. Large foreign investors still hesitated to locate in a Poland lacking infrastructure, tranquility, and a viable consumer market. Foreign commercial bankers railed that Poland had suspended interest payments on its private debt in 1990; that it wanted private debt forgiveness; that its total private debt was $22.9 billion; that alone it owed German banks $11.5 billion; that without restarting interest service and repayments on old loans, no new commercial loans would be made; that Western investors should bypass Poland and look to Hungary and Czechoslovakia.

True, the nation had cut costly imports; Germany had cancelled half of $5.5 billion debt owed by the government; the United States canceled 70 percent of the $3.67 billion owed; other members of the sixteen-nation Club of Paris began waiving approximately $11.2 billion under the tentative IMF plan conditioned on its approval of Poland's economic program; and the nation had been stripped of its foreign currency reserves, reducing its $46 billion international debt by 50 percent by February 1992. But popular discontent was nearly universal and might worsen or explode if the International Monetary Fund permanently suspended its loan agreement with Poland on the basis of its criticism that IMF targets were not met for controlling inflation and government-imposed budgetary austerity by cutting subsidies and social services.

Pacifying the public, the new government taking office 23 December 1991 under Prime Minister Jan Olszewski was a compromise lacking a working majority in Parliament, yet incorrigible to Western-imposed solutions, pledging to review the disaster-ridden economic policies of the previous two governments, calling for a speedup of privatization, increased government spending on services and credit for industry, guaranteed minimum prices for farmers, loosened wage restrictions at state-run companies involved in exports, and a gradual expansion of the money supply to finance government programs encouraging investment and exports—all this despite the obvious risk of a new round of inflation. "The channeling of more money in real terms to State run enterprises boils down to opening the gate for potentially strong inflationary pressure," said resigning Finance Minister Karol Lutkowski.

Prime Minister Olszewski was nonplussed, his focal point being the march away from state-owned companies by privatizing more than three-quarters of industrial production still employing more than 11 million people among Poland's 38 million. En masse bankruptcy of these enterprises was unacceptable, the prime minister said, leaving it up to Poland's still–Communist-dominated banks to lend money to economically viable firms. Yet reforming the banks by ousting former Communists was still incomplete in March 1992, Parliament rejecting President Lech Walesa's choice to replace the previous director, who was arrested.

No government program could overcome the 1991-elected parliamentary bloc opposing the government's reform plan either, and the public withdrew its support for rapid privatization, fearing government predictions that the early 1992 11 percent unemployment rate would reach 17 to 19 percent by the end of 1992. With the center-left wing of Solidarity represented by the Democratic Union party holding 14 percent of the seats and the swing vote in Parliament, moreover, budgetary funding for state enterprises would be limited, forcing these firms to move toward potential profitability.

Prime Minister Olszewski backed down only halfway, still trying to rescue some state-run companies and aiding farmers by deficit financing that with other costs would put the 1992 government budget in the red by $4.5 billion — about 5 percent of the state budget, a plan that the IMF was pressured to "approve with disgust," the prime minister said after paring his original $9-billion deficit plan.

Even without sufficient government subsidies, moreover, rehabilitation of Polish industry might become possible if, as President Lech Walesa told the Council of Europe, Western Europe stopped flooding the Polish market with goods while keeping their own markets closed and failing to invest in Polish production.

Clouds of Social Conflict

In the wake of layoffs, planned closing of unproductive coal mines and the sale of state-run industries to foreign investors, anxiety on questions of unemployment and the fear of exploitation by foreign investors accompanied heated exchanges over the not so distant future — impending social unrest, possibly strikes, even some form of authoritarian rule.

The core issue of full employment of 60 percent of the work force remained in the hands of the government — either to privatize or retain more than 8,000 state-run enterprises. To print money to subsidize state-sector companies, particularly those dependent on the collapsed Soviet market or on arms production, could keep workers employed and maintain their backing as part of the Solidarity movement, but such measures would run counter to IMF conditions for assistance as well as the repayment demands of foreign commercial lenders. Yet to overhaul inefficient, drastically technologically outmoded giant state factories required the government to generate vast sums of capital, either domestic or foreign. But as there were too few domestic resources, foreign capital seemed the only option.

In February 1992, General Motors Europe had agreed to a $75-million joint venture in Poland, creating a separate company in partnership with heavily indebted state-owned FSO, Poland's main manufacturer of midsized cars, FSO to provide land, buildings, and 1,000 of its 19,000 skilled auto workers. The government estimating that $1.5 billion worth of foreign cars were sold in Poland in 1991, GM Europe's president Robert J. Eaton said that the expected expansion of the Polish car market could lead to a three-labor-shift output of 35,000 cars annually, bringing the GM investment up to $300 million.

"The entrance of such an important company in our market makes Poland more credible in the world and is a very significant step on the road to negotiations with other foreign investors," offered Poland's minister of industry Andrzej Lipko.

Other foreign investors were still hesitant to invest millions that might be lost yet might soon follow the GM logic of deserting high-cost production in the West (that had led to a 1991 $4.45 billion loss) for lower-cost output near potential customers in Eastern and Western Europe. GM's strategic plan to operate companies where cars were sold would rely on Poland's parts makers and would help FSO redeploy its 18,000 workers to develop a replacement for inefficiently produced, shoddily worked 80,000 Polonezes each year.

Competition in the Polish car market had already begun, GM's Opel Astras to compete with the production of a subcompact for sale in Poland and Western Europe by a consortium of Poland's FSM and Italy's Fiat. German Volkswagen was also discussing a deal to make commercial vehicles in Poland. And although GM was to benefit from a portion of the 30,000 cars Poland imported duty-free from the European Community, France objected to plans to divide this quota equally among Fiat, GM, and Volkswagen.

Still the pace of foreign investments was too slow to employ sufficient Poles at high enough wages to raise living standards and too fast for workers and fervid nationalists who feared the destruction of state-held industries and foreign takeover.

Trapped

President Walesa was now trapped by the coalition government that he had opposed from its inception. Looser money and more help for the near-bankrupt state sector was the victory platform of candidates in the 1991 parliamentary elections. Walesa himself opposed the shutdown of unprofitable factories or coal mines, since these foci of employment were the only security blanket left for the working class, which Walesa and the government had failed to persuade to support the nation's pioneering economic program.

With the state budget too frail to support subsidies for failing enterprises and factory workers demanding that the government keep industry running, Walesa pointed out the absurdity of a democracy that might have rectified a failing socialism. "Only now, working people have rights and are free to proceed as they want," he said. "Therefore the full victory of Lenin has been achieved by us. In the moment when the proletariat finally feels they are proletariat, we propose to them capitalism." They protest government shutdowns of state industries, Walesa continued, "and we will not shoot."[16]

"Our own people are not getting the feeling that they are better off," Walesa told the Council of Europe, comparing Poland's Solidarity government with that of the ousted Communists. "The fruits of victory have turned sour. Already, one can hear some people wondering why we have even done it. Democracy is losing its supporters. Some people say, 'All right, let's go back to authoritarian rule.'"

Poland thus suffered under impending clouds of social conflict despite Walesa's earlier vision of a silver lining of available technology, mass production, full employment, low-priced bread, milk, and other basics as well as luxuries unknown in the past.

To realize this future, Poland would have to become a viable worker-run production state, perhaps neither socialist nor capitalist, guided by a coalition government designed to meet popular needs and vibrantly trading with both East and West. Thereby, one day the foreign debt might be repaid and Poland made economically free.

Section C:
The Outer Reach

The inner reach of a unified Germany linking Poland and Czechoslovakia to its commerce and providing a transit point to Western continental markets left the other liberated Eastern states relatively more isolated geographically and more desperate to establish links with the West to replace their old patterns of now-tenuous investments and trade:

- Hungary with Russia for oil, gas, other raw materials, and manufactures, and with those Western nations willing to take its best grades of shoes, buses, and other public transport vehicles;
- Yugoslavia with its six republics and two autonomous regions, and with Austria and southeastern Europe for markets;
- Bulgaria with the Soviet Union and Middle East for oil and gas; nations on its northern, western and southern doorstep for its agricultural goods; and assorted Western trading nations concentrating on its source of cheap labor, high skill, and nearness to regional markets;
- Romania with Iran and the Soviet Union for oil and gas, and with France, the rest of Western Europe, and the United States for manufactures.

Though these states in the outer reach were at a comparative disadvantage after their liberation in the late eighties and early nineties, nonetheless the future held great possibilities for their industrialization of land and factory, self-sufficiency and marketing, beyond their borders.

There were dangers that might impinge on their new freedom and self-determination too, for Western investors and traders operated by competitive market standards that these nations (save Romania to a degree) would quickly have to learn to secure their interests and protect their populations. Unregulated market dealing also promised to place units of monetary value on investments, labor, goods, and services, fostering the reemergence of social classes, polarizing access to wealth and poverty, and diversifying the human condition, degrading some, elevating others.

Chapter 10
Thumbnail Sketch in the Outer Reach

As the front of Eastern European communism was being transformed without Soviet influence or military strength, the United States, Britain, and the Western Continent sought to use NATO, debt relations, and other economic ties to draw central Europe into its sphere of influence and maintain this region as a future wedge to bring the former Soviet system into the democratic and market frame of the West, eliminating future expansion or military ambitions.

German unification became the focal point, to be parlayed by drawing Poland and Czechoslovakia into Western commercial ties. This would be followed by further indebting Hungary, watching Yugoslavia partition itself into six or more nation-states, and keeping Romania and Bulgaria on the new economic map drafted in the West.

More than simply a replay of the West's *cordon sanitaire* against spreading Bolshevik revolution after World War I or the Soviet's rigid Stalinism in Eastern Europe after World War II, a pan–European production and commercial zone of democratic independent states and republics was envisioned. Yet the question of underlying dependence remained, for Eastern Europe was deeply in debt to the West, its technological base and workers' skills were in desperate need of upgrading, and it held little experience in competitive world markets.

HUNGARY'S TRANSITION: FOREIGN DEBT, GOVERNMENT INTRANSIGENCE, AND POPULAR NEED

> People are growing impatient. They worry that this reform process is going to go on forever.
> —Former Hungarian finance minister Ferenc Rabar

Party leader Janos Kadar set the nation's economic chariot in motion, but could not stop it from severing his Achilles heel.[1]

Since 1968, the Communists had repeatedly tried disjointed schemes to improve economic conditions, but their central planning usually succeeded in making them worse. And Kadar's government was no better,

222

attempting an opening to the West for trade that ended in a $20-billion debt, an obligation that the lame-duck Communist government of 1989 could not repay, then had to put off by new obedience to strictures set by the International Monetary Fund (IMF).

For an added loan of $1 billion to carry current debt service and other outlays, the IMF had flexed its muscle, enforcing austerity that cut not only budgets but heartstrings. For the Fund's medicine of a 7 percent budget cut reduced government housing subsidies, raised consumer prices, eliminated fifty important though inefficient state-run companies, wiped out 100,000 jobs, and set forth a "debate" in Parliament about the precise measures to implement the program best.

In this grand drama of slavish legislative minutiae, the nation became both the first East European state to step toward a market economy and the last to enter the road to an alternative way of life.

First and Last on the Road to Liberation

By such steps, Hungary became Eastern Europe's showcase of a Communist government turning state companies into private ones, attracting Western investments, solidifying Continental commercial links, and creating a viable stock exchange.

Hungary was first in part because its Communist-run Parliament was flexible enough to sidestep an uprising in the face of a powerful opposition movement. It was last because its resources were not particularly needed in the West, so its internal transformation remained only partial and incomplete while its population was polarized into rich and poor.

Securing the future, the Communists had held on to political power by shadow-boxing with Western lenders and traders. For these goals they had

- changed their name to Socialist to win a public following;
- used secret negotiations with other political groups to outflank the liberal opposition Alliance of Free Democrats, thereby keeping the Communists in parliamentary power; and
- planned for a transition, soliciting Western trade and investments, preventing public participation in street demonstrations, and multiplying the political barriers put in the way of others by the single-party state.

The scheme did not go as planned, though. A 1990 referendum nominally offered Hungarians the first "free vote" in more than 40 years of Communist rule. But the people rejected this carefully crafted party plan for a one-month presidential election favoring the CP candidate Imre Pozsgay, who had hoped to secure a place in any new political order for members of the old.

And eventually a center-right coalition government was elected to office. Still, the technocrats were uneasy with government inaction, which included refusing to take painful measures removing price controls and devaluing the currency to make it fully convertible with those of the West, thus blocking or slowing the purchase of Continental and Anglo-Saxon technical equipment, machine components, computers, and consumer goods.

Letting Government Take the Blame

The left opposition was calculating, content to leave the center-right government and its supportive coalition Communists to make the shift to a free-market system, knowing it would necessarily undermine living standards, fuel raking criticism, and possibly set the stage for a second revolution and the opposition's taking power.

But the center-right coalition understood it was caught between the potential revolution from below and the left-wing parties waiting in the wings. "This Government," calculated Laszlo Lang, the director of the Budapest-based Central European Research Center, "does not like to take painful steps."

As Far Back as Their Grandfathers

To proceed with plans to privatize property and enterprises owned by the state, the government moved to compensate those unjustly deprived of their assets in the past. But in debating compensation for those stripped of their assets, Parliament was forced to pick a point in Hungary's painful history to account for these past injustices.

The Hungarian government set 8 June 1949, the day the first Communist government convened in Hungary, after much of the economy had already been nationalized. Opposition parties, surviving Jews, and ethnic Germans objected as earlier victims of the Hungarian state. For excluded were the 420,000 Jews ravished in Nazi concentration camps and their 337,000 properties turned over to the state after the war. Also excluded were the 200,000 remaining ethnic Germans of the 550,000 who lost their properties after the war, estimates of their expropriation covering 980,000 acres and 60,000 homes. Excluded too were small landholders who wanted the return of their agricultural land to secure their vesting under the 1945 land reform law, which was effectively abrogated during collectivization in the fifties, backing the Smallholders party as a condition of their continued support for the unstable parliamentary coalition.

Although legislation would provide compensation in the form of shares of state property, without guarantee of recovering their property, slated for recovery were an estimated 987 million acres, 3,970 small factories, and 400,000 dwellings and shops. The government's estimate of the cost of compensation hovered around 100 billion forints (about $1.43 billion), with vouchers offered pegged to the old value of each property, so that these claims could be used to buy any state property put up for auction. A ceiling of 5 million forints (roughly $70,000) was set on the amount any individual could claim, and in most cases former owners could use vouchers to claim only up to 20 percent of the value of their old properties.

Yet the scheme was threatened with almost immediate destruction, some 451 amendments being offered, the Free Democrats, the main opposition party, threatening to take any legislative measure to court, arguing that an avalanche of legal disputes of successive owners to identical property would seize attention, slow down privatization, and not cover compensation for other grievances such as the anti–Jewish law of 1938 limiting, then barring Jews from certain professions. Thus compensation for only some of the expropriated would lead to continued jealousies and future conflict.

The expropriators were also to be charged with high crimes under Parliament's 1991 mandate to remove the statute of limitations for earlier Communist crimes of murder and high treason that for political reasons were not prosecuted earlier. Applying the law to 80,000 former Communist officials would open a Pandora's box for actions carried out as government policy, including entering into relations with the Soviet Union as a foreign power.

Refusing to sign the bill, President Arpad Goncz (who had been jailed for several years as an opponent of the Communist government) sent the proposed legislation to Hungary's Constitutional Court for a ruling. "What really matters for the victims is recognition by society that they suffered, and financial aid, both of which are lacking," concluded Hungarian presidential legal adviser Andras Sajo.

These remained tasks to be completed in the nineties.

Exit Soviet Power

The end of the Warsaw Pact signaled Eastern Europe's opportunity to redefine its relationship with the Soviet Union, craft new plans, and design a foreign policy to guarantee its own security.

Hungary was in the forefront of these efforts. On 30 June 1991, Soviet troops marched out of Hungary and Prime Minister Jozsef Antall moved for a treaty with Moscow that would guarantee Hungary's right to enter into groups and alliances of its own choosing without any obligation to the Soviet Union. "We cannot take on any obligation that could disturb the European Community," he said, explaining Hungary's efforts to join the Western Continent in trade, and investment. "We would not like to accept [Soviet] draft wording that would say we could not join such a union."

Though Hungary had pledged that its territory would not be used as a staging area for any attack on the Soviet Union, the real issue, Prime Minister Antall said, was that "the Soviet union prefers to have a security zone between its borders and NATO. It is certain they are worried about being isolated." Hungary was to be a buffer state, a *cordon sanitaire* for Soviet security.

That was the plan before the 1991 failed military coup in the Soviet Union. Afterward, Hungary was on its own to accept or reject the role of security blanket for the new rulers in Moscow.

Restoring Economic Health and Prosperity

Political liberation had restored many social rights, but not economic health. For restoring material well-being involved reversing the patient's lack of care over several years, and this was yet to be done.

Hungarians in the eighties had experienced relatively slow inflation and a gradual rise in living standards. But the 1987–88 Communist government reversed the trend, with prices going up, incomes and living standards down. In 1988 alone, consumer prices jumped 15.7 percent, followed by another 17 percent in 1989. Salaries, bonuses, and social benefits also took a momentary dive, the government's consumption index going from 103 percent of the 1980 level to 95.7 percent.

A tight market for foreign consumer items meanwhile emerged, leaving only the wealthy few with city apartments, country villas, and Mercedeses controlling the hard-currency components of a smart purchase. True, government mandate limited each person to exchange only 3,250 forints (about $50) a year; true again, at that limit it would take about eight and a half years to pull together sufficient dollars to buy an inexpensive VCR or 40 years to buy a cut-price computer clone.[2] Yet these and other consumer hard goods were everywhere seen in the offices and homes of the middle and upper classes, who dealt directly in dollars and used forints only for Hungarian-produced goods and services.

Low-cost efficient production at living wages was the obvious key to economic well-being. The center-right government understood that if the cost of production and prices went up, the cost of living for the working population would also rise—and the contest of workers against both private and state employers would start with wage demands yet escalate to political ones.

To keep down such production costs, by the close of 1990, the government had refused to slash its industrial subsidies (comprising some 10 percent of GNP collected in taxes and borrowed funds) for fear of forcing inefficient enterprises to go out of business, thereby, throwing people out of work, pressuring industries to raise prices based on the real cost of production, and fueling worker demands for increased wages.

But without covering real production costs, there was no way to generate sufficient domestic surplus to pay off the foreign debt. So for the rest of the nineties it was likely that Hungarians would have to work harder to pay off the highest per capita foreign debt in Europe (about $18.5 billion in total in 1990) but would receive a worsening daily existence as the government cut subsidies that hitherto kept down prices of basic necessities, making these prices reflect real costs, and shut down unproductive enterprises, causing growing unemployment that would undercut consumer market growth and lever down the general wage scale.

Meanwhile, the most expropriated were cut free of land, work, and homes. Communist law imprisoned the "parasitism" of sleeping in public places or begging, requiring citizens to live at registered addresses, thus locking both dissidents and the rebellious into the triple oppression of unwanted family relations, unwanted state controls, and hated political restrictions. But postcommunism factory decisions to save money by closing down hostels that were once home to several hundred thousand single men combined with government amnesty in June 1989, freeing 3,000 prisoners with less than a year to serve on their sentences.

Some homeless were the victims of Budapest's chronic housing shortage—some alcoholics, underworld criminals, drifters. To their number were added 100,000 Romanians fleeing with their families from economic desperation at home. And by the closing months of 1990, some 20,000 Hungarians, mostly single men, were homeless, taking up residence in railway stations, parks, and bus stops.

Already beset by rising inflation and unemployment, there were few government resources to house and care for the homeless, save a $500,000 token program setting up 1,500 shelter beds and 300 daily free meals to take care of half the nation's homeless living in Budapest. Even here, residents set their own night rules—men and women cohabiting, drinking alcohol, young male graduates of state orphanages openly sniffing glue out of plastic bags.

The quest for freedom that had removed earlier Communist restrictions thus had its transitional price.

Government Programs

Government reforms turned on privatizing the economy to turn means of production, labor, and goods into marketable commodities on the domestic and international markets. As COMECON closed down and trade volume with the Eastern states was reduced and replaced with exchanges calculated in hard currencies, the drive for Western markets and investments intensified.

The limited flexibility of Hungarian state companies lacking means of exchange to invest in new technologies speeded the government's policy of privatization and access to foreign markets. The coalition government planned to reduce state ownership of production from the

90 percent level of 1990 to less than 50 percent by 1993–94. By the close of 1990, unified Germany was already Hungary's biggest trading partner, followed by the Soviet Union, Austria, Czechoslovakia, Italy, and the United States. As COMECON trading partners denominated their trade in hard currency in 1991, higher-quality imports from the West undercut Hungarian exports. So Hungarians strove to reorganize industry with Western capital, concentrate on lowering barriers to agricultural exports, and encourage tourism and health rehabilitation at its world-famous spas.

Foreign capital was seen as critical, despite Hungarian Supreme Court limitations on the First Privatization Program (1990–94) disposal of some twenty giant companies representing $1.12 billion of state assets by the Government Property Agency. With a highly skilled work force, low wages, government tax incentives, the right to repatriate profits in hard currency, the right to buy premises and land, and a perfunctory Finance Ministry license to take a controlling interest, the door was opened to the West.

Most of the 2,000 foreign joint-venture companies had been established before the transformation of 1988, some 120 being established from 1989–90, capped by the 1989 $150-million bargain sale of a controlling stake in the country's best-known global firm, the lighting manufacturer Tungsram, to General Electric. More than 60 percent of ensuing investment came from Austria and Germany in 1990. And by March 1992, foreign investments totaled more than $2.3 billion.

Yet the largest and most significant investment was by General Motors, designed to undermine the old COMECON production limits and fill the Hungarian market with the first Western car to be assembled in central Europe since communism went smash. COMECON, directed from Moscow, had designated which Eastern European nations would produce vehicles, autos being made in East Germany, Czechoslovakia, and Poland; trucks and buses in Hungary. The end of Soviet helotry brought a different formula for the market-oriented center-right government, encouraging GM's ultramodern auto plant employing highly skilled, low-paid workers at Szentgotthard, 120 miles west of Budapest.

Some 400 workers were promised double their domestic wages for an undisclosed sum under the confidential stipulation. The initial market for the 15,000 cars assembled annually was largely to businesses that could afford the price of between $13,310 and $14,610, far above the means of an average worker making $150 a month. And the balance would be sold to Hungary's nouveau riche that was already buying more expensive imported BMWs, Porsches, and Mercedes-Benzes.

GM Europe had broader plans too, its president, Robert J. Eaton, preparing to start production at its East German Eisenach assembly plant in the fall of 1992, to assemble cars at the Polish FSO auto plant and to operate in Russia and Ukraine within five years. "We are going to continue to move East, as we feel comfortable with the economic stability in those countries." He laid out plans for future competition with Suzuki Motor Company's October 1992 Esztergom, Hungary, production of the cheaper Swift subcompact, and Ford's planned spare parts manufacturing plant in Szekesfehervar.

Holding the controlling interest, confident of a shareholding compliant government, the repatriation of profits assured, the key was future market share. GM's initial investment totaled nearly $295 million, and the GM plant was owned two-thirds by GM Europe, 21 percent by the state-owned Raba Truck Works, and 13 percent by the State Development Institute. "This is a symbol of Hungary's economic rebirth," Prime Minister Antall exuded at the production line celebration of the first assembled Opel Astra. "It is another step along Hungary's road to national independence and a market economy."

Not Everyone Is Happy

With foreign investors getting all the breaks, though, not everyone in the work force was content with the 1990–92 average monthly wage of $150, not too far above the government poverty line of $85. As inefficient firms were shut down or taken over, thinning their work force, unemployment had risen, 20 percent inflation kept consumer goods out of the hands of most of the nation's 10.2 million, and the population reached the limits of their willingness to sacrifice.

If the government went further along the fast track to austerity, the population would see it as illegitimate. "We must avoid creating further uncertainty," Trade Minister Bela Kadar hedged. "Insecurity means no savings, no investment, no readiness to acquire new skills."

Exasperated with crises, failing living standards, and a complicated series of elections (two rounds of parliamentary votes, two separate referendums on the presidency, and local elections) as the rites of passage from a single-party state to multiparty democracy, the opposition parties pummeled the center-right coalition in the local elections of October 1990, though still not upsetting the balance of power in the national Parliament. Yet with one-fifth of the nation's population, the vote in Budapest awarded liberal opposition parties 50 percent of the vote against only 33 percent for the alliance of the Forum and Christian Democratic party, foretelling the future vulnerability of the center-right coalition, the rise of the Free Democratic Alliance under the leadership of many prominent Jews, and an effusion of anti–Semitic and chauvinistic propaganda.

And Now the Future

Expecting further changes in the mantle of power held by the coalition of the Hungarian Democratic Forum with the Christian Democrats and Smallholders party, the Free Democrats Alliance began constructing the framework for a democratic revolution. The Smallholders party, critical of the center-right coalition's survival, was loosing its rural following, having shown weak support even in the rural areas in the October 1990 local elections.

Yet once in power, the successful factions and fractions of the opposition would undoubtedly inherit the center-right government's structural inadequacies, institutionalized limitations, and economic restrictiveness. If these were not sidestepped, they might force any new government into new rounds of austerity: forced unemployment that the Communists would decry; too few consumer goods the people demand and want the government to provide; too many high-priced imports the many could not buy.

Free markets there might be, but consensus politics promised to crack along lines of class and caste. For in the Hungary of the early nineties, some denizens worked three jobs to cover escalating price levels. Over 2 million people, one-fifth of the nation's 11 million, lived below the legally ascribed "social minimum" of 4,300 forints per person per month. Others were more well positioned. In 1990–92, at least, wealth tightly held by one-quarter of the population represented 75 percent of all money in bank accounts in addition to forints and hard-currency cash on hand.

To conserve family resources, most Hungarian couples chose to have only one or two children; 1990 legal abortions were 72 per 100 live births. The population of 10.4 million might have been 2 million larger if it were not for the availability of abortions, and the government held no interest in changing the policy in the frame of rising needs for too few resources.

Living conditions also threatened longevity, the lowest in Europe at 65.1 years for men and 73.7 years for women. And desperation meanwhile ran high, the per capita suicide rate remaining the world's highest at 4,235 in 1990, although dropping from its 1983–84 peak.

Nor would popular feelings of exasperation and dismay much improve in the short term. For a squeeze long set in place by the $20-billion foreign debt, eating up currency reserves earned abroad, also meant fewer imports, more service charges in government taxes, thereby cutting net wages and living standards. And as no one ate on averages but only from income actually received, the family dilemma remains: With two working adults, average monthly family salaries totalling 10,000 forints faced annual 20 to 35 percent annual price hikes, ensuring downward mobility as the number of Hungary's poor rose in the early nineties.

Managers would thus have to contend with workers demanding more wages. State bureaucrats would likely face a public wanting more services and fewer taxes; politicians left, center, and right would be beset by those who once were supporters.

Perhaps the real issues would then emerge — Hungary debt-encumbered as part of the Western free market versus national self-determination based on establishing domestic egalitarian relations and material well-being.

Malaise and Scapegoat

But perhaps these issues would not even be raised. Or perhaps Hungary's population of Gypsies and Jews, the old scapegoats, would be identified to explain the malaise. Perhaps too, the stylization of the news and media opinion would be directed from press owners on the right spectrum. Perhaps the takeover of the Hungarian press would go forward, under the not so benign guardianship of Britain's now-deceased Robert Maxwell and Rupert Murdoch, France's right-wing press baron Robert Hersant (owner of the conservative *Figaro*), Germany's Springer chain and Bertelsmann group, and even the Swedish independent liberal daily *Dagens Nyheter*.

The latter, fulminated Hungarian minister Geza Jeszenszky, did not share the views of the center-right government. "It has a 'leftist-liberal' ideology, and does not stand on the national-liberal base that is so popular in Hungary," he wrote to the takeover client paper *Magyar Nemzet*, concerned about an overly hostile press during the government-imposed transition to market relations: "This paper regularly publishes disparaging articles not only about the Hungarian Government and its supporters, but about the issue of Hungarians living in Rumania, on which it shares the views of the Ceausescu-era propaganda. You must know that the Government does not want to control the paper but simply wants to avoid putting it in the hands of those who are either hostile or simply indifferent to the fate of the Hungarian nation."

The liberal *Dagens Nyheter* lost the bid, as the financing bank and the government-controlled publishing house with shares in the newspaper chose Robert Hersant to take over *Magyar Nemzet*, despite its news staff opposition to the sale, because of Hersant's "extreme rightist" views.

With the government thus favoring arch-conservative views, minorities, especially Jews, stiffened in apprehension of the future. True, of the 800,000 Jews who made Budapest one of the great centers of Jewish culture in Europe before the Nazi occupation, only 40,000 remain in the early nineties. And most of them have been reared in a secular climate of communism that has discouraged both Hungarian and Jewish identity.

Yet the renewed crisis of the early nineties has again given credence to the racism and xenophobia of right-wing philosophies, propounding the specter of Jews as money-driven "outsiders" undermining the nation's economy. Jews were being cajoled or forced to remain anonymous, or even to repress their own "Jewishness" out of fear of being ostracized.

"Pal, in these delicate moments, is it wise to provoke people?" asked a friend of noted Hungarian filmmaker Pat Schiffer when he tried to stage a "Jewish Film Festival" in Budapest in 1990. Long-term colleagues at his own studio now viewed his work as an "un–Hungarian" betrayal. "One of my best friends, a scriptwriter," he said, "reminded me when this started that I had personally never made a 'Jewish film.' He meant it as a compliment."[3]

Hungary stood thus: falling living standards; polarization of wealth and poverty; downward mobility for one-fifth or more of the population; foreign investors in search of assets selling below their real value, dirt-cheap labor and potential Eurasian markets; a center-right government inept and fearful to promote real reforms; patiently waiting parties of the Left planning for future parliamentary control; and a growing right-wing playing on myth and anti–Semitism as the rationale for the malaise. The future boded ill for most Hungarians, better for the rising upper classes, and best for foreign investors.

YUGOSLAVIA AND THE SIX-NATION POWER QUEST

> *Serbian President Slobodan Milosevic is a Bolshevik, at the beginning, in the middle and at the end. He is not capable of solving any problem of the Serbian people, because all their misfortunes were created by his Communist Party. He is like the Egyptian Pharaoh who could never lead the Jewish people out of Egypt.*
> —Vuk Draskovic, leader of the Movement
> for Serbian Renewal Party, 1990

> *Serbia's minimum requirement is that Serbs be in one common state. We must be prepared for different situations, especially where Serbs are in great danger. We must be ready. We have been robbed before. We cannot let that happen again.*
> —Law professor Budomir Kosutic

> *If you don't want to be a colony for outdated, polluting technology or be a pool of cheap labor, you must join the free market of Europe in a hurry.*
> —Roberto Boteri, editor of
> the Slovenian weekly *Mladina*

It was really six nations rolled into one—Croatia, Slovenia, Serbia, Macedonia, Montenegro, and Bosnia-Herzegovina—adding two autonomous regions, Kosovo and Vojvodina—all nationalists, each unyielding to relinquish full rights to the central government in the early nineties.[4]

A mosaic of nations, of peoples of Eastern Orthodox, Roman Catholic, and Muslim liturgy, each of the six republics had been dominated by an ethnic majority: the Serbs in Serbia, the Croats in Croatia, the Slovenes in Slovenia, the Montenegrins in Montenegro, the Macedonians in Macedonia, and the ethnic Muslims in Bosnia.

Allocation of political power thereby had its reflex in the welfare and economic policies of provincial ethnic populations. The issue was self-evident: central control versus ethnic autonomy by republics and locality.

Communists Past

With the weakening, teetering, and fall of Marshal Tito's ruling Communists in the late eighties, the quest for ethnic and democratic rights led to an effusion of political parties; the organized CP itself becoming fracturous by republic and ethnic affiliations.

For not all Communists agreed that power should flow from the center to reward some ethnic groups and republics and punish others. The party thus split ideologically from its old hierarchical ordering of political "line." And the Communist party as a whole was ready to release its central monopoly on a federal level, recognizing the path to future unity in a multinational state was to permit more local autonomy, cooling national resentments and stopping any moves toward secession and self-determination by individual republics or "autonomous" regions.

National resentments continued, though. In Serbia, the opposition that had opposed Stalin and Tito had long since suffered as Communist victims. Some Serbian Communists also objected to national multiparty elections. Yet many liberal intellectuals opposed exclusive or regional "democracy" by individual republics or ethnic groups, so their ideological stance effectively denied democratic rights to *all* ethnic communities and states.

With so many republics, parties, nationalities, interest groups, and Communist factions, the old federation could not last.

Centrist Austerity and Political Reflex

Federal centrist rule was becoming a surefire path toward downfall in Yugoslavia. Centrism had already destroyed the previous government, attempting to direct the transition from provincial to free markets. And whatever austerity measures might be imposed, central government price and wage policies would not be followed in the republics or their peripheries.

Prime Minister Branko Mikulic toppled in 1988 for placing a lid on prices and wages, living standards plummeting to their lowest level in two decades. Ante Markovic, the new prime minister in 1989, promised to reverse the 1,975 percent annual rate of inflation by the end of November through a four-point program conceived by Western sages who knew as much about Yugoslavia as the terrain of Mars: floating a new dinar, fully convertible with all Western currencies, worth some 10,000 old dinars; imposing a six-month wage freeze; setting price controls on electricity, gasoline, rail transport, rents, postal service, and medicine; and freezing interest rates hitherto set by the national bank.

Austerity thus imposed pleased foreign creditors. But 160,000 workers in Montenegro drew not a smile along their strike lines, followed in common protest by the laboring populations of Belgrade and Macedonia unifying against the centrist government.

Economic Doublethink

The cause of protest against economic downward mobility for the nation's multitude was the federalist plan, imposing a reduction in living standards on people in all the republics and autonomous regions. The plan had been designed to make the people pay for the mistakes of Communist governments, past and present. For these governments conceived and sought to repay Yugoslavia's massive foreign debt to the West—the 1990 central government reducing the sum from nearly $19 billion to $16 billion while enlarging hard-currency reserves to $7.5 billion and sharply increasing exports rather than accommodating home consumption—all accomplished "without a cent, not even a dollar, of support from abroad," Prime Minister Markovic boasted.

Markovic had moved simultaneously for economic independence and foreign market ties.[5] And seen through his lens as a Croatian *nationalist*, he spoke publicly of the other side, arguing that *the new central plan* was a *loosening* of the bureaucratic and economic stranglehold his predecessors held fast.

But the scheme was otherwise. Under his guidance, Belgrade would be the first link to the brave new world of finance, its stock exchange reopening 26 February 1990 after a break of almost half a century. Newly founded by four of Yugoslavia's largest banks, it was to be the first of three exchanges, would initially handle only government bonds but thereafter would trade stocks issued by private firms.

By itself, though, that would not yet allow a leap to financial capitalism amid the rocky economic times in the many republics, as wages were now frozen, the growth of money supply limited, state subsidies cut to enterprises thus throwing many into bankruptcy, and thousands out of work.

Opposition forces viewed the Markovic scheme differently: Was this state "decontrol" not encouraging private enterprise and foreign creditors and investors at the population's expense?

Secession, Civil War, and Benefits for Some

What could interrupt the move to federal unity—paying off the foreign creditors and imposing the austerities of incipient capitalism— would now be free elections in each republic followed by secession, or even civil war. Yet if Yugoslavia began to splinter into its component republics, ethnic violence and unrest would escalate, civil war might begin, and the political rivalries of the republics might end in a struggle that would drive them further apart.

Serbia, the largest of the six republics, held ambitions to create a Greater Serbia, either by strengthening the federal government or replacing it with an expansionist Serbian state. Thus had Serbia not only suppressed the Albanian minority of nearly 2 million in Kosovo but crossed swords with Croatia and Slovenia, the two most prosperous republics. And the latters' democratic elections in the spring of 1990 ended Communist rule, while Serbia retained a Communist government under President Milosevic, whose stir of Serbian nationalist passions set a self-determination policy that included withholding Serbian payments to the federal government and contesting Belgrade's authority to impose customs duties on goods entering Serbia from other Yugoslav republics.

Slovenia and Croatia sought autonomy within a confederation, threatening to secede from Yugoslavia if a confederation agreement could not be worked out. The first free balloting in Yugoslavia since World War II, taking place in these republics in early 1990, bringing nationalists to power, called for a transformation of Yugoslavia into a looser confederation. And the Slovene Parliament at the close of September 1990 approved a motion making the Slovenian Constitution the supreme law of its republic. This led in January 1991 to attempted secession and a military standoff with federal troops, momentarily resolved by a truce, awaiting a future showdown.

Croatia too was bent on independence. As a one-time province of Hungary, it was beset by religious conflicts of the Catholic Croatian majority and the Orthodox Serbian minority living adjacent to the border of Bosnia-Herzegovina. And heavily armed to stop the Croatian police from confiscating stolen weapons from police stations in Serb-populated counties in 1990, the Serbs took to the woods, barricaded Croatian roads, and continued the guerrilla war that had waged for years.

Given these divisions, local conflicts, and attempts at secession, Prime Minister Markovic saw federal authority under attack, warning on 15 November 1990: "The acts of the highest state organs of Slovenia, Serbia and, partly, Croatia inevitably lead to a straining of political relations in Yugoslavia and directly threaten the country's survival. The situation is characterized by growing nationalism and separatism and an alarming worsening of ethnic relations, all of which is expressed in violence, a drastic threat to public order, peace and citizens' safety."

With so many ethnic and nationalist groups, unity in a single nation almost defied the imagination. Integration of the 1.8 million Albanians among the 2-million population in the autonomous province of Kosovo, for example, would have to be based on full extension of rights by the controlling Serbians and allowing the Albanians to "integrate" into the larger Serbian community, or there would be an unending civil war. Yet fear captured the moment: Albanians armed, and the Serbs periodically went on house-to-house searches for their weapons, threatening and repeatedly killing Albanian protestors demanding independence for Kosovo.

Serbian nationalists were being led by the ruling Socialist party of Serbia, successor to the Communist League of Serbia, which hoped to restore its version of Serbia's rightful place in the Yugoslavian federation. For them, this meant regaining full control over the autonomous regions of Kosovo and Vojvodina, lost territories that marked nineteenth-century betrayals, genocide, and forced migrations.

Should the Yugoslavian federation break up, moreover, Serbian nationalists wanted retrieval of territories lost when Yugoslavia was first formed in 1918. And these demands were given credence by Serbian Socialist president Milosevic's campaigning in 1990 to restore sovereignty over Kosovo and deploying his party's control over the press, the Serbian Assembly, and the rewriting of the Serbian Constitution.

Serbian nationalists also planned to tear away Croatian territory by having the 4.7 million Serbians making up 11 percent of Croatia's inhabitants declare their autonomy from Croatia, threatening to form paramilitary groups to defend Serbs if the federal government in Belgrade refused to recognize and protect them, and using this as a pretext for the Serb-dominated Yugoslavian army and bureaucracy to stop Croatia from asserting its independence.

Tradition supported fears on both sides. For Croatian independence in World War II led to the slaughter of as many as 750,000 Serbians at the hands of Croatia's Fascist Ustashi, leading to revenge by the Communist Partisans' 1945 massacre of 100,000 Nazi-uniformed Croatian collaborators, though there were differences between Nazis and Ustashi on one side and the latter's repressed "sympathizers" on the other.

Slovenians Want Freedom Too

Among Slovenians, as the most prosperous and educated people of Yugoslavia's six republics, time seemed right for secession or a loose association in a confederation. Living in forests and valleys below the Alps near Austria, they manufactured with indigenous or cheaply imported raw materials, exporting manufactures, yet paid heavy taxes covering 27 percent of the federal budget, and received few services in return.

Tired of supporting the rest of the nation with these tax imposts and cheap manufactures, Slovenian nationalists wanted independence. Secession was the answer, insisted Roberto Boteri, editor of the provocative weekly *Mladina*. For Slovenia, with neighboring Croatia, was better situated than other republics and would benefit from freer markets to the West under a weaker central government.

Slovenians were also tired of Croats, Serbs, Montenegrins, and Macedonians dredging up ancient ethnic and religious quarrels. Many Serbs called Slovene democrats traitors, so the latter loved them not. And seeing themselves independent nations, both Slovenians and Croatians armed heavily to take on federal forces should they attempt to deprive them of their autonomy during the rest of the century.

Time of Reckoning

A time of reckoning fast approaching in the early nineties, the map of southeastern Europe was about to be redrawn. "Pluralism" was emerging — not in support of a unified nation but as six separate ones. The federation seemed to be breaking apart, shattering the old republican unity set up by the Communists in 1945 after a successful armed uprising against German and other occupiers. For now each Yugoslavian republic, autonomous region, nationalist group, political faction, and culture-bred community seemed determined to seek self-determination from centrist oppression for this or that people and region. Yet, mindlessly, each also used the rationale of hate and oppression of others as the blind fulcrum of self-emancipation.

The most logical future spelled loose confederation of the six republics and two autonomous regions, each governing itself yet trying to sidestep the Balkan strife of the past, each realizing its own limitations, isolation, and impoverishment; jettisoning the hatred of others based on past grievances; and overturning the narrow doctrine that the path to the freedom of its people was tramping on the ethnic and territorial rights of others.

More broadly, Yugoslavia's future was bound up with that of Eastern and central Europe, and partly, southeastern Europe — their combined destiny turning on the shattering of the Soviet Empire in the East, the unification of Germany in the corridor linking East and West, and the out-dating of nation-states in central Europe, undermining the post–Hapsburg ordering of nation-states that was first sponsored by Western nations establishing a *cordon sanitaire* after World War I, then demolished by Hitler's marching armies and restored by Allied victory and a new partition of Europe.

Sliding into the Abyss

And so came a rapid slide into the abyss of ethnic hatred and war, the breakup of Yugoslavia into its component nation-states, the rebalkanization of the old Balkans, and the intervention of the West — precise consequences unknown. Yugoslavia thus split asunder. The south Slavs (Serbs, Croats, Macedonians, Montenegrins, Bosnians, and Slovenes) could not agree on a federation led by Serbia, let alone a commonwealth or common market of independent states.

Declaring their independence, Croatia and Slovenia had forcefully seized border and customs posts to implement their power, bringing on a

Serbian-led attack on Croatia, the first major war on the European continent since 1945. With it came the death of over 10,000, thousands wounded, the destruction of billions of dollars' worth of infrastructure, factories, whole towns, undermining the economic prospects of 23.5 million people making up the six Yugoslav republics. Croatia broke free militarily, winning recognition by Western European states, bringing a brokered UN Security Council–approved cease-fire that after fourteen months of violations, was backed up by a 14,400-member peacekeeping force sent to war-ravaged Croatian villages.

But even this would not bring peace to the Serb-occupied territories in Croatia. For Croatian leaders wanted both revanchist control over the Serb-held areas and German financial aid for reconstruction. Though they insisted that the UN-protected areas must remain Croatian territory, and swore to use force to pry these regions from the controlling Serb rebels, the Serbs were backed by a formidable remnant of the Yugoslav army swearing the land would never be returned to Croatia. Foreseeing a political solution, Croatian leaders agreed to temporary rebel Serb governments in the crisis areas where Serbia and the Yugoslav army agreed to disarm Serb militants, to withdraw Serb army units to a point outside Croatia's official borders, and to create mixed Serb-Croat, lightly armed police forces in the protected areas, without allowing the Serbs to cement their control, discouraging Croatians from returning by blowing up their houses and intimidating them under the UN plan.

Meanwhile, by a March 1992 popular Slavic-Muslim-Croatian vote, the republic of Bosnia-Hercegovina to Croatia's south declared its independence, momentarily extinguishing the fuse on a powder keg ready to blow apart the frail remains of the republic, leaving Serbia as the rump. Boycotting the vote, the 31 percent Serbian minority opposing Bosnian independence threatened to derail secession and repeat the Croatian episode of carnage, railing against forced independence by the "tyranny of the majority," mobilizing their heavily armed militias backed up by the 100,000-strong Yugoslav army garrisoned in Bosnia to prevent a break with the Serb-controlled Yugoslav federation. But Serbia proper hesitated, momentarily joining the other groups in European Community negotiations to establish a Western-recognized sovereign Bosnia composed of semiautonomous ethnic cantons, each determined to secure its heritage and independence.

The March 1992 plan accepted by all parties would transform Bosnia-Hercegovina into an independent country divided into three ethnically defined regions—to be embodied in a draft constitution approved in an internationally supervised referendum. But the accord did not resolve crucial questions of the relationship of the Bosnian central government with the three ethnic regions or how the three parties would reach consensus on major issues of economic policy, foreign affairs, defense, withdrawal of the Serbian army, and running the government bureaucracy.

Though the republic would retain its current borders, no one knew exactly how to partition the three ethnically defined regions of 1.9 million Muslim Slavs, 750,000 Croats, and 1.4 million Serbs. "Drawing the map is going to be a nightmare," one Western diplomat bemoaned. "The urban areas are ethnically mixed. Families are mixed. Even apartment buildings are mixed."[6] Attacking Serbians brought on this Bosnian night.

Macedonia also declared its independence from the Yugoslav federation, rejecting requests by Serbia and Montenegro to join them in a new smaller Yugoslavia. Potential for conflict with others remained strong. For peopled by a mixture of Albanians, Gypsies, Turks, Slavs, and Walachians, the southern republic of Macedonia bordered Greece, which saw it usurping the name of Greek Macedonia, rekindling the violent conflicts of the early twentieth century over reuniting the fractured parts of Macedonia at Greece's expense. Lying astride the principal land route from the Middle East to Europe, Macedonia had also been the focal point of pre–World War I Balkan wars, now again facing potential territorial feuds with Bulgaria and Albania.

Matters reached an impasse when Macedonia's independence and sovereignty were accepted by a European Community commission in December 1991. But Greece disputed its self-description as "Macedonia" and its independence as a Slavic state. Then, as Serbian federal troops withdrew their occupation, Macedonian officials pleaded for European and U.S. recognition to protect their borders and access foreign protection and economic aid. Germany tried to force European Community recognition and UN troop occupation, even if Greece was opposed. "We recognize the sensitivities of Greece," a German official magnanimously provided, "but sooner or later we need a decision."

Meanwhile, Serbia itself imploded, crushed economically by annual inflation of 25,000 percent following its printing-press fiat currency financing the war on Croatia. Hard-currency deposits, long sought to import foreign technologies and goods, were frozen by some Belgrade banks, halting many imports essential for manufacturing. Other banks went bankrupt, their depositors losing everything. And not only production and home building ceased, unable to finance materials and wages, but the hyperinflation also destroyed the savings of hardworking Serbs at home and those who had labored as "guest workers" in the German Ruhr's twilight zones of grimy mining towns.

Unemployment surged, eroding support for the government's savage war on Croatia and Bosnia. Serbian monarchists demanded restoration of Crown Prince Alexander, whose family held the Yugoslavian monarchy until Hitler's Panzers put it in retreat to London in 1941. At the antigovernment rally on 10 March 1992, leader of the Serbian Renewal party Vuk Draskovic excoriated President Milosevic's failed hope to use the war on Croatia to rally Serbian nationalists to restore his sagging political support, drawing applause when he spoke of the president's having "whipped up a bloody war" that had alienated all of Serbia's traditional allies in Europe, including Britain and France, and "needlessly" sending thousands of Serbs to their deaths. Calling for a general strike to topple the president and his followers from power, Draskovic called attention to their hypocrisy—claims not to be Bolsheviks, yet using "notorious Bolshevik tactics," apparent from President Milosevic's obedient majority in Parliament and a military and police hierarchy obedient to the old Serbian Communist apparatus still in power.

Two days later, on 12 March, students taking to the streets called for the resignation of the president, trying to mobilize a following among workers in government offices and state-owned factories, the bulwark of the president's support. Expecting a full-scale popular assault, riot police and bulldozers sealed off the area and intersections around the president's home.

Yet for lesser matters, here and elsewhere local budgets for police protection were almost gone, and enforcement of law and order collapsed. Criminals seized the moment while many underpaid, demoralized soldiers demobilized themselves, selling or using their weapons in unauthorized ways, making the barrel of the gun a means for robbery, murder, collecting blood debts, and wiping out monies owed by eliminating aggressive creditors. And as the weapons bazaar expanded, fear escalated. There would be no immediate return to community tranquility in the Serbian remains of the Yugoslav federation.

BULGARIA: TAKING POWER IN HALF STEPS

> We're hearing of changes in nearby countries like Romania, even Albania, so we too demand democratic guarantees.
> — Petar Beron, Winter 1989

> I did everything. I even made mistakes (only two, though—not remarrying after my wife died in the 1980s, and not retiring a decade earlier). But I never committed crimes.
> — Todor Zhivkov, deposed Communist leader,
> 9 November 1990

> We need technical assistance.
> — Prime Minister Andrei Lukanov,
> winter 1989

The constitution guaranteed Communist supremacy. If that failed, there were the army, the police, and authoritarian controls imposed in the neighborhoods and at the workplace.[7] So those with power did not take kindly to the tiny initial opposition coalescing in the Union of Democratic Forces. These zealots of the deed thought freedom would come with a change of guards and bureaucrats, taking charge of ministries of state and outposts of police.

"Department Six," the secret police, seemed omniscient, well funded by periodic legislative reimbursement for a job well done. Todor Zhivkov, Communist and head of the government, relied on its services for up-to-the-minute information his collaborators could dispense to a long line of lesser guards, ensuring social stability and a "beneficent dictatorship."

Trouble in the Streets

"Czechoslovak students swept away totalitarianism like an epidemic and we will also sweep Bulgaria with 'Czechoslovak flu' this winter," student leader Emil Koshlukov warned the government in winter of 1989 as protestors filled Sofia's streets. Taking the opposition seriously, the government quickly removed the constitutional provision guaranteeing party supremacy, promising elections to avoid the consequences of the Czech and Slovak "flu."

But all was not fair in this coming electoral war of 1990. "How can we win elections in June when Department Six still exists and the mass media are still under dictatorship?" opposition speaker Ljubomir Sobajiev asked a crowd gathered in Sofia, demanding the Communists be ousted from control.

Still, the opposition grew bolder and stronger with each new revelation about Communist abuses and misuse of power against the people. For earlier rumors were now documented that Zhivkov's Stalinist government followed earlier ones in maintaining death camps for political prisoners in the forties and fifties, possibly into the early sixties when the camps were finally dismantled. Here tens of thousands were imprisoned and many thousands died, most families in this tiny nation of 9 million having a relative or friend that had been in, had seen, or had died in the camps.

Revelations in 1989 about the 1986 Soviet Chernobyl nuclear disaster then tipped the balance of public outrage against the Communist rulers. At the time of Chernobyl in 1986, Zhivkov had held technical conferences with his appointed commission of experts and top scientists and concluded that though the dangers of radiation were significant, public calm was essential. His ruling party publicly assured that there was no danger, that food and water supplies were not contaminated—at the same time that Communist leaders were using government foreign-exchange currencies, importing untainted food and water for themselves.

Change Cometh

On 9 November 1989, pressures building, a "palace coup" toppled Communist strongman Zhivkov, head of the party and iron-fisted leader for thirty-five years. It was a negotiated transition in power. The Communist party changed its name to Socialist but retained control over Parliamentary government. There was no full public accounting of the Communist party's misdeeds for decades.

June elections then changed the balance of power in Parliament, so the Socialists that took charge had to promote reforms if they were to stop the combined opposition parties from turning to the public and ousting the Socialist government.

Less than two months later, in July 1990, Zhivkov tried to make a deal, sending a "confidential" letter to the Socialist-run Parliament, offering to appear as a witness against allegations being readied against him by the public prosecutor's office, but the parliamentary Socialists, who had once been in his coterie, pressured him to withdraw his proposal for fear that wider circles of the apparat would be charged by the prosecutor. Zhivkov recalculated, following their lead.

Then, in November 1990, the students again called a strike at the University of Sofia, demanding in part that the Zhivkov government be brought to justice for its years of terror. The Socialist party once more defended, changing the focus with an early November 1990 rendition in their newspaper, admitting special rights were taken by the Zhivkov clique but delimiting them to economic largesse, not involving the underlying abuse of the population.

The Socialists argued that Zhivkov Communists had access to a government-financed cornucopia of sprawling apartments in Sofia and private villas, cars, and foreign currencies for purchase of Western goods and travel. But no longer. Yes, some Communist leaders involved still held power as Socialists, but their special benefits were a thing of the past. Besides, it was for the public prosecutor, not the general populace, to decide if they had done wrong.

Transition and Future Reform

The lame excuses convinced few, and steps for transitional reform went forward. With the November 1989 post–Stalinist government taking power under former Communist Andrei Lukanov as prime minister, the main coalition of opposition parties in the Grand National Assembly demanded a rapid shift to a market economy and held popular support and a bloc of votes to force the Socialist government to accede.

For the June 1990 elections had given the Socialists a slim parliamentary majority of 211 out of 400 seats only because they promised reforms, dropping their Marxist slogans and rhetoric. And they were still beholden to the population that backed the opposition parties and had to make good on bringing about reform.

Seizing the moment, Prime Minister Lukanov and his advisers then contacted several U.S. economists to help draw up a plan for reform, and a

600-page *Action Plan for Bulgaria,* drafted under the auspices of the U.S. Chamber of Commerce, was presented to the prime minister in early October 1990.[8] Its main provisions called for removal of economic impediments created by forty-five years of Communist rule, concentrating on

- "privatization of the means of production and distribution";
- "elimination of wage and price controls";
- a safety net to protect the disabled, unemployed, and poor from hardships;
- "basic reform of the monetary, banking and fiscal systems," including free circulation of foreign currencies and measures to control against hyperinflation.

The plan was quickly presented to the Socialist-controlled National Assembly as an essential program they had to accept. "They will be eager to proceed," said President Zhelyu Zhelev, "because otherwise the Government will fall."

Almost immediately, in November and December 1990, the government brought some 50 bills into Parliament, designed to turn the state-owned economy into a market-oriented system on Western designs. The privatization of industry, land ownership, and agriculture, still in its legislative formative stages, was largely a promise for the future, though speed was essential to deal with the impending crisis at home, growing ever more acute and unremitting.

Crises at Home and Abroad

By the early nineties, economic shortages in Bulgaria had become political metaphors for immediate reforms. Before the transition in power brokers, there had been few social rights but few shortages. The Soviet supply to Bulgaria's 9 million people with many essentials was based on links to Moscow going back to Tsar Alexander II's nineteenth-century end to Turkish domination of Bulgaria, its creation as a principality on 3 March 1878 by the Treaty of San Stefano, which ended the 1877–78 Russo-Turkish War, and Communist cooperation after the Bolshevik Revolution.

A year after the "palace coup" of 9 November 1989, the Stalinist Zhivkov was still insisting that under his regime people held jobs, the state provided security, stores were full, crime was minimized, and there were no "riots."

But this was before crisis within the Soviet Union led to new relations with its breakaway former satellites in late 1989, then the 1990 30 percent reduction in the flow of inexpensive Soviet oil once purchased by Bulgaria with its farm products and manufactured goods, sending gas prices up 100 percent, and the price of everything else impacted by energy costs—food, manufactured clothing, and other processed goods.

With zero growth in 1989 and a 9 to 10 percent shrinkage in 1990, Bulgaria's minister of foreign economic relations prepared for the worst: a 15 percent fall in industrial production between 1990 and 1992; some 45,000 people out of work; continued fuel and food shortages; and plummeting hard-currency reserves to import from, or pay on its already-defaulted debt to, the West.

The causes were not hard to locate: Soviet oil was either cut off or had to be paid for in hard currencies Bulgaria did not have; energy shortages led some plants to go half-time for lack of electrical power; and Baghdad's $1.2 billion trade debt to Sofia, to be paid in 2.6 million tons of Iraqi oil, was never delivered due to the UN-imposed trade embargo. Iran, Libya, and Algeria were to make up only 9 million of the 12 million tons of essential oil needed to keep Bulgaria working at full capacity.

To maintain these imports at world market prices, hard-currency export *earnings* were essential. Yet Bulgaria's infrastructure was not prepared for competitive market conditions; 80 percent of its trade until 1989 was with other Eastern European nations, and its most advanced technologies in computers were uncompetitive with those of market economies.

The future looked grim. Without sufficient petroleum products to run farm machinery, production would be cut; and without factory workers earning full wages at factories operating part-time due to energy shortages, there would be fewer consumers. With both farm and factory production down, there would be unemployment and need for a larger government-financed welfare system that the state could not pay for because the unemployed could not pay taxes. The increased shift of the tax burden to those still working would cut their consumption, ruining the market and their incentive to work hard.

Thus Bulgaria, the breadbasket of the Communist bloc, was now wanting for food, with shortages especially tight in Sofia. In November 1990, the government banned agricultural exports until March 1991 so that local stores could receive their quotas. Shortages were partly based on withholding crops from markets, farmers either refusing to harvest crops left to rot in the fields or withholding livestock from state slaughterhouses, waiting for a government-promised lifting of price controls.

Farmers set in conflict against store owners, truckers, and consumers, each group began hoarding and supplying the black market, where prices moved beyond the reach of most working people, fueling further rounds of inflation that reached well over 100 percent on basic foods like bread in the last few months of 1990, showing no signs of easing.

By mid–January 1992, unemployment was almost 25 percent, inflation exceeded 30 percent, and the foreign debt hovered around $11 billion.

A Nation That Cannot Reliably Borrow

The solution to the crisis was not to be found among foreign lenders, either. Past Communist governments had already borrowed $10.6 billion from the West, then, facing a spreading internal crisis and higher import costs, defaulted on interest and service charges in the spring of 1990. Without further access to trade credits or foreign capital, Bulgaria's foreign reserves were spent at an accelerated rate, going from over $1.2 billion in September 1989 to less than $200 million a year later. At that rate of decline, Bulgaria would use more than all its reserves by the end of 1990, and then would have to barter away its domestic industries and land.

And that is what happened as the new prime minister, Filip Dimitrov, tried to reestablish the Bulgarian state, seeking U.S. investments and aid, switching its national liberation day to 3 March from the previous 9 September 1944 when the Communists seized power under the Soviet army, and recognizing the independence of neighboring Macedonia given in the Treaty of San Stefano by the great powers to Bulgaria, then taken away four months later in the Treaty of Berlin.

A Second Revolution

In times past, a small independent nation with such a burden would have been easy prey for imperial lenders and investors, a process contemplated as Bulgaria's U.S.-designed economic plan and transition went forward in the early nineties.

And yet such encroachments would engender a second popular revolt, ousting the Socialist party running Parliament, then concentrating on new barter relations to exchange Bulgarian food and manufactures for oil from Iran, Libya, Algeria, Russia, and quite possibly a future Iraq. With access to oil, future domestic rehabilitation would likely be assured.

The revolution in the streets that began in the winter of 1989 over a lack of social rights was renewed the following winter over shortages and rationing when on 18 November 70,000 angry protestors packed the central square in Sofia demanding the resignation of former Communist prime minister Lukanov and his Socialist government.

"The Government's one-year credit is up!" shouted Petar Beron, leader of the main opposition group, the Union of Democratic Forces, to the angered throng from the Alexander Nevsky Cathedral steps. "It is time now for action! We will wait no longer. We will vote against the Government's budget draft."

That draft budget called for sharp increases in prices on twenty-one basic products, which would add to the pressures of existing government rationing of gasoline, electricity, and some food items. The opposition's view was that rather than adopt price increases reducing living standards, the government should allow its budget deficit to grow, borrowing the money at home or abroad, both unfeasible or practically impossible.

New elections were also demanded, the Union of Democratic Forces foreseeing that they would triumph, then join a coalition government on the condition that they be allowed to name the prime minister and several key cabinet members.

Though Prime Minister Lukanov narrowly survived a no-confidence vote on 23 November, action turned to a battle for the streets between 30,000 Lukanov supporters and opponents blocking the main boulevard in protest, leading to another mass demonstration by the opposition alliance on 25 November and a general strike called by the trade union confederation on 26 November. After the opposition's month-long campaign and three days of strikes, the Socialist government finally resigned at the end of November 1990.

But the Communists behind the Socialist party did not give up easily, doing battle with the Union of Democratic Forces to win popular backing, especially from the 2.3 million pensioners and new unemployed as the biggest losers.

With Bulgaria's first direct election for a figurehead president in January 1992 won by incumbent Zhelyu Zhelev, who in August 1990 had been appointed as head of state by the Bulgarian Parliament and was supported by the Union of Democratic Forces, the Union controlled both the presidency and the government (formed after winning 34.4 percent in the October 1991 general election). Control was consolidated as Zhelev also defended the nearly 1-million-member Turkish minority in its quest to win political rights and holding 24 of Parliament's 240 seats won in October 1991.

Though the president's only significant political prerogative was to send legislation back to Parliament for reconsideration, Zhelev sought to speed economic transformation, privatizing the state ownership of 93 percent of the nation's productive property, recognizing the continued hardships imposed on the newly unemployed, the retired, and others suffering falling living standards due to inflation and economic restructuring. "The presidential institution at this stage of our development is exceptionally important," said the Democrats' parliamentary leader, Alexander Yordanov. "If there's a parliamentary crisis, it's important that the presidency be in the hands of a democrat so Bulgaria won't return to a totalitarian system."

But it was an open question what the government would now do to eliminate unemployment, rising prices, cutbacks in electricity and gas, and restore the population's access to adequate food and sufficient medicine. A second revolution was in process, but the future was clearly uncertain.

The Future

During the early nineties, a coalition government operating through the Bulgarian Grand National Assembly Parliament will probably be forced to reorganize the nation, save and accumulate resources, provide affordable necessities (foods, medicines, toilet paper, petroleum products, fertilizers, and pesticides), and maintain a moratorium on payment of the foreign debt, part of which was stolen by individual Communists and Bulgarian secret police officers. If Bulgaria abrogates that debt, future Western loans and trade credits might be completely cut off.

The origin of part of the foreign debt resided in the many millions of dollars sent out of the country by the Communist-era secret police operating through 395 companies spread from Austria to Singapore in conjunction with high-ranking officials from foreign countries and foreign financiers like the British press magnate Robert Maxwell.

The chairman of the Bulgarian Parliament's National Security Committee, Yordan Vassilev, described the method by which phantom companies had been set up through a partnership between an official of a Bulgarian state enterprise, a secret police officer, and a Westerner with designs on stealing funds from a Western bank or other lender. With the three operatives establishing a company in a nation where there were weak financial controls, the company would then apply for bank loans, allegedly to establish another far-away enterprise buying a business or land. But rather than build a factory, the land was sold and the proceeds spirited away by the three agents, who also disappeared, so that only the loan outstanding remained, being demanded by a Western bank from Bulgaria's Foreign Trade Bank, thereby enlarging Bulgaria's foreign debt.

Even if some of the funds are eventually returned to the Bulgarian state, they will be a small portion of the total foreign debt. So will any return of the benefits showered on the old *nomenklatura* of Communists running Todor Zhivkov's government, following the dictator's immense legal and economic discretion demanding adherence to the secret 1962 decision ("Secret Protocol B-13") by the Communist Politburo ordering the Council of Ministers as the highest government body to transfer state funds to the secret police for distribution to privileged party members and government officials.

So the second revolutionary government will have to raise its own resources, go beyond its predecessor, and not be locked into attempting to implement a utopian Western-drawn plan for arms-length commercial investment and trade relations. For this might block Bulgaria's strong possibilities for bilateral barter and countertrade, as the nation sits astride the Black Sea to the west, bordering Greece and Turkey to the south, Romania to the north, Serbia and Macedonia to the east.

Bulgaria is thus destined once more to become Eastern Europe's breadbasket and the likely source of food and manufactures for the other nations on her doorstep. Such exports might conceivably finance eventual repayment of the national debt and empower those holding the mantle of government to protect domestic living standards. But precisely how this will be done without the revolution turning toward dictatorial controls or the nation becoming a Western appendage remains unknown.

Chapter 11

Romania and the End
of Party Dictatorship

Stasi, Gestapo, K.G.B., Sécuritaté: All bloodsuckers.
— Woman writing on the wall of invaded
Stasi spy headquarters in East Berlin

*That indelible image of Nicolae Ceausescu's lifeless body lying
on the ground could be the final scene in a modern-dress staging
of "Macbeth." The earlier images of Ceausescu and his partner in
dictatorship, his wife, Elena, staring down a military tribunal
could also be taken from Shakespeare's tragedy, as could the entire
Romanian nightmare of a married couple's lust for autocratic
power at any brutal price. When Lady Macbeth tells her husband
how she would even have "dashed the brains out" of "the babe that
milks me" to get what she wants, does one not recall the eyes of
that dead baby staring out of the photograph of the massacre at
Timisoara? . . .*
*The Ceausescus may come and go like the Perons and the Mar-
coses and so many before them, but there are always successors
waiting in the wings. Shakespeare wrote so that audiences might
recognize and maybe understand the pathology of evil.*
— Frank Rich,
The New York Times, 17 January 1990

Turkey owned it in 1856; France took it in the Crimean War, supported its rights to Transylvania after World War I, then turned Romania
into its own protectorate.[1] Stalin did the rest in 1940, his pact with Hitler
awarding the Reich northern Transylvania and Russian Bessarabia.
Fascist Marshal Ion Antonescu restored "order" until 1944.

Then came the postwar division of Eastern Europe. The Soviets
propped up the Romanian "Revolution," lasting forty-five years until a
new revolution brought an eager America and France to aid Romania,
momentarily outflanking West Germany in developing long-neglected
commercial ties.

The common link a Romance language, the French fluency of 65 percent of Romanian schoolchildren, might continue the century-old ties

between the two nations after the fall of the Great Dictator. And the United States saw both political and commercial opportunities in slipping between the new balkanized nations east of a unified Germany.

DATELINES

Ruling with an iron will in Europe's Eastern corridor, Stalinist president Nicolae Ceausescu tightened his grip in late 1989.

Decades earlier, on the heels of Soviet forces, Romania had become a client state. The king abdicated; the nation was renamed the Romanian People's Republic; and the state nationalized industry and banks, and set up a Soviet constitutional model, with Ceausescu made Communist party chief by 1965. Then came a sense of national independence from Soviet control: 1968 denunciations of the Soviet-led Warsaw Pact invasion of Czechoslovakia; setting up diplomatic relations with Israel after the 1967 war; recognizing West Germany.

Saving capital for his privately designed projects, austerity impositions were the next steps in the Ceausescu drama: moves to cut consumer spending and lowering energy use in order to eliminate $11 billion in foreign debts; arrests of protesting workers over declining living standards followed in November 1987.

March 1988 datelined a program to reduce living costs to accumulate more state capital by demolishing 8,000 villages for resettlement in "more efficient" housing complexes, some 50,000 Hungarians being thus moved against their will.

"GIVE US OUR DEAD!"

On 16 December 1989, another outrage: 200 to 300 known protestors (opposition leaders saying thousands) were killed by government Sécuritaté forces in Timisoara for the unconscionable act of demonstrating to protect a priest, Bishop Laszlo Tokes, defending their political and social rights.

Opposition polemicists declared hundreds were stripped naked to conceal their identity, garbage trucks hauling the dead to an open grave, the security forces shooting the drivers so no witnesses would be left to testify. Photographed corpses had hands missing; young children had been shot with high-power weapons, some several times; a woman's belly slit open, the fetus projecting, stillborn.

Verifiable or not, the city exploded. Tens of thousands took to the streets, chanting, "GIVE US OUR DEAD!"

Engulfed in a sea of humanity, every avenue was overflowing with demonstrators—waving Romanian flags with the Communist hammer and sickle cut from the midriff, others carrying banners emboldened with calls of "End Repression!"

Workers occupied factories, demanding the country's leadership "Resign!" demanding that the party, the military, and other officials whose actions wrought the human carnage be brought to account, that the dictator's security police units be withdrawn from the city.

Government officials, frightened, declared an emergency, putting their forces on combat readiness, banning public meetings and movements, trying to ensure the next day's normal production runs. All were to obey the law and, the government mandated, "take an active part in the normal course of social-economic activity." It was a living page of Orwellian fiction.

Tables turned, army men openly cried, aghast at the savagery of Sécuritaté, who, disguised, were wearing army uniforms. And alongside 50,000 marchers on Timisoara streets now stepped sympathetic uniformed soldiers and officers trailed by their own ensigns!

Military lines were confused but drawn as army units contested the authority of, fired on, the dictator's own security police.

SÉCURITATÉ!

Numbering in the hundreds of thousands, the security police had been recruited from state orphanages as young boys and among the impoverished peasantry, handpicked for abiding loyalty to the Ceausescus.

Most were paid well, some twice the wages of university professors, becoming part of a loyal institution, its sole function being protection of the dictator and his clique.

Not popular either were these president's men. For they were above and hated by the army, which viewed them as traitors against the ordinary populace from which the soldiers rose. Army men had been almost slaves, party orders forcing troops to raise crops and supply manual labor for grandiose Ceausescu projects. Ceausescu's party directing, the Sécuritaté maintained order and control of the army. The army seething with anger, neither party nor security police could wholly survive a popular uprising backed by the army.

But first many would die, be massacred, giving evidence and outrage for the army to erect a shield, move into attack formation against Ceausescu's Sécuritaté, this time under new political direction.

Then the mass graves in Timisoara were uncovered, city residents wildly guessing that 4,500 corpses had been dug up. "Not even Hitler killed his own children, and here they used automatic machine-gun bursts to shoot them down," said Slavomir Gvozdenovic, editor of *Timisoara Literary Review*. No one heard the few voices saying these dead were possibly from accident and hospital casualties and the city morgue.

Then, several days into the revolution, a liberal-minded chemical engineer in Timisoara, Dominic Paraschiv, was framed by the old authorities looking for a scapegoat, Paraschiv being shown on Romanian TV lying naked on a hospital bed covered only with a coarse fishnet and dying of gunshot wounds, depicted as "the butcher of Timisoara," accused of the massacre of eighty anti–Communists. Dominic's notoriety was so widely known that even seeking information about his involvement raised Sécuritaté questions about the investigator, the secret police thereby trying to continue their systematic repression of the past.[2]

BUCHAREST IN FLAMES

Word of *barbarosa* spreading like a prairie fire, the capital of Bucharest went up in flames. Security forces opened fire on demonstrators in the main squares, killing several hundred, shooting students first, then bayoneting the wounded, crushing their skulls, taking the corpses to unknown mass cremation graves, washing the streets of blood to conceal the carnage—Lady Macbeth reappearing once more, cleansing evil deeds.

Outraged, torching Ceausescu's Royal Palace residence, bombing the Central Committee building, setting the National Archives ablaze, the roving crowds grew more mindless, unruly, threatening.

Key army commanders, feeling betrayed, defected to the ranks of civilian protestors, taking thousands of their charges with them. Defense Minister Col. Gen. Vasile Milea refused to carry out Ceausescu's last official order to fire on the crowds, and Milea was shot in cold blood by the security forces loyal to the president.

Taking his place, chief of general staff Maj. Gen. Stefan Gusa swiftly called on antiterrorist army troops to come together at a central point, civilians gathering round. "Brothers," he told the crowd, "the Army throughout the country is at the side of the people. It is the people's Army. All Army units, all garrisons, and all our country's cities are quiet. Please, do understand that we have to put order into things in Bucharest as well. Therefore, you have to help the military to be able to go where they have missions to fulfill. The Army will always be with us and with you. We swear, we swear, we swear!"

- A.M., 23 December: Extending lines of fire between army and security forces rake the city, radio stations, and airport. Unarmed students take over the main radio stations, army tanks mobilizing to defend them against attack by heavily armed Sécuritaté. Down the avenue leading to University Square come thousands of people and army together, the crowds taking charge of Palace Square, the remains of the Central Committee building, climbing balconies to address their compatriots.
- P.M.: From the radio and television stations they hold, demonstrators take turns calling on the army and local militias to defend the interests of the people: "Shoot not them!" "Go into the streets,

peaceably!" "Occupy municipal councils!" "Take control in all cities, at all enterprises and establishments!"

Bucharest is falling to popular will amid disappearing army cordons; pandemonium reigns, horns blaring, people delirious with joy.

A Committee for National Salvation takes to TV, urging people amassed at Bucharest Square to leave it so the National Defense Ministry can destroy the terrorist forces of the State Security Service operating in the secret underground passages of the Central Committee building.

In the icy night of 23 December, fierce gunfire continues throughout the city; searchlights are everywhere; powerful explosions decimate gas lines. The army physically takes charge, putting the bureaus of the Ministry of Interior, with all its technological paraphernalia for repression, under its jurisdiction.

Crawling through secret underground tunnels beneath the Central Committee building, klieg lights darting, liberation forces move to liquidate fleeing members of the Central Committee.

The press liberates its libido, confessing that "until yesterday," it was "compelled to depict reality otherwise than it really was and systematically disinform the home and international public opinion."

POLITICS AND CONFLICT

Time of the essence now, the National Salvation Front provisionally organizes its public administration centered in Bucharest. "Our aim is to set up a new structure of political power," says Ion Iliescu of the Front; "the old structure — the party, the Government, and so forth — have actually been eliminated."

Timisoara's Committee for Social Democracy issues its own demands to Premier Constantin Dascalescu: immediate resignation of the entire political leadership of the country; free democratic elections; responsibility for those who issued orders to shoot at the masses of Timisoara; admittance of foreign journalists; publication of the Committee's demands in all Romanian media.

Revolution proceeding, outsiders also have their say. The voice of Romania past issues from Switzerland, King Michael calling for a constitutional monarchy, insisting he is still king and head of state, and has been so for the last forty years of expatriation in Geneva.

America lectures too, wanting influence in a future Romania bordering the Soviets, the U.S. administration speaking of "irresistible tides of reform." The State Department should know, having accommodated the dictator well over a decade. Reform, advises Washington, could not be halted, so great the costs, with those who oppose reform becoming "the chief victims," foreseeing too that Ceausescu's demise will "create a certain momentum for change in Moscow."

Many Romanians do not agree. Young people on the move seek to go beyond reform, setting up roadblocks everywhere to stop the security forces from consolidating their hold. They become the new guards at factories, identified by handlettered badges on their shirts; they frisk travelers at the entrances to Bucharest. You know them by their dress now — young men wearing red headbands, carrying new Kalashnikov assault rifles; women surrounded by piles of food and medicine.

Radio Free Romania is blaring: "Young people! Help the army effort by forming patriotic guards!" "Workers! Do everything at your units and factories to ensure no interruption in the supply line to the population, regardless of difficulty! Continue production full force to provide food, heating oil, and drinking water!" "People of Romania! Organize local committees of the National Salvation Front!"

It is 25 December, Christmas, snowing in Bucharest: The National Salvation Front Council joins the general staff and other military leaders to direct national operations from a secret protected center. Plans are firmed: Liquidate the scattered units of the security forces and terrorists bent on provocations, attacks against civilians, public institutions, industrial enterprises, military targets, trade outlets, hospitals, housing quarters.

The Front adopts extraordinary military and political measures: cease all firing of weapons; prevent vandalism, destruction, and personal revenge; turn over all arms and ammunition to the army; merge the Ministry of Interior with the Ministry of National Defense in order to command all troops and mobilize all weaponry; protect all social and production establishments; create new structures for democracy and freedom to restore order and reconstruct the nation; subordinate all forces to the Ruling Council; promote cooperation of creative forces, all nationalities, people of all social standing.

The plan to be put in action, freedom sounds on almost every tongue. Soldiers with aging automatic weapons fraternize with people on the street. Senior customs officers, border guards, and police wear proudly liberation armbands — striped yellow, red, and blue.

DÉMARCHE

Comes the démarche, Ceausescu's savage error.

Summoning a state TV-covered rally after the massacre at Timisoara, the president justifies the deed, igniting calls of "assassine!" — revealing for a fleeting moment a wild beastlike countenance, surprised, shocked, stricken with fear. For the first time, viewers see Ceausescu's face contorted in total disbelief that any in his realm might question his word and authority.

How could anyone have escaped his surveillance? Had he not eliminated political opponents, rotated individual officials between posts to prevent their creation of a power base, punished those expressing an opposing opinion? Was not one in four Romanians in his service an informer out of weakness and fear? Certainly the privileged inner circle was completely reliable. Were they not sustained with party privileges, an elite with villas, ski lodges, hunting resorts, special food shops and amenities? Sécuritaté—certainly they were faithful to the cause, bred and sustained from the president's special resources.

Calibrations of his enemies coursing his mind, fear seizes the president, giving orders to follow a preplanned route for escape. With their heavily armed, private guards, he and wife Elena now swiftly make their way through the secret palace tunnel to the airport, helicopter waiting, immediately taking to the air. The pilot, spotted on radar, tells the president that radio reports say the government has been overthrown.

Ceausescu quickly draws his weapon, holding helicopter pilot Lt. Col. Vasile Malutan at gunpoint:

> *Ceausescu:* No. Those are horrible lies. Are you not serving the cause?
> *Pilot:* We are seen and in danger of being blown up!
> *Ceausescu:* Land...
> *Ceausescu* (gun trained, leaving the helicopter): Are you serving the cause?
> *Pilot:* Which cause should I serve?

Ceausescu does not reply, sprints to a military vehicle radioed in flight, waiting to aid his escape. The hunt is on now, the Ceausescus and their military escort in disguise soon arrested by army forces near a rally in a nearby city. They are forced into an armored vehicle, then driven in circles for almost a dozen hours to stop the Sécuritaté from locating them so they can be secretly charged and tried.

Charges quickly leveled by the chairman of the prosecutor's office, their acts are depicted as

> crimes against the people. They carried out acts that are incompatible with human dignity and social thinking; they acted in a despotic and criminal way; they destroyed the people whose leader they claimed to be.

The Bill of Indictment contains the following points:

> 1. Genocide....
> 2. Armed attack on the people and state power.... The destruction of buildings and state institutions, undermining the national economy.... Obstruct[ing] the normal process of the economy.

CRIME AND PUNISHMENT

"They not only deprived the people of heating, electricity and foodstuffs," the prosecutor charges the Ceausescus in their fateful trial; "they also tyrannized the soul of the Romanian people."

"They not only killed children, young people, and adults in Timisoara and Bucharest; they allowed Sécuritaté members to wear military uniforms to create the impression among the people that the Army is against them. They wanted to separate the people from the Army."

Sécuritaté was under both Ceausescus' direct command, the prosecutor elaborates: "They used to fetch people from orphans' homes or from abroad whom they trained in special institutions to become murderers of their own people."

"You!" Finger pointing directly at the accused, the prosecutor exclaims: "You were so impertinent as to cut off oxygen lines in hospitals, and to shoot people in their hospital beds. The Sécuritaté had hidden food reserves on which [a malnourished] Bucharest could have survived for months, the whole of Bucharest."

"Was this butcher of Romania sane?" the prosecutor asks, ruminating: Mental illness — no, his Stalinist pathology of domination. Different too from the fixation of the mass murderer, brain twisted, eyes blinded by a mental picture predetermining the deed. For here sits Ceausescu, supremely rational, calculating, personifying the voice of the people he professes to represent yet brutally oppresses; the populace he claims he loves but refuses to reach, touch their heart, with compassion and empathy. This ruler, he is monster! charges the prosecutor.

> *Prosecutor:* You have never been able to hold a dialogue with the people. You were not used to talking to the people. You held monologues and the people had to applaud, like in the rituals of tribal people. And today you are acting in the same megalomaniac way.
> *Ceausescu:* I will only answer questions before the Grand National Assembly. I do not recognize this court. The charges are incorrect, and I will not answer a single question here.
> *Prosecutor:* There is still shooting going on. Fanatics, whom you are paying. They are shooting at children. They are shooting arbitrarily into apartments. Who are these Fanatics? Are they the people, or are you paying them?
> *Ceausescu:* I will not answer any question. Not a single shot was fired in Palace Square.... No one was shot.
> *Prosecutor:* By now [we have proven records], there have been thirty-four casualties.

Ceausescu sidestepping the substance of the charges, saying he "will only answer to the working class," questioning then moves to the point of authority of both prosecutor and the National Salvation Front that has dissolved the National Assembly. Ceausescu claims that he should be tried by the Parliament (he controlled), not by judges as ordinary citizens without authority to judge him, that a putsch against him was organized from abroad:

Prosecutor: The Grand National Assembly has been dissolved.

Ceausescu: This is not possible at all. No one can dissolve the National Assembly.

Prosecutor: We now have another leading organ. The National Salvation Front is now our supreme body.

Ceausescu: No one recognizes that. That is why people are fighting all over the country. This gang will be destroyed. They organized the putsch.

Prosecutor: The people are fighting against you, not against the new forum.

Ceausescu: No, the people are fighting for freedom and against the new forum. I do not recognize this court.

Prosecutor: Why do you think the people are fighting today? What do you think?

Ceausescu: As I said before, the people are fighting for their freedom and against this putsch, against this usurpation.

The prosecutor now calls for the death sentence and impounding the entire property of the accused Ceausescus:

> I would not call for the death sentence, but it would be incomprehensible for the Romanian people to have to go on suffering this great misery and not have it ended by sentencing the two Ceausescus to death. The crimes against the people grew year by year. They were only busy enslaving the people and building up an apparatus of power. They were not really interested in the people.

Ceausescu is accused of never having understood what was important in Romania, of never having understood the people. And, of course, he does not understand the seriousness of the current moment either.

"So far, they have always claimed that we have built this country [for the better]," the prosecutor tilts against the accused. "We have paid our eleven-billion-dollar foreign debts, but with this they bled the country to death and have hoarded enough money to ensure their escape."

Continuing, the prosecutor gestures toward them: "You might have achieved the understanding of the Romanian people if you had now admitted to your guilt. You should have stayed in Iran after the Sécuritaté slaughter in Timisoara where you had flown."

Both Ceausescus laugh, amused that the prosecutor would suggest they be accused, let alone would try to escape. "We do not stay abroad," Elena defends. "This is our home."

Court-appointed counsel for the defense, still unable to get the accused to cooperate in rebutting the substance of the underlying issues of crimes against the people, now speaks:

> Even though he — like her — committed insane acts, we want to defend them. We want a legal trial. Only a president who is still confirmed in his position can demand to speak to the Grand National Assembly. If he no

longer has a certain function, he cannot demand anything at all. He is then treated as an ordinary citizen. Since the old government has been dissolved and Ceausescu has lost his functions, he no longer has the right to be treated as the president.

The defense rests. There will be no recall of the dissolved National Assembly to try the former president. The military tribunal is in power now, and chairman of the new forum Council Ion Iliescu and General Militaru are overseeing the two-hour military proceeding, its verdict now being read: Death, and confiscation of all Ceausescu property!

"We have shouldered our responsibility as the Council," the self-appointed prime minister Petre Roman insists, "but we have used in every detail the existing legality of Ceausescu. That is to say, we have conducted a trial to which he had to submit because it was a military tribunal organized according to certain norms which were respected, including assessors [representative] of the people."

The Council fearing terrorist groups readied to attack to free the dictator, the Ceausescus are now taken to a military complex for execution. Facing the firing squad, Elena reminds the soldiers that she is above them, like a mother to them, being sharply rebuffed to think about the mothers who had been killed under her husband's rule.

The sentence is then immediately carried out, soldiers with automatic weapons firing under orders, the president's riddled body falling first, Elena, darting like a headless chicken across the military yard, an easy target for the executioners, the soldiers, wrath exploding, riddling their bodies.

"The sentence was definitive and was carried out," Council chairman Iliescu and General Militaru publicly announce. The Ceausescus are no more.

FIGHT TO THE FINISH

Make no mistake, though. The civil war was brutally alive. "We were in a circumstance which did not permit us to wait for another situation of instability," the prime minister said, justifying the secret trial and execution of the Romanian Caesars.

Despite Colonel General Vlad's order from his chair at the Department of State Security—that, the dictator dead, security troops side with the people and the army against Ceausescu's remaining clan—his order was not obeyed. Resistance from security forces powerfully continued, these highly trained street fighters turning to activities by night, mingling with liberation forces by wearing their armbands yet training their helicopter gunships on rail stations, airports, unsuspecting populations. The *engage* still numbered 25,000 to 30,000 against the army's swelled ranks of 175,000, but they were still no easy match, possessed of a paratrooper company, rocket grenade launchers, armored personnel carriers.

Intricate communication networks were everywhere in the capital: a unit of 1,500 specialized Sécuritaté assigned to guard the Ceausescus; a special force of 1,000 to combat "terrorism," using a vast system of secret tunnels and intelligence "safe houses"; caves and bunkers for storing months of food and ammunition supplies.

Having extended the old nineteenth-century Princely tunnel system used to defend Bucharest from the Ottomans, the Ceausescus' palace residence had been linked to the military academy, some twenty-five miles away and to the president's lakeside villas and two airports six miles away. Rumor held that those who dug these narrow burrows of security were shot to keep the dictator's confidence forever.

That was past now. The task at hand was to smoke out, gas, fire-bomb, starve, and shoot the security forces still holed up in this maze of crazy-quilted political magic. By Christmas day, most of the terrorists had either surrendered or dispersed into small groups drawing on hidden arms dumps, so the army ordered them captured alive to reveal any remaining cache of weapons.

Smokeouts began, following the caverns and tunnels of the dictator's madness: weapons, chemical- and germ-welfare supplies were uncovered, as were classified files documenting the lives of millions of "unreliable" citizens. Gunfire ricocheted through the narrow tunnels; flamethrowers singed walls; and trapped like rats, agents of the Sécuritaté put down their weapons, raised white flags, or emerged from sewers on the city streets — shivering, terror-stricken, some half starved.

Army men gave them no fine welcome either. Unprotected, they were punched and brutalized by the crowds. Some were shot point-blank, left to die on the street. Others pleaded their innocence of Ceausescu operations. Yet only a handful were ever tried, most filtering into Romanian civil life, perhaps for another terrorist adventure or hire as a soldier of fortune.

FILLING THE POLITICAL VACUUM

Abhorring the power vacuum, old and new parties quickly moved into the empty political space. But the opposition of more than a dozen parties, each publishing its thoughts and opinions, made future unity increasingly unlikely.

Here in contest were pro–Western, non–Communist leaders, the small National Salvation Front pursuing a program of free elections, a market-oriented economy, and socialism. The prewar Christian Peasant party surfaced, as did dozens of new groups, all viewing the Ceausescu Communists as slavish, backward, bureaucratic, authoritarian, repressive, and violent.

Small peasantry, few left after Ceausescu collectivization, came together behind the National Christian Peasant party (NCPP), once the party of the landlords, putting out their paper, *Reawakening*, proselytizing that a 2,000-year national backbone linked its cause, Christianity, moral rehabilitation, and peasant production. Christian morals and dignity of peasants, industrial workers, and intellectuals, the NCPP proclaimed, would promote unity, also ending the spiritual and material destruction of the Romanian peasant and villages. These forces would also block the governmental dismantling of producer cooperative farms, allowing the farmers to till their land alone or in free association. Such developments would set society on a renewed ecological foundation, provide equal church rights for all, with religion as a subject taught in school. For these goals, and feeding the nation, the Peasant party would adhere to the coalition National Salvation Front.

The old Liberal party, once beholden to conservative bankers and industrialists, was again calling for a free-market economy. In the past, both Peasant and Liberal parties had pumped nationalism, anti–Semitism, and chauvinism into the political mainstream. After World War I, they had gone after the Bolshevik Revolution and its followers; after the next world war, they faced the Communists in control; and after Ceausescu's fall, they again became the anti–Communist opposition, calling for Western-style democracy and becoming a participant in the Front.

Workers' and intellectuals' allegiance too was essential for the Salvation Front to survive. For at that point in Romania there was no labor "Solidarity" movement, as in Poland; no "Charter 77" among intellectuals, as in Czechoslovakia; no "Samizdat" intellectual underground papers to rally the opposition, as in the Soviet Union; and no ecological "Green" movement, as in the West.

Non-Communists had long been isolated from the wire-pulling apparati of state power, so the ten or so political parties in formation also faced the functionaries of a now villified regime.

Democratic structures completely lacking, new ways of viewing national decision-making were evolving, focusing on popular demands for atonement from the torturers and mass murderers to be brought to trial and firing squad.

But earth-turning political changes were not to come so quickly.

Delayed, with no time for elections, on 22 December a provisional government under former foreign minister Cornelia Manescu had emerged to take charge, representing many groups and the most important resistance forces—military officers, student leaders, literary figures and artists, former Communist officials.

Four decades without an alternative now awarded a handful of thirty-nine people composing the original Council of the National Salvation Front a powerful, totally unrepresentative voice as they emerged and took over from the nation's tiny and disparate dissident movement, now grown strong alongside others from the peasantry, liberals and those in Romania's arts.

FROM CHAOS TO ORDER AND DECEIT

Bringing order to chaos — that was the first task in eliminating the old government and its hirelings, asking for and receiving Western governments' recognition for the Front representing the "democratic will of the Romanian people."

A free democratic forum was to reconstruct the central economic plan, possibly establishing an open domestic market, perhaps carrying forward multilateral foreign commerce reaching Western Europe and the United States.

Proposing the future was to be the task of the provisional government's leader, Ion Iliescu — to adopt a pluralistic system, separation of state powers, a written constitutional system, restoration of civil rule, observation of human and national minority rights, restoration of small-scale agriculture, reorganization of trade, direction of foreign policy toward a united Europe, and, catering to Communist demands, continued membership in the Warsaw Pact.

On 26 December, four days into the life of the provisional government, there was sporadic gunfire in the capital, and several thousand converged for a mass meeting at Palace Square. Speakers, reading reports from various districts, announced that local committees of the Front were still composed of old leaders and incompetent Communists. In one district, a report read, the new local bodies refused to talk to the students that made the revolution.

"No deceit! No deceit!" the rally began chanting. "The army is with us!" "We will not go away!"

From the rostrum appeals were made to TV and the leadership of the National Salvation Front to come to the square and take part in the dialogue. But come the self-selected leaders did not. Rather, Free Romanian Television announced that the Council of the National Salvation Front had nothing to do with calling the meeting and that in the Council's opinion, the situation in Bucharest was not conducive to holding mass meetings.

"Nomenklatura," "Communist technocrats," "the old order" — these images raced through the student movement. "Have we, the students whose blood washed the streets of Bucharest — have we won the revolution to again be ruled by new oppressors?"

OPENING TO THE COMMUNIST RIGHT

No easy step was freedom's path from the tyrant's penal order of political repression and enforced immiserization. Military moves now required a political sequel, stepping away from the Stalinist model of draconian repression, megalomaniac central planning, and atavistic thinking that pervaded the old system of bureaucratic centralism.

Yet, the Council began to sift out and demote the non–Communists, a founder of the Front, Valentine Gabrielescu, vigorously opposing the character of the emerging government. Striking at Ion Iliescu, the head of the Council's cabinet (also Ceausescu's former cabinet minister and Communist party secretary), Gabrielescu, charged that Iliescu was given the political edge because of the political ineptitude of amateurs. "These Communists," he criticized, "push themselves and one another forward. I am convinced these are the types who will try to put a rosy face on communism. Did we overthrow Ceausescu to have the Communists back again?"

It was fact: To preserve its own hold on state power, the party jettisoned the Ceausescus, reformatted their political policies, and appeared as libertarians calling for free elections, democracy, and trade. Party chief, now new Council president, Iliescu did no more than they asked.

The first revolution of the children of Romania, supported by the army and the police, had been returned to the Communists, their consensus, their bureaucratic methods.

PARTY, ARMY, SÉCURITATÉ, AND ORDER

The population was not pacified by the self-appointed transitional government's use of the army and reorganized Sécuritaté to maintain order.

Without new leaders, the provisional government had relied on the remaining experienced Communist bureaucrats. And the Communists relied on the army that had reasserted its power, yet faced a population that was traditionally anti–Communist, anti–Russian, anti–Hungarian, and lacking knowledge of the methods of multiple-party democracy.

Here was a formula for either a new system of government or a reincarnation of the old, with party, army, and order imposed on the people who had just won their freedom.

On 27 December, old party hands in charge of the new Council announced emergency measures to strike at the lingering threat from the Sécuritaté. Special military tribunals were created to try terrorists who did not immediately surrender the next day, 28 December, with a promise of immunity to those who surrendered themselves and others under the decree. No one believed there would be no retribution, the population that had most suffered viewing the Communist-led transitional government as unreliable, vowing an eye-for-an-eye against all security forces.

Council duplicity was in store. The old Communists in the Council had formally sent the Sécuritaté into retirement, but from its structure had created another security force and prepared the reserve secret police for future deployment.

This had been accomplished by transferring the operations and personnel of the Sécuritaté from the Interior Ministry to the Council run by the defense minister, so that some of the same people who carried out security functions of the Sécuritaté now administered the same under defense minister Council authority.

To make the transition feasible, the popular loyalist Gen. Nicolae Militaru was removed and Council loyalist General Stanculescu was installed as the new defense minister. Stanculescu proceeded to arrest only members of the secret police who were "directly involved" in the December repressions of demonstrators, transferring the rest—some 1,844 secret police from Bucharest to surrounding areas for reserve duty; another 1,739 to operate between units around the country. Still another 611, who had *actively attacked* the revolutionary movement as part of Ceausescu's elite counterespionage unit of 2,400, were now put on reserve duty.

Arresting only an initial seven of the many thousands of Sécuritaté, General Stanculescu exonerated the rest because, he said, they "became aware during the first hours of the revolution of the necessity of the fight for liberty and democracy and fought against the terrorists."

This was blatantly false, as the opposition movement charged. And the Sécuritaté operating underground again sent anonymous threats— several to General Popa, who as chief of the military tribunal condemned Ceausescu and his wife to death.

In possession of critical firsthand evidence, General Popa mysteriously committed "suicide" just as the trial of twenty-one former secret police officers began in March 1990. They were charged with scores of deaths at Timisoara: Maj. Gen. Emil Macri and six others with genocide, facing life imprisonment; fourteen others with shooting unarmed civilians, facing up to twenty years.

The case was moved to Bucharest under sharp protest of Timisoara residents, who accused the prosecutors of failing to substantiate and dropping the original charges of genocide. And on 9 December 1991, the Supreme Military Court in Bucharest reached a majority verdict to jail eight Communist officials and members of the Sécuritaté for up to twenty-five years for aggravated murder and complicity in murder for the massacre of ninety-seven people and the wounding of hundreds of others in Timisoara. Six of the original defendants were acquitted, one died in prison, and ten others were found guilty of lesser charges but were freed for time served and under a 1990 presidential amnesty. Henceforth, the Sécuritaté would not have to worry about being charged with crimes against humanity.

Again on the offensive, the Sécuritaté had renewed their terror, National Peasant party's spokesman Valentine Gabrielescu documenting one of his own party workers being assaulted, slain, and his tongue cut out as he left church in the Bacau area.

Cabinet minister Corneliu Bogan also began a series of not-so-veiled threats against the opposition's political right to criticize, saying, "There can be no opposition party because there is no party in government."

Contrite and untrue, the Communists again in charge, Bogan insisted that the Front was a "remarkable consensus," had a program, required tranquility — and that might mean using the army against any opposition.

The situation thus begun, December 1989 continued into the early nineties: The new government Council empowered the Communists at the expense of its non–Communist members, dividing supporters. Four million people making up the pool of former Communist bureaucrats were mobilized by the new government to keep the state operating, and there was no witch-hunt to do away with Ceausescu supporters of the Sécuritaté.

"The first question will be competence," cabinet minister Bogan began the new ordering of apparat. "There are some people who expressed their views and suffered under Ceausescu, and some complied under his regime. We have to remember that not everyone can be a hero." Thus the Communist-led government kept its "competent" Communist bureaucracy.

REVOLUTION AND ECONOMIC SURVIVAL

Whatever its failings, the revolution freed Romanians to speak, think, write, organize — and worry about their future. The Romanian population of 22 million declined between 1989 and the end of 1991, and quickened emigration accompanied a fall in the birth rate as frightened families limited the number of mouths to feed.

Still, typewriters — and now computers — no longer had to be registered with the police.

The destruction of churches and national monuments was declared illegal.

Abortion as a primary means of birth control was legalized.

Spontaneous demonstrations were allowed (there had been hundreds of them by early 1992), and citizens were no longer legally obliged to address one another as "Comrade" this or that.

Yet the military tribunals that were to track, try, and punish Ceausescu's armed supporters largely failed to accomplish their political task under the reign of the new Communist-led government. And, though illegal, retaliation by personal vendetta continued.

Residence laws that restricted mobility of peasants and workers were abolished.

The government also promised to repay citizens for money forcibly subtracted from their paychecks for so-called economic development under the dictator's megalomaniac building schemes.

The hated modernization program that razed villages and destroyed old viable structures and homes was halted, but the peasantry were not rehabilitated.

True, under the land-return law for up to twenty-five acres per farm family, the peasantry were again to be able to own and work small plots of land and bring their produce to market. But though cooperatives legally ceased to exist as of 1 January 1992, the government blocked small farmers either by giving deeds to only 16,000 of over 6 million who entered claims or by pressuring collectives to transform themselves into agricultural associations entitled to borrow state equipment and receive state subsidies when selling their output to the state.

By contrast, small plots received no government aid, over 12.3 million acres going unsown in early 1992. "The state does not want to recognize the right of people who lost their lands, and it certainly does not want to give up its property," explained Viorel Pasca, representing the National Peasants party in February 1992. "The land is left fallow because the peasants don't know where their plots of land are, they would have no [government] tractors to cultivate it if they did, and there was no gasoline available during the planting season anyway."[3]

REVOLUTION NOT OVER

The revolution was not over, a second coming increasingly likely. For the first Romanian revolution in 1989 turned on deeper, still-unfulfilled tasks, including, besides a new social order and the role of the army in any crisis, economic survival.

Self-sufficiency had been muted by the dictator's export program to eliminate the foreign debt of $11 billion. A hungry people had faced export of their farmers' grain and workers' output. Imports of Iranian oil and gas were exchanged, and Romania became Iran's second largest trading partner in Eastern Europe.

Romanian food was also sent to the Soviet Union as its largest market, further impoverishing the people, requiring the provisional government to reverse these exports immediately to reorganize the nation's economic lifeline.

Reducing such exports, the provisional government was able to take food off rationing, meeting the immediate needs of the population. So three days after Ceausescu was ousted, Romanians were allowed to turn on gas and oil for heat and cooking in their apartments, ending the "austerity" of wearing overcoats at home. On 27 December, Romanian-raised chickens, oranges, and lemons were the first diverted from export to the Soviet Union, so Bucharest had its first taste of a real holiday season in decades.

Then came the terrible truth: The 60 million tons of grain Ceausescu claimed were stored were only 16.8 million; the 25,000 tons of stored meat would not meet the 60,000 tons monthly requirement for 23 million people.

France and the United States sent in airlifts of donated medicine, medical help, and food. Other Western aid was conditional. Elections on the agenda for May 1990, the United States asked that they be fair and unfettered, promising benefits if they were. Through grants or highly subsidized prices, Washington would also benefit U.S. farmers by shipping $80 million worth of cattle feed and butter. Free elections would bring other aid too, including a waiver of trade restrictions and U.S. support for Romanian efforts to join the General Agreement on Tariffs and Trade and the International Monetary Fund.

But there would not be completely fair elections, for not all parties were equal in gaining television coverage, buying newsprint, or using government funds. And the future might not be better unless the economy, social structure, and political situation were equitably reorganized.

On 1 February 1990, a new arrangement for sharing political power had been agreed upon by the opposition forces, designed in part to defuse building political tensions and distrust, in part to restore some semblance of stability, in part to give all political parties a clear field to run in coming elections, but mostly to stop the demonstrations that woud prevent reorganization of a fast-deteriorating economy.

These nuances and complications eliminated the Front's domination of the Council, creating a more balanced one awaiting the national election. For it was now evident that the Communists controlling the government, backed up by the army, could not rehabilitate an economy where the people were unwilling charges. Yet rule momentarily they did. "We say in Romania that miracles endure for three days," said Mircea Dinescu, head of the Writers Union. "Like our revolution: after three days the professionals of power took over. The master was killed, his servants took over."

Romanian officials would now worry about demonstrators storming back to the streets to oppose this or that former party or government official, these spies and Sécuritaté, those great and small tyrants. "No more Communists, no more Ceausescu!" remained the opposition's threat that no Romanian government could ignore.

In October 1990, ten months after Ceausescu was ousted, the economy had virtually collapsed, output plummeting and the trade deficit growing. Prime Minister Petre Roman accelerated the government three-year plan for privatizing at least half of bloated and outdated state-owned companies, with employees to be awarded preferential rights to purchase shares in the privatized sectors of agriculture, the food industry, light industry, housing construction, services, tourism, trade, and transport. Allowing prices of most goods to rise 100 to 125 percent to "market" levels, the state planned to subsidize energy, fuel, and rent for a year, and the government was to control prices for basic foods and services. Social security measures were to protect retirees and housewives, with pensions indexed to prices for nonessential goods and services.

"We have reached a point of no return," the prime minister said. "We must implement reforms. Not only pay lip service to it. The solution is a shock therapy, included in the basic principles of the government reform." But these and other reforms in banking, tax imposts, and a conditioned foreign-financed trade deficit promised to build an unemployed army of 1 million in 1992, bringing a sharp response from the working population, pressuring managers to let wages rise even as output plummeted in 1990.

THE LOGIC OF POLITICAL PARTIES, FOREIGN AID, AND A MARKET ECONOMY

A market economy required production for self-sufficiency and exports to pay for essential energy and other imports. In the first nine months of 1990, however, people had stopped working at capacity and half of Friday and Saturday, production dropping 28 percent and exports falling 46 percent.

Dictating a workweek including two Saturdays a month, the government increased the average from 40 to 44 hours a week, with the population still caught in a wage-price freeze. And thus the government lost its popular authority, urban support for the National Salvation Front largely gone by February 1992, leaving 1,340 small towns and villages still supporting its mayoral candidates. In Bucharest and other major cities like Brasov, Constanta, and Sibiu, the union of fourteen opposition parties backing the Democratic Convention won the initial mayoral posts awaiting the spring runoff elections.

"These elections are the first stage of Romania's true democratization," heralded victorious Timisoara mayoral candidate Viorel Oancea. And a multiplicity of parties now pitted one ethnic and vested interest against another—2 million ethnic Hungarians backing the Democratic Union of Hungarians, taking several Transylvanian cities; the anti–Hungarian, extreme-right Romanian National Unity party winning the city of Cluj in Transylvania.

The logic of parties thus had an economic foundation. And in its early stages of redesign, all economic plans would go to shreds, as would the parties that promised reforms and higher living standards. Like other newly liberated Eastern Europe states, the Romanian government Communists had initially sought foreign aid and trade. And on 30 January 1991, the European Community, the United States, and Japan had begun to extend economic aid to Romania on the alleged basis that the government had ceased violent repression of protestors. The IMF promised about $1 billion in aid on condition that the government swiftly put a free market in place.

But the conditions proved too harsh. Under the Communist government leaders still in charge, state subsidies were to be eliminated except for energy; price controls on food were removed and most restrictions on foreign exchange abolished in 1991. Yet by passing on the "true costs of the necessities of life" and pushing unemployment as high as 500,000 to 1 million, the government risked renewed protests.

"We have made an error," bemoaned Alexandru Birladeanu, the Senate president, an 80-year-old economist who had resigned from the Ceausescu leadership in 1968. "We are going too fast. In creating the Romania of the year 2000, we are making the Romanians of 1991 pay too high a price."

And thus the time warp in seeking reforms: public outrage at hyper-inflation of 100 to 125 percent in 1990 alone; the June 1990 bands of Communist miners defending the Communist-led government with axes and bats after a day of opposition protest; the fears by foreign investors seeking social order as the basis for investment projects totaling $2 billion; future plans for economic and cultural ties reuniting Moldova and Romania, separated in 1940 when Bessarabia (the section of Moldova north and east of the Prut River) was incorporated into the Soviet Union under the 1939 secret pact between the Soviets and Nazi Germany.

ROMANIAN LIES AND ETHNIC WARS

Ethnic clashes between Slavs in northern Moldova declaring their Trans-Dniester Republic against the Romanians making up two-thirds of Moldova's 4 million people were complicated by Romanian rumors creating tension and rifts with Hungarians in Transylvania.

By late 1990, the division between Romanians and the nation's 2 million Hungarians had already been accentuated by economic conflict. The Hungarians resided largely in the area of Timisoara, focused on Transylvania and other western borderlands that were historically part of Hungary. Their superior education and business acumen were sharply resented by the Romanians.

And the Romanians also feared the Democratic Hungarian Union and its key figure, Bishop Laszlo Tokes, the clergyman whose arrest in December 1989 had set off the revolt against the Ceausescu regime. The Union commanded the loyalty of virtually the entire Hungarian population in Romania and had polled the second largest number of votes among the eighty-four parties represented in Romania's May 1990 elections.

Spreading rumors that Tokes was far less central to the events of December 1989, Romanians claimed he had left the country for Budapest or America, which was untrue, though Tokes had visited New York to drum up aid and investment capital for Romania's failing economy.

Elections alone could never solve such problems now, and there were related issues too: the need for local democracy, a restructured economy, the elimination of the new secret police, the need for compassion among all ethnic groups to build the nation. By early 1992, these problems had not been adequately aired, had barely been discussed or resolved. The revolution that brought high expectations and temporary relief in food, heat, and power lay in shambles. And it was apparent that the nation's inefficient factories would have to be retooled or closed. There were too few apartments to house the population adequately.

In Timisoara, prices were out of reach for necessities; water in apartments was either nonexistent or ice cold. Universities closed for lack of dormitory heat. Factories furloughed workers due to raw material shortages. And electricity for street cars and tram lines was expected to be cut. The December Romanian Supreme Court had convicted and sentenced only eight of the twenty-four Communists and secret police charged with participating in suppressing the Timisoara uprising. The rest were freed, and the public was bitter and would never know who shot, killed, and wounded their people—and why. "Today, we Timisoarians have the right to ask whether there is reason to celebrate," Reformed Church minister Tokes told his congregation in the second week of an icy December 1991. "Is it worth continuing what we started, or hoping, or trusting again?"[4]

Solutions were avoided by tough new laws to curtail popular rights, turning to agencies of repression. Government buildings were now "protected" from demonstrators, and some 4,500 new police agents and a new internal security force were organized. "We didn't have a revolution to demonstrate in parks," a poster near the university complained of regulations limiting protests to the areas easily controlled.

And so yesterday's disenfranchised, especially the irrepressible students who started the first revolution, might again became today's protestors and perhaps tomorrow's revolutionaries of a second coming. Hear them out; they may well be Romania's future:

> We have no language of liberty, only applause and cheers.
> Our revolution has been stolen by the old faces.
> No *perestroika*, no Communists.

For it is not government hierarchy that they hold dear, but freedom, self-determination of each people, each region, each community, perhaps joining together by their own volition in a broader movement for unity.

Part V:
Arms and the New
Balance of Power

We, the expellees, renounce all thought of revenge and retaliation.
— 1950 Charter of Federation of German Expellees from Poland, Czechoslovakia, and the Soviet Union

The Government of the People's Republic of Poland has decided to renounce the payment of compensation to wartime claimants as of January 1, 1954, in order to make a further contribution for the solution of the German question in the spirit of democracy and peace.
— Polish government declaration, 23 August 1953

A state cannot have Soviet and American troops on its territory as a definitive solution. That would be a kind of unprecedented paradise on earth.
— Italian prime minister Giulio Andreotti, March 1990

The unity of the two Germanys is reachable only on the basis of total equality. West Germany must offer freedom, unity, democracy and social justice. But the German Democratic Republic does not come this way with empty hands. The people there carried the heavy portion of German history.
— Hans-Dietrich Genscher, West German foreign minister, February 1990

Guaranteed borders are the cornerstone of a securely unified Germany. More, they are the foundation for a secure, post-cold-war Europe.
— Editorial, The New York Times, 28 February 1990

271

Until today, the conflict of interest of each country was suppressed by the conflict between the United States and the Soviet Union.
        —Gen. Hiroomi Kurisu, Japan's former
        chairman of the Joint Chiefs of Staff

We want a President to be Commander in Chief, not Commander in Chicken.
        —Georgia state representative Mabel Thomas,
        introducing Senator Bob Kerrey

Just as the 1980s will be remembered for the unraveling of the communist faith, so the 1990s may well see the unraveling of the opposite idea—the notion of Western democracy as a universally applicable model.
        —Robert Wright and Doyle McManus,
        Flashpoints: Promise and Peril in a New World

We have to conclude the Uruguay Round of this GATT negotiation. It is critical to the security of Europe, the security of the United States and the security of Asia.
        —U.S. vice president Dan Quayle
        mid–February 1992

The people of the former Soviet Union have inspired the world with their courage in struggling to create a stable democracy out of the ruin of Communism. These same people need our assistance now to help them keep their children alive and healthy. To balk at providing assistance at a time of desperate need could doom their fragile democracy and the peaceful world order. The children of the former Soviet Union, to whom we can give the gift of life, and our own children, to whom we can give the gift of peace, deserve no less.
        —Arthur Hartman, former U.S. ambassador
        to the Soviet Union, 1981–88

The Warsaw Pact was largely a Soviet invention: Eastern European armies were actually part of the Soviet army.[1] Soviet units made up four-fifths of the Warsaw forces of some 6 million troops, and Moscow bore 80 percent of its costs. Soviet military officers were largely in control and linked training to Soviet methods, equipment, and instruction in Russian war colleges. In all Warsaw Pact nations, moreover, military portfolios remained in Communist hands.

But then came change—nationalist revolutions in Eastern Europe shaking the Red Army to its core as the armies of the East retreated to domestic defense, a buffer between their sovereignty and the Soviet Union, between themselves and any potential threat from the West.

In the overlapping Eastern European revolutions of 1989–91, the Warsaw Pact thus lost resources and will for military action. No longer viewing their forces as the front line for the Soviet army, nationalists established their own autonomous military units as a future front to secure their own nations' borders against any foreign impositions.

The armies of Poland, East Germany, Czechoslovakia, Hungary, Bulgaria, and Romania would no longer fight to preserve Soviet power, seeing no threat to themselves from the West, viewing NATO as a force to prevent German revanchism.[2]

For the West, especially the United States, the critical question became not merely shifting from the production of armaments to provide for needy domestic populations but extending prosperity and trade to generate the resources to provide for the desperate of former Communist nations. For these ends, the United States tried to force Europe and GATT to adopt subsidy-free trade that would generate many billions of dollars worth of additional U.S. agricultural exports, threatening that the American troop commitment to defend Western Europe depended on trade progress.

Chapter 12
A Military Matter

Between German unity and revanchism stood NATO forces.[1]
Chancellor Kohl had proved himself a merchant of equivocation, a fore-
taste for the world of how a united Germany would behave once it rees-
tablished unity and full sovereignty. For Kohl had waivered on the German border question with Poland, the Soviet Union, and Czechoslovakia.
In the Sudetenland of western Czechoslovakia, those expelled had had
their property seized and much of it nationalized when the Communists
came to power in 1948. And Kohl had paid more attention to the "chauvinistic escapades of expellee officials" than the "historically understandable
wishes of our Polish and other European neighbors," charged Horst
Ehmke, the Social Democrats' parliamentary leader.

As Kohl pursued his plan for a unitary state within the frame of NATO,
he had sought to bargain on the fears of Poland, Czechoslovakia, and the
USSR, appeasing the 12 million Germans evicted from their ancestral land
and rights in the East, including the 2.2 million Germans in the Federation of Expellees, who, harboring revanchist hopes, supported Kohl's
Christian Democrats.[2]

This was untenable in the frame of NATO. Yet the original one-to-one
agreement between the United States and Kohl's Germany for *Grossdeutschland* kept united Germany in NATO but provided no promise of
border security for the Soviets, Poland, and Czechoslovakia. This meant
Soviet troops would remain on East German territory until such guarantees were offered. But Italy flatly refused such a "solution" to the balance
between power blocs.

A single German government could not impose this on the rest of
Europe, Italian prime minister Giulio Andreotti warned; the United
States could not align with Germany in a one-to-one agreement to keep
a united Germany in NATO under such conditions. For keeping Soviet
troops in East Germany to stop any future revanchist moves would effectively align the United States with the Soviet Union against Western
Europe.[3]

The question of divided loyalties would not fit in the new alignments
of bloc power, then. And with a new groundswell of support, no longer
needing the reactionary backing of German expellees to win a landslide

275

election, in 1990 Kohl's Christian Democratic Union made a treaty for the security of the German-Polish border with Poland's Prime Minister Mazowiecki.

Later, on 27 February 1992, Chancellor Kohl and Czechoslovakian president Vaclav Havel signed a treaty for neighborly relations and friendship, recognizing that the 1945 Potsdam Agreement, calling for the "humane and orderly transferral" of millions of Germans from the regions they inhabited for generations, was in fact an "expulsion" and "act of force." Though the treaty provided for no compensation for the lost German property or Czechoslovakia's claims for human and material damages wrought by the *Wehrmacht*, the resettlement of Germans in Czechoslovakia was agreed upon.

Neither side appeased its followers, though. Chairman Franz Neubauer of the League of Expelled Sudeten Germans accused Prague of "systematically auctioning off" former German property to Czechs and Slovaks as part of its campaign to privatize business and property, again pressuring Chancellor Kohl to protect their right for supportive spring 1992 votes from the descendants of Sudeten Germans living in the south German states such as Baden-Wurttemberg. Chancellor Kohl played their hand, knowing Havel wanted unqualified German support for Czechoslovakia's entrance into the European Community, strongly urging Prague, "with a view to your sought-after membership in the European Community," to enact legislation "as quickly as possible" to ease the settlement of foreigners, including Germans, in Czechoslovakia.

Czechs and Slovaks feared a new revanchism, that the 1938 Munich Agreement empowering Nazi Germany to dismember Czechoslovakia might be replayed by Prague bowing to German pressure, readmitting the German minority to its old property rights. Now it would be a peaceful reconquest, President Havel noting that "as quickly as Czechoslovakia is able to open to Europe, and as quickly as we are able to adjust our legal system to Europe, in that measure will it become possible for any European, Germans included, if they want to live in our country, work in our country, and invest here, to come here."[4]

NATO would meanwhile remain the centerpiece of Western détente and peace with the East.

NATO AS CENTERPIECE OF DÉTENTE

Teutonic power remained, though. West Germany alone had a standing army of 478,000 in 1990, with more than 300,000 NATO forces stationed on its territory. East Germany had a people's army of 175,000 and and nearly 400,000 Russian troops on its soil. The balance favored West Germany by 200,000 troops, so that even if the Soviets stayed to stop German revanchist moves to pre–World War II borders, no solution by arms would be feasible, at least not without several million dead.

West German schemes to merge with the East also meant military merger, to be approved by NATO following Western interests. If Soviet forces then left East German soil, German forces could still conceivably secure German prewar eastern territories across the Oder and Neisse rivers into Poland and part of the Soviet Union.

East Germany Objects, for the Moment

Unity of the German state posited revanchist designs on Poland, then. So the political trick facing German politicians was to unify and make the other powers believe Germany would keep Polish borders inviolable.

Grossdeutschland was seen by the East German Communists as an opening to German reclamation of Poland, though.[5] "If one border falls" between the two Germanys, argued new Communist chairman Gysi in 1989, "all the others, from Bessarabia to Tyrol, are endangered. Peace in Europe has existed since the Second World War really only because nobody really altered the borders or put them in serious question."

Premature unification of the Germanys, he argued, would endanger Poland's borders as conservative Germans demanded recovery of lost German territories to the east, and the United States, France, Britain, and the USSR, as the postwar occupying powers, "would be forced to make a terrible choice, as at Munich, between giving in piecemeal or remaining firm."[6]

Gysi and the Communists had repeatedly misread the new testament of détente. For the East could maintain neither social stability nor economic security, requiring the West for both as well as for promised respect of Polish borders.[7]

Negotiating the New Bloc Alignments of Power

Balancing military power by bloc alignments was still the moment of European history. Soviet concern over a reunified, militarized Germany led to delays in negotiating the hardware and troop ratios for NATO and the Warsaw Pact, the Soviets calling for 700,000 to 750,000 troops on each side of central Europe.

The purpose was to limit the size of the West German military, which in early 1990 was already planning to cut its conventional forces. But the Soviets were also speaking for a Poland that wanted the two Germanys to initial a peace treaty guaranteeing existing borders before final affirmation of their treaty creating a single German state. When Chancellor Kohl objected, the Soviets and Poles hunkered down to win their demands.[8]

Making an end run around the Soviet position, West Germany then sought to quicken the process by uniting the German delegation under one flag in dealing with (and manipulating) the post–World War II Big Four treaty powers. Ignoring all formulas, West Germany first won its way with the United States, then stampeded France, Britain, and the USSR as the other three treaty powers, and thereafter sidestepped the twelve-nation EEC, the sixteen-nation NATO, and the thirty-five-nation Conference on Security and Cooperation in Europe.

Under U.S. tutelage, Germany effectively undercut the old military-bloc alliances, though England, fearing Teutonic potential, planned to keep the Continental powers at odds. London wanted to slow Bonn's drive for rapid unification and France's push for Common Market integration. For it seemed clear to the Bank of England and the Thatcher government that a reunited Germany in the EEC would subserviate both British bankers and traders.[9]

Paris and Washington held other views, seeking a unified Germany for reasons of their own. The United States envisioned a Continent of harmony to absorb a united Germany—thereby responding to the German Social Democrats, the Russian revisionists, the Polish Solidarity government, and Italy's prime minister—to pressure Bonn to renounce revanchist aims. France sought to unify the Continent under its own influence without U.S. domination of NATO, thereby managing change in Europe, so the Mitterrand government moved to accelerate EC integration to enclose a united Germany.

Other European nations, both in and outside the EC, viewed the battle of the Big Four over the body of Germany as keeping them powerless, favoring their own selfish interests and territories. And Washington took advantage of the splits, its *formulae diplomatique* ("one-three-one and a half") giving the U.S. president the initiative to style the Western bloc, forcing Britain, France, and the Soviet Union to deal individually with Washington and empowering the United States to dictate to West Germany and its new pawn in the East. The real formula was "one-one": the United States, as the most powerful military state, and West Germany, as Europe's most viable economy, would decide the future shape of the Western Continent.

The merits of this design were reviewed by President Bush and Chancellor Kohl on 25 February 1990, a critical dateline for understanding the fallout that would beset Europe in the early nineties. For thereafter, U.S. forces would remain stationed in a united Germany and elsewhere in Europe to guarantee the stability of the power balance that would restrain a unified Germany while overseeing a balkanized Eastern Europe.

Teutonic-American will in command, the United States *and* West Germany reaffirmed the current borders of Europe, formally recognizing the German-Polish border. A united Germany was now to be part of NATO, as Chancellor Kohl expounded:

> One thing is clear: A united Germany cannot belong to two different Pact Systems....

Neutralism would be a very false solution for us. I can't see that there would ever be any majority in the Federal Republic or in a united Germany for a neutralized Germany. I think we have learned lessons and we do not want to repeat the errors of history. But one mistake in the times of the Weimar Republic . . . was that Germany was isolated in Europe. One must make Germany a part of the whole.[10]

Though the post–World War I Weimar state was not the most cogent example of German mistakes—for the superliberal republic was replete with Social Democrats fronting for the *Grossbanken,* the great industrialists, and the general staff—it led in part to deindustrialization and disarmament, isolation (in the sense that Germany was economically weakened), lost resources and trading partners.[11]

To make united Germany part of the whole of Europe, moreover, would mean new bloc alignments. The United States would be the Continental policeman, a united Germany Europe's economic superpower. U.S. military forces in Germany would ensure that Eastern Europe would remain geographically balkanized, politically isolated, and militarily passive, while both the United States and Germany targeted its resources, investment opportunities, and markets. Overwhelming armed might, the fatal error President Bush fixated and seized upon, would keep a united Germany in NATO, linked to U.S. arms and obligation to keep the Polish border intact—a huge budgetary cost, but no small political item in appealing to the considerable ballot-box clout of millions of Polish Americans.[12]

But now came the difficult part—risk of a future, German state that might lay claim to Poland's East Prussia and Silesia, where many ethnic Germans still live, and to Czechoslovakia's Sudetenland. Unalloyed too were French fears of German economic might and potential dominance, as well as the disquietude in British boardrooms foreseeing German demands for *Lebensraum.*

Lebensraum and the Chancellor's Ace

Poland's *Solidarity Weekly* caught the drift: The old German song of "Unity, Law, Freedom," the official German anthem once sung as "Deutschland, Deutschland über Alles," brought jitters to the Poles across the Oder.

If and when German attitudes might again change, unified and pathologically riding high, the revanchism of the past would seek to reverse the Polish borders set at Yalta and Potsdam without Polish participation.

For now, though, Poles would not grant the right to millions of Germans living in their midst who sought unity with the "fatherland." So too, the millions of Germans expelled from Silesia, East Prussia, Pomerania, and Sudetenland, the region of Czechoslovakia that borders on Poland, called fruitlessly for compensation, lost property, and minority rights.

These expellees threatened to walk out of Chancellor Kohl's Christian Democratic Union and kill his chance for reelection if he fixed borders and made the nonaggression pledge the Poles demanded.[13]

The chancellor then played his ace. Knowing that there was no way to reverse the fact that Silesia and Pomerania were awarded by the Soviet Union to its World War II Polish ally in compensation for Soviet occupation of Eastern Poland, knowing too the Polish Western border was actually guaranteed by his own Christian Democratic Union, Kohl sidestepped the issue with ambiguities, refusing to guarantee the border integrity in provincial German campaigning so as not to confront the expellees and the right-wing nationalist Republican party.

"Our assessment is that Kohl personally understands full well that the German-Polish border cannot be changed and will not," said a U.S. administration official. "He is a man who is facing a close election and is concerned that if he adopts a totally ambiguous stance, he is going to have some critical votes siphoned off."[14]

Now the puzzle pieces fell in place. The Left in East Germany was forced to its knees. West German political parties took charge of their compatriot parties in the East. "If the Social Democrats control the government after the elections or if the Christian Democratic Alliance does, they are absolute puppets of their West German brother parties," expounded East German cabinet minister Pflugbeil. "Now East German parties behave exactly like the old Communist officials against whom we stood together."[15]

The rest of the story is now history. East Germany voted Christian Democratic, Kohl's party, the critical Soviet cave-in also coming under joint U.S.-German pressure.

The Soviets Cave In

The Soviets worried. "We should not overlook the impending danger of the accelerated reunification of Germany, or in fact, the engulfment of the German Democratic Republic," Soviet theoretician Ligachev warned the Central Committee. "It would be unpardonably short-sighted, a folly not to see that on the world horizon looms a Germany with a formidable economic and military potential. Real efforts of the world community, of all democratic forces, are needed in order to prevent in advance the raising of the issue of the revision of post-war borders and not allow a new Munich."[16]

Ligachev played well in West Germany. Chancellor Kohl immediately sought compromise, stipulating that Western military forces would never be sent to East Germany, a position backed by the United States, Britain, and France.

Backed too by the Soviet foreign minister Shevardnadze, East German prime minister Modrow sought to slow unification, with both German states detaching themselves from their respective military alliances to form a neutral Germany. But both Washington and Bonn opposed such control over German armed potential.

Certain that its own 400,000 troops would be pressured out of East Germany by a Social Democratic (or more unlikely, Christian Democratic Union) victory at the 18 March 1990 East German election, the Soviets tried to get Western European nations to disarm unilaterally. And after his secret diplomacy to unify Germany, Foreign Minister Shevardnadze also called for the thirty-five nations in the Conference of Security and Cooperation in Europe (CSCE) — composed of sixteen NATO nations, seven Warsaw Pact members, and twelve neutral countries — to demilitarize, lock a united Germany into a new "pan–European" political structure for its own safety, and stop the right-wing revanchists in Germany from claims to Pomerania, Silesia, and parts of East Prussia, now located in Poland or the Soviet Union.

This would have meant that independent Eastern European states would coalesce with NATO forces in the CSCE. And under an Italian proposal, a single European security system would have required members to respect one another's sovereignty and observe human rights.[17]

Thus was a three-stage process to be put in place: the two Germanys would unite; the Big Four would redesign their own military balance of strength; and the other 43 nations of the CSCE would unilaterally disarm and enter a nonaggression pact. The Soviets thereby hoped to gain security.

German nonaggression guarantees might also be warranted within NATO. "Europeans have bitter memories of Nazi Germany and are genuinely uneasy about reunification," recounted a senior Pentagon official. "Eastern Europeans and Poles in particular fear German *revanchism* and see German membership in NATO as a guarantee of good behavior."

France, Britain, and other NATO allies were also uneasy about German reunification, wanting to bind Chancellor Kohl to two commitments: a reunified Germany would remain in NATO; to appease the Soviet Union, NATO forces would not be deployed in East Germany, even allowing some Russian forces to remain there temporarily. The latter would prevent a unified Germany from giving renewed life to the Warsaw Pact.

Eastern Europe surprised NATO members by demanding the same — that a united Germany be within NATO to prevent revanchism; that without such membership, they would again be forced to look to the Soviet Union as protector. Even a neutralized Germany would not satisfy an Eastern Europe wary of German expansion. And as Soviet forces in the early nineties left under Eastern European pressures, the last remaining skeleton troops would be in East Germany, linked to a supply line running through Poland. Poland, apprehensive still, even if the two Soviet divisions remaining there in 1990 were removed, would likely allow Soviet transit rights to supply their remaining East German forces.

Poland might also keep Soviet troops on hand in case a united Germany reached beyond its existing borders. In February 1990, President Jaruzelski told the World Economic Forum in Switzerland that though Poland did not arbitrarily fear German reunification, it nonetheless conjured memories of Nazi occupation, raising questions of whether Poland's northern and western borders with East Germany, as defined by post–World War II mandates, would be respected by a unified Germany. This, Jaruzelski explained, was the main reason Poland had not followed Czechoslovakia and Hungary in requesting the withdrawal of Soviet troops. "When the issue is resolved and security guarantees are satisfactory," he concluded, "at that time the need for Allied [Soviet] forces will no longer exist."

Poland thus demanded inviolability of its borders from a united Germany, and in the long run that might not be possible without the accelerated integration of the rest of Eastern and Western Europe.

"Neutrality is an issue that concerns not just the two Germanys, but also all of Europe," East German prime minister Hans Modrow solemnized. German reunification of "one people" in "one Fatherland" could sidestep Hitler's formulation of "one *Führer*" only by the rest of Europe approving German unity at various stages of consolidation.[18]

Short of the mark again, part of Modrow's formula was filtered through NATO. For a defensive realignment of NATO promised to keep German forces under NATO's multinational military command, headed by a U.S. general. Yet Soviet forces were scheduled to be withdrawn from Eastern Europe, temporarily leaving 195,000 to 225,000 soldiers in East Germany.[19]

The military solution was now obvious: some U.S. forces would remain in West Germany; a united Germany would remain in NATO; and other NATO and Warsaw Pact forces would be cut, creating the following potential alignment in the early nineties:

	February 1990	Planned 1993–95
Soviet Forces		
Soviet Republics	5,440,000	1,200,000
East Germany	400,000	195,000
Poland	35,000	0
Rest of Eastern Europe	125,000	0
All Eastern Europe	560,000	195,000
Old Warsaw Pact	6,560,000 (est.)	1,395,000
U.S. Forces		
West Germany	243,000	120,000
NATO Flanks	110,000	30,000
All Europe	353,000	150,000
European Forces	594,000	400,000
NATO Forces	1,300,000 (est.)	700,000

The Soviet Union was in desperate need to save outlays on stationing troops in East Germany and for an infusion of Western aid to get through several hard winters of mass discontent and the repositioning of its military forces at home. In Poland, 35,000 Soviet troops remained in early 1992, the Russians promising to leave by the end of the year, each side billing the other for services rendered, Poland also demanding compensation for environmental damage, wanting to take possession of all Soviet property.[20]

These pressures influenced Russia's military rapprochement. Based on July 1990 Soviet talks with West Germany, the Soviets had agreed to withdraw all remaining 370,000 troops in central Europe by 1994 in return for security assurances and $7.5 billion in aid as part of the understanding on German reunification.

This made the earlier agreements null and void. The Soviets were still unable to get the United States to commit itself to eliminate its forces in West Germany. And the scorecard of troops in Germany by 1994 would likely be near zero for the Soviets and an indeterminate number for the United States.

True, Vice President Quayle threatened to cut U.S. troops in Europe if Western Europeans, particularly France, did not eliminate export subsidies and price supports the twelve-member European Community pays its farmers in violation of GATT rules. But the Europeans called his bluff. And the Socialist party's President Mitterrand, protecting French farmers protesting any subsidy cuts as Europe's largest producers of farm products, held fast. "His Government is weak in the polls," said Harry Freeman, executive director of Multilateral Trade Negotiations, a group backed by 14,000 U.S. companies supporting a free-trade pact. "If Mitterrand hurts French farmers, I think you can say goodbye to the Socialist Party's chance of winning an election for a long time to come. I don't know if they would compromise even if the rest of the E.C. puts them under extreme pressure." Dan Quayle ate crow, denying any linkage between U.S. troop levels defending Europe and progress on free trade.[21]

America seemed to be potentially the only military superpower left in Europe. But a united Germany was standing in the wings—East and West.

The New All-European Architecture

To resolve the "German Question," Chancellor Kohl concluded, "it must be embedded in the architecture of all Europe. We must take into account the legitimate interests of our neighbors, friends and partners in Europe and the world."[22]

The meaning was vague. But East Germany was facing debts West Germany was willing to cover with its strong currency. Trade between East Germany and the Soviet Union was three times West Germany's and covered long-term contracts for Eastern German machine tools and other heavy industrial products vital to the Soviet economy, items that West German capital infusions in the East would ensure. "We can arrive at an agreement satisfactory to the Soviet Union, even if all these East German factories were absorbed into the West German economic system," Chancellor Kohl expounded.[23]

Economic unification would thus be a lever to gain Russian approval for both political and military consolidation. Bonn thus pledged 12 billion marks to East Germany but would not release the funds until after the 1990 elections provided Kohl his landslide victory, eliminated East German Communist power, and advanced the economic consolidation process.

The Soviet Union had cornered itself between an Eastern Europe that wanted Soviet troops to leave, a Western Europe that wanted U.S. troops to stay, and an Eastern Germany that without Soviet troops would be little more than a West German outpost. The Soviet Union was no longer a European power but now needed its army to face internal rebellion from its republics and a possible future revanchism from a united Germany.

And thereafter the United States successfully imposed unequal troop cuts on the Soviets, maintaining U.S. superiority in Western, central, and, by withdrawal of Soviet troops, Eastern Europe. Soviet negotiators backed down, agreeing to a larger number of U.S. forces in central Europe than the Soviets kept in place in the East.[24]

But not for long, once the army reasserted its hold in the Politburo in late 1990. Realizing the Soviets had been outflanked by their own internationalists negotiating the withdrawal of Soviet forces from Eastern Europe and making greater weapons cuts than the West, the Kremlin moved powerfully in February 1991 to reinforce three motorized infantry divisions for defense, exempting them from the Strategic Arms Treaty by reclassification as "naval shore defense units" and throwing the army into action to contain nationalist movements at home to preserve the structure of power—or to move backward to the status quo before the words *glasnost, demokratia,* and *perestroika* were part of Soviet people's vocabulary.

All this was to change again with the failed coup of 1991, opening a new era of nuclear disarmament and self-containment of the military forces of the new republics within their respective boundaries, eliminating Russia and the other republics as world miltary powers.

NATO, RUSSIA, AND A PARED MILITARY DEFENSE

The logic of NATO was lost with the breakup of the Soviet Union into separate republics lacking a common military offensive for defense and empire. The nuclear capability of Russia was undermined by its self-

imposed "spear search" designed to undermine its military-industrial complex by dismantling its nuclear arsenal, reemploying its nuclear-bomb
designers in peaceful projects, and tapping U.S. aid for such purposes
while extracting further loan guarantees so that Russia could borrow
money to buy more American grain[25] to pacify hungry populations suffering under hyperinflation.

And yet these populations might be unable to disarm completely and
adopt Western democracy as a universally applicable model. For weaponry
itself might become the driving force in production by former socialist
states bent on exports to earn foreign exchange.[26] And traditional mechanisms of domestic and international control might disappear, elevating
uncertainty in power relationships and creating the political and military
climate for a "Darwinian free-for-all." The scarcity of the means of production and existence might lead to popular, nationalist, and ethnic strife,
questioning the legitimacy of governments in power—left, right, or
center. And armed rebellion by small discontented sects and groups might
remain possible. Rather than acceptance of liberal democracy (as author
Fukuyama has theorized), then, the old nation-states might split apart,
balkanized territories might again redivide, and the Western concept of
liberal democracy might never emerge in Eurasia.[27]

The former Soviet republics agreed on Russia's proposal for nuclear
disarmament. But they were polarized and realigned around those wanting an all–Commonwealth military and those favoring independent
armies that would not fall under a common dictatorial central command.
The first group was led by Russia and adhered to by Kazakhstan, Armenia,
Turkmenistan, Kyrgyzstan, and Tajikistan; the second was spearheaded
by Ukraine, joined by Azerbaijan and Moldova, leaving Belarus and
Uzbekistan with military reservations.

Asserting that in signing Commonwealth documents "there are no
instruments of control and no mutual obligations," Kazakhstan president
Nursultan Nazarbayev stressed that the main defense issue should be
managing a huge military establishment made increasingly restless by the
politicians' dispute over its future.

True enough, Ukraine, Kazakhstan, Belarus, and Russia pledged placing nuclear weapons under the care of Moscow central command. Yet the
necessity for international nuclear disarmament agreement was all the
more urgent because the moment of Commonwealth agreement might
not last. For conventional forces, by early 1992, strong nationalist sentiment in Ukraine made it virtually impossible for its leadership to agree to
any common army with the Russians, who traditionally had dominated
the 3.5-million Soviet military. Ukrainian president Kravchuk was exercised about the military issue severely straining society as well, saying that
Moscow was misrepresenting Kiev as demanding the entire Black Sea
fleet when in reality it wanted only its fair share and that profiteers were
attempting to sell parts of the merchant fleet and navy "in secret."

INVENTING MILITARY SCENARIOS

Thereafter, NATO, and the Pentagon as its principal backer, could only invent scenarios for new enemies that had not yet emerged as global dangers, Chairman of the Joint Chiefs of Staff Powell stating in January 1992 that "the real threat we now face is the threat of the unknown, the uncertain."[28] Deposed president Gorbachev reaffirmed that the years spent "plunged in the cold war made losers of us all."[29]

But now there was no longer a real danger absent a bipolar military world, only a multiplicity of small military powers facing America as the single great monolith of firepower. True, Russia might help supply them, reopening its arms factories in Izhevsk, maintaining full employment of restless millions by shifting 70 percent of production dependence on Soviet military contracts to new world-class commercial, secretive, competitive arms manufacture for export to earn hard currencies.[30] Besides, the United States said it sought Russian competition, and America was the greatest arms salesman on the planet.

The Commonwealth military services posed no threat to NATO either. Though the army, navy and air force were still largely united in early 1992, they remained "self-restrained" and highly organized, rejecting "all attempts to draw them into political gambles," said Commonwealth commander Marshal Yevgeny I. Shaposhnikov.

Nuclear disarmament need not be put off, then, though Russia's President Yeltsin was opposed to U.S. unilateral launching of space weapons as likely to breed distrust among nations, proposing instead that because Russia remained more vulnerable than the United States to a Third World missile threat, shared antimissile technology was a way to win American cooperation, expertise, and money—coddling his generals by also raising salaries. But the United States was already spending $4.15 billion on star wars "brilliant pebbles" research in 1992, and for 1993, President Bush requested $5.4 billion to put 1,000 of them in orbit. It was left to Congress to cut the program as unnecessary.[31]

America had hitherto relied on a nuclear triad of long-range bombers, submarines, and missiles, the subs armed with so many warheads that it would have been prohibitively expensive to operate them as nuclear weapons platforms if the United States went below the level of 4,500 warheads, with 2,500 being proposed by Russia. Thus the U.S. State Department looked for an intermediate stage of nuclear disarmament, while Congress cast a jaundiced eye at, and wielded a potential budgetary ax over, the Pentagon's new guesswork of warmaking proposals.

To try to prop up support for its $280-billion-a-year budgets, the Pentagon exaggerated the threats facing the U.S. and the West, painting testimonial pictures of "illustrative," "not predictive," internal budgetary military needs to guide defense planners making up administration policy in supporting worldwide U.S. military and political aims after the cold war.[32]

A few of the seven sketches of war preparedness were plausible: A coup by right-wing elements allied with Colombian drug traffickers against Panama's civilian leaders might close the Panama Canal, which remained essential for global trade. A revived heavily armed Iraq might invade both Kuwait and northeast Saudia Arabia with 21,000 tanks and 21 divisions, seeking to capture oilfields, air bases, and seaports. North Korea might use the cover of a peace initiative to attack South Korea with 300,000 troops and 5,000 tanks, seeking to capture Seoul. A Philippines coup might degenerate into factional fighting, with some forces seizing hostages at the Subic Bay naval base and threatening 5,000 Americans still living in the area.

Two other grimmer, if implausible, scenarios called for a bigger military budget still: Simultaneous war by Iraq and North Korea might tax U.S. support forces and supply lines. An antidemocratic expansionist Russia might align militarily with Belarus by 2001 and, Ukraine neutral, launch an attack through Poland, seizing Lithuania, and threatening U.S. and NATO interests.[33]

The latter seemed particularly absurd as Sweden, Finland, and Norway moved not only to join the European Common Market but to build a regional market covering St. Petersburg and Russia on the eastern flank, the northern coasts of Poland, a reunited Germany, and the three newly constituted Baltic nations of Latvia, Lithuania, and Estonia. No longer was military neutrality crucial in Scandinavia to stay out of European war, as political and economic integration was the thrust of the future.[34]

Still, General Powell said that the scenarios helped the Pentagon "size the force and also more importantly, size the power projection capability" needed to move troops, tanks, and artillery on transport aircraft and cargo ships to distant potential war zones.[35]

By February 1992, though, the illogic of Pentagon scripting to reconstitute large-scale U.S. military forces was already obvious to a Congress called by constituents to secure the economic home front. The Congressional Budget Office had released a study concluding that the purported $180 billion in Pentagon spending cuts announced in 1991 would ultimately increase economic growth if the savings were used to reduce budget deficits. Yet the Pentagon budget by 1997 would still be over $200 billion (in 1992 dollars), one-third the 1992 budget, yet diminishing the "peace dividend" that was to produce extra dollars for domestic priorities and deficit reduction.

Rather than follow Senator Sam Nunn's efforts to create new jobs for military personnel in education and put unneeded military bases to other uses, both Democratic and Republican congressional leaders saw the Pentagon as an employment station, worried that cuts in the military budget would close bases, swell the army of the unemployed, and ruin their chances for reelection.

But nuclear disarmament would mean budget outlays and jobs for those dismantling 2,000 nuclear weapons annually and storing the grapefruit-size balls of plutonium thermonuclear triggers, radioactive toxic metals and their lethal by-products posing dangers to the environment and terrorist attacks.[36]

Publicizing the secret fifties cables of China's Mao to Stalin revealing China's defense of North Korea under the "title Volunteer Army," director of Central Intelligence Robert M. Gates also went the last mile to keep up the illusory need for big military budgets, testifying before the House Foreign Affairs Committee that the North Korean government could possess a nuclear weapon from within a few months to a few years. But Gates neglected to state any factual information supporting his belief that North Korea was hiding parts of its nuclear weapons program, despite its pledges to join South Korea in making the peninsula nuclear-free and to open its installations to international inspection.[37]

Some congressmen were meanwhile insisting, though, that the keys to America's future were massive investments and greater productivity promoting greater stability at home and abroad. Others asserted that even a half cut in the U.S. military would maintain its preeminent global power, for well over half of the pre–1992 defense budget was devoted to countering Soviet threats.

The Senate Armed Services Committee openly challenged the Defense Department's war scenarios shaping their forces and military budgets for 1994 through 1999, Michigan Democratic senator Carl Levin telling the press that "some of these scenarios are incredibly unlikely. If they are used for budget rationale, they could undermine the strength of the Pentagon's budget request."

Central, then, was the issue of military spending well into the next century to sustain forces capable of fighting and winning one or more of these seven hypothetical conflicts. "We can see through these scenarios," the Armed Services Committee's Virginia Republican John W. Warner adumbrated. "I don't think Congress should put limits on their hypothetical planning, but then we have a right to be critical of them."

"The question for the [armed] services really is, are you [Congress] prepared to deal with scenarios like these, and if so, what kind of shortfalls in munitions or spare parts might you expect?" defended Vice Chairman of the Joint Chiefs of Staff David E. Jeremiah.

Congressional expectations were limited, though, for the Pentagon had refused to give the classified scenario documents to the committee, the chairman, Senator Sam Nunn, saying that the refusal put senators in the untenable position of making decisions on military spending without the same information *The New York Times* had secured in making the initial public disclosures. "We're in the position of demanding it now," Senator Nunn recounted, the Pentagon having frequently given committees classified documents in the past. "We're entitled to anything *The New York Times* gets."[38]

It was time to end the costly U.S. protective shield for Western Europe and Japan. And the liberal media took the cue, *The New York Times* editorializing:

> An Iraq-size threat won't permit the Pentagon to preserve its Base Force—12 carrier task forces, 26 tactical air wings, and an Army of 12 active-duty and 6 reserve divisions. Such a threat won't warrant all the present capacity to project power around the globe. And it can't conceivably justify the current pace of U.S. modernization.
>
> That's why the Pentagon imagines having to take on Iraq and North Korea *simultaneously.* Yet even fighting two wars in two different parts of the globe won't justify maintaining the Base Force at current levels. Only the rapid resuscitation of a global threat by Russia on the enormous scale once posed by the Soviet Union would provide a threat commensurate with the Pentagon's excessive force structure.[39]

"The striking thing about the Pentagon list is how far its planners had to stretch to come up with any plausible threats," conservative columnist Leslie Gelb wrote, pointing to the ticking political bombshell about to detonate. "A resurgent Iraq or an attack by North Korea on South Korea are practically off imaginable charts. And the U.S. along with its allies could deal with them crushingly with only a small fraction of curent military power, as happened in the Persian Gulf war. As for protecting American citizens in places like the Philippines or Panama, a few battalions and a few air squadrons could do the job easily. And as for worrying about some new world military power, none is near any horizon."[40]

President Bush had sought $281 billion for the military in fiscal year 1992–93, which for five fiscal years could total $1,405 billion. Yet only modest cuts of $91 billion for 1992–97 were proposed by Chairman Les Aspin of the House Armed Services Committee, leaving the Pentagon $191 billion a year. Other military experts recommended spending of $160 billion to $180 billion a year by the end of the nineties.[41]

The NATO military bill paid by the United States was $150 billion a year, about half of all Pentagon outlays. If the United States followed Canadian plans to pull out all its combat forces from Europe by the end of 1994 in the name of a "peace dividend" necessitated by internal budgetary constraints, U.S. forces would be cut back from the 350,000 deployed during the most intense phases of the cold war to its February 1992 level of 220,000 to its planned reduction of 150,000 by 1995—to zero sometime in the future.

Canada's Finance Minister Don Mazankowski had justified the acceleration to zero of the planned Canadian cut from 6,600 to 1,100 soldiers and fliers by end of 1995, explaining that "since September 1991, the world has changed a great deal," insisting that the peace dividend was possible "without lessening our commitment to NATO solidarity." The savings in five years would be $2.2 billion, reducing the total $12 billion a year on defense, cutting Canada's accumulated debt and heavy annual interest charges.

Under internal political pressure, the United States might one day be forced to follow the Canadian lead. If that happened, said Simon Serfaty, a specialist in Atlantic relations of the Johns Hopkins University School of International Studies in Washington, "it will confirm the perception that all of the New World is going home, and it might increase European interest in developing an autonomous defense entity that would be distinct from NATO." This, he said, would be the culmination of mid-eighties European discussions about reviving an abortive early fifties initiative calling for a European Defense Community to exist alongside the European Community.

But meanwhile, NATO secretary-general Manfred Wörner noted Ottawa's action "with considerable regret, given the political and military importance of the presence of Canadian forces in Europe." And the Bush administration angrily reacted to the Canadian decision to withdraw its troops from NATO's European theater, fearing that it would increase congressional pressure for faster U.S. withdrawal and unravel the forty-three-year-old North Atlantic Treaty Organization.[42]

Not satisfied, the Pentagon then came up with a one-power thesis: an outline for a $1.2-trillion strategy to prevent any other nation from challenging U.S. military supremacy, "to discourage them from challenging our leadership or seeking to overturn the established political or economic order." But this would not fly in a Congress that had already received $54 billion from its allies, mostly from Germany and Japan, to finance the Gulf war, that faced a projected 1992 budget deficit of $400 billion, and that was aware that foreign investments in the United States exceeded U.S. investments abroad by as much as $500 billion.

Nor would Congress be much of a defense miser either. Under congressional scrutiny, the "base force" of 1.6 million troops might be cut a nominal 140,000, the B-2 bomber might be scrapped, the army's tactical missile system might go the way of the stone ax, and new aircraft carriers might never be built. But these were nominal cuts at best. The Pentagon retained broad-based support in Congress and in those communities that had lived forty-seven years on the U.S. military dole.

The Blind Spot and Disarmament Reconversion

Fear and the blind spot in all the new Pentagon scenarios had a subtext: the right of the U.S. to intervene in the internal affairs of other countries rather than pull back America's military machine and convert its industries, mobilizing its population for peacetime production.

Elections in the offing in early 1992, members of Congress feared cutting the military budget too steeply, thereby increasing unemployment lines in a recession. Representative Aspin's fiscal 1993 cuts were planned not to affect active military forces. Yet, estimating that more than 2 million military-related jobs would be lost by 1996, Senator Nunn proposed allowing military personnel a year's leave to attend college or undertake vocational training to prepare for civilian life, also supporting increased retirement pay for military personnel going into teaching and law enforcement. And the Democratic budget plan sought to divert Pentagon money into domestic program—housing, AIDS research, preschool programs like Head Start, and assistance for laid-off workers in military industries.[43]

Reconversion could also upgrade the nation's entire infrastructural and technological base, just as happened in postwar Japan and Germany, rather then remaining bogged down by cold war corporate and defense managers and engineers trained in Pentagon "cost-maximizing practices" undercutting industrial efficiency. For these professionals, conversion to peace production would mean an end to subsidies as well as retraining for unfamiliar cost-minimizing skills and the technologies of civilian production. President Bush's six-year (1992–97) plan for 1.3 million people to lose their jobs in the defense industry and military services would be overshadowed by this massive reconversion, which could mobilize the energies of both management and labor for long-term civilian production—selecting new products, estimating their market, retraining employees, altering production methods, and retooling and redesigning plant facilities. "The first-hand knowledge possessed by defense company employees is essential for conversion," writes Chairman Seymour Melman of the National Commission for Economic Conversion and Disarmament. "Thus, conversion must be done locally; no remote central office can possess the necessary knowledge of people, facilities and surroundings."

America would also be renewed, Melman says, listing what converted factories could produce: "Products we now buy abroad such as machine tools, electric locomotives, farm machinery, oilfield equipment and consumer electronics. Besides, the modernizing of America's infrastructure will require construction machinery and capital goods of many kinds. In sum, conversion is crucial to creating a full-employment, productive U.S. economy."[44]

After forty years and more than $11 trillion to wind down the cold war, conversion would be a long time coming. The 1992–97 presidential plan for $43 billion in cuts from the $1.2-trillion five-year defense budget that was sent to Congress held on to the Pentagon's concept of the base force. Yet, the "base force," conceived in 1990 before the collapse of the Soviet Union and the splintering of its military forces, was bolstered by seven future military combat scenarios that Congress could not swallow. And the centrist compromise turned on Representative Aspin's $91-billion cuts over these five years, reducing defense employment and spending the savings not on deficit reduction but on industrial reinvestment and domestic programs.[45] At best, then, these were token cuts, not steps toward disarmament.

Congress, under pressure to cut the military budget for social programs, would take a small slice of the Pentagon's budgetary pie to share it out to repay part of the national debt, social entitlements, public health, education, environment, and science programs.

Without full employment, moreover, tax-financed social programs would become more necessary to pacify and provide for the deprived. And without such programs, the lack of welfare and education would degrade large numbers, creating an underclass that would strive for survival by almost any means. For as Andrew Schotter, chairman of the Economics Department at New York University, has written: "The price capitalism pays for its failure to provide proper incentives to the underclass so that its members can seek honest rather than criminal employment is readily visible."[46]

FUTURE SCENARIOS

Precise future scenarios uncertain, a new era of peace and social production had clearly begun, though it might take decades to bring it to fruition.

Rather than a contest of two nuclear superpowers, there were now half a dozen minipowers facing off with a NATO that Russia sought to join in order to secure itself and the flank of central Asian republics bordering Iran, Afghanistan, and western China. The Commonwealth of Independent States even refused to use its armed forces to take sides between warring former Soviet republics, withdrawing the last successor to the Soviet army from Nagorno-Karabakh and away from the Armenian-Azerbaijan border at the end of February 1992.[47]

Moving into the vacuum, the forty-eight-nation Conference on Security and Cooperation in Europe called for an immediate cease-fire in the enclave, members of CSCE being encouraged to impose an embargo on supplies of weapons and ammunition to the warring parties, though both Armenia and Azerbaijan had appealed to Czechoslovakia to ensure humanitarian assistance and the exchange of hostages.[48]

The United States meanwhile remained unready for complete nuclear disarmament in 1992, the key issue being a mutual U.S.-Russian reduction in both offensive and defensive nuclear weapons. If both sides reduced offensive weapons and only the United States retained defense weapons, any remaining Russian offensive missiles would be useless, and the remaining U.S. offensive weapons would constitute a nuclear monopoly. President Yeltsin thus insisted that any defensive U.S. system must "strengthen stability against a background of sharp cuts in strategic offensive arms."

But the United States was unwilling to cut its planned unilateral defense, either a multibillion-dollar limited antimissile defense to protect against ICBM attacks across the North Pole or a massive costly defense to protect against offshore submarine-launched missiles, airplane- and cruise-launched missiles, or suitcase-smuggled bombs. With hard-liners in Washington wanting to take advantage of Moscow's weakness by deploying defenses unilaterally, Moscow had only two responses: to revive centrist rule and its military-industrial complex or to cooperate with the United States on defense.

The first effort at sharing military technology was blocked by the Bush administration. Though the Russian arsenal and space program were up for sale to earn hard currencies by early 1992, the U.S. government only reluctantly made it possible for federal and civilian bargain hunters to buy advanced rocketry and space equipment cheaply — reasoning that since many space products held potential military uses, the best course would be to stop their production, defuse any potential military threat, and redirect Russian nuclear bomb designers into peaceful scientific work. Though the acquisition of Moscow's superior technology could save both federal budgetary resources and American industry many billions of dollars in development costs as well as help the United States compete with foreign rivals, Deputy Secretary of Defense Donald Atwood told the Senate committee that considers defense appropriations that the administration had "great concerns" about aiding the military-industrial complex of the former Soviet Union. True, most of Moscow's space complex was tied to military operations, but nonetheless Moscow space assets might aid the U.S. civilian space program that Senator Mikulski, chair of the Appropriations Subcommittee overseeing NASA, said was an opportunity foreign rivals were sure to seize if America did not. And though leaders of the Pentagon's star wars research program were pressing to buy more than fifty Russian high technologies such as the RD-170 advanced rocket engine and other space items of superior quality or not made in the West, the administration remained skeptical that Russia was really trying to shift from a military to a civilian economy,[49] thus trying to disarm Russia so it could not react to Western deployment of an antimissile system.

Russian officials were incredulous, publicly expressing growing frustration with the ban on purchases and the lack of cooperation among technical experts of East and West, wanting to pass from words to deeds. Former presidents Nixon and Reagan quickly joining the chorus to buy Russia's major high technologies, the White House relented on $14 million of bargain-price space and nuclear equipment — the Topaz-2 nuclear reactor for space power and the Hall Thrusters for moving objects in space, useful for both exploration and star wars projects.

Even such purchases would not go beyond easing Russia's economic crisis and discouraging Russian scientists from becoming nuclear mercenaries, though. In the short term, the best the United States would offer was to join twenty-four other nations in signing the Open Skies Treaty for surveillance flights by once-hostile neighbors, relaxing tensions between insecure states to stop them from building up their military forces in central Europe. A joint global defense system remained a premature plan in early 1992.

The benefits of future mutual defense were obvious. The possibility of a joint Russian-U.S. ballistic missile early-warning center, the sharing of star wars technology alongside deep cuts in long-range nuclear missiles, would undoubtedly pit any aggressive minor power against a monolithic enemy in control of the most sophisticated technology on the planet, tying together all NATO and Russian radar, staellite, and other early-warning assets in a single location where all participants could monitor virtually any ballistic missile launching worldwide. But Yeltsin's concept of cooperation was much more comprehensive than anything Washington was ready to embrace in early 1992. Rather, star wars officials were interested in buying Russia's critical technologies, not offering U.S. Strategic Defense Initiative technology that would subsidize Russia's protection or consulting with Russia over U.S. use of its own ABMs.[50]

Still, peaceful cooperation might gradually overlap with future joint defense.

In March 1992, the federal government planned to hire the services of 116 Russian scientists to help the United States harness the vast energy of nuclear fusion using the Russian pioneer technology of donut-shaped magnetic fields to contain a heavy form of easily extracted hydrogen (deuterium) from water, heated with microwave beams at 200 million degrees Centigrade to weld the atoms of light elements, using the kind of thermonuclear fire that lights the sun. The one-year $90,000 contract covered $65 a month per scientist, equal to 6,500 rubles per month, more than seven times the unofficial national average monthly wage of 900 rubles. For America, the contract purchased the equivalent of millions of dollars' worth of fusion research in the United States. The Russian work was to be directed by the privately owned San Diego company General Atomics, whose director, Dr. Thomas C. Simonen, also directed his firm's comparable fusion program. Russia lacking its own funds to go forward, the work was to be done at the Kurchatov Institute of Atomic Energy, named after Dr. Igor V. Kurchatov, the father of the Soviet A-bomb, though for decades little weapons work was done, focusing instead on making innovative reactors, including ones for use in space.[51] There was little doubt, however, that star wars technology would also reap a future advantage.

An early-warning center would also be the first explicit concrete defense cooperation between the United States and Russia, Secretary of State James Baker explaining that besides linking Russia and former Soviet republics with the United States, the proposed arrangement would also bring together the United States and its allies in NATO. "We hope that our NATO allies would want to participate in such an early warning center and have no reason for our part to exclude participation of any other countries which would want to participate in a responsible way," Secretary Baker said, opening the door to join the American megalith. "We saw during the Gulf War what happens when we have a proliferation to irresponsible nations of ballistic missiles."[52]

Perhaps the United Nations would provide the future military forces for consolidated effort against such nations. With the end of the cold war, major powers looked to peacekeeping as a less costly route than allowing local conflagrations to flare into endless wars. And as such UN operations became more ambitious, complex, and costly, engineered political solutions were sought, whether in the Middle East, Cambodia, or Yugoslavia.[53]

With the United States automatically responsible for 30 percent of the cost of every UN peacekeeping operation — roughly equal to the total assessment of all European Community nations and two and a half times the amount billed to Japan — the Bush administration asked for an increased outlay from $115 million in 1991 to $107 million in 1992 to an added $810 million for 1992–93 for troop deployment in Yugoslavia and Cambodia. These were designed to cover the cost of the growing UN army increasing its sphere of peacekeeping operations:[54]

	Number (1991)	Estimated Cost (in millions)
Cambodia	22,000*	$1,900.0*
Yugoslavia	14,300 +	634.0 +
Lebanon	5,900	151.5
Western Sahara	2,700 +	140.9
Iraq and Kuwait	540	80.2
Angola	440	52.1
Golan Heights	1,300	37.8
Cyprus	2,200	31.0
Arab-Israeli Conflict	300	31.0
El Salvador	1,000	13.2
India and Pakistan	40	5.0

*Projected 1992–93.
+ Projected 1992.

In the future, the U.S. conception of a "new world order" could be backed by deploying financial wizardry with hidden presidential or State Department funds, or using defense budget allocations, to bolster UN rapid-deployment forces as both military defenders and peacemakers, saving the United States billions of dollars by imposing part of the cost of policing the world on other nations.[55]

Third World nations were meanwhile being heavily armed by the Big Five powers, role-playing as arms restrainers as permanent members of the UN Security Council. Under the pressure of their respective arms merchants, the United States and the other four accounted for almost $9 out of every $10 of weapons sold worldwide. In 1992, the United States hoped to add some $5 billion to the nearly $14 billion in arms sales to Saudi Arabia made between August 1990 and February 1992, militarily unbalancing the Middle East power quest by selling the most advanced F-15 fighter aircraft and unsettling U.S. competitor arms merchants cartelizing regional production, markets, and prices. "Coordination among the five members is critical since overseas contractors are ready to sell Tornadoes or European Fighter Aircraft (both joint projects of several European nations) if the U.S. reneges on the F-15 sale," wrote Deputy Director Natalie J. Goldring of the research group British American Security Information. "The Saudis cannot turn to suppliers outside the five countries if they expect to purchase aircraft nearly as advanced as the F-15."

The Saudis and other buyers were also positioned to play one technological arms seller against the others. In 1968, the Saudis had sidestepped congressional resistance by agreeing to deals with Britain. In 1992, the United States had to consult with Britain to ensure that an American decision to forgo the sale would not immediately be followed by a British-Saudi deal. In any case, the U.S. sale would break the cartel's marketing agreement not to rearm the Middle East at one another's expense. "If this sale goes forward," Goldring wrote in March 1992, "it will undermine hopes for limitations on arms sales. The other permanent members will cite it as evidence that the U.S. is continuing to sell arms to its allies while expecting them to exercise restraint."

The logic of the Big Five continuing to sell their advanced weapons would also make it difficult for their own military forces to retain a technological edge against potential foes, fueling more weapons research and development and production of high-tech weaponry.[56] War preparedness without end might thereby be promoted in the name of security.

IS THIS THE START OF A NEW REVANCHISM?

On the European continent, German politicians were just as sure, refusing to rely solely on weapons preparedness. For more than the tortured fears held by Pentagon planners, the Strangeloves of a united Germany held broader ambitions east and west.

Germany looked east for economic success, political alignments, and arms agreements. All three were linked, moreover, because eastern German trade with the former Soviet republics was essential to the prosperity that would ease the economic unification of Germany and enable Kohl's Christian Democratic party to maintain its popularity in at least four of the five new eastern German states, while also breaking the Washington-Bonn military link that one day would allow an all–German army to act as a counterweight to any remaining forces in Eastern Europe.

Bonn feared Washington in part because U.S. foreign policy might continue to mediate arms and peace negotiations for Germany. In the recent past, the United States may have determined that Germany would be reunified, the Berlin Wall destroyed, and Russian disarmament would proceed. But Germany sought the complete unhinging of Russian nuclear capability, the safety of geographically close Russian and Eastern European civilian nuclear plants to secure Germany from the faulty design of Soviet reactors, and thereby security from the growing political power of the vocal Green movement.

Bonn also looked to the antipathy eastern Germans felt toward the United States, NATO, the presence of American forces, and the lack of German political self-determination. And Chancellor Kohl moved into the empty political space, designing a new *Anschluss* with Austria, Croatia, and Slovenia. The chancellor thus backed Austria for full membership in the Common Market. To solidify the link, he made alliance with the former Nazi Austrian president Kurt Waldheim, thereby offending Jewish organizations worldwide and appeasing conservative voters in Baden-Wurttemburg and Schleswig-Holstein to win them from backing the far-right Republican party. And playing on German sympathy for the embattled separatist Yugoslavian republics, he developed a distinctive Teuton policy to drag Germany's Western European allies and the European Community into recognizing Croatia and Slovenia, irreparably making them dependent on both Germany and the West.

UNHINGING TURMOIL AND NUCLEAR MERCENARIES

Western aid was meanwhile the answer to some of the military and political problems throughout former Soviet territories. Though the International Monetary Fund held some $15 billion available for loans to nations in need, Russia required $6 billion in ruble-stabilization funds and $12 billion to help it finance crucial imports. Ukraine and other republics needed more than $10 billion. And the IMF moved to assess capital increases from its members, the United States holding out for domestic political purposes in an election year and not wanting any assessments that would reduce Washington's portion of total funding as well as reducing its IMF voting power (and veto power over policy decisions) to 14 percent from about 19 percent.[57]

In the new Commonwealth, former nuclear bomb designers held a powerful wedge as a once favored group. Like the army, former Soviet atomic scientists also sought security, asking Secretary of State Baker for $25 million of the $400 million in aid appropriated by Congress to eliminate the Soviet arsenal to speed the transformation of their jobs to civilian social purposes.

The framework was set with the transfer of some 3,000 tactical warheads to Russia from the other republics, bringing the Russian total to

12,000, leaving 3,000 in Belarus and Ukraine. Plans for Russian relocation of the 12,000 long-range nuclear weapons in Russia, Ukraine, Belarus, and Kazakhstan would also eventually lead to their dismantling, leaving 100 tons of weapons-grade plutonium and 400 to 500 tons of highly enriched uranium, materials to be stored at sites subject to international monitoring if Washington agreed to similar inspections.

Conversion of all ten nuclear weapons plants and realignment of their workers for commercial production or other alternative uses would be complemented by establishing an international science and technology center in Russia to support unemployed scientists and engineers of the former Soviet Union to redirect their military expertise to civilian purposes, thereby blunting the temptation of these Soviet nuclear experts to sell their services to aspiring nuclear powers like Iraq, Iran, Libya, or North Korea. And with budgets for nuclear weapons labs slashed 50 percent in 1992, crash programs for alternative deployment took an economic twist.

Employing 16,000 people, including 9,000 technicians and 7,000 production engineers and scientists, Chelyabinsk-70 was prepared for a new era. "Our institute is well equipped with scientific research equipment," offered Yevgeny N. Avrorin, scientific leader of the Institute of Technical Physics at Chelyabinsk-70, one of the two Russian research centers for nuclear weapons design that since 1988 had devoted 50 percent to military research and 50 percent to nonmilitary. "This has come at great expense to our taxpayers, and we understand that now is the time to give this back. We have a huge scientific research potential, and therefore conversion to different types is not so painful. We have no shortage of ideas. But we have no sufficient financing for them."

The problem, he explained, was that conversion to civilian projects was expensive and that without commercial customers there was no way for the institute to cover its costs. "The task will be to find projects with a maximum profit return," he concluded, conceding that the former Soviet scientific community had much to learn about Western-style supply-and-demand practices.[58] And the West was destined to invest commercially, perhaps with government guarantees as well as customs and tax breaks.

Disarmament in Russia would thus proceed, awaiting like measures in the United States and Europe, so that long after the death of the Warsaw Pact and the demise of NATO, there would be a realignment of blocs of military power by regions—possibly the Commonwealth alongside some armies of independent republics of the former Soviet Union; likely a linkage of Western and central Europe; almost certainly an alliance of the United States, the Middle East, the Far East, and Latin America; and conceivably Japan and East Asia.

The need for civilian production in the former Soviet republics was an obvious way to reemploy former military experts and production workers. The new Commonwealth could produce only 15 to 20 percent of the medical supplies it required and lacked hard currency to import these or other goods in short supply. A frighteningly large proportion of medical personnel were not well trained; most hopsitals were filthy, dark, and cold, and could not replace equipment that broke down. Shortages of sterilization equipment and syringes led to their dangerous reuse, creating both a danger of AIDS and a lack of immunization. Some twenty-seven of forty vaccines produced in the Commonwealth were "unfit for human or animal use," the World Health Organization found, the dangers increased by storage without refrigeration beyond their effective dates.

Devastating medical consequences might follow these deficiencies. In 1989, one-quarter of Soviet children who should have been vaccinated against polio were not, the following year bringing 312 reported cases. In 1989 one-fifth of children were not immunized against diphtheria, 1990 reporting several hundred cases in Moscow alone. One-third did not get whooping cough vaccination in 1989, and without remediation, a breakdown in sanitation might be responsible for more deaths related to paratyphoid, typhoid, and hepatitis A. Annually, some 120,000 new cases of Commonwealth tuberculosis were reported.[59]

Not only in the medical field but elsewhere the opportunity for redeployment of Commonwealth scientists and military production workers was enormous. Swords could be transformed into tractors and new technology; medical supplies and food output could replace the production of guns and missiles. Arms reduction had transformed, and would continue to change, the balance of power in Eurasia and the world. It would also elevate the condition and dignity of the peoples of the former Soviet Union.

Chapter 13
COMECON's Quiet End

> *The Council for Mutual Economic Assistance has exhausted itself, but the economic "space" of its member countries is not a myth but a reality. This must be taken into account, and member countries should not break traditional economic links between them.*
> —Tass (Moscow), 5 January 1991

> *There is a possibility to rebuild COMECON, but my feeling is there is no need if we can enter into a common European home with the European Community.*
> —Prague economist Milos Zeman

> COMECON, *in the way that it existed, has exceeded its possibilities and does not correspond to the existing economic and social conditions of its member states. These countries are, however, linked to one another by established economic ties, and it would be pointless for any of them to cut these ties and reject one another right away.*
> —Stefen A. Sitaryan, Soviet deputy prime minister, 5 January 1991

> The theory was all right if you believed in central planning. The problem was that central planning failed in one country after another on a national level, and attempts to elevate it to a supranational level inevitably failed too. And there was that rather unpleasant aspect of Big Brother in Moscow telling us what to do in Budapest or Warsaw or Prague. You always suspected that he benefited more from the deal than you.
> —Z. Zygot, Hungarian senior economist, 5 January 1991

Pravda for once spoke truth: "The move by COMECON members toward market economies exposed serious defects in this international organization. The bulky, bureaucratic structures of COMECON had become legendary."[1]

Ceasing to be a functioning organization in 1989, since 1949 the Council for Mutual Economic Assistance (COMECON) had provided the Soviet Union a veil for its economic imperialism in Eastern Europe.

300

As a Soviet response to the U.S. Marshall Plan rebuilding the economies of Western Europe, COMECON was designed to integrate its members' economies through central direction, pooling capital, resources, and expertise to promote specialized production in different states and regions. The alleged aim was to promote the division of labor on the basis of the location of resources, labor, and the advantages of large-scale production, supposedly achieving low-cost economies of scale and improving the quality of output.

All this was largely myth. Moscow centrally planned the economies of the nine other COMECON members, dictating the sites for development of specialized industries of the members and combining their investment funds in a way that most benefited the Soviet Union.

No dynamic production apparatus was ever created either, though at its high point allegedly 30 percent of global industrial output was under its aegis. Rather, COMECON members were placed in a bilateral relationship with Moscow that deprived them of technology and know-how, allowed them to drift into specialized production without computing the costs of essential inputs in relationship to the value of output, and made their attempted commodity exports beyond COMECON both low quality and uncompetitive.

COMECON AS SOVIET HELOTRY

COMECON had appeared as an umbrella covering Soviet methods, essentially making bilateral trade agreements into pure barter transactions. Equivalent "prices of production" were arbitrarily placed on the exchange of goods, each compacting different real costs. Exchange of more cost-based value for less cost-based value thereby became the basis of barter COMECON-style, the Soviet Union usually reaping the better half of the bargain.

Hence, the unequal terms of trade — with clumsy Soviet manufactures, oil, and natural gas priced high, and Eastern European crude manufactures and materials priced low — meant monetary imbalances whereby more labor was expended by Eastern European workers to produce commodities, which were then exchanged for less Soviet labor crystallized in their exported goods.

Annual bilateral pacts and the systemic restraints of five-year plans locked Eastern Europe into the narrow economic formula Moscow imposed on the goods to be traded as well as their quantities and prices. And such neomercantile extortion might have continued if the Soviet Union could have provided the tools and manufactures of the modern industrial world.

But Soviet technological backwardness had spelled inferior goods, a lack of variety, and unfair competitive prices. Eastern Europe had thus looked to the West, scrambling to acquire hard currencies by requiring trade within COMECON to be based on dollars, Deutsche marks, and market prices rather than barter in backward products, artificial prices, and inconvertible currencies. To win hard currencies, moreover, each COMECON member secretly reserved its highest-quality product lines for Western markets.

And then came conflict as the Soviet Union, playing omniscient director, refused to pay either Hungary or Czechoslovakia in hard currencies, so that though each was running a $1-billion 1989 trade surplus with Moscow, the imperial master refused to remit its debt in dollars as these nations of skilled workers asked.

The Soviets also felt themselves losing through COMECON, some $10 billion each year being unrequited under terms of trade whereby the Soviets provided low-cost oil, gas, and other commodities in exchange for poor-to-mediocre manufactures from Eastern Europe.

The truth was deeper, though. For Soviet economic strength was 28 to 50 percent of what the official figures revealed for Gross National Product, agriculture being only 55 to 85 percent of America's output level. Soviet officials, having disguised the nation's true economic condition so long, had believed their own tortured statistics and discovered their dismal condition only when the opposition and the CIA revealed why they could not adequately clothe, feed, or house their millions.[2]

Moscow was in desperate need of both food and technology imports, to be paid from the Kremlin's short supply of hard currencies. To add to these, to win dollar returns by trade, in January 1990 the Soviets proposed that COMECON exchange take place at significantly higher world market prices and that payments be made in hard currencies.

The straw thus laid broke the camel's back. COMECON was soon to be no more.

COMECON DISSOLUTION

On 5 January 1991, the members of COMECON agreed on plans to dissolve the organization, to replace it with a new body that would promote the integration of its members into international trade, and to adopt the Western standards of supply costs in relation to competitive demand prices.

"At first, though, almost everyone wanted to withdraw, break existing contracts, in order to exit fast and completely," an official at COMECON headquarters observed as the meeting opened on 5 January 1991. "Then they looked at the Western markets in which they would be forced to compete and decided that a prolonged transition would better meet their needs, so long as all future COMECON trade would be valued and paid in U.S. dollars or, preferably, German marks."

Foreseeing a switch from central planning to their own market economies in 1988–89, Poland, Czechoslovakia, and Hungary wanted to move out of COMECON as quickly as possible. And by the close of 1990, they especially sought COMECON payment in marks so they could trade with a unified Germany.

The process would be drawn out for several years, though, because each COMECON member sought to preserve its existing sources of energy, raw materials, and markets, giving the Soviets an opportunity to cut military costs of occupying Eastern Europe while making these COMECON members pay in hard currencies for the import of Soviet oil and gas.

IMPERIAL POLITICS AND HARD-CURRENCY RATIOS

For forty years, unknown values exchanged under COMECON's Soviet direction had been accounted for by transferring rubles for positive trade balances. Moscow enforced Eastern European dependency by providing not only manufactures but inexpensive oil, natural gas, and assistance.

Such leverage in bilateral trade could not be deployed once Eastern European nations asserted their independence and entered other markets based on competitive prices.

Breakaway from COMECON was also essential for Poland, East Germany, and Hungary, each carrying huge hard-currency debts repayable to the West. Unable to limit themselves to bilateral trade and Soviet-remitted "transfer rubles," they sought to export to the West and beyond, to win markets worldwide for shoes and buses manufactured in Hungary, machine tools in Czechoslovakia, and the like.[3]

Even then, it would take Eastern European countries at least a decade to pay off their mountains of debt if only trade channels were used.

TRANSITIONAL SHELL

As COMECON trade plummeted in 1990 and seemed likely to continue its slide in 1991, a transition group, audaciously named the Organization for International Economic Cooperation, attempted to preserve what little trade remained, switched from value calculations in rubles to world prices in convertible currencies, and moved from Moscow dictation to coordination of mutual development.

The new relationship was certainly uncertain. But henceforth there would be no Moscow "coordination" of government development and investment plans. Rather, the new organization would try to continue or expand trade by bringing together buyers and sellers from member nations representing individual enterprises or specific industries.

The effort nonetheless seemed passé, at least in seeking to end the isolation of an Eastern Europe that had freed itself from Soviet rigidities and exploitation. The Soviet vision to delay the economic independence of Eastern Europe was resented by nations far more adept at reaching the

West than the incorrigible Kremlin apparatchiks. It was the Soviets who had lagged in entering Western European markets.

Albania had left COMECON in 1961. Yugoslavia was simply an observer, participating in the projects that might benefit its autonomy and independence. And Romania traded with the West in defiance of Stalin and his followers.

Lesser involvement in COMECON was taken by those who tried to emulate the Soviets' centrally planned economy from afar—Afghanistan, Angola, Ethiopia, Laos, Mozambique, South Yemen, and Vietnam. But the mainstay of COMECON, East Germany, dropped away when it united with West Germany in October 1990. In the early nineties, Czechoslovakia, Hungary, and Poland also sought International Monetary Fund loans, hoping to recapitalize their economies and move out of COMECON's mercantile framework into Western markets as quickly as possible. And left in COMECON at the outer reach of Eastern Europe was Bulgaria; in the Caribbean, Cuba; and in Asia, Mongolia.

The Soviets wanted Yugoslavia to participate again as a supplier of food, Germany to be an observer as a potential purveyor of critical materials and extended markets, and Albania to be the last hope of socialism under attack.[4]

CONSUMPTION VS. BUILDING AN INVESTMENT BASE

But the reality in Eastern Europe and the former Soviet Union demanded immediate changes COMECON could not negotiate. After years of central plans adopted and abandoned, of reforms started and forgotten, and a failed coup that led to the end of the seventy-four-year-old command system, by early 1992 the new economic reforms were not stimulating production. Black marketeers were periodically raiding money supplies. Cash and credit were in short supply for industries and farmers needing to buy materials and pay wages. The government's deficit-reducing program was in a shambles. The breakup of state industries and trade monopolies promised to create a wave of unemployment expected to rise to 10 percent of the work force by the fall of 1992. And the foods, manufactures, and raw materials the Soviet Union once imported from its Eastern European satellites were at a trickle. The most critical import shortage was medicines and pharmaceuticals, from syringes and aspirins to antibiotics, which Eastern Europeans would sell only for the hard currencies Commonwealth governments simply could not pay. The old supply lines had run out.

"In the border market in Yekaterinburg, where people come each day to swap anything for anything," in one scene in central Asia, "reporters found a man holding up a flimsy piece of cardboard upon which were displayed a few adhesive bandages, some packets of aspirin and several unidentified medical supplies. He was apparently bartering them for food."[5]

Eastern Europe faced its own dilemma. Massive investments in technology and other means of production were still required to provide the foundation for self-sufficient production to raise domestic living standards. But to make such investments from domestic sources alone would require limitations on consumption enforced by the state, the very authoritarian controls the newly liberated states were attempting to overthrow. Foreign capital might again be borrowed, as the Communist regimes had done. But what if the sums borrowed were again used for current consumption or misused?

Rather than build up a capital and investment base, political pressures in Poland and the rest of Eastern Europe demanded the use of foreign credit to finance such personal consumption, so that Eastern Europe would again be heavily indebted with an unrepayable financial burden to the West.

The past certainly provided a clue to the misuse of foreign debt. When the Communists still held power at the close of 1988, foreign debt was both massive and unrepayable in hard currencies:

Debtor Nation	Debt Per Capita
Hungary	$1,820
East Germany	1,250
Poland	1,030
Bulgaria	870
Yugoslavia	790
Czechoslovakia	430
Soviet Union	170
Romania	80

After the revolutions, Eastern Europe still needed massive sums to upgrade technologies, foster production and employment, regulate costs and prices, and provide a safety net for those unable to cope under the new conditions. By the close of 1989, Poland alone needed $10 billion. Western governments offered only $1 billion in emergency resources.[6]

More loans were reluctantly forthcoming. But the illogic of unrepayable debts by nations that looked to the West for new loans and trade would keep them in the category of high-risk states forced to succumb to terms imposed by creditor nations and institutions. Germany forgave half of the Polish debt in early 1992. And even joining the International Monetary Fund in order to borrow (on conditions of deflation, closing outmoded factories, and imposed unemployment) involved grants or borrowing hard currencies from wealthy nations. If the former Soviet republics took a 4.25 percent stake in the IMF to borrow to the limit of three or four times their capital stake, they would have to put up about $5.1 billion, one-fourth in hard currency and the balance in their own currencies. But that would also pressure rich member nations to increase the fund's overall capital from $120 billion to $180 billion, the United States delaying approval of its $12-billion share of the increase until after the 1992 elections.[7]

MEANWHILE, BACK IN RUSSIA, MORE PRINTING-PRESS MONEY

Without sufficient foreign capital, Russia and the other Commonwealth nations tried to fuel production by printing phantom currencies and borrowing saved rubles from both individuals and companies, squeezing resources for investment by further reducing current consumption.

In the wake of the government's desperate dash to enlarge production to meet the population's essential needs, Russian speculators from the old *nomenklatura* legally privatized state properties, then tried to sell them off for private profit. Inexperienced, the Yeltsin government fell into the trap of planning to sell off some 100,000 state shops representing 70 percent of the consumer marketplace by the end of 1992, then discovered that the regional and local government agencies that would negotiate the sales were often the bulwarks of old Communist methods, awarding party factory managers an inside track to use their training as managers, their considerable influence in post–Communist business and government circles, and their accumulated monetary resources legally to privatize assets. Though the Yeltsin government opposed privatization by the *nomenklatura* in the form of closed stock companies masking ownership by mixing private partners and corporate entities, and scheming to sell off large-scale military assets for private profits, initially the government had no way to stop the old party elite from building a new kind of monopoly for themselves. For they had inherited party resources and had most-favored status in obtaining easy credit from the state banking system.[8]

The logic of Russian Central Bank procedures accommodated *nomenklatura*-controlled industries. For bank policy was to print rubles to lend to these essential industries, particularly state-owned farms and farm-equipment makers, to keep the nation supplied with food by subsidizing agriculture with cheap credit.

The central bank also loaned to some dozen or so government-owned commercial banks at high interest rates (20 percent in February 1992), accounting for most of the nation's banking. Though these commercial banks also had outside investors, the government was the largest shareholder in early 1992, continued to get most of its funds by borrowing from the Russian Central Bank, was a depository for people's savings, and loaned the funds to critical industries and, by relending to the central bank, to the government to cover the budget deficit.

This shell game, switching printing-press money and people's savings, was best negotiated by the government-owned giant Sberbank, holding the savings of millions of Russians, lending the lion's share of its deposits to the central bank to help finance government deficits and the small balance to commercial borrowers. The central bank also used these switched deposits and newly minted rubles to loan to government-owned commercial banks such as Agroprombank and Promstroibank to relend to agricultural and industrial borrowers at high interest rates. But if their loans or interest due was not repaid, commercial bank losses could end in bankruptcy and losses for Russians salting away their labor-earned savings to garner 20 to 50 percent a year.

To finance smaller companies, cooperatives, and other enterprises emerging in the swath of privatization of the economy yet unable to borrow from government commercial banks, hundreds of privately owned banks blossomed under *perestroika* in the late eighties, only to find the central bank unwilling to finance them and the source of their funds coming from their shareholders, loans from other banks, and depositors — mainly companies, but individuals, too.

These limited resources put some 1,200 Russian and 800 commercial banks in other republics at great risk in lending to commercial firms that might be unable to repay either their loans or 1992 50 percent interest charges. Though they were positioned to recall their loans and deny new credit to shaky company borrowers, bad debts could quickly wipe out both these banks and their uninsured depositors. Without central bank oversight to regulate these commercial banks' lending closely and flag those loans unlikely to be repaid, the private commercial banks kept thousands of companies afloat, replacing the old Soviet government allocation of funds to state enterprises, so they could pay their suppliers, invest in new projects, pay salaries, and cover losses.[9]

THE WEST MOVES IN

As demand moved up, the United States readied its export of capital technology for trade and investment to reach some 400 million people in Eastern European nations, lifting in December 1989 some of its earlier curbs on the export of telecommunications equipment, computers, and other sophisticated products embargoed during the cold war.

Strategic threats from the Soviet bloc eroding, the controls expressing that threat were drawn away for Poland and Hungary. The United States had used a nonobligatory Western and Japanese group (COCOM) to keep warmaking technology out of Soviet hands, but the U.S. now pared the interdicted list of hardware to the strict category of "strategic technology," not including items like computers that could be used for industrial production or even nuclear plant safety.

The COCOM restriction list was now a dead letter, releasing West

German eagerness to sell advanced technology. Former under secretary of commerce for export administration Paul Freedenberg warned: "The U.S. is trying [so assiduously] to balance the strategic risk of taking things off the list versus genuine risk that you could see COCOM collapse if we are out of step with [competitive] reality."[10]

And with large chunks of East Germany's wounded economy, and 17 percent unemployed, dependent on contracts with the former Soviet republics, official policy from Bonn would look to the East to maintain all–German prosperity.

A deeper critique also issued. For the Western-financed export of technology for efficient Eastern European industrial production with low-wage workers would then place foreign industrialists in command.

INVESTMENT OPPORTUNITY KNOCKS

The key factor in Eastern European production with low-wage skilled labor was nearness to the heart of Western European markets. International GATT trade negotiations might collapse because of domestic farming interests in France and the United States, but investments in Western and Eastern Europe portended access to an extended market.

For Samsonite Corporation, the world's largest luggage producer, making luggage for sale in Western Europe in its own factory would raise quality and productivity above that of purchased luggage from manufacturers in Korea or Taiwan, without having to pay the shipping cost to Europe.[11]

By the start of 1990, the Industrial Bank of Japan saw Eastern Europe as a potential investment sphere and market. It already held 98.3 percent of IBJ Schroder (once the British merchant bank of L. Henry Schroder Wagg & Co. Ltd., whose parent now owned the Schroder balance of 1.7 percent), which was increasingly becoming active in Eastern European transactions, representing such big-name clients as Electrolux, A.B., the Swedish appliance maker; Hoechst, G.m.b.H., the West German chemical producer; and YKK, the Japanese zipper manufacturer.

And this was only a start for Japanese, U.S., and Western European investors and traders looking east. The nineties would witness their increasing presence and, for better or worse, the likely transformation of political economy throughout Eastern Europe.

Chapter 14
The Quest for Freedom: Revolution and the Transformation of Europe

My blackest dream is that we will take all our Communists and send them to Siberia. And then what will we have? Communism without Communists.
— Adam Michnik, editor of Poland's
leading newspaper, 13 March 1992

In many of the remote republics, the centrifugal forces are moving at such speed that they cannot be stopped without violence and blood, and it should not be done at any price. Everything is racing forward so haphazardly that in any case the Soviet Union will fall apart anyway. . . . We can only move a little faster to prevent new misfortunes so that the split will take place without extra suffering of the people.
— Aleksandr Solzhenitsyn, 18 September 1990

Salvation may not lie in erecting borders but in gradually integrating the republics into the common European bosom. And if some republics feel ready for this integration sooner than others, their chance cannot be taken away by brute force. It is better to have a well-disposed neighbor like Finland than a republic determined to escape and filled with hatred for those who won't let it go.
— Yevgeny Yevtushenko, 19 January 1991

The industrial handicap in European countries has been accentuated by prohibitive custom barriers and other nationalistic economic priorities. The difficulties in this connection were enhanced between the two wars by provisions of the Treaty of Versailles, which increased by 50 percent the number of independent European countries. Each of the newer countries was seeking to buttress its political independence by attempting to achieve economic self-sufficiency. The political uncertainty in which Europe lived throughout the period between the two wars strengthened the powerful tendency towards economic nationalism. In

309

> *short, nearly every country sought to develop within its own ter-*
> *ritory the key industries which were considered essential to their*
> *national defense as well as to their economic well-being.*
>   *In the existing situation there was a tendency in each of the*
> *European countries for small scale independent producers to be*
> *replaced by one or a few large companies. Even so, the domestic*
> *market was usually not large enough to permit the realization of*
> *the full advantage of large scale enterprise. With still larger plants,*
> *unit costs could be reduced. Hence there was a tendency to expand*
> *the size of establishments and "dump" a portion of the product in*
> *foreign countries for whatever price might be obtained.*
>   —Louis Marlio, director of the
>   world aluminum cartel, 1930s

The breakaway of republics in the USSR and nations in Eastern Europe spelled not simply freedom from Soviet and Communist domination but self-segregation and future balkanization of the region.

The next steps were soon put in motion: desperate attempts to establish national self-sufficiency and the competitive building of enterprises to supply domestic markets and sell abroad for whatever price in hard currencies could be won.

To accomplish these, republics and nations were not organized as capitalist or market economies, and the future contours and destinies of the former Soviet republics and Eastern European nations began to project the centrist and hierarchical structures of both the past and the moment.

EUROPE TIMES PAST

World War I had provided a watershed for the balkanization of Eastern Europe. The titanic conflict had severed all trade between enemy states and the myopic Treaty of Versailles had created 7,000 long miles of new frontiers that soon surrounded themselves with tariff walls and other trade barriers.

Britain had led, and the United States followed, a three-point program seeking (1) to confine Germany to Europe, (2) to keep Germany at odds with militarized France, and (3) to weaken, undermine, and overthrow the 1917 Russian Revolution by fortifying Germany at Russia's expense. As the spread of Bolshevik revolution threatened Germany and the rest of Europe, Britain's Lloyd George successfully insisted Germany must not be dismembered but rather strengthened as a major Continental power.

Hence, Versailles bore bitter fruit in the name of "security," and large chunks of Eastern Europe were balkanized as a buffer against Soviet expansion. Britain and the United States together made sure that the Hapsburg monarchy was broken up and that Germany and Russia were stripped of their "alien" fringes. From the western lands (Finland, Latvia, Estonia, Lithuania, Poland, and Bessarabia) torn by the German-led Central Powers from war-weakened Russia, the victorious Entente powers created a *cordon sanitaire*, stretching across Europe almost from the Arctic to the Black Sea.

This was one way to "contain" the new Soviet Russia. For the units of *cordon* were either given a nominal independence or (as in Bessarabia) turned over to a state like Romania, all of them obedient to France or Britain. Even Ukraine was slated to come under French rule, while areas around the Caspian Sea and the rich oil deposits of the Caucasus were designated for British domination, plans undermined by Bolshevik defenses and publication of the secret agreements for partition made by the Western Entente during the war.

The Soviet Union was in no position to stop this division of central and Eastern Continental territory or the rebuilding of German power. Fully occupied in beating back counterrevolution at home and the armies of Western intervention, Russia turned to build socialism in one country, holding little interest in spreading revolution or unification with capitalist Europe.[1]

As Russia left the capitalist marketplace, traditional markets once held by industrialized Western nations also failed to revive their prewar vigor. The move toward autarchy witnessed national markets being filled from domestic workshops and factories, blocking imports from others. True, Belgium and northern France devoted their factory systems to restoring capital equipment destroyed in the war, but even their boom of 1919–20 was modulated by the lack of markets. True, capitalist nations soon tried to restore the exchange of goods by laying the foundation for the exchange of currencies on a fixed basis, facilitated by international financial conferences in 1920 and 1922. But these nations soon decided that trade could not be restored if the industries of trading powers were not uplifted, leading to U.S. and British captial being loaned and invested in Austria (1920); Hungary (1924); Italy, Czechoslovakia, Romania, and Bulgaria (1925); and Germany (1920s). With trading partners and means of steady exchange of currencies established, U.S. and British policymakers believed world commerce could be restored.

But it never was. Anglo-Saxon capital merely put weak nations on steady economic feet, reinforcing their ability to produce for the same markets U.S. and British exporters hoped to win. Brave hopes for unfettered trade were the only products of the League of Nations, the International Chamber of Commerce, and the International Labor Office. Their aficionados could speak firmly of equal application of trade barriers and tariff clauses, commercial settlements and taxation procedures, but they had no power to prevent nations from trying to accomplish self-sufficiency behind walls that blocked out foreign goods.[2]

More hopes were expressed in 1927 at the World Economic

Conference: Tariffs and duties should be lowered to encourage free trade and stimulate production worldwide. But again, as few were listening, only a handful of schedules were lowered.

In the course of the twenty-two years between wars, moreover, the struggle for markets and economic empire reached a high pitch, taking on political and military attributes both within and outside Europe. Exaggerated economic nationalism, which World War I had fanned to red heat in the old and new states of the world, produced new tariff wars, new imperialistic rivalries, new jealousies, new armament races, and new political intrigues. Military and naval rivalries had not been abolished. And as new military alliances were established, the army and navy budgets of the world were larger than ever. Imperialistic rivalries were as rife as they had been before the war, and the nations of the world were again on the verge of conflict.

Class divisions in Europe were also more distinct than ever before as the centralization of capital in the hands of a few financiers led to a worsened condition for the vast majority of working people. But the population did not silently bear this burden, forming rebellious popular fronts in both France and Spain. In 1931, the Spanish Republic was established after the electoral defeat of the monarchy and the withdrawal of King Alfonso. In France, the Popular Front put the government of Léon Blum in office. These two Western European republics then became part of a "democratic belt" that stretched from the south across Europe through the central nations of Switzerland, Germany, Austria, Czechoslovakia, and Poland to the USSR in the east. In all these republics an antimonarchist and antilandlord sentiment prevailed, and in most of these nations there were traces of anticapitalism as well.

But as these political developments terrified the aristocracy and the bourgeoisie, they moved to protect their interests in land, factories, and banks, at the same time moving to suppress the growing popular movements. Not only did they fear these majorities, but they feared one another as well, and they prepared to use national government power to counter their equals in other countries. At the same time, they joined forces to repress the republican belt of governments, their newly installed reactionary regimes arming themselves and buying time by mutual nonaggression pacts.

By these means, popular movements were soon undermined or destroyed. France's Popular Front lost its following when the Blum government proved too timid to aid republican Spain. And in Spain, the Popular Front was totally destroyed in 1939 by a combination of Italian armies, German war materials, Franco's Fascist bands, and the policy of the British Tory government, which prevented both Moscow and Washington from rendering the aid the republican government required.

Throughout Europe, privileged classes looked upon Hitler's Nazis as their saviors, but even before the Nazis violated Austrian and Polish borders, the upper classes had solidified their power, replaced republican constitutions, established dictatorships, and suppressed popular protest. In Germany, Austria, and Czechoslovakia, the Nazis moved powerfully to trample republicanism and established Fascist rule.

Yet as the reactionaries broke popular governments, each national bourgeoisie began to compete against the others — the foreigners — to divide the globe in a way most favorable to themselves. They also aligned themselves into blocs of nations, their measures by treaty, entente, and rapprochement increasing as the years passed.

The collapse of world commerce was behind many of the new political alignments, for autarchy in production and protection of domestic markets made trade increasingly impossible. Sound currencies exchangeable for one another on a stable basis were lacking since some nations owned gold to back up their bank notes and others did not. Since gold was *the* way for capitalist nations to value their accumulated wealth, the currencies of those have-not nations could not be stabilized, so that trade with these nations became impossible if they could not pay in commodities or gold itself.

Trade soon crumbled because buying nations could not pay in gold; they could not pay in gold because they had no way to earn it by exports; and they could not export because world markets were either not rebuilt after the Great War or because they collapsed under increasing pressure on nations to produce but not to consume, to sell but not to buy, to export but not to import.

By 1940, every vestige of the cooperative international capitalist system of trade had disappeared. Preparations for war had replaced negotiations for commerce. The concern for international currency stability had been displaced by dealings over ratios of military hardware, and marching armies made the struggle for peace obsolete.

World War II followed, ending with a Europe divided into two major political camps that solidified in 1948, placing Stalin at the height of his domestic power, able to mobilize internal resources and send the Red Army and Communist commissars to Eastern Europe.

Communism already had three distinct ideological wings. Eastern Europe and major Western European parties in Italy and France followed Moscow's lead in organizing industrial workers; Mao Tse-tung looked to the peasant, not an industrial base China lacked, for ideological support. And Yugoslavia unified six distinct nations under Marshal Tito's refusal to bow to Kremlin controls. Nor could orders from the Soviet Central Committee direct the economies of Czechoslovakia, Poland, or Hungary. Despite COMECON efforts at unequal trade favoring Moscow, there never was a commonwealth of Communist states under Stalin's political thumb. And though the Soviet bloc existed by military puissance, political supranational mandate, and economic exchange, the illegitimacy of the center repeatedly expressed itself at the periphery in the forms of impatience in waiting for the material benefits that communism promised and a general recognition of fear of the authorities, who refused to grant personal freedoms that might be taken.[3]

With Stalin's death in 1953, Soviet bureaucratic centralism deployed hierarchical stratums of apparatchiks whose sinecures and defined functions directed the economy and maintained controls through the secret police and the military-industrial complex. By the early sixties, the official doctrines of socialist society were still generally believed, but by the late sixties, they were being questioned by repression in Czechoslovakia and the inability of the system to deliver the material rewards of productive labor. By the early eighties, moreover, there was general stagnation in Communist Europe, unrelenting central controls and a clear deterioration in both living standards and the quality of daily life. By 1985, Mikhail Gorbachev played to popular dismay, exposing the center's failings and proposing needed reforms—leading to the switchback trail of Soviet politics, the pullback from Eastern Europe, the disintegration of the Eastern bloc, the start of new democratic institutions, the latter's turn toward dictatorial ways under conditions set by financial institutions in the West, and a return to narrow nationalist formulations, autarchy, and threats to one another's security.[4]

Yet precisely what would come afterward was still unknown. There was obviously a rapid European reversion to political focus on nationalist, ethnic, and religious identities. The partition of the Soviet Union into states and microstates was going forward. Yugoslavia was in the throes of civil conflict, being balkanized into its several nation-states, each of which might be divided again by ethnic heritage, religion, and language. Western Europe had also returned to nationalist concerns, neglecting to take critical steps to political unity and concentrating on the power balance of domestic political life.

Germany was meanwhile breaking its axis with France in the European Community, forcing its wishes on its European partners in the West, entrapping its debtors and beneficiaries in the East, economically whipsawing England across the Channel, and rather than join France in a military venture to oust the United States from its strategic position in Europe, encouraging Washington to keep its military forces on the European side of the Atlantic. New calculations thereby accompanied the reemergence of old German ambitions.

OUTLINE OF THE FUTURE

Would the old alignments of blocs of powerful nations be recreated in the heat of the latest recurrent rounds of crises? Would a new balkanization cut Eastern Europe into slivers of autonomous states and republics lacking the ability either to produce efficiently or trade and import essentials competitively?

Would these states be saddled with Communist institutions handed down from the past, while the Communists themselves were kept out of administrative positions momentarily to direct, dismantle, and transform them?

Would the Western powers create new spheres of influence in the East and subjugate or otherwise exploit its territories, resources, and working populations?

Old Alignments Possibly Reemerge

Long-term answers to these questions remained uncertain in the early nineties. But in the short term Western nations would set the frame for external trade, infusions of capital, and the extraction of wealth from the new Eurasian nation-states caught in limbo between the old bureaucratic party centralism and the new balance of forces promoting centrist-directed transformation.

The newly liberated zones were meanwhile unprepared to reorganize national production, the labor force, or distribution, haggling over political ratios of power and government control mechanisms while their desperate populations suffered under the weight of high rates of unemployment, hyperinflation, rapidly falling living standards, and homelessness for those most exploited.

Discarding one bondage also weakened liberated nations, making them vulnerable to new masters, and the latter might uphold standards furthering their own extraction of resources and wealth from those weaker than themselves. Thus looking to the West as instructor of marketplace methods and source of financial infusions, debtor republics faced dangers, possibly new oppressors replacing old and the contours of earlier empires reemerging with unknown permutations. There need be no avaricious drive to shape such relations, only the external links of money and markets that place not equity but exchange value on all things, labor and human relations among them. Thereby exogenous forces might shape Eastern Europe's reach, underlying atavistic motives residing in the distant past, perhaps replaying a nineteenth- and twentieth-century amalgam and design, with Russia, England, the United States, Germany, France, and a host of lesser powers moving their pieces on the Eurasian chessboard for a checkmate game.

Russian Reversion to Past Rigidities

Returning to its earlier draconian ways, the Soviet Union through August 1991 had moved for internal stability—the party, KGB, and army together putting aside *perestroika*, planning to reverse, limit, and guide the earlier freedoms of *glasnost* and the Congress of People's Deputies, that democratic parliamentary forum of the popularly elected all–Soviet assembly whose creation in 1989 represented the triumphant apogee of political reforms set afoot by Mikhail Gorbachev.

Pressured by the Kremlin in early 1991, state-run TV had backed up undemocratic Politburo policy decisions with complete stylization of the "news"; and the opposition press and TV beat a fast retreat to stop cancellation of their government "franchise" and air rights. Interfax and Baltfax were still reporting, they knew not how long, the contours of the restoration of centrist controls and the crackdown under way, reversing the previous four years of experimentation with open discussion, democracy, and talk of economic reforms:[5]

- September 1990. Troop movements around Moscow signify the army exerting not-so-subtle pressure on the liberals, Parliament, and the reformists; Gorbachev blackmail on the food shortage begins.
- September 1990. Gorbachev's shelving of the "500-day Plan" designed by the *perestroika* liberals, pending restoration of order to the streets, the republics, and the Union.
- September–November 1990. A new relationship established between the president able to rule by postdated *ukaz* and the Supreme Soviet with after-the-fact veto power once decisions were in process of implementation.
- October–November 1990. Unexplained Kremlin slowing of international arms negotiations.
- October–December 1990. KGB chief Vladimir A. Kryuchkov and Defense Minister Dmitri T. Yazov issue militant public statements demanding order, accompanied by a din of conservative party speeches in Parliament and reactionary press articles criticizing Gorbachev's *glasnost* and *perestroika* as creating the frame for dissident activities, street demonstrations, armed secessionist revolt, and the breakup of the Union.
- November–December 1990. Replacement of liberals surrounding President Gorbachev with party functionaries and apparatchiks. Party clone Gennadi I. Yanayev becomes vice president, relaying Gorbachev's authoritarian orders. Economic apparatchik Valentin Pavlov becomes prime minister, enunciating the new Gorbachev line. Reactionary Latvian party and KGB chief Boris K. Pugo becomes minister of interior in charge of Interior Police used to create party "Committees of National Salvation" to forward Kremlin controls, hence violence, in Vilnius, Lithuania, Riga, Latvia, with similar plans for other republics and cities in the future.
- 12 December 1990. Secret KGB warning to the Politburo that soldiers must be readied to stop revolts planned in Lithuania, Latvia, and Estonia, and to oversee possible supportive demonstrations in Moscow and other cities.
- 12–15 December 1990. Gorbachev cabinet and "brain trust" review a

series of measures that will ensure domestic "stability" and prevent the Baltic republics from breaking away.

- 12–19 December 1990. Liberals in the *perestroika* "brain trust" resign, fearing a turn toward renewed totalitarian controls, the most famous Stanislav S. Shatalin, Vadim V. Bakatin, Nikolai Y. Petrakov, and Aleksandr N. Yakovlev.
- 20 December 1990. Foreign Minister Eduard A. Shevardnadze resigns, warning of a coming dictatorship.
- 22–31 December 1990. Presidential decree implemented for KGB and the police to "cooperate" with newly established worker vigilante committees to monitor food collection and distribution to catch, accuse, and summarily punish those involved in theft, illegal diversion, and speculation.
- 21 December 1990–10 January 1991. Minister of interior clandestine plans go forward to use military force against the parliaments and independence forces in Lithuania, Latvia, and Estonia. Interior Ministry troops and army to attack television stations, airports, public buildings, and interfering protestors or others impeding control.
- 15–27 January 1991. Interior troops with army and special forces storm and bloodily attack citizens in Vilnius and Riga per planned scenario. Gorbachev denies knowledge after the fact and makes no effort to chastise the constitutionally illegal, party-directed "Committees of National Salvation" that allegedly called for help from the Interior troops, reifying party direction of KGB and army used to subjugate the Baltics during and after World War II.
- 22 January 1991. Gorbachev decree ordering 50- and 100-ruble bills to be withdrawn from circulation and that banks offer new currency or credit only for sums equal to the average earnings of each citizen or a strict accounting for the source of currency beyond such limits.
- 25 January 1991. Gorbachev decree that armed soldiers join police in patrolling major cities starting 1 February 1991.
- 26 January 1991. Gorbachev decree granting sweeping powers to KGB and police to search private business premises to confiscate documents to combat "economic sabotage"; to demand and receive from banks and other finance-credit enterprises current and accounting information about the credit and monetary operations and foreign economic affairs carried out by enterprises, institutions, and organizations, regardless of the form of ownership; and to freeze the assets and documents of any business. Alleged purposes: to discourage fledgling moves toward free enterprise by Soviet cooperatives, joint ventures, and foreigners; to block the use of cooperatives as cov for black market operations selling at exorbitant prices for d and drawing goods from scarce state supplies through illega nels; to regularize the supply of food and consumer goods to ulation.

By all these measures, Kremlin law and order took precedence over democracy, private accumulation, speculation, separatist movements, and foreign commerce. Encumbered by the internal struggle to keep its republics under central dictatorship, the party centrist forces concentrated on domestic controls, no longer seeking either external empire or foreign military might. Yet by concentrating on repressive domestic controls, Gorbachev and his party momentarily offended and closed down ties with the West. Soviet planners held on to the naïve and fervid hope to industrialize under socialism using Western capital and technologies and entering world markets.

As lines for domestic conflict tightened and six republics moved for independence, on 17 March 1991 a majority of voters in nine of the Soviet republics still called for maintaining a unified state, giving Gorbachev a new opening for added Kremlin rigidities. But this populist vote carried apparent weight only until the August 1991 failed coup revealed the putschists Gorbachev himself had empowered, pursuing their own narrow careers, political aspirations, and hopes to take power in the wake of popular disillusionment with *perestroika* reforms, currency scandals, military maneuvers, attempted assassinations, and wheel-of-fortune politics.

This swing from the political left to the right became Gorbachev's fatal error that also led to his refusal to give Yeltsin due credit for saving both the government and Gorbachev from a renewed Stalinist dictatorship. And Gorbachev's reaffirmation of the popularly hated Communist party quickly led to the destruction of any popular hope for a unified nation.[6]

The Congress of People's Deputies was then suspended, and after the Soviet state was itself disbanded, the Parliament of the Russian Republic declared its dissolution on 2 January 1992.

The former republics now separate states, production was disorganized, state employment uncertain. Supplies shipped between the former republics were interrupted by corrupt diversion, autarchic schemes, quotas on trade, coupon rationing, and currency ratios. A new class of traders and middle agents moved goods and materials at ever-higher prices. Unemployment and poverty escalated, living standards fell, com-
diseases rose. Police enforcement and authority structures
property crimes went up; the battle of political par-
d blaming the others for society's ills; and
e republics began calling or moving for
tion.

in March 1992. Nationalism was rife in each
guided by Communists in charge of the gov-
ht-left bloc knit the traditionally antithetical
ists and Communists, respectively demanding
onarchy and the Soviet state! While the first

wanted the tsar's heirs reinvested with power, the latter denounced the "Gorbachev-Yeltsin clique" and "pseudo-democrats" for "selling out the Union of Soviet Socialist Republics to Western capitalism," leading the country to disintegration.

Not contented, the Communists thus regrouped, calling for the reconvening of the Congress of People's Deputies on 17 March 1992. They proclaimed this as a meeting of the *veche*, the ancient Slavic communal assembly at which major decisions were to be made, its organizers arguing that Russia had no authority to dissolve the Congress or the Soviet Union.

Their plans for delegates, the election of a new Soviet president, and thereby the creation of a new Communist government were banned by both the Russian Parliament and the prime ministers of the Commonwealth of Independent States formed by eleven former Soviet republics, the latter denouncing them as "interference in the internal affairs of sovereign states." And when they met at the Voronovo state farm auditorium without electricity one candle-lit night, with fewer than a fourth of the former deputies nominating army general Albert Makashov as their president, the impotence of the old-line Communists was never clearer.

Nor was there immediate political life in the concurrent 17 March rally outside the Kremlin of 10,000 die-hard champions of the old Soviet Union mingled with monarchists, anarchists, and neo–Fascists. "We do have a real government. Only it's in prison," Soviet-nationalist TV host Aleksandr Navzorov said, drawing loud applause for the jailed August putschists.[7] For indeed the Yeltsin and other republic governments were not yet at any significant risk.

Russia was nonetheless weakened by factions, destruction of its state-financed press and subsidized Union of Soviet Writers, fights with Ukraine over military forces and territory, and dozens of autonomous regions within Russia demanding independence from grasping centrist controls. Though the Communist government of the Tatar Autonomous Republic in central Russia thus took on a nationalist cast, speaking of the rights of Tatarstan in a successful referendum on independence, Vice President Aleksandr V. Rutskoi defended the central government, calling for a state of emergency on 15 March 1992 to forestall the disintegration of Russia. And so it went—boundaries and matters of government unsettled and in flux, appealing to and facing Western pressures and interests.

The two points of departure were a return to narrow autarchic nationalism or opening up to Western capital, markets, and aid. "Economically, we are not even on the edge of an abyss—we're fully in it," President Kravchuk said of the first jump-off point on 20 March 1992. "If this continues, the entire existence of the Commonwealth of Independent States is questionable."[8]

And continue it did. Bred of Russian and Ukrainian efforts to extract material wealth from one another under IMF pressure, Russia's planned oil prices to rise as much as 10 times, to be sold for rubles or hard currency to Ukraine. To buy Russian petroleum products, however, Ukrainian salaries would have to be raised to Russian levels, and holding only 17 percent of all rubles in circulation, Ukraine worried that higher-paid Russians would use rubles to buy cheaper Ukrainian goods. To protect its goods, the Ukraine Parliament adopted a set of economic goals that included completely replacing the ruble with local currency coupons or foreign convertible currencies for external and internal dealings. This withdrawal from the "ruble zone" was "equivalent to withdrawal from the Commonwealth of Independent States," said Vladimir Grinyov, a founder of the opposition New Ukraine.[9]

Meanwhile, pursuing the second point of departure, Russia looked to the West. "The Russians are moving very fast, said Stanley Fisher, a former World Bank chief economist. "They have done a lot on the budget side. They have tightened their monetary policy. With external support they can go the last few yards."[10] Indeed, Socialist economics had utterly failed. The collapse of the attempt at communism here and throughout Eastern Europe was certain, as Nobel Prize–winning economist Friedrich von Hayek had predicted before the close of World War II.[11] In the quest for freedom and free markets, former Communist states now looked to the West.

NEW SPHERES OF WESTERN INFLUENCE

External support was seen as the savior throughout Eurasia. With the disintegration of the Soviet colossus and its Eastern European helotry, both were balkanized, each state planning for self-sufficiency yet unable to rebuild production and commerce without Western links—mostly with and through Germany; less with the United States, Britain and France; even less, Japan and economically weaker powers.

Ties westward had placed waiting, credit-offering Germany in the driver's seat. Positioned in mid–Europe, unified economically, it would one day capture Eastern influence and commerce as well as dominate the Western Continent with its capital and manufactures.

The United States, slower to invest in former Communist Eurasia, had suffered a crisis in internal production and failing trade competitiveness. Its basic industries had been gutted, only partially upgraded technologically and displaced by a revolution in power sources, automated manufacturing, and output of computer-directed robots. Hierarchical in industrial organization, its workers had lost skills, union power (unionization declined from about 32 percent of the work force in the thirties to 12 percent in industry and 6 percent in government in 1992), real wages, and almost all direction over the production process, thereby being discouraged from putting forth their best efforts. Its social security system weakened, the senior labor force often worked for wages to retire, not to ensure a job well done. Overall production inefficiencies had forced up domestic costs and prices, leading to calls for protectionist measures as U.S. companies tried to stop imports by increasing complaints directed to GATT of foreign dumping on the American market.[12]

The U.S. government had meanwhile lost its budgetary balance between social services and military outlays. America's educational system had been degraded, its teachers underpaid and held in low esteem. Its population was in conflict, struggling for jobs and wealth, divided by race, class, ethnic communities, and gender. The United States had also been weakened by forty-six years of military outlays, a war it could not afford against Iraq, and a NATO it could not sustain alone.

And as Japan momentarily reversed its eighties investment of hundreds of billions of dollars in the United States and elsewhere and foreign investors became the largest purchasers of deflated Japanese stocks and bonds, instead of $100 billion or more annually flowing out of Japan, $30–$40 billion a year began flowing inward in 1991–92. This swing in Japanese capital movement placed upward pressure on U.S. interest rates to attract foreign capital into Treasury and other bonds, thereby reducing the American outflow of loan and investment capital to others, including Eastern Europe and the former Soviet Union.[13]

Limiting their financial risks in Eurasia, most Western nations were at loggerheads, divided by separate interests and blocs. England opposed Continental unity. France also moved against German domination on the Western Continent, the Dutch and Danes fearing a German-directed central bank almost as much as England. Together they viewed a united Germany as again seeking *Lebensraum*, east and west.

England and France took the lead to limit future Teutonic hegemony. But America viewed Germany as its stalking horse to rehabilitate the former Soviet republics and Eastern Europe, planning to step into any future economic vacuum, blind that German political calculations could someday change.

Little-Englanders vs. Continental Unity

In the early nineties, Britain carried a double burden: a deep economic downturn at home and too little capital to export to the Western or Eastern Continent to combat Germany's aggressive power. Emergent spheres of European influence were already defining themselves, Western European efforts to consolidate the Continent faltering on Britain's questioning the establishment of a central bank, single currency, and political integration that would likely fall under German control.

Britain, politically astute and trying to keep its U.S. ally by securing America's dulled edge in time of overstretch (an economic crisis at home, an expensive military encounter in the Middle East), had sought to continue its centuries-old policy of ensuring there would be no single dominating force in Europe, neither economic nor political, neither ideological nor military. Britain thus opposed a single Western European state as well as a political federation, a financial confederation, or banking uniformity.

For this, Tory England would seek to keep the U.S. budget afloat to maintain the "Atlantic Alliance" against unification of the Western Continent. Prime Minister Thatcher thus became the self-appointed treasurer collecting monies for the United States to act as intermediary to defend the oil and other interests of Europe and Japan against Iraq in the Middle East. "We cannot conceivably accept that a country can simply march into a neighbor, which is an independent country and a full member of the U.N., and annex it," she said during one of her last months in public office.[14]

And though "Island Englanders" would remain with this foreign policy for the rest of Thatcher's term and beyond, the United States sought to use the united Germany it fostered as a buffer, and entrée, to the East, pressuring reluctant Britain to join a united Western Continent. Thus a half year before the Berlin Wall crumbled, in May 1989, Washington already spoke of Germany as its joint "partner in leadership" on the Continent.

Britain certainly favored the realignment of political forces in Europe, Prime Minister Thatcher telling Parliament on 22 November 1990 that the disarmament agreement and plans for a new CSCE ensured "a new order in Europe, and I hope, a very successful peaceful one." But Britain played a close hand, watching just how far France would allow German Continental domination to proceed, how U.S. policymakers would respond to Teutonic expansion while America paid the cost in a military presence, and whether Russia and Ukraine would disarm in the face of the emerging German *Weltpolitik*.

There were also domestic pressures shaping British opposition to a unified Western Continent. In late 1990, with considerable popular backing, Parliamentary member Janner of the Labour party had sharply criticized the prime minister's lack of emphasis on domestic matters, so deeply concerned were his constituents that she was leaving the nation in an economic mess. "Is she," asked he, "aware that they are desperately worried about [the per capita] poll tax, about deepening recession, about the health problems, and . . . are worried about the educational system and about the whole poor shambles?"[15]

This lack of social programs represented the accumulation of poverty over decades, the fact that making up the deficit in unfilled needs would involve new investments, high wages, greater welfare benefits, and social services. England could not afford simultaneously to resolve its domestic crisis, risk imports of cheaper continental products wiping out English industries, and export much capital for operations on the Continent. For such exports would mean accelerated impoverishment, unemployment, and disaccumulation at home, leading to Thatcher's displacement by Prime Minister John Major and eventually the fall of the Tory government.

To resolve domestic problems, moreover, England would have to retain full sovereignty and could not be subject to a fiscal or monetary union with a central governmental budget and a foreign central bank setting common EC policies for Britain.

Britain opposed the formation of a central EC bank by 1994. England would think twice before approving a future single Common Market currency. And aligning Little-Englanders with the working class and the impoverished on fixed or no incomes, British policymakers were more right than wrong for their survival against a German-dominated Common Market with its disparate rates of growth, production, and inflation.

To maintain its autonomy from German reach, Britain would not now, perhaps never, agree to surrender to a European central bank the right to decide how many pounds should be circulated in Britain or what they should be worth. So the tactic for Britain was not a single common currency but a supplemental common currency based on a European currency unit, so there would be no permanent locking of exchange rates.

The Little-Englanders backing the Thatcher Tories had thus opposed a federated Europe. "We want you to tell Froggie Common Market chief Jacques Delors exactly what you think of him and his countrymen," *The Sun*, England's broadest mass-circulation tabloid, said, encouraging xenophobia in attacking the EC's French Socialist president. "At the stroke of noon tomorrow, we invite all true blue Brits to face France and yell 'Up Yours, Delors.'"[16]

It was this ungainly alliance of Tories opposing a Continental bank and currency, vulnerable common people seeking improved conditions, and Labour party support that would keep England from *full* Common Market participation and subjugation under a raking German presence.

And fearing the new alliance that could turn the Conservatives from office, Prime Minister John Major tried to assure Chancellor Helmut Kohl of British support, minus an EC central bank, should he remain after the contest with the Labour party in the April 1992 general elections.

England would also try to keep Eastern and Western Europe apart. And for this purpose, England in the nineties would likely extend increasing aid, trade, and investments to both the Commonwealth of Independent States and Eastern Europe, an historical counterweight to German unity and strength on a continent already overwhelmed by Teutonic trade and finance.

European Unity

Germany's expansionary lens focused east and west in the early nineties. From its view westward, some "degree of harmonization of the economies" of EC member states would obviously be necessary, advised Frankfurt Commerzbank senior economist Pete Pietsch in 1990. Following such logic, Chancellor Kohl successfully pushed for a 1 January 1994 deadline to establish the EC central bank. He understood that once German inflation fighters were in charge, a common central bank could effectively crack down on high-inflation countries like Greece and Portugal, creating domestic unemployment that might lead to political upheaval yet also award Germany the opportunity to take up investment and market opportunities in their failed economies. Herein resided Western transcontinental opportunities for Germany, so a future *Lebensraum* would obtain economically.

Yet any integration in Western Europe might take decades, not years, as Italy's Foreign Minister Gianni de Michelis told the German-sponsored Bertelsmann Foundation at its late 1990 meeting. Italy's Emilio Colombo added it was impossible to build a "community without sovereign institutions" and wanted an organized European power that could "sit alongside the U.S. as an equal." And such European unity might prevent the reemergence of the competitive European power blocs that prevailed between the two world wars, thereby aligning groups of rival states seeking markets, security, and support. But the question remained whether there could be real unity on the Western Continent with financially dominant Germany in the EC.

In central Europe, meanwhile, West Germany had successfully pursued its revanchist policy, formally merging East and West Germany, now obliged by interests, equity, and politics to pursue a new *Anschluss* with Austria, Croatia, and Slovenia; reindustrialize Russia and the rest of Eurasia; and, mobilizing Western capital, establish a backdoor entrance to the Polish, Czechoslovakian, and Hungarian economies.

Expectations of a decade of pouring West German capital into its eastern wing might limit German-owned investments elsewhere, but surprises were likely as Germany became the Continental entrepôt of Western capital and pushed heavy private investments in Eastern Europe.

Lebensraum in the 1990s

Germany's unified future was still in formation in the early nineties. The cost of reviving East Germany between 1991 and 2000 would come to some $1 or $2 trillion, about equal to ten or twenty years of expected German budget deficits, as the five new states of Eastern Germany borrowed beyond their capacity to tax or repay. The cost in 1991 was 140 billion marks ($85 million), promising to rise to 180 billion marks in 1992 and averaging out to $85 billion a year thereafter.[17]

There was also the matter of paying for the Middle East war and Germany's new imperial aims. For normal budgetary means could not finance both German reindustrialization and contributions of rising sums to the U.S.'s widening military front. Germany promised $2.2 billion when the U.S. air war on Iraq began in mid–January 1991; the figure was already raised to $6.7 billion on 23 January; and German aspirations for a new sphere of Middle Eastern influence brought promises of financial aid to oil-supplying Egypt, oil-shipping Jordan, and trading partner Turkey.

The result was an escalating German budget deficit: up from $73.3 billion in 1990 to well over $100 billion in 1991, perhaps as high as $121 billion with the surge of borrowing by the new eastern German states in 1992.

And who would pay? There were four paths to raise the needed capital, each with political consequences: new taxation, further government borrowing, wage controls through the central bank's interest rate structure, and draining other nations in the Common Market.

Chancellor Kohl favored lifting taxes (the chancellor's December 1990 reelection campaign had promised *not* to), disguising the finance of German unification in Bonn's alleged contribution to the United States to fight Iraq in the Persian Gulf.* "I would call his statement a fig leaf," said Warren Oliver, conservative economist with UBS Phillips and Drew in London. "Everyone has been expecting tax increases because the costs of unity are proving greater than anticipated. The Gulf War provided an unassailable excuse."

Kohl also reasoned that higher taxes would reduce the nation's need to borrow, thus easing pressure on higher interest rates, in turn relayed to the rest of Western Europe, raising their ire and cutting their ability to stimulate economic growth in times of an economic turndown. To stop large pay increases demanded by unionized labor, moreover, the Bundesbank had maintained living standards by modulating inflation. Bank president Karl Otto Pöhl maintained a restrictive stance, keeping interest rates high to counter the potential inflationary effects of soaring government deficits, themselves the cause of borrowing that fueled competition of government deficit spenders with the buying public. By preventing inflation, Bundesbank logic ran, the deutsche mark would remain stable, protecting it in the hands of consumers who could maintain their buying power without demanding higher wages, which in turn would force up the German cost of production.

Infallible the logic might be for internal German expansion in rebuilding the East, but it switched the burden of *Grossdeutschland* reindustrialization to France and others in Western Europe. For a stable

---

*Some recalled that Germany had done nearly the same after World War I, borrowing capital from Wall Street and withholding war reparations while using both for reindustrialization.

deutsche mark and high German interest rates locked other Common Market currencies into a narrow range of exchange through the operation of the European monetary system. As high Bundesbank interest rates were relayed to France and other European nations, their economic growth slowed, and to stimulate domestic investment, they elevated their budgetary spending yet could not upgrade their levels of savings, investment, employment, production, and marketing.

Without these sources of accumulation and wealth creation in France and the other Common Market partners, moreover, German policies to enhance its concentration of wealth were destined to divide the Economic Community anew. Germany might one day produce and accumulate more in a reindustrialized East, but present Teutonic gains were at the expense of France and others in the EC. "It is vain to think you can compensate for [German] budgetary policy which is too expansionary with [Bundesbank] monetary policy which is too restrictive," French finance minister Pierre Bérégovoy criticized the German posture in late December 1990.[18]

But by then the fears and burdens of German unification and reindustrialization were being powerfully visited on the Common Market. The Bundesbank, using the interest rate structure, and the European monetary system, regulating exchange rates, were together draining capital from other nations to build German puissance for tripartite expansion in eastern Germany, Eurasia, and the Western Continent.

Only Britain pulled up its monetary security blanket. The Bank of England was independent of Chancellor Kohl's scheme to tax the Continent for Teutonic strength, also independent of Herr Pöhl's Bundesbank policies to dampen inflation at home but cut production elsewhere on the Continent. Fallen Tory leader Margaret Thatcher had correctly foreseen the dangers of entanglement in the Common Market and European monetary system.

And a new alignment in the Common Market and Europe was in sight as Germany took in and supported the majority of refugees from Eastern Europe; planned to raise taxes beyond the 1991 "one-time" 7.5 percent surcharge on personal income and an increase in several consumer taxes; clogged its courts with conflicting ownership claims to Nazi- and Communist-seized properties in East Germany; planned to take over and renovate much of eastern Germany's labor-intensive heavy industry as an interim measure leading to privatization; provided about 60 percent of all 1991–March 1992 Western aid to the former Soviet republics; and to lessen the financial strain while conquering Europe economically, urged the United States to maintain its 300,000 troops in Europe rather than reduce them by half while more than 225,000 Russian troops remained in eastern Germany.

Germany meanwhile perfected a two-tier eastern policy to transform united Germany from a frontline zone against future chaos in the former

Soviet Union into a secondary zone behind the buffer states of Poland, Czechoslovakia, and Hungary. To stop turmoil in Russia and the other Commonwealth states and bring the rest of Eastern Europe into its sphere, Germany thus placed over half (some $50 billion) of all Western aid in Eastern Europe from 1990 to March 1992. And to gain new production and market opportunities fortifying the new eastern buffer zone, German state grants and credits backed business investments in Poland, Czechoslovakia, and Hungary.

All these forces empowering Germany meanwhile put fear in the heart of France. For it was not merely the move eastward that would strengthen Germany's future industrial base and trade zone but the use of that power to overwhelm and weaken Western Continental resistance.

France as Third Force

French policy had two fronts: Anglo-Saxon divisive designs and Germany's preference for an eastern sphere at the expense of EC solidarity. On the first front, seeking to consolidate the continent against Anglo-American efforts to do away with Common Market subsidies that might weaken its members' economies and introduce political dissention, France again emerged as tradition's third force in Europe.

France saw the United States as trying to foster economic trade conflict, seeking to embroil and divide France and Germany politically. French farmers relying on Common Market farm subsidies had already crossed swords with the United States, Canada, and other nations dependent on agricultural exports seeking EC subsidy cuts by as much as 36 percent. In 1991 the United States had sold $696 million of corn gluten, its main export cereal substitute to Europe, wanting a still broader market by the elimination of EC subsidies. And though Chancellor Kohl had promised Washington he would press France on the issue in 1990, he delayed in order to pursue U.S.-backed German reunification and elections, delaying again in 1992 for fear of conflict in the EC and interference with Germany's new Eastern European sphere of influence designed to turn Czechoslovakia, Poland, Hungary, and Croatia into buffer states against conflicts farther east. French farmers and workers voted "No" on Teutonic Rule.

The U.S. recourse was to waylay French exports by blocking completion of GATT trade negotiations. "Any agreement which puts a cap on corn gluten exports will severely upset Midwestern agricultural interests since this is the type of value-added export we are trying to increase," Senator Charles E. Grassley, Agricultural Committee member from corn-growing Iowa, wrote a Bush adminsitration official. Farm lobbyists like the U.S. Feed Grains Council also sought to ensure rejection of the whole GATT agreement if it limited their access to European agricultural markets.[19] And under such lobbying pressure, the constitutional allotment of two senators from each state put the nation's agricultural areas in command of the Senate, rejecting any U.S. agricultural treaty. France would lose GATT export rights to the American market unless Germany pressured France to change its policy.

Germany might plead, but France would not budge, President François Mitterrand protesting that reduced subsidies would destroy a productive social class that was the fount of French self-sufficiency in food.

On its second front, France understood the danger posed by the growing political and economic power of a united Germany, France seeking to ally with Russia, Poland, Czechoslovakia, and Hungary politically and economically, to encircle and cloister Germany in times of possible future discord. To strengthen its position in the East, French aid to Romania was also offered, as were investments in Hungary and the western Balkans after the 1992 partition of Yugoslavia.

But this might be a frail defense against German economic muscle after thirty-five years of Franco-Teutonic cooperation in the Common Market, an alliance that had frayed when President Mitterrand tried to slow the pace of German unification in 1990. By 1992, French officials could only complain about Germany rebuilding its traditional sphere of influence in central Europe. And Germany's role in the EC changed from being the Western continental paymaster to aid giver to the Eastern Continent; from help for Spain, Portugal, Greece, and Ireland as the poorest members of the EC to bringing Poland, Czechoslovakia, Hungary, Estonia, Latvia, and Lithuania into the Common Market as even poorer associate members; from promoting greater economic and political unity of the EC (by creating a central bank and common currency as the cat's paw of a Franco-German alliance against Britain) to using the new associate members as a hodgepodge of German client states diluting any future common foreign and security policies.

The fallout would be a return to narrow European nationalism and competitive spheres of power. As France and Germany slowly parted ways, Britain would successfully divide the Western Continent, undermining French aspirations to grandeur yet liquidating British Continental influence, and empowering Germany as the economic and political hub in the European Community and Eastern Europe.

The United States would meanwhile attempt to retain its power through Germany and Britain, appeasing both by maintaining some semblance of military operations in Europe in the nineties; forcing the French plan for the nine-nation Western European Union regional defense system to come under NATO command, compelling any Franco-German military force to pay for their own operations, and ensuring that a continued American presence in Europe would oversee any future threats from either Germany or the Middle East.

Outflanked, France would thus seek a tripartite defense against potential isolation: against Anglo-Saxon division of the Western Continent, against German domination east and west, and against a German-Eurasian alliance developing Eastern European industries and exports jeopardizing French interests.

EASTERN POLITICAL INDEPENDENCE

To varying degrees, with or against their will, the smaller Western nations would be aligned with these larger powers and their policies, all of them facing the newly balkanized eastern wing, hemmed in by the uncertain destiny and needs of Russia and a united Germany. The U.S. presence was the only remaining linchpin keeping France, Germany, Britain, and Russia from one another's jugular.

"The only element of stability and predictability in this world in transition is the transatlantic axis," NATO secretary general Manfred Wörner said, calling attention to NATO's remaining function. "If the United States disengages, I foresee a certain temptation for Western European nations to revert to past patterns of power politics."[20]

Germany was stretching its political muscle, bowling over French and English opposition in the West, creating a new *cordon sanitaire* in the East, and foreseeing that the United States would one day leave and give it a free hand, economically or otherwise. "If the United States leaves, Germany will be the dominant European power," Berlin writer Peter Schneider surmised in 1992. "No one likes the idea; many Germans don't want it. But it will happen anyway."[21]

Eurasia was secured by German wealth. For political independence of the new states was not possible without, or with, massive infusions of foreign economic aid. But could future prosperity coexist with Western prescriptions for austerity and demands for loan repayments? And under such exogenous pressures, what elements of commonality might become critical for development, peace and prosperity in Europe for the rest of the twentieth century?

Conditions of Change

There were no precise answers in the early nineties. The conditions essential for change might be framed by a new round of revolutions and reforms pursued by, or in the name of, the people in each nation, republic, or region. Undoubtedly, parliaments, premiers, presidents, and cabinets would be frequently replaced, juggling their personnel, without much altering the basic framework for administering power.

The conditions of, and necessities for, "pluralism" would also likely be set by the competition of vested groups and special interests, initiating and backing their political parties and factions. By these means, structured parliamentary and presidential elections would be held periodically to ensure that each nation promised either traditions or a democratic path.

There would surely be popular attacks on the remnants of Communist-held bureaucracies with their vested rights and positioned sinecures handed down from past regimes, protecting apparatchiks, more or less incompetent, inefficient, and corruptible.

And deeper ideological questions would also be raised about the way social and economic life should be organized and proceed. In some nations and ministates, a second, third, or other revolution would doubtlessly ensue. But in any event, only then was it likely that real transformation would proceed—or become entrapped by old habits, ways of thinking, and material pressures. Dichotomies of socialism or market economies would also likely be seen as subsidiary to questions of economic survival, social viability, and the production of quality output to ensure safe manufacturing, equitable distribution, and the preservation of human life.

In these ways, states in Eastern Europe and Eurasia would travel the long and bumpy path to prosperity, equitable or otherwise.

Emergent Spheres of Influence

But these states might also undo their independence and well-being. Their outreach for investments from and commerce with other nations and states might establish new spheres of Western influence, causing tensions and discord. For in the early nineties, Eastern Europe broke completely free of the Soviet helotry, the Soviet empire self-destructed, the independent states of Eurasia moved toward Western ties—more or less falling into either an inner reach by way of German territory or an outer reach by several circuitous paths that made it possible for the West efficiently to invest, capture regional markets, and replace decaying commercial ties with the former republics of the Soviet Union.

The Inner Reach

The consolidation of the two Germanys in 1990 unified *Grossdeutschland* politically, promised to do so economically, and raised the question whether it would ever do so militarily. Teutonic unification also meant that common borders with Poland and Czechoslovakia would provide a future opportunity for heavy commercial traffic, exchanging technology, labor, manufactured goods, and services. A united Germany promised the territorial integrity of both Poland and Czechoslovakia, but such promises spoke to artificial boundary lines the military was never to cross, not the probable integration of their economies, not the political influences of one another.

Thus was established an inner reach locking Germany to the Western Continent and enticing Poland and Czechoslovakia to use *Grossdeutschland* as a way station for commerce not only with Germany but with the entire Western zone. Hereafter it would be impossible to speak of German unification in isolation from its immediate eastern neighbors. Hence, it was probable that

- West Germany, destined to link politically and socially with its eastern wing, would ultimately ensure economic parity between its two regions and then tighten its influence over Poland and Czechoslovakia.
- Czechoslovakia, landlocked between powers east and west, would likely solidify ties with Germany, linked by a new economic *Anschluss* with Austria and the western Balkans, and become a major producer of high-quality goods and services for Western Europe and the United States.
- Poland too would probably tighten ties with German, other Continental, and Anglo-U.S. interests that remained determined to produce with highly skilled cheap labor to market in both Western and Eastern Europe.

The Outer Reach

The inner reach of a unified Germany linking Poland and Czechoslovakia to its investments and commerce and providing a transit point to Western Continental markets left the other liberated Eastern states relatively more isolated geographically, estranged from old and failing patterns of investment and trade, and trying to build an autarchic base linked to more prosperous nations—leaving desperate Romania to look to France and others in the West; partitioned Yugoslavia to seek out its own regions and southern and central Europe; Hungary to explore ties with the republics of the old Soviet Union and those Western nations willing to take its best grades of shoes, buses, and other public-transport vehicles; and Bulgaria with assorted Western joint venturers and nations.

These states were clearly at a comparative disadvantage after liberation in the early nineties. But the future held great possibilities for their reindustrialization, self-sufficiency, internal trade, and marketing beyond their borders.

There were dangers that might impinge on their new freedom and self-determination too, for Western investors and traders operated by competitive standards of the market and profit ratios that these nations, save Romania, would quickly have to learn to secure their interests and protect themselves.

At the outer reach in the nineties, it was possible that

- Hungary might become the economic appendage of the Western alliance and its austerity-minded International Monetary Fund, a client nation with heavy foreign debt and investments, cheap expendable labor, high unemployment, displaced populations, meager domestic resources, and high culture.

- Romania too might become an outpost of Western domination, controlled by an increasingly democratic forum at home, appealing for loans, investments, and commerce to exploiting interests abroad.
- Yugoslavia, fractured into many feuding cultures, nations, and regions, each momentarily thinking itself self-sufficient, might discover tomorrow that all are compelled to create a new federation to survive economically and negotiate for commerce with other nations.
- Bulgaria would probably become part socialist, part capitalist, remaining out of direct foreign controls yet succumbing to the pressure of foreign commercial interests.

Conjecture these thoughts may be, but the overall material and political tendencies now in motion in the early nineties are likely to fulfill themselves in a new capitalization of the West, balkanization and indebtedness of the East, and empowerment of Western states extracting resources and wealth at the expense of those in Eurasia.

The quest for freedom will undoubtedly remain irrepressible in the republics of the former Soviet Union and Eastern Europe in the coming decade, but real freedom will be won only when the people of each nation and region establish democratic controls over the material conditions that bind their lives.

Notes

1. TSAR AND SOVIET

1. By comparison, so-called record-breaking rates of industrial growth in the thirties were based on unfulfilled five-year plans and "mendacious statistics" bringing local production figures up to centrist bureaucratic expectations. So too, the so-called successes of the command economy of the fifties were based on centrist Gosplan dictation of local quotas that were reaffirmed by production units regardless of real output levels, justifying and reaffirming (what Marshall Goldman, the associate director of the Harvard University Russian Research Center, inappropriately calls) "Western standards" of economic life. Thus the gyrations and periodic decline of GNP began long before the end of Gorbachev's illusive *Perestroika* in 1990. See Marshall I. Goldman, *What Went Wrong with Perestroika?* (New York: W. W. Norton, 1992).

2. See Goldman, *What Went Wrong*. The absurd and shocking extent of the apparatchiks' ignorance, incompetence, pretentions and inflexible controls was the foundation for the atavistic malaise that made *Perestroika* under Gorbachev impossible, forcing him momentarily to swing backwards to pick up their support, then unsuccessfully try to go forward to bring *Perestroika* to fruition. Gorbachev's fatal error was that he miscalculated how the apparat, the army, KGB et al. would react to his renewed effort to undermine the traditional bureaucracies of government, security, and military force. See Chapter 2.

3. Anatoly Sobchak, *For a New Russia: The Mayor of St. Petersburg's Own Story of the Struggle for Justice and Democracy* (New York: Free Press, 1991).

4. Associated Press (Moscow), 14 January 1992.

5. "News Conference: Deputy Chief Prosecutor Yevgeny Lisov," Interfax (Moscow), 21 January 1992.

6. See Mikhail Gorbachev, *The August Coup: The Truth and the Lessons* (New York: Harper Collins, 1991); Sobchak, *For a New Russia*; John Morrison, *Boris Yeltsin: From Bolshevik to Democrat* (New York: Dutton, 1991).

7. Morrison, *Boris Yeltsin*.

8. Ukraine was the second largest republic and the Soviet breadbasket, providing over 22 percent of all output and 18 percent of all consumer goods. See *Europe World Yearbook*, Vol. 2, 1990; *U.S.S.R.: Facts and Figures Annual*, 1990; Interfax (Moscow), 30 November 1991.

9. Morrison, *Boris Yeltsin*.

10. *Ivzestia* (Moscow), 5, 6 December 1991.

11. See David K. Shipler, "Democracy Is a System, Not a Man," *The New York Times*, 9 January 1992.

12. Tass (Moscow), 6 December 1991.

13. Vladimir Bukovsky, "Tumbling Back to the Future," *The New York Times Magazine*, 12 January 1992, 42.

14. "Another Outbreak of Populism against a Backdrop of Empty Shelves," *Izvestia*, 14 January 1992.

15. Bukovsky, "Tumbling Back to the Future," 42.

16. The "Democratic Reform Movement" was created by St. Petersburg mayor Anatoly Sobchak, Moscow mayor Gavril K. Popov, and former KGB general and Politburo member Eduard A. Shevardnadze. The "People's Party of Free Russia" was founded by the former Central Committee member and later vice president of Russia Aleksandr V. Rutskoi. The "Party of the Socialist Choice" was created by the former Central Committee member and critical historian Roy A. Medvedev (Bukovsky, "Tumbling Back to the Future," 44).

17. Ibid.

18. Louis Uchitelle, "Moonlighting in Moscow," *The New York Times*, 28 January 1992.

19. Interfax (Moscow), 12 January 1992.

20. Bukovsky, "Tumbling Back to the Future," 39.

21. Ibid.

22. Interfax (Moscow), 13, 14 January 1992.

23. See Interfax (Moscow), 13 January 1992; *Pravda Buryaty* (Moscow), 3 January 1992.

24. Interfax (Moscow), 14 January 1992.

25. Louis Uchitelle, "Getting the Most from Each Ruble," *The New York Times*, 14 January 1992.

26. Interfax (Moscow), 14 January 1992.

27. Quoted in Craig R. Whitney, "Yeltsin, in Britain, Warns of Peril of Russian Unrest," *The New York Times*, 31 January 1992.

28. Institute for Strategic Studies, *Current Estimates*, London: ISS, 1991.

29. "Future of the Ukrainian Armed Forces," Kiev, Ukraine: Parliament Building, 9 January 1992, reported by Interfax.

30. Ibid.

31. Tass (Moscow), 9 January 1992.

32. "Interview: Admiral Chernavin," *Sovetskaya Rossya*, 9 January 1992.

33. Associated Press (Sevastopol), 8 January 1992.

34. *Nezavisimaya Gazeta*, 11 January 1992.

35. *Sovetskaya Rossya*, 11 January 1992.

36. See James F. Clarity, "Ukraine and Russia Discuss Disputes, *The New York Times*, 14 January 1992, interview with President Leonid M. Kravchuk.

37. Interfax (Moscow and Movorossisk), 27, 28 January 1992.

38. Reuters (Moscow), 11 January 1992; Interfax (Belarus), 11 January 1992.

39. Interfax (Moscow), 10 January 1992.

40. Bukovsky, "Tumbling Back to the Future," 42.

41. Interfax (Moscow), 9, 10, 11 January 1992.

42. Interfax (Moscow), 10, 11, 12 January 1992.

43. See Clarity, "Ukraine and Russia Discuss Disputes."

44. Louis Uchitelle, "Ad Hoc Ukraine Money Drives Out Ruble," *The New York Times*, 13 February 1992.

45. Foreign aid was conditioned on austerity measures enforced by the IMF.

Thereby external IMF pressure would require that subsidies and social services be cut to reduce the budget deficit, that energy prices be raised to world levels, that trade barriers between republics be lowered — measures that would further cut living standards. Using such criteria, in 1992 the IMF was to provide Russia with up to $4 billion and other republics up to $2.3 billion. Over three years, 1992–95, the IMF total could reach as much as $18 billion. As its share, the U.S. Congress was to vote on an additional $12 billion contribution to the IMF as well as $600 million in technical and humanitarian assistance. By early 1992, Germany had provided some $35 billion, half of all Western aid, to the former Soviet Union, much of it earmarked to help Soviet troops exit former East Germany. See Steven Greenhouse, "IMF Endorses Russian Plan for Economy, Clearing Way for Aid and for Membership," *The New York Times*, 1 April 1992.

46. On 31 March 1992, Russia, containing 150 million people spread over at least thirty-nine nationalities and scores of ethnic groups, signed a federal treaty with eighteen of its twenty main subdivisions to form the basis of a new post–Soviet state. The treaty spelled out the relationship between Moscow and Russia's local authorities, granting them more political and economic autonomy, especially over their natural resources, while binding them to a single federal state. Moscow was to handle federal matters of defense, money supply, the federal budget, foreign policy, and foreign trade. Standing aside, the predominantly Muslim republics of Chechen-Ingush and Tatar sought control over their oil and other resources. But in each republic there was no uniformity of goals, and eventually they might join the new federation. Though Tatar's referendum for sovereignty and equal status with Russia was approved by 61.4 percent of voters at the end of March 1992, the chairman of its Parliament sought to negotiate a treaty to bind Tatar to Russia on a new basis. Chechen-Ingush also declared its independence in November 1991, but that might not last long, as already on 31 March 1992 the opposition mobilized and seized the television broadcast center in the capital of Grozny, President Dzhokhar Dudayev declaring a state of emergency. See Steven Erlanger, "Most Pieces of Russia Agree to Coalesce, for Now," *The New York Times*, 1 April 1992.

PART II : THE GREAT LEAP FORWARD

1. George Laqueur, *Stalin: Revelations of Glasnost* (New York: Macmillan, 1990), 22–23.
2. Ibid., 22–24.
3. Richard Krooth, *Arms and Empire: Imperial Patterns before World War II* (Santa Barbara: Harvest Publishers, 1981), 45–47.
4. Laqueur, *Stalin*; Andrei Sakharov, *Memoirs* (New York: Random House, 1990).
5. Boris Yeltsin, *Against the Grain* (New York: Simon and Schuster, 1990).
6. Martin Malia, "The Soviet Union Has Ceased to Exist," *The New York Times*, 31 August 1990.
7. "500 Days That Can Shake the World," *The New York Times*, 5 September 1990.
8. Sakharov, *Memoirs*.

336 Notes

9. Yeltsin, *Against the Grain; Without Force or Lies: Voices from the Revolution of Central Europe in 1989–90,* ed. William M. Briton (San Francisco: Mercury House, 1990).

2. THE "SUCCESS" AND FAILURE OF THE SOVIET ECONOMY

1. Basil Dmytryshyn, *U.S.S.R: A Concise History* (New York: Charles Scribner's Sons, 1965); Merle Fainsod, *How Russia Is Ruled,* rev. ed. (Cambridge: Harvard University Press, 1964).
2. William Blackwell, *Beginnings of Russian Industrialization, 1800–1868* (Princeton: Princeton University Press, 1968); Michael T. Florinsky, *Russia: A History and an Interpretation,* 2 vols. (New York: Macmillan, 1954).
3. Edward Hallett Carr, *The Bolshevik Revolution, 1917–1923* (New York: Macmillan, 1952); Vasil Ryabov, *The Great Victory* (Moscow: Novosti Press Agency, 1985).
4. Ryabov, *The Great Victory;* Alexander Worth, *Russia at War, 1941–1945* (New York: Dutton, 1964); Ian Grey, *The First Fifty Years: Soviet Russia 1917–1967* (New York: Coward-McCann, 1967); Nikolai Voronkov, *900 Days—The Siege of Leningrad* (Moscow: Novasti Press, 1982).
5. Harnon Tupper, *The Moscow Kremlin* (Berkeley: University of California Press, 1954); N. N. Baransky, *Economic Geography of the U.S.S.R.* (Moscow: Foreign Languages Publishing House, 1956).
6. Aleksandr Solzhenitsyn, *Komsomolskaya Pravda* (Moscow), 18 September 1990.
7. Sakharov, *Memoirs,* 142–48.
8. James S. Gregory, *Russian Land—Soviet People: A Geographical Approach to the U.S.S.R.* (Racine: Western, 1968); Fainsod, *How Russia Is Ruled.*
9. Celestine Bohlen, "Gorbachev Rebukes Solzhenitsyn for Opinions 'Entirely in the Past,'" *The New York Times,* 26 September 1990.
10. Celestine Bohlen, "Gorbachev Seeks Sweeping Powers to Meet a 'Crisis,'" *The New York Times,* 22 September 1990.
11. *New Times* (Moscow), 10–29 September 1990; Celestine Bohlen, "Soviets Are Deep in Military Rumors," *The New York Times,* 27 September 1990.
12. A. M. Rosenthal, "The Gorbachev Era Ends," *The New York Times,* 21 September 1990.
13. *New Times* (Moscow), 1–30 September 1989.
14. Peter Passell, "Gorbachev's Unease," *The New York Times,* 21 September 1990; *Washington Post,* 22 September 1990.
15. *New Times* (Moscow), 20–23 September 1989; *Los Angeles Times,* 22 September 1990; Francis X. Clines, "For Kremlin Economist, Always a Plan," *The New York Times,* 21 September 1990.
16. *New Times* (Moscow), 20–23 September 1990; *Los Angeles Times,* 22 September 1990.
17. "Excerpts from Gorbachev's Talk on Plans for Economic Revisions," *The New York Times,* 18 September 1990.
18. Allen Kassof, ed., *Prospects for Soviet Society* (New York: Praeger, 1968); *New Times* (Moscow), 20–30 September 1989; *Los Angeles Times,* 21–30 September 1990.

19. "Boris Yeltsin, Reconsidered," *The New York Times*, editorial, 18 September 1990.

20. Fainsod, *How Russia Is Ruled*; *New Times* (Moscow), 22–30 September 1989; *Los Angeles Times*, 24–30 September 1990.

21. Bill Keller, "Boris Yeltsin," *New York Times Magazine*, 23 September 1990, 32.

22. Jerome Blum, *Lord and Peasant in Russia from the Ninth to the Nineteenth Century* (Princeton: Princeton University Press, 1961); *Revolutionary Russia: A Symposium*, ed. Richard Pipes (Cambridge: Harvard University Press, 1968).

23. "Interview, Prime Minister Ryzhkov," Novotni Press Agency (Moscow), 23 September 1990.

24. Ibid.

25. Ibid., 24 September 1990; Celestine Bohlen, "Premier of Soviet Union Warns the Nation of Poor Harvest," *The New York Times*, 24 September 1990.

26. I. Binder and A. Ul'masov, "A Critique of Bourgeois Conceptions of Economic Development in Soviet Central Asia," *Problems of Economics*, Vol. XIV, No. 5 (1971), 74–93; *New Times* (Moscow), 10–30 September 1990.

27. *New Times* (Moscow), 10–30 September, 1–7 October 1990.

28. *New Times* (Moscow), 1–31 August, 10–30 September 1990.

29. "Interview, Boris Yeltsin," Novotni Press Agency (Moscow), 24 September 1990.

30. *New Times* (Moscow), 24 September, 1990; Celestine Bohlen, "Soviet Parliament Grants Gorbachev Emergency Powers," *The New York Times*, 25 September 1990.

31. Fainsod; Grey, *The First Fifty Years*.

32. Solzhenitsyn, *Komsomolskaya Pravda* (Moscow), 18 September 1990.

33. Bill Keller, "Gorbachev Says 6 Months Are Needed to Prepare for New Economy," *The New York Times*, 1 September 1990.

34. Solzhenitsyn, *Komsomolskaya Pravda* (Moscow), 18 September 1990.

35. *New Times* (Moscow), 1–31 August, 1–30 September 1990.

36. Francis X. Clines, "In Moscow, a City of Bare Shelves, Consumer Rage Turns on Cabinet," *The New York Times*, 17 September 1990.

37. *New Times* (Moscow), 21–30 September 1990.

38. *New Times* (Moscow), 26–30 September 1990.

39. Francis X. Clines, "Economic Plan: A Kremlin Intrigue," *The New York Times*, 11 September 1990.

40. "The Soviet Economic Morass," *The New York Times*, 16 September 1990.

41. "Public Interviews," Novotni Press Agency (Moscow), 24–30 September 1990.

42. Ibid.

43. Ibid.

44. Ibid.

45. Francis X. Clines, "From Moscow, a Plan to Junk Communism in 500 Days," *The New York Times*, 9 September 1990.

46. Parliamentary Documents, *Yeltsin-Shatalin Proposal* (Moscow: Prepublication Fax Edition, July–August 1990).

47. *New Times* (Moscow), 12 September 1990.

48. Francis X. Clines, "Gorbachev Endorses a Proposal for Free Enterprise in 500 Days," *The New York Times*, 12 September 1990.

49. *New Times* (Moscow), 1–7 October 1990.

50. Bill Keller, "Gorbachev's Hesitation," *The New York Times*, 12 September 1990.

51. See Dusko Doder and Louise Branson, *Gorbachev: Heretic in the Kremlin* (New York: Praeger, 1990); Gail Sheehy, *Man Who Changed the World* (New York: Praeger, 1990).

52. Though subsequent investigations only turned up 7 billion rubles ($64 million at February 1992 exchange rates) in Soviet bank accounts and other assets, including property, the party allegedly had a treasure of as much as $50 billion, 60 tons of gold, 150 tons of silver, and 8 tons of platinum—all assets the Russian Republic later moved to nationalize. Russian Parliament, hearings, testimony of Deputy Prosecutor Yevgeny K. Lisov, 10 February 1992. See Celestine Bohlen, "Gorbachev Authorized Investments by Party," *The New York Times*, 11 February 1992.

53. Lydia S. Rosner, "Bureaucratic Hangover," *The New York Times*, 19 January 1992.

54. See Russian Deputy Prime Minister, *Plan for Economic Reform*, Boris Yeltsin Government, Cabinet Document, January 1992, fax ed. " Prof. Jeffrey Sachs: News Conference," Interfax, 15 January 1992.

55. Interfax, 16 January 1992.

56. Interfax, 23 January 1992.

57. "Prof. Jeffrey Sachs: News Conference," Interfax, 15 January 1992.

58. "Interview: Chairman Ruslan Khasbulatov," *Moskovsky Komsomolets*, 16 January 1992, fax ed.

59. "No Time to Be Stingy with Russians," *The New York Times*, 22 January 1992, editorial.

60. Francis X. Clines, "Kazakhs Travel Smoother Road to Capitalism," *New York Times*, 27 January 1992.

61. Interfax (Moscow), 16 January 1992.

62. Interfax (Moscow), 23, 24 January 1992.

63. Louis Uchitelle, "In Russia, Long Lines for Plentiful Bread," *The New York Times*, 22 January 1992.

64. Celestine Bohlen, "Moscow Puzzle: Milk Is Costlier but Still Scarce," *The New York Times*, 7 February 1992.

65. Interfax (Moscow), 23 January 1992; Tass (Moscow), 23 January 1992.

66. "Yeltsin's St. Petersburg Tour," Interfax (St. Petersburg), 15 January 1992.

67. Interfax (Moscow), 23 January 1992.

68. "Interview: Nusultan A. Nazarbayev," Interfax (Moscow), 16 January 1992.

69. "Ruble-Rich Ukrainians Looking for Bargains," *The New York Times*, 29 January 1992.

70. William E. Schmidt, "Finns Watch Russian Border for Smugglers and Refugees," *The New York Times*, 4 February 1992.

71. Louis Uchitelle, "The Art of a Russian Deal: Ad-Libbing Contract Law," *New York Times*, 17 January 1992.

72. Roger Cohen, "Easing Trade Barriers Is Urged," *The New York Times*, 3 February 1992.

73. Interfax (Moscow), 16 January 1992.

74. Associated Press (Moscow), 5 February 1992.

75. Celestine Bohlen, "Russia Outlines a Program to Sell State-Owned Shops," *The New York Times*, 8 February 1992.

76. Celestine Bohlen, "Yeltsin Deputy Calls Reforms 'Economic Genocide,'" *The New York Times*, 9 February 1992.

77. Cohen, "Easing Trade Barriers," *The New York Times*, 3 February 1992.

78. Michael Wines, "Yeltsin Is Annoyed, and U.S. Is Puzzled," *The New York Times*, 3 February 1992.

79. Celestine Bohlen, "Russia Trying to Keep Track of Aid from Abroad," *The New York Times*, 23 January 1992.

80. Roger Cohen, "East Meets West, Dollars Apart," and Francis X. Clines, "U. S. Embassy Seeks to End Its Social Isolation in Moscow," *The New York Times*, 5 February 1992.

81. Cohen, "East Meets West."

82. European Economic Association, *Aid to the Commonwealth of Independent Nations*, January 1992. Also cited in *The New York Times*, 23 January 1992.

83. Bohlen, "Russia Trying to Keep Track."

84. Cohen, "East Meets West."

85. Thomas L. Friedman, "Bush to Press Congress to Approve $645 Million for Ex-Soviet Lands," *The New York Times*, 23 January 1992.

86. Elaine Sciolino, "CIA Casting About for New Missions," *The New York Times*, 4 February 1992.

87. Elaine Sciolino, "CIA Chief Says Threat by Ex-Soviets Is Small," *The New York Times*, 23 January 1992.

88. "Interview with President Boris N. Yeltsin," BBC News (Moscow), 25 January 1992.

89. Russian Mission, United Nations, Speech by Russian President Boris N. Yeltsin to the Security Council, 31 January 1992.

90. Michael Wines, "Bush and Yeltsin Declare Formal End to Cold War," *The New York Times*, 2 February 1992.

91. Russian Mission, Speech by Yeltsin.

92. Eric Schmidt, "U.S. Is Considering Sharp Cuts in Multi-Warhead Nuclear Missiles," *The New York Times*, 23 January 1992.

93. Eric Schmidt, "Military Proposes to End P."

94. "The Rise and Fall of MIRV," *The New York Times*, editorial 27 January 1992.

95. See *The Philadelphia Inquirer*, 26 January 1992; *Washington Post*, 26 January 1992.

96. Thomas L. Friedman, "Ex-Soviet Lands to Get Swift Aid," *The New York Times*, 24 January 1992.

97. Eric Schmidt, "Pentagon Warns Panel against More Budget Cuts," *The New York Times*, 25 January 1992.

98. Steven Greenhouse, "Economists Cite Benefits of Arms Cuts," *The New York Times*, 3 February 1992.

99. R. W. Apple, Jr., "White House Race Is Recast: No Kremlin to Run Against," *The New York Times*, 6 February 1992.

100. Russian Mission, Speech by Yeltsin.

101. Alison Mitchell, "Yeltsin, on Summit's Stage, Stresses His Russian Identity," *The New York Times*, 1 February 1992.

102. "Wheat Prices in Wild Ride as Ex-Soviets Buy Again," *The New York Times*, 25 January 1992.

103. "Moscow Needs More Than a Gesture," *The New York Times*, editorial, 24 January 1992.

104. Louis Uchitelle, "Ad Hoc Ukraine Money Drives Out Ruble," *The New York Times*, 13 February 1992.

105. Friedman, "Ex-Soviet Lands."

106. Steven R. Weisman, "Money, Greed and Power: Sect Divided," *The New York Times*, 10 February 1992.

107. Stephen Engelberg, "Eager If Uneasy, East Europe Accepts German Investments," *The New York Times*, 23 January 1992.

108. Ferdinand Protzman, "Germany Curbs Trade Aid for Former Soviet States," *The New York Times*, 23 January 1992.

109. Ferdinand Protzman, "Several Dark Spots Emerge to Mar Germany's Economy," *The New York Times*, 8 February 1992.

110. Cohen, "Easing Trade Barriers."

111. See *Stern* (Bonn), 23 January 1992, editorial.

112. Cohen, "Easing Trade Barriers."

113. Cohen, "East Meets West."

PART III : HISTORY WITHOUT END

1. Francis Fukuyama, "The End of History," *The National Interest*, 1989; Francis Fukuyama, *The End of History and the Last Man* (New York: Free Press, 1992).

2. See Francis Fukuyama, "Rest Easy. It's Not 1914 Anymore," *The New York Times*, 9 February 1992; Kenneth M. Jensen, ed., *A Look at "The End of History?"* (Washington, D.C.: United States Institute of Peace, 1990); Joseph Campbell, *Myths to Live By* (New York: Bantam Books, 1988).

3. CENTRIST STATE, SOCIAL THEORY, AND MARKET ECONOMY

1. See Frederick Engels, "The Wages System," in *The British Labour Movement* (New York: International Publishers, 1940), 14; Samuel Gompers, *Seventy Years of Life and Labor* (New York: Dutton, 1957), 251.

2. Engels, "Wages System," 13–14; see E. P. Thompson, *The Making of the English Working Class* (New York: Vintage, 1967).

3. The sources of this capital were land producing revenue from output and rents; merchant accumulations through buying low and selling high; financial accumulation from lending during the Middle Ages; and bullion and other wealth extorted or otherwise extracted from peoples on other continents. See Richard Krooth, ed., *The Great Social Struggle*, vol. 2 (Santa Barbara: Harvest Publishers, 1979).

4. Adam Smith, *An Inquiry Into the Nature and Causes of the Wealth of Nations* (New York: Modern Library, 1937), 69, 73–74, 77–79.

5. See Karl Marx, *Capital: A Critical Analysis of Capitalist Production*, 3 vols. (Moscow: Foreign Languages Publishing House, 1961); Smith, *An Inquiry*, 69, 73–74, 78–79.

6. David Ricardo, *Principles of Political Economy and Taxation* (London: Everyman's Library, 1911), 52, 64, 192, 225; P. Sraffa, ed., *The Works and Cor-*

respondence of David Ricardo (Cambridge, England: Cambridge University Press, 1951), vol. 2, 421ff; vol. 4, 312ff, 379ff.

7. Thomas Robert Malthus, *Principles of Political Economy Considered with a View to Their Practical Application* (London: British Museum Manuscript Edition, 1820), 8, 38–39, 463.

8. Karl Marx, "Estranged Labour," in *Economic and Philosophical Manuscripts of 1844* (Moscow: Foreign Languages Publishing House, 1961), 81; Marx, *Capital: A Critical Analysis*, vol. 1, 616.

9. Frederick Engels, "Outlines of a Critique of Political Economy," in *Economic and Philosophical Manuscripts of 1844*, appendix, 198–203.

10. Nassau W. Senior, *An Outline of the Science of Political Economy* (London: British Museum Manuscript Edition, 1836), 153, 168ff.

11. John Stuart Mill, *Principles of Political Economy* (New York: Longmans, Green, 1909), 199–201ff.

12. See M. Maximova, *Economic Aspects of Capitalist Integration* (Moscow: Progress Publishers, 1973).

13. See Zbigniew Brzezinski, *Ideology and Power in Soviet Politics* (New York: Praeger, 1962).

14. See Andrei Almarik, *Will the Soviet Union Survive until 1984?* (New York: Harper, 1969).

15. See Zhores Medvedev and Roy Medvedev, *A Question of Madness* (New York: Knopf, 1971); Boris I. Nikolaevsky, *Power and the Soviet Elite: "The Letter of An Old Bolshevik" and Other Essays* (London: Pall Mall Press, 1966).

16. Artyom Borovik, *The Hidden War: A Russian Journalist's Account of the Soviet War in Afghanistan* (New York: Atlantic Monthly Press, 1991).

17. Roy Medvedev and Giulietto Chiesa, *Time of Change: An Insider's View of Russia's Transformation*, trans. Michael Moore (New York: Pantheon Books, 1989).

18. Peter Passell, "Economic Scene: Bread, Sausages, Hyperinflation," *The New York Times*, 26 December 1990.

19. Medvedev and Chiesa, *Time of Change*, 297.

20. Ibid., 297–98; emphasis added.

21. *Izvestia* (Moscow), 16 October 1990.

22. Medvedev and Chiesa, *Time of Change*, 298.

23. Ibid., 298–99.

24. Ibid., 299.

25. President Mikhail S. Gorbachev, "Proposed Economic Program," submitted on 16 October 1990 to the Soviet legislature. *Izvestia* (Moscow), 17 October 1990.

26. George Soros, "Gorbachev's Reform Plan Is a Bust," *The New York Times*, 19 October 1990; emphasis added.

27. See G. Bruce Knecht, "From Soviet Minister to Corporate Chief," *New York Times Magazine*, 26 January 1992, 24–26, 28.

28. "Poland's Industry Grinds to a Halt When Russia Cuts Off Gas Supply," *The New York Times*, 30 January 1992.

29. Interfax (Moscow), 17 January 1992.

30. Celestine Bohlen, "Russians Take a Flier on Oil in Capitalism for the Masses, *The New York Times*, 19 January 1992.

31. American Economic Association, annual meeting, 10–12 January 1991, "Panel: Key Issues of Soviet Economic Reform," presentation by Padma Desai.

32. *Komsomolskaya Pravda* (Moscow), 20 January 1992.

33. American Press International (Moscow), 19 January 1992. Interfax (Tashkent), 16–19 January 1992.

34. Interfax (Moscow), 9 February 1992.

35. Francis X. Clines, "Tug of War, with Rallies, Is Played Out in Moscow amid Mood of Discontent," *The New York Times*, 10 February 1992.

36. Reuters (Atlanta), 13 February 1992, reporting the Centers for Disease Control findings of the U.S. team visiting Russia from 16 January to 6 February 1992.

37. Francis X. Clines, "Yeltsin Vows to Ease Impact of His Economic Program," *The New York Times*, 14 February 1992.

38. Interfax (Tashkent), 18 January 1992.

39. Interfax (Tashkent), 19 January 1992.

40. Tass (Moscow), 18 January 1992.

41. Russian Information Agency (Moscow), 18, 19 January 1992.

42. Reuters (Tbilisi), 17 January 1992.

43. Tass (Moscow), 18 January 1992.

44. Reuters (Washington, D.C.), 24 March 1992.

4. IN THE LAND OF THE BLIND

1. See V. I. Lenin, "Letter to the Congress," *Kommunist* (1956); Joseph Stalin, supervisor, *A Concise History of the All-Union Communist Party (Bolsheviks)* (Moscow: Lenin Institute, 1933).

2. See Medvedev and Chiesa, *Time of Change*.

3. *New York Times Magazine*, 28 October 1990, 32.

4. Vitaly A. Korotich, *Ogonyok* (Moscow), 16 October 1990.

5. Yelena Bonner and Andrei Sakharov, *Human Rights*, delivered at the Berkeley Human Rights Symposium, University of California, Berkeley, summer 1989.

6. Yelena Bonner, *SDS and Human Rights*, delivered at the University of California Berkeley meeting of Scientists for Sakharov, Orlov, and Shraransky, Berkeley, 1986.

7. See Richard Krooth, ed., *The Great Social Struggle*, vol. 2 (Santa Barbara: Harvest Publishers, 1981).

8. Bolis Kagarlitsky, *The Dialectics of Change*, delivered at the Colloquium Series 1990, Sociology Department, University of California, Berkeley, 22 March 1990.

9. Ibid.

10. Alexander Dallin, Chair, "Reform and Nationality Problems," *The Nationalities Question: Session I, the Future of the Soviet Union*, a panel delivered at the XIV Annual Stanford-Berkeley Conference, Stanford University, 16 March 1990.

11. Wayne Vucinich, Chair, "Varieties of National Movements," *The Nationalities Question: Session IV, The Future of the Soviet Union*, Stanford-Berkeley Conference.

12. Gregory Freidin, Chair, "The Future of the Multi-National System," *The Nationalities Question: Session V, The Future of the Soviet Union*, Stanford-Berkeley Conference.

13. See Geoffrey Hosking, *The Awakening of the Soviet Union* (Cambridge: Harvard University Press, 1990).

14. Mikhail Shatrov, *The Dictatorship of Conscience* (Moscow: Foreign Languages Publishing House, 1985).

15. *New York Times Magazine,* 28 October 1990, 71.

16. Peter Gumbel, "Gorbachev's Change of Heart on Reforms May Have Been to Save His Political Skin," *Wall Street Journal,* 26 October 1990.

17. Peter Gumbel, "Resisting Reform, Soviet Town Shows How Hard It Will Be to Install Free Market," *Wall Street Journal,* 26 December 1990.

18. "X" [aka George F. Kennan], *Foreign Affairs* (July 1947).

19. Alan Riding, "Yeltsin, Showing Annoyance at Delays, Urgently Appeals for Aid," *The New York Times,* 6 February 1992.

20. Steven R. Weisman, "Dispute over Seized Islands Is Delaying Japanese Aid to Russia," *The New York Times,* 7 February 1992.

21. David Binder, "U.S. Selects 5 to Be Envoys in New Republics," *The New York Times,* 8 February 1992.

22. Reuters (Riga, Latvia), 6 February 1992.

23. David Binder, "4 New Republics Provide Details on Dismantling Ex-Soviet Arsenal," *The New York Times,* 7 February 1992; Thomas L. Friedman, "U.S. to Offer Plan to Keep Scientists at Work in Russia: Fears on Weapons," *The New York Times,* 8 February 1992.

24. John Noble Wilford, "U.S. Is Seeking Soviet Expertise for 'Star Wars,'" *The New York Times,* 8 February 1992.

25. Thomas L. Friedman, "Tajikistan to Curb Sales of Atom Arms Equipment," *The New York Times,* 14 February 1992.

26. Thomas L. Friedman, "U.S. to Counter Iran in Central Asia," *The New York Times,* 6 February 1992.

27. "Winking at Aggression in Baku," *The New York Times,* editorial, 14 February 1992.

28. "No Demons in Central Asia," *The New York Times,* editorial, 7 February 1992.

PART IV : THE EASTERN EUROPE THAT WAS

1. Frank Viviano, "Identity Crisis in the Eastern Bloc," *San Francisco Chronicle,* 23 October 1990. See Clyde Haberman, "Gorbachev Lauds Religion on Eve of Meeting Pope," *The New York Times,* 1 December 1989.

2. Andrew H. Malcolm, "The Man Behind the Match for the Man of Steel," *The New York Times,* 18 February 1992.

3. James Brooke, "Latin Lure to 'New World' for Eastern Europeans," *The New York Times,* February 17, 1992.

4. Francis X. Clines, "It's Not Yet Capitalism, but Ruble Is Healthier," *The New York Times,* 18 February 1992.

5. Ibid.

5. CAPTIVITY AND BREAKAWAY IN EASTERN EUROPE

1. For a remarkable artistic depiction of wartime fascism in Eastern Europe, see Art Spiegelman, *Maus: A Survivor's Tale: And Here My Troubles Began* (New York: Pantheon Books, 1986, 1991).

344 Notes

2. See Elie Wiesel, *Night*, trans. Stella Rodway (New York: Bantam Books, 1982); Robert Conquest, *The Great Terror* (Oxford University Press, 1990); Georg Von Rauch, *A History of Soviet Russia*, 5th ed., trans. Peter and Annette Jacobson (New York: Praeger, 1967); Felix Greene, *The Enemy* (New York: Vintage Books, 1970); Spiegelman, *Maus*.

3. H. Seaton-Watson, *The Eastern European Revolution* (London: Methuen, 1946); see Richard Pipes, *Some Operational Principles of Soviet Foreign Policy* (Washington, D.C.: U.S. Government Printing Office, 1972).

4. Hanna Krall, *Shielding the Flame: An Intimate Conversation with Dr. Marek Edelman, the Last Remaining Surviving Leader of the Warsaw Ghetto Uprising*, trans. Joanna Stasinska and Lawrence Weschler (New York: Henry Holt, 1986).

5. See Lazar Pistrak, *The Grand Tactician: Khrushchev's Rise to Power* (New York: Praeger, 1961).

6. G. Ionescu, *The Breakup of the Soviet Empire in Eastern Europe* (London: Penguin, 1965); see Bertram D. Wolfe, *Khrushchev and Stalin's Ghost* (New York: Praeger, 1957).

7. Alexander Dubček with Jiri Hockman, *The Autobiography of Alexander Dubček* (New York and Tokyo: Kodashna International, 1992). Prepublication copy.

8. George Shaw Wheeler, *The Human Face of Socialism* (New York: Hill and Wang, 1970); Harry Schwartz, *Prague's 200 Days* (New York: Praeger, 1970).

9. See James R. Wright, *Industrialized Building in the USSR* (Washington, D.C.: U.S. Department of Commerce, National Bureau of Standards, 1971); Elizabeth K. Poretsky, *Our Own People* (Ann Arbor: University of Michigan Press, 1970).

10. M. Kaser, *COMECON* (Oxford: Oxford University Press, 1963).

11. Krooth, *Arms and Empire*, chapter 1.

12. Krooth, *Arms and Empire*, chapters 1, 2.

13. Don Cook, *Floodtide in Europe* (New York: G. P. Putnam's Sons, 1967).

14. See *Speech of Nikita Khrushchev Before a Closed Session of the XXth Congress of the Communist Party of the Soviet Union on February 25, 1956* (Washington, D.C.: Senate, Committee of Judiciary, Subcommittee to Investigate the Administration of Internal Security Act and Other Internal Security Laws, 1957); see also *The Soviet Approach to Negotiations* (Ibid., 1969).

15. D. P. Calleo, *Europe's Future* (London: Hodder and Stoughton, 1967); Andrei D. Sakharov, *The Letters of Andrei D. Sakharov* (Minneapolis: Lazear Agency, 1991); Andrei Sakharov, "Thoughts on Progress, Peaceful Coexistence and Intellectual Freedom," *New York Times*, 22 July 1968.

16. Krooth, *Arms and Empire*, chapter 1.

17. R. Mayne, *The Community of Europe* (London: Gollancz, 1958); R. Broad and R. Jarrett, *Community Europe* (London: Oswald, Wolff, 1967).

18. M. Camps, *What Kind of Europe?* (Oxford: Oxford University Press, 1965).

19. Ibid.

20. See Pierre Salinger, *With Kennedy* (New York: Doubleday, 1966).

21. Calleo, *Europe's Future*; Henry Kissinger, *The Troubled Partnership* (New York: McGraw-Hill, 1969).

22. J-J Servan-Schreiber, *Le Défi Américain* (Paris: Denoel, 1967).

23. N. Beloff, *The General Says No* (Harmondsworth: Penguin, 1963); Harold Wilson, *Industrial Helotry* (London: Penguin, 1970).

24. See Richard Krooth, *Bicentennial Appraisal* (Santa Barbara: Harvest Publishers, 1976).

25. Robert B. Reich, *The Next American Frontier* (New York: Times Books, 1983), 117–19.

26. See Robert B. Reich, "The Real Economy," *Atlantic Monthly*, February 1991, pp. 35ff; Richard Krooth and Hiroshi Fukurai, *Common Destiny: Japan and the United States in the Global Age* (Jefferson, N.C.: McFarland, 1990).

27. See James T. Reitz, *Soviet Defense-Associated Activities outside the Ministry of Defense* (McLean, Va.: Research Analysis Corp., 1969); Andrei D. Sakharov, *Letters*; Andrei Sakharov, "Thoughts on Progress, Peaceful Coexistence and Intellectual Freedom."

28. "Soviet Timidity? No Caution," *The New York Times*, editorial, 10 December 1989; see Jensen, ed., *A Look at "The End of History?"*

29. See Jensen, ed., *A Look.*

30. *New York Times*, 17 October 1990.

31. Hans Kohr [aka Leopold Kohr], "Disunion Now: A Plea for a Society Based upon Small Autonomous Units," *Commonweal*, 26 September 1941; Francis Fukuyama, "Rest Easy. It's Not 1914 Anymore," *The New York Times*, 9 February 1992. Even in Western Europe, there seemed no end to the need for interdependence; still the Spanish Basques, the Bavarians, the Sicilians, the peoples of Euskadi, French-Brittany, and Scotland, North Ireland, and others would momentarily deny this need in order to establish themselves as self-determined and politically autonomous from the *diktat* of a central governing force or other exogenous region. Yet one day all these independent and protesting regions would have to cooperate in the Common Market or other commercial region, possibly reuniting economically or politically.

32. Thomas L. Friedman, "Uzbek Chief, of Course, Says Yes to Democracy," *The New York Times*, 17 February 1992.

33. Henry Kamm, "Struggling Ukrainian Miners Are Put Off by Diet of Nationalism," *The New York Times*, 16 February 1992.

34. See Stephen Sestanovich, "The Revolution: A Case for Optimism," *The New York Times*, 23 December 1991.

35. See Yelena G. Bonner, "Why Is the West Afraid of Freedom?" *The New York Times*, 6 December 1991.

36. Reuters (Minsk, Belarus), 15 February 1992.

37. Reuters (Istanbul), 15 February 1992.

38. Edward A. Gargan, "A 'Chastened' Pakistan: Peace with U.S. Is Aim," *The New York Times*, 19 February 1992.

39. "Muslim Regional Group Welcomes Ex-Soviet Central Asians," *The New York Times*, 17 February 1992.

40. "New Leader, New Role for Turkey," *The New York Times*, editorial, 15 February 1992.

41. See Krooth, *Arms and Empire*, chapters 3, 4, 5; Hans Kohr [aka Leopold Kohr], "Disunion Now: A Plea for a Society Based Upon Small Autonomous Units," *Commonweal*, 26 September 1941; Fukuyama, "Rest Easy;" Vladimir Kvint, "Opportunity in a Shattered Land," *The New York Times*, 19 January 1992.

42. Serge Schmemann, "Fears Deep as Russia's Snow, but Poetry, Too," *The New York Times*, 17 February 1992; "In Dire Times, Every Little Kopeck Helps," *The New York Times*, 19 February 1992.

43. Steven Greenhouse, "7 Top Industrialized Nations Plan a Fund to Aid the Ruble," *The New York Times*, 15 February 1992.

44. Louis Uchitelle, "Russia's Central Bank Resists Cuts in Lending," *The New York Times*, 16 February 1992.

45. Anthony Lewis, "For Want of a Nail," *The New York Times*, 16 February 1992.

6. ENTERING A EUROPEAN HOME

1. *Internal Memo*, Politburo, CP, USSR, Moscow, November 1988.

2. George Saunders, ed., *Samizdat: Voices of the Soviet Opposition* (New York: Monad Press, 1974).

3. See Nikita Khrushchev, *Khrushchev Remembers*, ed. and trans., Strove Talbott (Boston: Little, Brown, 1970); *Speech of Nikita Khrushchev Before a Closed Session of the XXth Congress of the Communist Party of the Soviet Union on 25 February 1956*.

4. Saunders, ed., *Samizdat*; Natalia Ivanova, "Literature: Traditions and Changes," *Soviet Literature and Art Almanac* 89 (1990), 21.

5. Ivanova, 21.

6. "The Joke Factory and the Wall," *The New York Times*, 7 November 1989.

7. Steven Greenhouse, *The New York Times*, 28 November 1989.

8. See Adam Schesch, *An Outline History of Vietnam* (Madison, Wis.: National Coordinating Committee to End the War in Vietnam, 1965); "Third World Liberation Movements," Ph.D. diss., University of Wisconsin, 1992; Richard Krooth, *The Political Economy of the War in Vietnam* (Madison, Wis.: National Coordinating Committee to End the War in Vietnam, 1965).

9. Craig R. Whitney, "Is East Europe Too Amazing for the West?" *The New York Times*, 28 October 1989.

10. John Tagliabue, "Shevardnadze Calls for End of Military Treaties," *The New York Times*, 27 October 1989.

11. John Tagliabue, "Police in Prague Move to Break Up Big Protest March," *The New York Times*, 29 October 1989.

12. Owen Harris, "As Ideology Dies, Analogies Rise," *The New York Times*, 28 October 1989.

13. Kissinger, *The Troubled Partnership*.

14. William Safire, "Bring on CSCE," *The New York Times*, 15 October 1990.

15. Ivanova, 8-9.

16. Shelia Rule, "Gorbachev Gets Nobel Peace Prize for Foreign Policy Achievements," *The New York Times*, 16 October 1990.

7. PRAGUE SPRING REDUX

1. *The New York Times*, 2 January 1990. This chapter is based on Czechoslovakian Academy of Sciences, Economics Institute, reports and data (Prague: 1989-92); Czechoslovakian Finance Ministry (Prague: 1990-92); with the help of Czech and Slovak emigres living in the U.S. and Switzerland.

2. John Tagliabue, "Czech Communists Replace Party Chairman, *The New York Times*, 21 December 1989.

Notes   347

3. Craig R. Whitney, "Havel Is Elected Czech President," *The New York Times*, 20 December 1989.

4. *The New York Times*, 2 January 1990.

5. Ibid.

6. "Excerpts from Statements by Czech Leaders and Opposition," *The New York Times*, 29 November 1989.

7. Thomas L. Friedman, "East Bloc Trip Buoys Baker, yet Alerts Him to the Odds," *The New York Times*, 12 February 1990.

8. Henry Kamm, "Prague to Scrap Its Defenses along Austrian Border," *The New York Times*, 1 December 1989.

9. Serge Schmemann, "Czech Party Aide Sees Free Ballot within Next Year," *The New York Times*, 30 November 1989.

10. John Tagliabue, "Prague Would Cut Defenses along West German Border," *The New York Times*, 16 December 1989.

11. John Taligabue, "Party in Prague Is Suspending," *The New York Times*, 22 December 1989.

12. Henry Kamm, "Spirit of 1968 Is Still Alive, Still Distinct," *The New York Times*, 30 November 1989.

13. John Tagliabue, "Dubcek Expected to Support Havel in Czechoslovakia," *The New York Times*, 17 December 1989.

14. John Tagliabue, "Prague Marchers Rally for Havel," *The New York Times*, 18 December 1989.

15. William H. Luers, "Czech History: A Waiting Game," *The New York Times*, 16 December 1989.

16. Steven Greenhouse, "Czechs Fault Policies of Hard-line Communists as a Cause of Industrial Lag," *The New York Times*, 1 December 1989.

17. AP (Prague), 25 November 1990.

18. Steven Greenhouse, "Year of Economic Tumult Looms for Eastern Europe," *The New York Times*, 31 December 1990.

19. Steven Greenhouse, "Czechs Begin Shift to a Free Market," *The New York Times*, 1 January 1991.

20. *Rude Pravo* (Prague), 19 February 1992.

21. "Czechoslovakia to Return Property Confiscated in the Communist Era," *The New York Times*, 27 February 1991.

22. "Czechs by the Millions Are Investing $35 in a State Bargain," *The New York Times*, 21 January 1992.

23. John Tagliabue, "Hot to Invest? Trust a Man with a Harvard Past?" *The New York Times*, 6 March 1992.

24. Stephen Engelberg, "Eastern Europe Foils All but the Hardiest of Western Investors," *The New York Times*, 5 March 1992.

25. Steven Greenhouse, "Deal Is Near for a Czech Auto Maker," *The New York Times*, 5 October 1990; Reuters (Prague), 16 March 1992.

26. Engelberg, "Eastern Europe."

27. "With Democracy, Prague Discovers Street Crime," *The New York Times*, 18 December 1991.

28. Burton Bollag, "Havel Asserts Nation Faces Breakup," *The New York Times*, 11 December 1990. Slovak nationalism, suppressed during four decades of Communist rule, was a product of earlier repression as well. Slovakia was dominated by Hungary for centuries, became part of the newly created state of Czechoslovakia with the post–World War I breakup of the Austro-Hungarian Empire, and from 1939 to 1944 was made a nominally independent Nazi puppet

state headed by the Catholic priest Jozef Tisa (later executed as a war criminal for deporting Slovak Jews to Nazi death camps). The Communists took over in 1945.

29. John Tagliabue, "Arms Exports Bring Profits and Pain to Czechs and Especially to Slovaks," *The New York Times*, 19 February 1992.

30. John Tagliabue, "Sign on Capitalist Road—Recession," *The New York Times*, 25 February 1992.

31. Henry Kamm, "Top Prague Party Is Splitting in Two," *The New York Times*, 12 February 1992.

32. Lawrence E. Joseph, "Prague's Spring into Capitalism," *The New York Times Magazine*, 20 December 1990, 22.

33. Milos Forman, "Czech Communists Forget So Easily," *The New York Times*, 30 October 1990.

34. Henry Kamm, "Thousands Rally in Prague to Denounce Communists," *The New York Times*, 12 October 1990.

35. Burton Bollag, "In Czechoslovakia, Hunt for Villains," *The New York Times*, 3 February 1991.

36. "In Former Communist Lands, Fear That Justice Is Vengeful," *The New York Times*, 26 December 1991.

37. "Taking the Communists to Court Can Be Nettlesome, Czechs Find," *The New York Times*, 24 January 1992.

38. Joseph, "Prague's Spring into Capitalism," 36.

39. Karel Dyba (Czechoslovakian Minister of Economic Policy Development) and Daniel J. Arbess, "Prague Has to Drive Fast in Economic Mud," letter, *The New York Times*, 21 January 1992.

40. Pavel Solc, "Lustration Is Necessary," letter, *The New York Times*, 21 January 1992.

41. Jan Sammer, "Ban Proven Agents," letter, *The New York Times*, 21 January 1992.

42. Vaclav Havel, "The End of the Modern Era," *The New York Times*, 1 March 1992. Many Western scientists want politicians and governments to support their research and theories that have the potential to improve the human condition—viewing Havel's turn to individual subjectivity as a dangerous obscurantism that will undermine the scientific attitude and lead to a turn away from solving the world's problems. See "With Apologies to Havel, Let Reason Rule," Letters, *The New York Times*, 17 March 1992.

43. John Tagliabue, "Prague Turns on Those Who Brought the 'Spring,'" *The New York Times*, 24 February 1992.

8. DEUTSCHLAND ÜBER ALLES

1. This chapter was written with the help of German citizens and émigrés living in the United States. Data from the following sources: In Moscow, Foreign Minister Shevardnadze, *Report*, Politburo, 15 February 1990. In Frankfurt, Deutsche Bank, A.G.; Dresdner Bank, A.G.; and Commerzbank, A.G. In Berlin, Deutsche Kreditbank. In Bonn, various agencies of the German government. Quotes and data from *The New York Times* as indicated.

2. Serge Schmemann, "East Berlin Faults Opposition on Raid," *The New York Times*, 17 January 1990.

3. Serge Schmemann, "East Berlin Chiefs Listen to Torrent of Public Outrage," *The New York Times*, 30 October 1989.

4. Serge Schmemann, "Central Committee Ends Session with Program of Radical Change," *The New York Times*, 11 November 1989.

5. See Craig R. Whitney, "East German Communists Confront Party Collapse," *The New York Times*, 17 December 1989.

6. See Serge Schmemann, "The Germans: Second Thoughts on Open Border," *The New York Times*, 15 January 1990.

7. "Neo-Nazi Skinheads Mar Leipzig's Rally for German Unity," *The New York Times*, 6 February 1990.

8. See Craig R. Whitney, "East Germans See Crisis and Change," *The New York Times*, 18 December 1989.

9. Craig R. Whitney, "German Momentum," *The New York Times*, 19 December 1989.

10. Serge Schmemann, "Leipzig Marchers Tiptoe around Unification," *The New York Times*, 19 December 1989.

11. Henry Kamm, "Brandt Hails the German People for a Display of 'Human Unity,'" *The New York Times*, 14 November 1989.

12. Serge Schmemann, "East Berlin Cabinet Adding Members from Opposition," *The New York Times*, 6 February 1990.

13. Shevarnadze, *Report*.

14. Thomas L. Friedman and Michael R. Gordon, "Steps to German Unity: Bonn as a Power," *The New York Times*, 16 February 1990.

15. Shevarnadze, *Report*; Steven Greenhouse, "Polish Official Vows to Defend Border," *The New York Times*, 21 February 1990.

16. Shevarnadze, *Report*; *Pravda* (Moscow), 16, 17 February 1990.

17. Ibid.

18. "Gorbachev Remarks on a United Germany," *The New York Times*, 21 February 1990.

19. See David Binder, "East Germans React Coolly to Kohl Plan for Closer Ties," *The New York Times*, 30 November 1989.

9. POLAND'S DEMOCRATIC STEP

1. Information and data for this chapter are from Adam Smith Institute (Warsaw: 1989–92); the staff of *Solidarity Weekly* (Warsaw: 1988–92); the Polish Finance Ministry, Foreign Affairs Ministry, and Agricultural Ministry; and Polish citizens and émigrés living in the United States and Germany. Quotes and data from other sources as indicated.

2. "Farmers, Fearing a Drop in Prices, Criticize Poland's Economic Plan," *The New York Times*, 19 December 1989.

3. Steven Greenhouse, "In Poland, a Small Capitalist Miracle," *The New York Times*, 19 December 1989.

4. Floyd Norris, "Eastern Bloc Shift Worries to Western Banks," *The New York Times*, 4 January 1990.

5. Neil A. Lewis, "Walesa Welcomed by Unions in the U.S.," *The New York Times*, 15 November 1989.

6. "Excerpts from Address by Walesa," *The New York Times*, 16 November 1989.

7. "Poland's Brave New Economics," *The New York Times*, editorial, 22 December 1989.

8. Steven Greenhouse, "'Shock Therapy' for Poland: It Might Be Too Damaging," *The New York Times*, 26 December 1989.

9. "Talking Business," *The New York Times*, 26 December 1989.

10. Steven Greenhouse, "In Poland, Capitalism Brings Hope Tempered with Worry," *The New York Times*, 1 January 1990.

11. "Poland's Brave Plunge," *The New York Times*, editorial, 3 January 1990.

12. Steven Greenhouse, "Austerity in Poland," *The New York Times*, 3 January 1990.

13. Steven Greenhouse, "Poland's New Vanguard: The Jobless," *The New York Times*, 5 February 1990.

14. John Kifner, "Poland Changes to a Free Market Show Early Gain," *The New York Times*, 3 March 1990.

15. Steven Greenhouse, "Poles Find Crime Replacing Police State," *The New York Times*, 4 March 1990.

16. Quoted in Stephen Engelberg, "Facing Strikes, Walesa Laughs at History's Joke," *The New York Times*, 14 January 1992.

10. THUMBNAIL SKETCH IN THE OUTER REACH

1. This section is based on information from Directorate, Central European Research Center (Budapest: CERC, 1990–92); Hungarian Secretariat, Minister of Finance (Budapest: MF, 1990–92); Hungarian Secretariat, Privatization Ministry (Budapest: MP, 1990–92); and various other agencies of the Hungarian center-right government (Budapest, 1990–92).

2. Secretariat, Finance Ministry, *Statistical Survey*, March 1990–February 1992; Directorate, Central European Research Center (Budapest: CERC, 1991–February 1992).

3. Quoted in Frank Viviano, "Identity Crisis in the Eastern Bloc," *San Francisco Chronicle*, 23 October 1990.

4. This section is based on information from Secretariat, Government Finance Ministry (Belgrade: Finance Ministry, 1990); Roberto Boteri, editor of Slovenian *Mladina*; Vuk Draskovic, Serbian Renewal Party (Belgrade: SRP, 1990); Law Professor Budomir Kosutic (Belgrade: Serbian Constitutional Committee, 1990); Central Intelligence Agency, *Yugoslavia: National Intelligence Estimate* (Washington, D.C.: CIA, November 1990).

5. A similar move was made by Ceausescu in Romania during the eighties.

6. Quoted in Chuck Sudetic, "Yugoslav Groups Reach an Accord," *The New York Times*, 19 March 1992.

7. This section is based on information from "Interview: Todor Zhivkov," *Trud (Labor)* (Sofia), 9 November 1990; Bulgarian Office of Foreign Economic Relations (Sofia: Minister of Foreign Economic Relations, 1990–February 1992); Bulgarian Socialist Party, Budget Proposal, 1990–91, Assorted Documents 1991–92 (Sofia: Socialist Party, 1990–92); Bulgarian Public Prosecutor's Office (Sofia: PPO, 1991–92); Richard W. Rahn, ed., *Action Plan for Bulgaria* (Washington, D.C.: U.S. Chamber of Commerce, September 1990).

8. Rahn, ed., *Action Plan for Bulgaria*.

11. ROMANIA AND THE END OF PARTY DICTATORSHIP

1. This chapter was written with information provided by Bishop Laszlo Tokes; Slavomir Gvozdenovic, editor of *Timisoara Literary Review*; National Defense Ministry (Budapest); Timisoara's Committee for Social Democracy; Radio Free Romania (Bucharest); Interior Ministry (Bucharest); National Prosecutor's Office, Chairman (Bucharest); National Christian Peasant Party; National Salvation Front; and Council of National Salvation Front.
2. Hemdale Film Corporation, *Requiem for Dominic*, produced by Norbert Blecha, directed by Robert Dornhelm, screenplay in German with English subtitles, Berkeley, Calif., Pacific Film Archives, 1991.
3. Quoted in "Romanians Can't Afford to Farm Their Lands," *The New York Times*, 12 February 1992.
4. Quoted in "A City in Romania Faces New Enemy," *The New York Times*, 17 December 1991.

PART V : ARMS AND THE NEW BALANCE OF POWER

1. Part V is based in part on information from Soviet negotiators under Foreign Minister Shevardnadze, East German prime minister Modrow, Interfax (Moscow 1989–91), and Soviet, German, U.S., British, and other negotiators of subsequent agreements. See also Clyde Haberman, "Italy Says German Unity Talks Should Include Other Nations," *The New York Times*, 3 March 1990; Michael R. Gordon, "Outlook Is Cloudy for an Arms Deal by U.S. and Soviets," *The New York Times*, 6 February 1991.
2. See Bernard E. Trainor, "With Reform, Tough Times for the Warsaw Pact," *The New York Times*, 20 December 1989.

12. A MILITARY MATTER

1. Chapter 12 is based in part on reports by Interfax (Moscow), 1989–92; *New Times* (Moscow), 1989–91. See Serge Schmemann, "Kohl Calls for Guarantees from Warsaw If Any Accord on Borders," *The New York Times*, 3 March 1990.
2. Serge Schmemann, "For German 'Expellees,' the Past Is a Future Vision," *The New York Times*, 4 March 1990.
3. Haberman, "Italy Says German Unity Talks Should Include Other Nations."
4. John Tagliabue, "Kohl and Havel Sign Pact but Issue Remains," *The New York Times*, 28 February 1992.
5. Hans Modrow, *"Grossdeutschland"* (Berlin: Politburo, 10 December 1989).
6. Craig R. Whitney, "East German Asks Help of U.S. in Keeping His Country Separate," *The New York Times*, 5 December 1989.
7. Modrow, *"Grossdeutschland."*
8. See Michael R. Gordon, "Soviets Now Seeking Broader Troop Limits in Central Europe," and Serge Schmemann, "Bonn Again Dodges Warsaw's Demands for Guarantees on Borders," *The New York Times*, 23 February 1990.

9. See *The Banker* (London), January–December 1990.

10. "Excerpts from the News Conference Held by Bush and Kohl," *The New York Times*, 26 February 1990; see Alan Riding, "Western Europe Is Edgy over the U.S. and Much Else," *The New York Times*, 25 February 1990.

11. Krooth, *Arms and Empire*, chap. 2.

12. Robert Pear, "Bush and Kohl Try to Allay Fears of a Reunified Germany's Power," *The New York Times*, 26 February 1990.

13. Serge Schmemann, "Kohl's Political Math," *The New York Times*, 28 February 1990.

14. Thomas L. Friedman, "West Berlin Mayor Critical of Kohl on Boundary Issue," *The New York Times*, 27 February 1990.

15. Henry Kamm, "Some East Germans See Their Hopes Eclipsed by Bonn's Ascendancy," *The New York Times*, 28 February 1990.

16. "Excerpts from Speech by Ligachev to Party," *The New York Times*, 7 February 1990.

17. Paul Lewis, "Shevardnadze Calls for Meeting This Year on German Reunification," *The New York Times*, 16 February 1990.

18. Alan Riding, "Fear on Germany Is Focus at East Europe Meeting," *The New York Times*, 5 February 1990.

19. See Bernard E. Trainor, "Shift in the Western Alliance's Focus: From Moscow to a United Germany?" *The New York Times*, 18 February 1990.

20. Stephen Engelberg, "Leave, but Pay Us, Poles tell Russia," *The New York Times*, 23 February 1992.

21. Ferdinand Protzman, "World Leaders Urged to Save Trade Pact," *The New York Times*, 25 February 1992.

22. Craig R. Whitney, "Kohl Says Moscow Agrees Unity Issue Is up to the Germans," *The New York Times*, 11 February 1990.

23. Craig R. Whitney, "German Whirlwind," *The New York Times*, 12 February 1990.

24. Thomas L. Friedman, "U.S. Hesitates to Cash in on a Cold War Victory," *The New York Times*, 13 February 1990.

25. Thomas L. Friedman, "Baker and Yeltsin Agree on U.S. Aid in Scrapping Arms," *The New York Times*, 18 February 1992.

26. Celestine Bohlen, "Arms Factory Can Make Bricks, but, Russia Asks, Is That Smart?" *The New York Times*, 24 February 1992.

27. Robert Wright and Doyle McManus, *Flashpoints: Promise and Peril in a New World* (New York: Alfred A. Knopf, 1992).

28. U.S. Congress, *National Military Strategy, Fiscal 1993* (Washington, D.C.: Fax edition, January 1992).

29. Mikhail S. Gorbachev, "No Time for Stereotypes," *The New York Times*, 24 February 1992.

30. Bohlen, "Arms Factory Can Make Bricks."

31. William J. Broad, "Serious Sharing of 'Star Wars'? Not in This Millennium," *The New York Times*, 23 February 1992; Flora Lewis, "It's Lunacy to Keep 'Star Wars' Alive," *The New York Times*, 22 February 1992.

32. Patrick E. Tyler, "War in 1990s? Doubt on Hill," *The New York Times*, 18 February 1992.

33. Patrick E. Tyler, "7 Hypothetical Conflicts Foreseen by the Pentagon," *The New York Times*, 17 February 1992.

34. William E. Schmidt, "In a Post–Cold War Era, Scandinavia Rethinks Itself," *The New York Times*, 23 February 1992.

35. Patrick E. Tyler, "Pentagon Imagines New Enemies to Fight Post–Cold War Era," *The New York Times,* 17 February 1992.

36. Keith Schneider, "Nuclear Disarmament Raises Fear on Storage of 'Triggers,'" *The New York Times,* 26 February 1992.

37. Seth Faison, Jr., "Mao's '50 Cable Gives Evidence of Korea Plan," *The New York Times,* 26 February 1992; Elaine Sciolino, "C.I.A. Chief Doubts North Korean Vow on Nuclear Arms," *The New York Times,* 26 February 1992.

38. See U.S., 92d Congress, Senate Armed Services Committee, *Hearings,* 20 February 1992 (Washington, D.C.: U.S. Government Printing Office, 1992).

39. "War Games, Money Games," editorial, *The New York Times,* 19 February 1992.

40. Leslie H. Gelb, "What Peace Dividend?" *The New York Times,* 21 February 1992.

41. Patrick E. Tyler, "Top Congressman Seeks Deeper Cuts in Military Budget," *The New York Times,* 23 February 1992.

42. Clyde Farnsworth, "Ottawa to Pull Out Combat Force from Europe by the End of 1994," *The New York Times,* 27 February 1992.

43. Eric Schmitt, "Move to Shift $15 Billion from Military Gains Support in House," *The New York Times,* 28 February 1992.

44. Seymour Melman, "Shaping a Civilian Economy," *The New York Times,* 27 February 1992.

45. Patrick E. Tyler, "How Big a Military Does a Superpower Need?" *The New York Times,* 1 March 1992.

46. Andrew Schotter, "Improve Capitalism. Use Some Socialism," *The New York Times,* 29 February 1992.

47. Interfax and Reuters (Moscow), 28 February 1992.

48. Reuters (Prague), 29 February 1992.

49. William J. Broad, "U.S. Moves to Bar Americans Buying Soviet Technology," *The New York Times,* 1 March 1992.

50. "Don't Rush to Deploy ABMs," *The New York Times,* 27 February 1992.

51. William J. Broad, "U.S. Plans to Hire Russian Scientists in Fusion Research," *The New York Times,* 6 March 1992.

52. Thomas L. Friedman, "U.S. and Russia See New Arms Accord for a July Summit," *The New York Times,* 19 February 1992.

53. Paul Lewis, "As the U.N.'s Armies Grow, the Talk Is of Preventing War," *The New York Times,* 1 March 1992.

54. See "The New World Army," editorial, *The New York Times,* 6 March 1992; Barbara Crossette, "Spending for U.N. Peacekeeping Getting a Hard Look in Congress," *The New York Times,* 6 March 1992.

55. See Leslie H. Gelb, "Banana Republic, U.S.A.," *The New York Times,* 6 March 1992.

56. Natalie J. Goldring, "The Insecurity Council," *The New York Times,* 23 February 1992.

57. Steven Greenhouse, "Delay by the U.S. Said to Imperil Aid to Ex-Soviet Lands," *The New York Times,* 23 February 1992.

58. Thomas L. Friedman, "Ex-Soviet Atom Scientists Ask Baker for West's Help," *The New York Times,* 15 February 1992; Eric Schmitt, "Soviet Atom Move Is Ahead of Schedule," *The New York Times,* 28 February 1992.

59. Arthur Hartman, "Life or Death for Russian Children," *The New York Times,* 23 February 1992.

COMECON'S QUIET END

1. *Pravda* (Moscow), 4 January 1991.
2. "C.I.A.–Soviet Economists Report," Washington Economic Conference, Washington, D.C., 23–27 April 1990.
3. Steven Greenhouse, "East's Turn to West Puts COMECON in Peril," *The New York Times*, 16 December 1989.
4. COMECON Conference (Moscow, COMECON Headquarters), 5 January 1991.
5. Thomas L. Friedman, "By Trip's End, Moscow Looks Good," *The New York Times*, 20 February 1992.
6. Steven Greenhouse, "Eastern Europe Awaits the Storm," *The New York Times*, 17 December 1989.
7. Steven Greenhouse, "Ex-Soviet Nations May Join I.M.F. Soon," *The New York Times*, 25 February 1992.
8. Francis X. Clines, "Russia to Fight Private Sell-Offs by Ex-Officials," *The New York Times*, 29 February 1992.
9. Louis Uchitelle, "The Roulette of Russian Banking," *The New York Times*, 29 February 1992.
10. Clyde H. Farnsworth, "U.S. Said to Weigh New Export Rules for Eastern Bloc," *The New York Times*, 17 December 1989.
11. Robert J. Cole, "Talking Deals: It's Slow Going in Eastern Europe," *The New York Times*, 4 January 1990.

14. THE QUEST FOR FREEDOM

1. Krooth, *Arms and Empire*, 45–46.
2. Ibid., 62.
3. See Adam B. Ulam, *The Communists: The Story of Power and Illusions: 1948–1991* (New York: Charles Scribner's Sons, 1992).
4. See Walter Laqueur, *The Long Road to Freedom: Russia and Glasnost* (New York: Praeger, 1992).
5. Interfax, Baltfax, September–December 1990, January–February 1992.
6. Vladimir Pozner, *Eyewitness: A Personal Account of the Unraveling of the Soviet Union* (New York: Random House, 1992).
7. Quoted in Serge Schmemann, "Soviet Die-Hards Fume by Candlelight," *The New York Times*, 17 March 1992.
8. Serge Schmemann, "Ukrainian Uses Summit to Berate Russians and the Commonwealth," *The New York Times*, 21 March 1992.
9. Quoted in Serge Schmemann, "Ukraine's Parliament Votes to Replace the Ruble," *The New York Times*, 21 March 1992.
10. Steven Greenhouse, "U.S. Is Working on Soviet Aid Package," *The New York Times*, 21 March 1992.
11. Friedrich A. von Hayek, *The Road to Serfdom* (Chicago: University of Chicago Press, 1944).
12. General Agreement on Tariffs and Trade, *Review of American Trade*, Geneva, 12 March 1992, fax edition.
13. James Sterngold, "Japanese Shifting Investment Flow Back towards Home," *The New York Times*, 22 March 1992. Already in a deep recession, America's demand for Japanese capital was low, sparing the United States a further production downturn.

14. Craig R. Whitney, "Thatcher Warns Europeans on Slow Response to Crisis," *The New York Times,* 31 August 1990.

15. Transcript of Parliamentary Proceedings, Federal News Service, Washington, D.C., 23 November 1990.

16. "Up Yours, Delors," *The Sun* (London), 1 November 1990.

17. Ferdinand Protzman, "Bonn Is Warned About Cost of Unification," *The New York Times,* 20 March 1992.

18. Ferdinand Protzman, "Kohl Says Gulf War May Bring Tax Rise," *The New York Times,* 24 January 1991.

19. Stephen Kinzer, "Kohl, Visiting Bush, Is Expected to Discuss Europe and Trade," *The New York Times,* 21 March 1992.

20. Quoted in Alan Riding, "At East-West Crossroads, Western Europe Hesitates," *The New York Times,* 25 March 1992.

21. Ibid.

Calleo, David Patrick. *Britain's Future*. London: Hodder and Stoughton, 1968.
_____. *Europe's Future: The Grand Alternatives*. London: Hodder and Stoughton, 1967.
Campbell, Joseph. *Myths to Live By*. New York: Bantam Books, 1988.
Camps, Miriam. *Britain and the European Community, 1955-63*. London: Oxford University Press, 1964.
_____. *What Kind of Europe? The Community Since de Gaulle's Veto*. London: Oxford University Press, 1965.
Carr, Edward Hallett. *The Bolshevik Revolution, 1917-1923*. New York and London: Macmillan, 1952.
_____. *International Relations Between the Two World Wars, 1919-39*. London: Macmillan, 1955.
_____. *The Soviet Impact on the Western World*. London: Macmillan, 1946.
_____, and R. W. Davies. *Foundations of a Planned Economy, 1926-1929*. New York: Macmillan, 1976.
Central Intelligence Agency (unofficial version). *Yugoslavia: National Intelligence Estimate*. Washington, D.C.: C.I.A., November 1990.
"C.I.A.-Soviet Economists Summary Report." Washington Economic Conference Proceedings, Washington, D.C., ECP, 23-27 April 1990.
"A City in Romania Faces New Enemy." *The New York Times*, 17 December 1991.
Clarity, James F. "Ukraine and Russia Discuss Disputes." *The New York Times*, 14 January 1992 (interview with President Leonid M. Kravchuk).
Clines, Francis X. "Anxiety over Anti-Semitism Spurs Soviet Warning on Hate." *The New York Times*, 2 February 1990.
_____. "Economic Plan: A Kremlin Intrigue." *The New York Times*, 11 September 1990.
_____. "Elections in Soviet Republics Slow Murky Transformation of Politics." *The New York Times*, 25 February 1990.
_____. "From Moscow, a Plan to Junk Communism in 500 Days." *The New York Times*, 9 September 1990.
_____. "Gorbachev Calls Lithuania's Move an 'Alarming' Step." *The New York Times*, 13 March 1990.
_____. "Gorbachev Endorses a Proposal for Free Enterprise in 500 Days." *The New York Times*, 12 September 1990.
_____. "Gorbachev Gains Support in Raucous Debate on Rules of Party, Delegates Report." *The New York Times*, 7 February 1990.
_____. "In Moscow, a City of Bare Shelves, Consumer Rage Turns on Cabinet." *The New York Times*, 17 September 1990.
_____. "It's Not Yet Capitalism, but Ruble Is Healthier." *The New York Times*, 18 February 1992.
_____. "Kazakhs Travel Smoother Road to Capitalism." *The New York Times*, 27 January 1992.
_____. "Kremlin Bypassed in Mediation Bid." *The New York Times*, 30 January 1990.
_____. "Money System Fails, Kremlin Is Warned." *The New York Times*, 14 September 1990.
_____. "Nationalists Victorious in Lithuanian Elections." *The New York Times*, 26 February 1990.
_____. "Soviet Shopping: The Lines Worsen." *The New York Times*, 30 September 1990.

————. "Tug of War, with Rallies, Is Played Out in Moscow amid Mood of Discontent." *The New York Times,* 10 February 1992.

————. "U.S. Embassy Seeks to End Its Social Isolation in Moscow." *The New York Times,* 5 February 1992.

————. "Yeltsin Vows to Ease Impact of His Economic Program." *The New York Times,* 14 February 1992.

Cohen, Roger. "Easing Trade Barriers Is Urgent." *The New York Times,* 3 February 1992.

————. "East Meets West, Dollars Apart." *The New York Times,* 5 February 1992.

Cole, Robert J. "Talking Deals: It's Slow Going in Eastern Europe." *The New York Times,* 4 January 1990.

COMECON Conference. Moscow, COMECON Headquarters, 5 January 1991.

"COMECON Meeting." Tass (Moscow), 5 January 1991.

Commerzbank, A. G. *Internal Research Reports.* Frankfurt: Commerzbank, A. G., 1989–91.

Conquest, Robert. *The Great Terror. Stalin's Purge of the Thirties.* Oxford: Oxford University Press, 1990.

————. *The Nation Killers: The Soviet Deportation of Nationalities.* London: Macmillan, 1970.

————. *Power and Policy in the USSR: A Study of Soviet Dynastics.* London: Macmillan, 1961.

————. *Russia after Khrushchev.* London: Pall Mall Press, 1965.

———— *Soviet Studies Series.* London: Bodley Head, 1967.

Cook, Don. *Floodtide in Europe.* New York: G. P. Putnam's Sons, 1965.

Council, National Salvation Front. *Answer to Inquiry; Assorted Documents.* Bucharest, 1989–91.

C. P. Politburo, USSR. "Internal Memo." Moscow: Politburo, November 1988.

Crossette, Barbara. "Spending for U.N. Peacekeeping Getting a Hard Look in Congress." *The New York Times,* 6 March 1992.

Csicsery, George. "The Other War." *Express* (Berkeley, California), 8 February 1991.

"Czechoslovakia to Return Property Confiscated in the Communist Era." *The New York Times,* 27 February 1991.

Czechoslovakian Academy of Sciences, Economic Institute. "Reports & Data, 1989–92." Prague: CAS, 1989–92.

Czechoslovakian Finance Ministry. *Reports, Data and Interviews.* Prague: CMF, 1989–91.

"Czechs by the Millions Are Investing $35 in a State Bargain." *The New York Times,* 21 January 1992.

Dallin, Alexander, Chair. "Reform and Nationality Problems." *The Nationalities Question: Session 1, The Future of the Soviet Union,* XIV Annual Stanford-Berkeley Conference, Stanford University, 16 March 1990.

Deutsche Bank, A. G., Research Staff. *Internal Research Reports.* Frankfurt, Germany: Deutsche Bank, A. G., 1989–91.

Deutsche Kreditbank, Research Staff. *Internal Reports.* Berlin: Deutsche Kreditbank, 1989–90.

Directorate, Central European Research Center. *CERC Reports.* Budapest: CERC, January 1991–92.

————. *Reports and Surveys.* Budapest: CERC, 1990–92.

Dmytryshyn, Basil. *USSR: A Concise History.* New York: Charles Scribner's Sons, 1965.

Doder, Dusko, and Louise Branson. *Gorbachev: Heretic in the Kremlin.* Updated version. Viking Penguin, 1991.

"Don't Rush to Deploy ABMs." *The New York Times,* 27 February 1992.

Draskovic, Vuk. *Answers to Inquiries.* Belgrade: Serbian Renewal Party, 1990–91.

Dresdner Bank, A. G. *Internal Research Reports.* Frankfurt, Germany: Dresdner Bank, A. G., 1989–91.

Dubček, Alexander, with Jiri Hockman. *The Autobiography of Alexander Dubček.* New York: Kodashna International, 1992.

Dyba, Karel, and Daniel J. Arbess. "Prague Has to Drive Fast in Economic Mud." *The New York Times,* 21 January 1992, letter.

The Economist (London), 1–7 November 1990.

Engelberg, Stephen. "Eager If Uneasy, East Europe Accepts German Investments." *The New York Times,* 23 January 1992.

————. "Eastern Europe Foils All but the Hardiest of Western Investors." *The New York Times,* 5 March 1992.

————. "Facing Strikes, Walesa Laughs at History's Joke." *The New York Times,* 14 January 1992.

————. "Gloom and Economic Anxiety Overtake Poles." *The New York Times,* 6 February 1992.

————. "Leave, but Pay Us, Poles Tell Russia." *The New York Times,* 23 February 1992.

Engels, Frederick. "An Outline of the Science of Political Economy." In *Economic and Philosophical Manuscripts of 1844,* appendix. Moscow: Foreign Languages Publishing House, 1961.

————. "The Wages System." In *The British Labour Movement.* New York: International Publishers, 1940.

Erlanger, Steven. "Most Pieces of Russia Agree to Coalesce, for Now." *The New York Times,* 1 April 1992.

Europe World Yearbook, vol. 2. New York: E.W.Y. Assn., 1990.

European Economic Association. *Aid to the Commonwealth of Independent Nations.* Davos, Switzerland: EEA, January 1992.

"Excerpts from Address by Walesa." *The New York Times,* 16 November 1989.

"Excerpts from News Conference Held by Bush and Kohl." *The New York Times,* 26 February 1990.

"Excerpts from Remarks by Soviet Ambassador." *The New York Times,* 8 February 1990.

"Excerpts from Speech by Ligachev to Party." *The New York Times,* 7 February 1990.

"Excerpts from Statements by Czech Leaders and Opposition." *The New York Times,* 29 November 1989.

Fainsod, Merle. *How Russia Is Ruled.* Rev. ed. Cambridge, Mass.: Harvard University Press, 1963.

————. *International Socialism and the World War.* Cambridge, Mass.: Harvard Political Studies, 1935.

Faison, Keith, Jr. "Mao's '50 Cable Gives Evidence of Korea Plan." *The New York Times,* 26 February 1992.

"Farmers, Fearing a Drop in Prices, Criticize Poland's Economic Plan." *The New York Times,* 19 December 1989.

Farnsworth, Clyde H. "Ottawa to Pull Out Combat Force from Europe by the End of 1994." *The New York Times,* 27 February 1992.

————. "U.S. Said to Weigh New Export Rules for Eastern Bloc." *The New York Times,* 17 December 1989.

Federal Republic of Germany. *Government Reports.* Bonn: Federal Republic of Germany, 1989–92.

Fedorov, Boris (1989–91 finance minister). *Reports.* Moscow: Russian Federation, 1989–91.

Fein, Esther B. "Gorbachev Hints He Would Accept Multiparty Rule." *The New York Times,* 4 January 1990.

Florinsky, Michael T. *Russia, A History and an Interpretation.* 2 vols. New York: Macmillan, 1953.

Forman, Milos. "Czech Communists Forget So Easily." *The New York Times,* 30 October 1990.

Freidin, Gregory. "The Future of the Multi-National System." *The Nationalities Question: Session V, The Future of the Soviet Union,* XIV Annual Stanford-Berkeley Conference, Stanford University, 16 March 1990.

Friedman, Thomas L. "Baker and Yeltsin Agree on U.S. Aid in Scrapping Arms." *The New York Times,* 18 February 1992.

————. "Bush to Press Congress to Approve $645 Million for Ex–Soviet Lands." *The New York Times,* 23 January 1992.

————. "By Trip's End, Moscow Looks Good." *The New York Times,* 20 February 1992.

————. "East Bloc Trip Buoys Baker, yet Alerts Him to the Odds." *The New York Times,* 12 February 1990.

————. "Ex–Soviet Lands to Get Swift Aid." *The New York Times,* 24 January 1992.

————. "Ex–Soviet Scientists Ask Baker for West's Help." *The New York Times,* 15 February 1992.

————. "Tajikistan to Curb Sales of Atom Arms Equipment." *The New York Times,* 14 February 1992.

————. "U.S. and Russia See New Arms Record for a July Summit." *The New York Times,* 19 February 1992.

————. "U.S. Hesitates to Cash in on a Cold War Victory." *The New York Times,* 13 February 1990.

————. "U.S. to Counter Iran in Central Asia." *The New York Times,* 6 February 1992.

————. "U.S. to Offer Plan to Keep Scientists at Work in Russia: Fears on Weapons." *The New York Times,* 8 February 1992.

————. "Uzbek Chief, of Course, Says Yes to Democracy." *The New York Times,* 17 February 1992.

————. "West Berlin Mayor Critical of Kohl on Boundary Issue." *The New York Times,* 27 February 1990.

————, with Michael R. Gordon. "Steps to German Unity: Bonn as a Power." *The New York Times,* 16 February 1990.

Fukuyama, Francis. "The End of History." In *The National Interest.* Washington, D.C., 1989.

————. *The End of History and the Last Man.* New York: Free Press, 1992.

————. "Rest Easy. It's Not 1914 Anymore." *The New York Times,* 9 February 1992.

"Future of the Ukrainian Armed Forces." Interfax, 9 January 1992.

Gargan, Edward A. "A 'Chastened' Pakistan: Peace with the U.S. Is Aim." *The New York Times,* 19 February 1992.

Gelb, Leslie H. "Banana Republic, U.S.A." *The New York Times,* 6 March 1992.

————. "What Peace Dividend?" *The New York Times,* 21 February 1992.

"German Unification." *Pravda* (Moscow), 16–17 February 1990.

"Germany's Duty to Ugly History." *The New York Times*, 28 February 1990.

Goldman, Marshall I. *What Went Wrong with Perestroika?* New York: W. W. Norton, 1992.

Goldring, Natalie J. "The Insecurity Council." *The New York Times*, 23 February 1992.

Gompers, Samuel. *Seventy Years of Life and Labor.* New York: E. P. Dutton, 1957.

Gorbachev, Mikhail. *The August Coup: The Truth and the Lessons.* New York: Harper Collins, 1991.

————. "No Time for Stereotypes." *The New York Times*, 24 February 1992.

————. "Proposed Economic Program Submitted 16 October 1990 to the Supreme Soviet." *Izvestia* (Moscow), 17 October 1990.

————. "Proposed Program." *Supreme Soviet.* Moscow: Supreme Soviet, 16 October 1990.

"Gorbachev Remarks on a United Germany." *The New York Times*, 21 February 1990.

Gordon, Michael R. "Outlook Is Cloudy for an Arms Deal by U.S. and Soviets." *The New York Times*, 6 February 1990.

————. "Soviets Now Seeking Broader Troop Limits in Central Europe." *The New York Times*, 23 February 1990.

Greene, Felix (research by Richard Krooth). *The Enemy.* New York: Vintage Books, 1970.

Greenhouse, Steven. "Austerity in Poland." *The New York Times*, 3 January 1990.

————. "Czechs Begin Shift to a Free Market." *The New York Times*, 1 January 1991.

————. "Czechs Fault Policies of Hard-Line Communists as a Cause of Industrial Lag." *The New York Times*, 1 December 1989.

————. "Deal Is Near for a Czech Auto Maker." *The New York Times*, 5 October 1990.

————. "Delay by the U.S. Said to Imperil Aid to Ex–Soviet." *The New York Times*, 23 February 1992.

————. "Eastern Europe Awaits the Storm." *The New York Times*, 17 December 1989.

————. "East's Turn to Put COMECON in Peril." *The New York Times*, 16 December 1989.

————. "Economists Cite Benefits of Arms Cuts." *The New York Times*, 3 February 1992.

————. "Ex–Soviet Nations May Join I.M.F. Soon." *The New York Times*, 25 February 1992.

————. "I.M.F. Endorses Russian Plan for Economy, Clearing Way for Aid and For Membership." *The New York Times*, 1 April 1992.

————. "In Poland, a Small Capitalist Miracle." *The New York Times*, 19 December 1989.

————. "In Poland, Capitalism Brings Hope Tempered with Worry." *The New York Times*, 1 January 1990.

————. "Poland's New Vanguard: The Jobless." *The New York Times*, 5 February 1990.

————. "Poles Find Crime Replacing Police State." *The New York Times*, 4 March 1990.

————. "Polish Official Vows to Defend Border." *The New York Times*, 21 February 1990.

————. "7 Top Industrialized Nations Plan a Fund to Aid the Ruble." *The New York Times*, 15 February 1992.

————. "'Shock Therapy' for Poland: It Might Be Too Damaging." *The New York Times*, 26 December 1989.

————. "U.S. Is Working on Soviet Aid Package." *The New York Times*, 21 March 1992.

————. "Year of Economic Tumult Looms for Eastern Europe." *The New York Times*, 31 December 1990.

Gregory, James Stothert. *Russian Land—Soviet People: A Geographical Approach to the USSR*. Racine, Wis.: Western, 1968.

————. *The USSR: A Geographical Survey*. New York: John Wiley, 1946.

Grey, Ian. *Catherine the Great: Autocrat and Empress of All Russia*. London: Hodder & Stoughton, 1961.

————. *The First Fifty Years: Soviet Russia. 1917–1967*. New York: Coward-McCann, 1967.

————. *Ivan the Terrible*. London: Hodder and Stoughton, 1964.

————. *Ivan III and the Unification of Russia*. New York: Collier Books, 1967.

————. *Peter the Great: Emperor of All Russia*. Philadelphia: Lippincott, 1960.

————. *The Romanovs: The Rise and Fall of a Dynasty*. Garden City, N.Y.: Doubleday, 1970.

Grigoriev, Leonid. *Reports; Interview*. Moscow: Institute of World Economy and International Relations, 1989–91.

Gumbel, Peter. "Gorbachev's Change of Heart on Reforms May Have Been to Save His Political Skin." *Wall Street Journal*, 26 October 1990.

————. "Resisting Reform, Soviet Town Shows How Hard It Will Be to Install Free Market." *Wall Street Journal*, 26 October 1990.

Gvozdenovic, Slavomir (ed. *Timisoara Literary Review*). *Answer to Inquiry*. Timisoara, 1990.

Haberman, Clyde. "Gorbachev Lauds Religion on Eve of Meeting Pope." *The New York Times*, 1 December 1989.

————. "Italy Says German Unity Talks Should Include Other Nations." *The New York Times*, 3 March 1990.

Harris, Owen. "As Ideology Dies, Analogies Rise." *The New York Times*, 28 October 1989.

Hartman, Arthur. "Life or Death for Russian Children." *The New York Times*, 25 February 1992.

Havel, Vaclav. "The End of the Modern Era." *The New York Times*, 1 March 1992.

"Havel New Year's Address." *The New York Times*, 2 January 1990.

Hewett, Edward (Soviet economy expert). *Reports*. Washington, D.C.: Brookings Institution, 1989–91.

Hosking, Geoffrey Alan. *The Awakening of the Soviet Union*. Cambridge: Harvard University Press, 1990.

————. *The Russian Constitutional Experiment: Government and Duma, 1907–1914*. Cambridge: Cambridge University Press, 1973.

Hungarian Government. *Reports, Policy Statements*. Budapest, 1990–92.

Hungarian Secretariate, Minister of Finance. *Reports*. Budapest: MF, 1990–92.

Hungarian Secretariate, Privatization Ministry. *Privatization Reports*. Budapest: MP, 1990–92.

"In Former Communist Lands, Fear That Justice Is Vengeful." *The New York Times*, 26 December 1991.

Institute for Strategic Studies. *Current Estimates*. London: ISS, 1991–92.

Institute of International Economic Studies (Oleg Bogomolov, director). *Reports*. Moscow: Institute of International Economic Studies, 1989–91.

Interfax (Belarus), 11 January 1992.
Interfax (London) (Moscow) (Vilnius, Lithuania) (Riga, Latvia), November 1989–January 1992.
Interfax (Moscow), 30 November 1991.
Interfax (Moscow), 10 January 1992.
Interfax (Moscow), 12, 13, 14 January 1992.
Interfax (Moscow), 16 and 23 January 1992.
Interfax (Moscow), 17 January 1992.
Interfax (Moscow), 23, 24 January 1992.
Interfax (Moscow), 9 February 1992.
Interfax (Moscow), 28 February 1992.
Interfax (Moscow and Movorossisk), 27, 28 January 1992.
Interfax (Tashkent), 16–19 January 1992.
Interior Ministry. *Internal Documents*. Bucharest, 1990–91.
"Interview: Admiral Chernavin." *Sovetskaya Rossiya*, 9 January 1992.
"Interview: Chairman Ruslan Khasbulatov." *Moskovsky Komsomolets* (Moscow), 16 January 1992.
"Interview: Nusultan A. Nazarbayev." Interfax (Moscow), 16 January 1992.
"Interview: Todor Zhivkov." *Trud(Labor)* (Sofia), 9 November 1990.
"Interview with President Boris N. Yeltsin." CBS News (Moscow), 25 January 1992.
Ionescu, Ghita, ed. *Between Sovereignty and Integration*. London: Croom Helm, 1974.
_____. *The Breakup of the Soviet Empire in Eastern Europe*. Harmondsworth: Penguin, 1965.
_____. *Communism in Romania, 1944–1962*. London: Oxford University Press, 1964.
_____. *The Politics of the European Communist States*. London: Weidenfeld and Nicholson, 1967.
_____. *The Reluctant Ally. A Study of Communist Neo–Colonialism*. London: Ampersand, 1965.
Ivanova, Natalia. "Literature: Traditions and Changes." In *Soviet Literature and Art Almanac 89*. Moscow: Novotni Press Agency Publishing House, 1990.
Izvestia (Moscow), September 1989–January 1991.
_____. 5, 6 December 1991.
Jensen, Kenneth M., ed. *A Look at 'The End of History?'* Washington, D.C.: United States Institute of Peace, 1990.
"The Joke Factory." *The New York Times*, 7 November 1989.
Joseph, Lawrence E. "Prague's Spring into Capitalism." *New York Times Magazine*, 20 December 1990, 22.
Kagarlitsky, Bolis. "The Dialectics of Change; and Questions and Answers." Colloquium Series 1990, Sociology Department, University of California, Berkeley, 22 March 1990.
Kamm, Henry. "Brandt Hails the German People for a Display of 'Human Unity.'" *The New York Times*, 14 November 1989.
_____. "Prague to Scrap Its Defenses along Austrian Border." *The New York Times*, 1 December 1989.
_____. "Some East Germans See Their Hopes Eclipsed by Bonn's Ascendancy." *The New York Times*, 28 February 1990.
_____. "Spirit of 1968 Is Still Alive, Still Distinct." *The New York Times*, 30 November 1989.

————. "Struggling Ukrainian Miners Put Off by Diet of Nationalism." *The New York Times*, 16 February 1992.

————. "Thousands Rally in Prague to Denounce Communists." *The New York Times*, 12 October 1990.

————. "Top Prague Party Is Splitting in Two." *The New York Times*, 12 February 1992.

Kaser, M. *COMECON. Integration Problems of the Planned Economies.* London: Oxford University Press, 1965.

————. "Report to the Social Science Research Council on a Study on Industrial Management and Development in Eastern Europe, Paper No. 2, 1971." *Papers in Eastern European Economics.* Oxford: Centre for Soviet and Eastern European Studies, 1971.

————, with Hans-Hermann Homann and Karl C. Thalheim, eds. *The New Economic Systems of Eastern Europe.* London: Weidenfeld and Nicolson, 1975.

————, ed. "Economic Development for Eastern Europe." Proceedings of a Conference Held by the International Economics Association. Plovdiv: IEA, 1968.

Kassof, Allen, ed. *Prospects for Soviet Society.* New York: Praeger, 1968.

Keller, Bill. "Azerbaijan Talks Start in Latvia." *The New York Times*, 2 February 1990.

————. "Azerbaijan Vows to Secede If Soviet Troops Stay." *The New York Times*, 23 January 1990.

————. "Baltics Say Kremlin Blocks Economic Shifts." *The New York Times*, 11 February 1990.

————. "Did Moscow Incite Azerbaijanis?" *The New York Times*, 19 February 1990.

————. "Force as a Last Resort: Armed Power Salvages Moscow's Fading Authority." *The New York Times*, 28 January 1990.

————. "Gorbachev Issues Emergency Decree over Azerbaijan." *The New York Times*, 16 January 1990.

————. "Gorbachev Says 6 Months Are Needed to Prepare for New Economy." *The New York Times*, 1 September 1990.

————. "Gorbachev's Hesitation." *The New York Times*, 12 September 1990.

————. "In Soviet Speeches, 2 Nightmares: Europe's Ideologies, or Its Armies." *The New York Times*, 7 February 1990.

————. "Lithuanian Sees Completely Different Future for Communism." *The New York Times*, 7 February 1990.

————. "Lithuanians Seek to Remove KGB." *The New York Times*, 24 February 1990.

————. "Morning After in Lithuania: Pride Is Tempered by Doubt." *The New York Times*, 13 March 1990.

————. "Moscow's Envoys Seek to Reassure Lithuania." *The New York Times*, 18 January 1991.

————. "Party Asks Calm at Sunday Rallies." *The New York Times*, 23 February 1990.

————. "Soviet Faction Sees Split within Party." *The New York Times*, 11 February 1990.

Keller, John. "Poland Changes to a Free Market Show Early Gains." *The New York Times*, 3 March 1990.

Khrushchev, Nikita. *Khrushchev Remembers.* Translated and edited by Strobe Talbott. Boston: Little, Brown, 1970.

Kinzer, Stephen. "Kohl, Visiting Bush, Is Expected to Discuss Europe and Trade." *The New York Times,* 21 March 1992.

Kissinger, Henry. *The Troubled Partnership.* New York: McGraw-Hill, 1969.

Knecht, G. Bruce. "From Soviet Minister to Corporate Chief." *New York Times Magazine,* 26 January 1992, 24–26, 28.

Kohr, Hans. "Disunion Now: A Plea for a Society Based upon Small Autonomous Units." *Commonweal,* 26 September 1941.

Komsomolskaya Pravda, 20 January 1992.

Korotich, Vitaly A. (contributor). *Ogonyok,* Moscow, 16 October 1990.

Kosutic, Budomir (law professor, Serbian Constitutional Committee). *Answers to Inquiry.* Serbia: Constitutional Committee, 1990.

Kozol, Jonathan. *Rachel and Her Children: Homeless Families in America.* New York: Fawcett Columbine, 1988.

Krall, Hanna. *Shielding the Flame: An Intimate Conversation with Dr. Marek Edelman, the Last Remaining Surviving Leader of the Warsaw Ghetto Uprising.* Translated by Joanna Stasinska and Lawrence Weschler. New York: Henry Holt, 1986.

Krooth, Richard. *Arms and Empire: Imperial Patterns before World War II.* Santa Barbara: Harvest, 1981.

_____. *Empire: A Bicentennial Appraisal.* Santa Barbara: Harvest, 1976.

_____. *The Political Economy of the War in Vietnam.* Madison, Wis.: National Coordinating Committee to End the War in Vietnam, 1965.

_____, and Hiroshi Fukurai. *Common Destiny: Japan and the United States in the Global Age.* Jefferson, NC: McFarland, 1990.

_____, ed. *The Great Social Struggle.* Santa Barbara: Harvest, 1979.

Kvint, Vladimir. "Opportunity in a Shattered Land." *The New York Times,* 19 January 1992.

Lapidus, Gail W., ed. *Analyzing the Gorbachev Era: Working Papers of the Students of the Berkeley-Stanford Program.* Palo Alto and Berkeley: Berkeley-Stanford Program in Soviet Studies, 1989.

Laqueur, George. *Stalin: Revelations of Glasnost.* New York: Macmillan, 1990.

Laquerur, Walter. *Europe in Our Time: A History 1945–1992.* New York: Viking, 1992.

_____. *The Long Road to Freedom: Russia and Glasnost.* New York: Viking, 1992.

Lenin, V. I. "Letter to the Congress." *Kommunist* (Moscow), 1956.

Lewin, David. *From Purge to Coexistence. Essays on Stalin's and Khrushchev's Russia.* Chicago: Henry Regnery, 1964.

_____. *The New Soviet Empire.* London: Hollis and Carter, 1951.

Lewis, Anthony. "For Want of a Nail." *The New York Times,* 16 February 1992.

Lewis, Flora. "It's Lunacy to Keep 'Star Wars' Alive." *The New York Times,* 22 February 1992.

Lewis, Neil A. "Lithuanians Spur Offer by Moscow." *The New York Times,* 13 January 1990.

_____. "Tough Choice for the U.S.: Baltic States or Gorbachev." *The New York Times,* 13 January 1990.

_____. "Walesa Welcomed by Unions in the U.S.A." *The New York Times,* 15 November 1989.

Lewis, Paul. "As the U.N.'s Armies Grow, the Talk Is of Preventing War." *The New York Times,* 1 March 1992.

_____. "Shevardnadze Calls for Meeting This Year on German Reunification." *The New York Times,* 16 February 1990.

Ligachev, Yegor K. *Memorandum on Position of the Party.* Moscow: Politburo, 1990.

"Lithuania's Declaration." *The New York Times,* 13 March 1990.

Luers, William H. "Czech History: A Waiting Game." *The New York Times,* 16 December 1989.

Malcolm, Andrew M. "The Man behind the Match for the Man of Steel." *The New York Times,* 18 February 1992.

Malia, Martin. "The Soviet Union Has Ceased to Exist." *The New York Times,* 31 August 1990.

Malthus, Thomas Robert. *Principles of Political Economy Considered with a View to Their Practical Application.* London: British Museum Manuscript ed., 1820; 2d ed., 1836.

Marlio, Louis (director of the World Aluminum Cartel in the 1930s). *The Aluminum Cartel.* Washington, D.C.: Brookings Institution, 1947.

Marx, Karl. *Capital: A Critical Analysis of Capitalist Production.* 3 vols. Moscow: Foreign Languages Publishing House, 1961.

――――――. "Estranged Labour." In *Economic and Philosophical Manuscripts of 1844.* Moscow: Foreign Languages Publishing House, 1961.

Maximova, M. *Economic Aspects of Capitalist Integration.* Moscow: Progress, 1973.

Mayne, Richard J. *The Community of Europe.* London: Victor Gollancz, 1962.

――――――. *The Europeans: Who Are We?* London: Weidenfeld and Nicholson, 1972.

――――――. *The Recovery of Europe: From Devastation to Unity.* London: Weidenfeld and Nicolson, 1970.

Medvedev, Roy, and Giulietto Chiesa. *Time of Change: An Insider's View of Russia's Transformation.* Translated by Michael Moore. New York: Pantheon Books, 1989.

Medvedev, Zhores, and Roy Medvedev. *A Question of Madness.* Translated by Ellen de Kadt. New York: Knopf, 1971.

Melman, Seymour. "How Big a Military Does a Superpower Need?" *The New York Times,* 1 March 1992.

Meyer, Stephen M. "From Afghanistan to Azerbaijan, Discord Undermines the Red Army." *The New York Times,* 28 January 1990.

Mill, John Stuart. *Principles of Political Economy, with Some of their Applications to Social Philosophy.* 2 vols. New York: Longmans, Green, 1909.

Mitchell, Alison. "Yeltsin, on Summit's Stage, Stresses His Russian Identity." *The New York Times,* 1 February 1992.

Modrow, Hans (former prime minister, German Democratic Republic). *Grossdeutschland; Assorted Documents.* Berlin, Politburo, 10 December 1989, 1990.

Morrison, John. *Boris Yeltsin: From Bolshevik to Democrat.* New York: E. P. Dutton, 1991.

"Moscow Needs More Than a Gesture." *The New York Times,* 24 January 1992. Editorial.

Muller, Father Protr. "Sunday Sermon on Soviet Occupation." Vilnius, Lithuania: Russian Orthodox Church, 1991.

"Muslim Regional Group Welcomes Ex–Soviet Central Asians." *The New York Times,* 17 February 1992.

National Christian Peasant Party. *Answer to Inquiry.* Bucharest, 1990.

National Defense Ministry. *Internal Reports.* Bucharest: MDN, 1990.

National Geographic Society, Library and News Collection; Records Library;

Translations Division; Pre-Press Division. *Maps and Reports*. Washington, D.C.: NGS, 1989–92.

National Prosecutor's Office, Chairman and Personnel. *Answer to Inquiries; Assorted Documents*. Bucharest: MI, 1990.

National Salvation Front. *Recordings; Assorted Documents; Answers to Inquiries*. Bucharest, 1990–91.

"Neo-Nazi Skinheads Mar Leipzig's Rally for German Unity." *The New York Times*, 6 February 1990.

"New Leader, New Role for Turkey." *The New York Times*, 15 February 1992. Editorial.

"The New World Army." *The New York Times*, 6 March 1992. Editorial.

"News Conference: Deputy Chief Prosecutor Yevgeny Lisov." Interfax (Moscow), 21 January 1992.

News reports and interviews. Novotni Press Agency, 1989–91.

Nezavisimaya Gazeta, 11 January 1992.

Nikolaevsky, Boris Ivanovich. *Power and the Soviet Elite: "The Letter of an Old Bolshevik" and Other Essays*. Edited by Janet D. Zagoria. London: Pall Mall Press, 1966.

————, with David Lewis and David J. Dallin. *Forced Labor in Soviet Russia*. London: Hollis and Carter, 1948.

"No Demons in Central Asia." *The New York Times*, 7 February 1992. Editorial.

"No Time to Be Stingy with Russians." *The New York Times*, 22 January 1992. Editorial.

Norris, Floyd. "Eastern Bloc Shift Worries to Western Banks." *The New York Times*, 4 January 1990.

Pacific Film Archives. Clemov Collection. Berkeley, Calif.: Pacific Film Archives, 1989–90.

Padma Desai. "Key Issues of Soviet Economic Reform." Annual Meeting, American Economic Association, Washington, D.C., 10–12 January 1991.

Passell, Peter. "Economic Scene: Bread, Sausages, Hyperinflation." *The New York Times*, 26 December 1990.

Pear, Robert. "Bush and Kohl Try to Allay Fears of a Reunited Germany's Power." *The New York Times*, 26 February 1990.

Pipes, Richard. *Some Operational Principles of Soviet Foreign Policy*. Washington, D.C.: U.S. Government Printing Office, 1972.

Pistrak, Lazar. *The Grand Tactician: Khrushchev's Rise to Power*. New York: Praeger, 1961.

"Poland's Brave New Economics." *The New York Times*, 22 December 1989. Editorial.

"Poland's Brave Plunge." *The New York Times*, 3 January 1990. Editorial.

"Poland's Industry Grinds to Halt When Russia Cuts Off Gas Supply." *The New York Times*, 30 January 1992.

Polish Agricultural Ministry. *Reports*. Warsaw: AM, 1990–91.

Polish Finance Ministry. *Reports*. Warsaw: PFM, 1990–91.

Polish Foreign Affairs Ministry. *Reports*. Warsaw: FAM, 1989–92.

Politburo, C.P. USSR *Internal Memorandum*, November 1988.

Poretsky, Elizabeth K. *Our Own People. A Memoir of 'Ignace Reiss' and His Friends*. Ann Arbor: University of Michigan Press, 1970.

Pozner, Vladimir. *Eyewitness: A Personal Account of the Unraveling of the Soviet Union*. New York: Random House, 1992.

Pravda Buryaty, Moscow, 3 January 1992.

Protzman, Ferdinand. "Bonn Cancels Half of Debt Poland Owes." *The New York Times*, 20 February 1992.

———. "Bonn Is Warned about Cost of Unification." *The New York Times*, 20 March 1992.

———. "Germany Curbs Trade Aid for Former Soviet States." *The New York Times*, 23 January 1992.

———. "Kohl Says Gulf War May Bring Tax Rise." *The New York Times*, 24 January 1991.

———. "Several Dark Spots Emerge to Mar Germany's Economy." *The New York Times*, 8 February 1992.

———. "World Leaders Urged to Save Trade Pact." *The New York Times*, 25 February 1992.

"Public Interviews." Novotni Press Agency (Moscow), 24–30 September 1990.

Radio Free Romania. *Answer to Inquiry*. Bucharest, 1990.

Rahn, Richard W., ed. *Action Plan for Bulgaria*. Washington, D.C.: United States Chamber of Commerce, September 1990.

Reich, Robert B. *The Next American Frontier*. New York: Times Books, 1983.

———. "The Real Economy." *Atlantic Monthly*, February 1991.

Reitz, James T. *Soviet Defense-Associated Activities Outside the Ministry of Defense*. McLean, Va.: Research Analysis Corp., 1969.

Report of the Center for Disease Control, Findings of the U.S. team visiting Russia from 16 January to 6 Febrary 1992. Reuters (Atlanta), 13 February 1992.

Riasanovsky, Nicholas (moderator). "The Strength and Character of Conservative and Reactionary Forces." *Beyond Leninism in Eastern Europe and the Soviet Union*. Conference proceedings, Berkeley: University of California, 1991.

Ricardo, David. *Principles of Political Economy and Taxation*. London: Everyman's Library, 1911.

Rich, Frank. "'Macbeth,' with Lessons Ever Apt and Ever New." *The New York Times*, 17 January 1990.

Riding, Alan. "At East-West Crossroads, Western Europe Hesitates." *The New York Times*, 25 March 1992.

———. "Fear on Germany Is Focus at East Europe Meeting." *The New York Times*, 5 February 1990.

———. "Western Europe Is Edgy over the U.S. and Much Else." *The New York Times*, 25 February 1990.

———. "Yeltsin, Showing Annoyance at Delays, Urgently Appeals for Aid." *The New York Times*, 6 February 1992.

"The Rise and Fall of MIRV." *The New York Times*, 27 January 1992.

"Romanians Can't Afford to Farm Their Lands." *The New York Times*, 12 February 1992.

Rosenthall, A. M. "The Gorbachev Era Ends." *The New York Times*, 21 September 1990.

Rosner, Lydia S. "Bureaucratic Hangover." *The New York Times*, 19 January 1992. Letter.

"Ruble-Rich Ukrainians Looking for Bargains." *The New York Times*, 29 January 1992.

Rude Pravo, 19 February 1992.

Rule, Shelia. "Gorbachev Gets Nobel Peace Prize for Foreign Policy Achievements." *The New York Times*, 16 October 1990.

Russian Deputy Prime Minister. "Plan for Economic Reform." Cabinet Document, Boris Yeltsin Government, January 1992.

Russian Information Agency. *Report*, 18, 19 January 1992.

Russian Mission, United Nations. "Speech by Russian President Boris N. Yeltsin to the Security Council." New York: United Nations, 31 January 1992.

Ryabov, Vasil. *The Great Victory*. Moscow: Novosti Press Agency Publishing House, 1985.

Sachs, Jeffrey. "News Conference." Interfax, 15 January 1992.

Safire, William. "Bring On CSCE." *The New York Times*, 15 October 1990.

Sakharov, Andrei D. *The Letters of Andrei D. Sakharov*. Unedited prepublication edition of letters, collected by Tanya Sakharov and Mikhail Liberman, ed. Minneapolis: Lazear Agency, 1991.

_____. *Memoirs*. New York: Random House, 1990.

_____. "Thoughts on Progress, Peaceful Coexistence and Intellectual Freedom." *The New York Times*, 22 July 1968.

Salinger, Pierre. *With Kennedy*. New York: Doubleday, 1966.

Sammer, Jan. "Ban Proven Agents." *The New York Times*, 21 January 1992. Letter.

Saunders, George, ed. *Samizdat: Voices of the Soviet Opposition*. New York: Monad Press, 1974.

Schesch, Adam. *An Outline History of Vietnam*. Madison, Wis.: National Coordinating Committee to End the War in Vietnam, 1965.

_____. "Third World Liberation Movements." Ph.D. diss. University of Wisconsin, 1992.

Schmemann, Serge. "Bonn Again Dodges Warsaw's Demands for Guarantees on Border." *The New York Times*, 23 February 1990.

_____. "Central Committee Ends Session with Program of Radical Change." *The New York Times*, 11 November 1989.

_____. "Czech Party Aide Sees Free Ballot within Next Year." *The New York Times*, 30 November 1989.

_____. "East Berlin Cabinet Adding Members from Opposition." *The New York Times*, 6 February 1990.

_____. "East Berlin Chiefs Listen to Torrent of Public Outrage." *The New York Times*, 30 October 1989.

_____. "East Berlin Faults Opposition on Raid." *The New York Times*, 17 January 1990.

_____. "Fears Deep as Russia's Snow, but Poetry, Too." *The New York Times*, 17 February 1992.

_____. "For German 'Expellees,' the Past Is a Future Vision." *The New York Times*, 4 March 1990.

_____. "The Germans: Second Thoughts on Open Border." *The New York Times*, 15 January 1990.

_____. "In Dire Times, Every Little Kopeck Helps." *The New York Times*, 19 February 1992.

_____. "Kohl Calls for Guarantees from Warsaw if Any Accord on Borders." *The New York Times*, 3 March 1990.

_____. "Leipzig Marchers Tiptoe around Unification." *The New York Times*, 19 December 1989.

_____. "Shadow of Moscow Darkens Lithuanian Independence Vote." *The New York Times*, 9 February 1991.

_____. "Soviet Die-Hards Fume by Candlelight." *The New York Times*, 17 March 1992.

_____. "Ukraine's Parliament Votes to Replace the Ruble." *The New York Times*, 21 March 1992.

————. "Ukrainian Uses Summit to Berate Russians and the Commonwealth." *The New York Times,* 21 March 1992.

Schmidt, Eric. "Move to Shift $15 Billion from Military Gains Support in House." *The New York Times,* 28 February 1992.

————. "Pentagon Warns Panel against More Budget Cuts." *The New York Times,* 25 January 1992.

————. "Soviet Atom Move Is Ahead of Schedule." *The New York Times,* 28 February 1992.

————. "U.S. Is Considering Sharp Cuts in Multi-Warhead Nuclear Missiles." *The New York Times,* 23 January 1992.

Schmidt, William E. "Finns Watch Russian Border for Smugglers and Refugees." *The New York Times,* 4 February 1992.

————. "In a Post-Cold War Era, Scandinavia Rethinks Itself." *The New York Times,* 23 February 1992.

Schmitter, Philippe (moderator). "Building Democratic Institutions." *Beyond Leninism in Eastern Europe and the Soviet Union.* Conference proceedings, Berkeley, California, University of California, 15 March 1991.

Schneider, Keith. "Nuclear Disarmament Raises Fear on Storage of 'Triggers.'" *The New York Times,* 26 February 1992.

Schotter, Andrew. "Improve Capitalism. Use Some Socialism." *The New York Times,* 29 February 1992.

Schwartz, Harry. *Prague's 200 Days.* New York: Praeger, 1969.

Sciolino, Elaine. "C.I.A. Casting About for New Missions." *The New York Times,* 4 February 1992.

————. "C.I.A. Chief Doubts North Korea Vow on Nuclear Arms." *The New York Times,* 26 February 1992.

————. "C.I.A. Chief Says Threat by Ex-Soviets Is Small." *The New York Times,* 23 January 1992.

Seaton-Watson, H. *The Eastern European Revolution.* London: Methuen, 1946.

Secretariat, Government Finance Ministry. *Reports.* Belgrade: 1990–92.

Secretariate, Finance Ministry. *Statistical Surveys.* Budapest: March 1990–February 1992.

Secretariate, General Agreement on Tariffs and Trade. *Review of American Trade.* Geneva: GATT, 12 March 1992. Fax edition.

Senior, Nassau W. *An Outline of the Science of Political Economy.* London: British Museum manuscript edition, 1836; G. Allen and Unwin, 1938.

Servan-Schreiber, J-J. *Le Défi Américain.* Paris: Denoel, 1967.

Sestanovich, Stephen. "The Revolution: A Case for Optimism." *The New York Times,* 23 December 1991.

Shatrov, Mikhail. *The Dictatorship of Conscience.* Moscow: Foreign Languages Publishing House, 1985.

Sheehy, Gail. *The Man Who Changed the World: The Lives of Michail S. Gorbachev.* New York: Harper Collins, 1990.

Shevardnadze (USSR Foreign Minister). *Internal Report on German Unification,* Politburo, 15 February 1990.

————. (USSR Foreign Minister). *Report on the German Democratic Republic.* Politburo, 15 February 1990.

Shevardnadze and Soviet Negotiators. *Answer to Inquiries.* Moscow and Canada, 1990.

Shipler, David. "Democracy Is a System, Not a Man." *The New York Times,* 9 January 1992.

_____. "A Reporter at Large: Between Dictatorship and Anarchy." *New Yorker,* 22 June 1990.

Sitaryan, Stefen A. (Soviet Deputy Prime Minister). *Answer to Inquiry.* Moscow, COMECON Meeting, 5–6 January 1991.

Smith, Adam. *An Inquiry into the Nature and Causes of the Wealth of Nations.* New York: Modern Library, 1937.

Smith, Martin (senior producer). *Frontline: Guns, Tanks and Gorbachev.* Soviet Tanks Moving in on Vilnius, Lithuania. Correspondent Hendrick Smith. New York: PBS, 19 February 1991.

Sobchak, Anatoly. *For a New Russia: The Mayor of St. Petersburg's Own Story of the Struggle for Justice and Democracy.* New York: Free Press, 1991.

_____. "Press Interview, Mayor of Leningrad." Interfax, 1990–91.

Solc, Pavel. "Lustration Is Necessary." *The New York Times,* 21 January 1992. Letter.

Solidarity Weekly, 1988–91.

Solzhenitsyn, Alexsandr. "How to Revitalize Russia." *Komsomolskaya Pravda* (Moscow), 18 September 1990.

Soros, George. "Gorbachev's Reform Plan Is a Bust." *The New York Times,* 19 October 1990.

Sovetskaya Rossya, 11 January 1992.

The Soviet Approach to Negotiations. Senate, Committee of Judiciary, Subcommittee to Investigate the Administration of Internal Security Act and Other Internal Security Laws, 1969.

"Soviet Commander in Azerbaijan Sees Troop Pullback Starting Soon." *The New York Times,* 1 February 1990.

"The Soviet Economic Morass." *The New York Times,* 16 September 1990.

"Soviet Timidity? No Caution." *The New York Times,* 10 December 1989. Editorial.

Speech of Nikita Khruschchev before the Closed Session of the XXth Congress of the Communist Party of the Soviet Union on 25 February 1956. Washington, D.C.: Senate Committee of Judiciary, Subcommittee to Investigate the Administration of Internal Security Act and Other Internal Security Laws, 1957.

Spiegelman, Art, *Maus: A Survivor's Tale, And Here My Troubles Began.* New York: Pantheon Books, 1986, 1991.

Sraffa, Piero, ed. *The Works and Correspondence of David Ricardo.* Cambridge, England: Cambridge University Press, 1951.

Stalin, Joseph. *A Concise History of the All-Union Communist Party* (Bolsheviks). Moscow: Lenin Institute, 1933.

Steiner, Jon M. *Reflections on Experiences in Nazi Death Camps.* Sonoma State University: unpublished copyrighted manuscript, 1992.

Stern (Bonn). January 1992. Editorial.

Sterngold, James. "Japanese Shifting Investment Flow back towards Home." *The New York Times,* 22 March 1992.

Sudetic, Chuck. "Yugoslav Groups Reach an Accord." *The New York Times,* 19 March 1992.

Summers, Lawrence. "Gorbachev Should Pay Lithuania." *The New York Times,* 14 March 1990.

Supreme Soviet, Parliamentary Documents. *Yeltsin-Shatalin Proposal.* Moscow, prepublication fax ed., July–August 1990.

Tagliabue, John. "Arms Exports Bring Profits and Pain to Czechs and Especially to Slovaks." *The New York Times,* 19 February 1992.

————. "Czech Communists Replace Party Chairman." *The New York Times*, 21 December 1989.

————. "Dubcek Expected to Support Havel in Czechoslovakia." *The New York Times*, 17 December 1989.

————. "Hot to Invest? Trust a Man with a Harvard Past?" *The New York Times*, 6 March 1992.

————. "Kohl and Havel Sign Pact but Issue Remains." *The New York Times*, 28 February 1992.

————. "New Pariahs Have Eastern Europe Astir." *The New York Times*, 18 March 1992.

————. "Party in Prague Is Suspending." *The New York Times*, 22 December 1989.

————. "Police in Prague Move to Break Up Big Protest March." *The New York Times*, 29 October 1989.

————. "Prague Marchers Rally for Havel." *The New York Times*, 18 December 1989.

————. "Prague Turns on Those Who Brought the 'Spring.'" *The New York Times*, 24 February 1992.

————. "Prague Would Cut Defenses along West German Border." *The New York Times*, 16 December 1989.

————. "Shevardnadze Calls for End of Military Treaties." *The New York Times*, 27 October 1989.

————. "Signs on Capitalist Road—Recession." *The New York Times*, 25 February 1992.

"Taking Communists to Court Can Be Nettlesome, Czechs Find." *The New York Times*, 24 January 1992.

"Talking Business." *The New York Times*, 26 December 1989.

Tarasov, Artyom (member of Parliament). *Interviews*. Moscow, 1989–91.

"Testimony of Deputy Prosecutor Yevgeny K. Lisov." Hearings, Russian Parliament, 10 February 1992.

Thatcher, Margaret. "Presentation to Czechoslovakian Parliament." *Parliamentary Records*, 18 September 1990.

Thompson, E. P. *The Making of the English Working Class*. New York: Vintage Books, 1967.

Timisoara Committee for Social Democracy. *Answer to Inquiry*. Bucharest, 1990.

Tokes, Bishop Laszlo. *Answer to Inquiry*. New York, 1990.

Trainor, Bernard E. "Shift in the Western Alliance's Focus: From Moscow to a United Germany?" *The New York Times*, 18 February 1990.

————. "With Reform, Tough Times for the Warsaw Pact." *The New York Times*, 20 December 1989.

"Transcription of Parliamentary Proceedings." *Federal News Service* (Washington, D.C.), 23 November 1990.

Tupper, Harnon. *The Moscow Kremlin*. Berkeley: University of California Press, 1954.

Tyler, Patrick E. "Pentagon Imagines New Enemies to Fight Post-Cold-War Era." *The New York Times*, 17 February 1992.

————. "7 Hypothetical Conflicts Forseen by the Pentagon." *The New York Times*, 17 February 1992.

————. "Top Congressman Seeks Deeper Cuts in Military Budget." *The New York Times*, 23 February 1992.

_____. "War in the 1990s? Doubt on the Hill." *The New York Times*, 18 February 1992.

Uchitelle, Louis. "Ad Hoc Ukraine Money Drives Out Ruble." *The New York Times*, 13 February 1992.

_____. "The Art of the Russian Deal: Ad-Libbing Contract Law." *The New York Times*, 17 January 1992.

_____. "Getting the Most from Each Ruble." *The New York Times*, 14 January 1992.

_____. "Moonlighting in Moscow." *The New York Times*, 28 January 1992.

_____. "The Roulette of Russian Banking." *The New York Times*, 29 February 1992.

_____. "In Russia Long Lines for Plentiful Bread." *The New York Times*, 22 January 1992.

_____. "Russia's Central Bank Resists Cuts in Lending." *The New York Times*, 15 February 1992.

Ulam, Adam B. *The Communists: The Story of Power and Illusions, 1948–1991.* New York: Charles Scribner's Sons, 1992.

"Up Yours, Delors." *The Sun* (London), 1 November 1990.

UPI October 1989–March 1992.

U.S., 92d Congress, Senate Armed Services Committee. *Hearings*, 20 February 1992. Washington, D.C.: U.S. Government Printing Office, 1992.

U.S. Bureau of the Census. *Statistical Reports and Diagrams.* Washington, D.C.: USBC, 1987–91.

U.S. Congress. *National Military Strategy.* Washington, D.C.: fax ed., January 1992.

USSR: Facts and Figures Annual. Moscow: Progress Publishers, 1990.

USSR Interior Ministry. *Report on Baku.* Politburo, 15 January 1990 (summary of classified report).

Viviano, Frank. "Identity Crisis in the Eastern Bloc." *San Francisco Chronicle*, 23 October 1990.

von Hayek, Friedrich A. *The Road to Serfdom.* Chicago: University of Chicago Press, 1944.

Von Rauch, Georg. *A History of Soviet Russia.* Translated by Peter and Annette Jacobson. New York: Praeger, 1967.

Voronkov, Nikolai. *900 Days — The Siege of Leningrad.* Moscow: Novasti Press Agency Publishing House, 1982.

"Vremya." Soviet News Program (Moscow), 1989–91.

Vucinich, Wayne (moderator). "Ethnic Conflicts." *Beyond Leninism in Eastern Europe and the Soviet Union.* Conference proceedings, Berkeley, California, University of California, 15 March 1991.

_____. "Varieties of National Movements." *The Future of the Soviet Union.* XIV Annual Stanford-Berkeley Conference, Stanford University, 16 March 1990.

"Vzglyad" (Viewpoint). TV *Magazine* (Moscow), 1990.

"War Games, Money Games." *The New York Times*, 19 February 1992. Editorial.

Ward, Benjamin (moderator). "Economic Transitions." *Beyond Leninism in Eastern Europe and the Soviet Union.* Conference proceedings, Berkeley, California, University of California, 15 March 1991.

Weber, Steve (moderator). "International Influences on the Transitions." *Beyond Leninism in Eastern Europe and the Soviet Union.* Conference proceedings, Berkeley, California, University of California, 15 March 1991.

Weinberg, Lev. *Reports; Interview.* Moscow: Soviet Association of Joint Ventures, 1989–91.

Weisman, Steven R. "Dispute over Seized Islands Is Delaying Japanese Aid to Russia." *The New York Times,* 7 February 1992.

————. "Money, Greed and Power: Sect Divided." *The New York Times,* 10 February 1992.

Wells, Herbert George. *The Country of the Blind.* London: Strand, 1904; Thomas Nelson, 1911.

"Wheat Prices in Wild Ride as Ex-Soviets Buy Again." *The New York Times,* 25 January 1992.

Wheeler, George Shaw. *The Human Face of Socialism.* New York: Hill and Wang, 1970.

Whitney, Craig R. "East German Asks Help of U.S. in Keeping His Country Separate." *The New York Times,* 5 December 1989.

————. "East German Communists Confront Party Collapse." *The New York Times,* 17 December 1989.

————. "East Germans See Crisis and Change." *The New York Times,* 18 December 1989.

————. "German Momentum." *The New York Times,* 19 December 1989.

————. "German Whirlwind." *The New York Times,* 12 February 1990.

————. "Havel Is Elected Czech President." *The New York Times,* 20 December 1989.

————. "Is East Europe Too Amazing for the West?" *The New York Times,* 28 October 1989.

————. "Kohl Says Moscow Agrees Unity Issue Is Up to the Germans." *The New York Times,* 11 February 1990.

————. "Powers That Be." *The New York Times,* 16 September 1990.

————. "Thatcher Warns Europeans on Slow Response to Crisis." *The New York Times,* 31 August 1990.

————. "Yeltsin in Britain, Warns of Peril of Russian Unrest." *The New York Times,* 31 January 1992.

Wiesel, Elie. *Night.* Translated by Stella Rodway. New York: Bantam Books, 1982.

Wilford, John Nobel. "U.S. Is Seeking Soviet Expertise for 'Star Wars.'" *The New York Times,* 8 February 1992.

Wilson, Harold. *Industrial Helotry.* London: Penguin, 1970.

Wines, Michael. "Bush and Yeltsin Declare Formal End to Cold War." *The New York Times,* 2 February 1992.

————. "Yeltsin Is Annoyed, and U.S. Is Puzzled." *The New York Times,* 3 February 1992.

"Winking at Aggression in Baku." *The New York Times,* 14 February 1992. Editorial.

"With Apologies to Havel, Let Reason Rule." *The New York Times,* 17 March 1992. Letters.

"With Democracy, Prague Discovers Street Crime." *The New York Times,* 18 December 1991.

Wolfe, Bertram D. *Khrushchev and Stalin's Ghost.* New York: Praeger, 1957.

Worth, Alexander. *Russia at War, 1941–1945.* New York: E. P. Dutton, 1964.

Wright, James R. *Industrialized Building in the USSR.* Washington, D.C.: U.S. Department of Commerce, National Bureau of Labor Standards, 1971.

Wright, Robin, and Doyle McManus. *Flashpoints: Promise and Peril in a New World.* New York: Knopf, 1991.

"X" (aka George F. Kennan). "Foreign Affairs and Russia" [Containment of Communism], *Foreign Affairs*, Washington, D.C. July 1947.

_____. *Russia Leaves the War*. New York, 1956.

Yeltsin, Boris. *Against the Grain*. New York: Simon and Schuster, 1990.

"Yeltsin's St. Petersburg Tour." Interfax, 15 January 1992.

Yevtushenko, Yevgeny. "Mud and Blood Are Sisters." *The New York Times*, 19 January 1991.

Zeman, Milos. *Answer to Inquiry by Czechoslovakian (Prague) Economist*. Moscow: COMECON Meeting, 5–6 January 1991.

Zygot, Z. (pseudonym). *Answer to Inquiry by Hungarian Senior Economist*. Moscow: COMECON Meeting, 5–6 January 1991.

Index

Tatars 26, 27
Terekhov, Aleksandr 49
Tokes, Bishop Laszlo, representative of Democratic Union of Hungarians 268–269
Treaty of Versailles 310
Tsar Nicholas II 32; abolishing serfdom 32
Turkey: chain-of-command from Washington 167; ownership of Romania 249; President Turgut Ozal 166–167; relations with U.S. 142

Ukazy 3; *see also* Russia; Soviet Union
Ukraine 3; *see also* Soviet Union
Union of Soviet Writers 319
U.S.: aid 140; aid to Soviet Union 170; buying critical Russian technology 141; diplomatic ties with Central Asian republics 142–143; financing Soviet nuclear scientists 141; Pentagon logic about Cold War, post–Cold War threats 99–101; Sixth Fleet 53; State Department "Soviet Desk" 140; threats to withdraw American troops from Europe if Europe, GATT refuse subsidy-free trade 273
Uzbekistan Popular Movement (*Berlik*) 126

Vlad, Romanian Colonel General 258

Walesa, Lech: as prime minister over crisis-ridden economy and 1991–92 economic plans gone awry 216–217, 219; as Solidarity spokesman 206; as spokesman to the Council of Europe 218; *see also* Poland, Solidarity
Warsaw Pact: as Eastern Europe

looks to NATO to prevent German revanchism 273; as Soviet invention 272; loss of resources, will for military action 272–273; *see also* NATO
Wells, H. G., author of *The Country of the Blind* 129
West Germany 7; foreign minister Hans-Dietrich Genscher 175; *see also* Germany
Western advisors 9
Western Entente 311
Western Europe: American challenge 159–160; British divide-to-rule policy 156–157; conflicts over continental unity 155–156; Continental System under French control 156; European Coal and Steel Community 156; European Free Trade Association 157; Hallstein Doctrine 156; Marshall Plan 156; Mitterrand on construction of Europe 177; Monnet Plan 156; potential of united Europe against U.S. power during American imperial overstretch 160–161; Treaty of Rome 157, 158; vulnerability to U.S. military plans 158–159; West German revanchism and military subjugation 155–157; *see also* Eastern Europe; Europe
Western private capital 8; *see also* Eastern Europe; Soviet Union; U.S.
Wonder Woman 145
World Bank 46, 55, 127
World Economic Conference of 1927 311–312
World War I 7
World War II 7
Wörner, Manfred 329

Yakunin, Father Gleb, insurgent leader of Communist-Fascist alliance 125
Yazov, Dmitri T. 45
Yeltsin, Boris 45; government and revolution from below 48; shock reforms 89–91, 94–95; surrounded by rivals and under siege 88, 91–94